Robert Bruce Flanders ✾

NAUVOO ✾ *Kingdom on the Mississippi*

UNIVERSITY OF ILLINOIS PRESS ✾ URBANA, 1965

Illini Books edition, 1975   ISBN 0-252-00561-9

A grant from the Ford Foundation has helped to defray the cost of publishing this work.

Preface

Nauvoo, Illinois, is a quiet village of a thousand inhabitants located on the Mississippi between Keokuk and Fort Madison, Iowa. It has no railroad, and is today an out-of-the-way place. The town covers more than six square miles, much of it open fields and tangled brush. Houses are scattered about at wide intervals, some inhabited, some empty, some in ruins. Superimposed upon the whole is a gridiron of old streets, some in use, others almost but not quite reincorporated into the surrounding fields and woods. Nauvoo is a semi-inhabited ghost city. Although some historic buildings have been restored, the marks of the past predominate. The scene readily stimulates the imagination to recall the "City Beautiful" of the Mormon Prophet Joseph Smith, which was in 1845 the largest city in the state of Illinois.

The Mormons came to the Prairie State in 1839, built Nauvoo, and were driven out in 1846. Those few years were of great significance in the history of the sect. In Nauvoo the young latter-day prophet made his most prodigious effort to establish a utopian community. He shaped it to his own vision, and sealed the work with a martyr's blood. Nauvoo served as a prototype for the Mormon communities founded by Nauvooans in the valleys of the Great Basin. The pattern of much that was basic to Mormon society in the West began in Nauvoo: forms of social organization and control, the union of ecclesiastical and civil government, the notion of an independent Mormon nation-state within the American Federal Union, peopling a new country with convert-immigrants, and the polygamous family system. Utah had its roots in Nauvoo; without that seven years' experience in Illinois the development of the Great Basin, and of the West, would not have been the same.

In addition, the Nauvoo experience caused a permanent division in the Mormon Church. The dissolution of the city was also in a sense the dissolution of the church corporate into hostile factions, despite the efforts of Brigham Young to prevent the split. Although the numerous Mormon sects which arose in the ensuing generation were divided by complex controversies over doctrine, there was also in the separation a simple dichotomy. On the one hand were those who favored or at least acquiesced in the vision of a corporate or "political" Mormonism as it had been expressed in the building of Nauvoo. On the other hand were those who came to oppose what Nauvoo stood for and who wished for a simpler, more orthodox manifestation of the faith. The death of Joseph Smith in 1844 dissolved bonds of personal fealty for many Saints, and made opposition to Church authority easier; and the breakup of corporate Mormonism in Illinois assured the division of the Church. The largest group followed Young to Utah and founded another corporate Mormon society that dwarfed the one attempted in Illinois. The others, cast in a dissenter's role, drifted for years without strong leadership or a sure sense of identity. Their rebellion expressed itself not as criticism of Smith and his city by the Mississippi, but as criticism of the successor, Brigham Young, and his city by the Great Salt Lake.

The presence of Joseph Smith dominates this book just as it dominated Nauvoo. Yet there is no pretense here of biographical writing. The account of Smith is not a balanced one if for no other reason than that it does not treat him as a great religious teacher, evangelist, and lawgiver, though it is this facet of his career that has been most revered by successive generations of Latter-day Saints. The image which emerges in the following pages is of a man of affairs—planner, promoter, architect, entrepreneur, executive, politician, filibusterer—matters of which he was sometimes less sure than he was those of the spirit. Such an image is inevitable however in a study of Nauvoo. Central to Smith's religious vision was the conviction that the men of God must be men of affairs, fashioning the Kingdom of Heaven into a kingdom of this world. Nauvoo was his supreme effort to accomplish that end. It was to be a new Jerusalem, the beginning of a society that would, in the metaphor of the ancient prophet, roll forth and fill the whole earth.

I am grateful for the kind assistance given me during the preparation of this book by the Graceland College Library, the Illinois State Historical Library, and the staff of the Utah Room of the University of Utah Library; by Mr. John Gorby and Mr. Preston Kimball, attorneys of Hancock County, Illinois; by Mr. Kenneth Stobaugh and Mr. Floyd Fears of the Joseph Smith Historic Properties at Nauvoo; and, over a period of many years, by the staff of the Wisconsin State Historical Society. Particular thanks are due to Dr. T. Edgar Lyon of Nauvoo Restoration, Incorporated; to

Professor Leonard J. Arrington of Utah State University for his painstaking reading of the manuscript, his valuable criticisms and suggestions, and his encouragement; to Miss Tess Morgan of the Graceland faculty for her expert technical reading of the manuscript; to my old friend and Graceland colleague Alma Blair, whose interest and encouragement have been constant; and to my teacher and mentor Professor Vernon Carstensen, now of the University of Washington, under whose wise and astute direction I wrote at the University of Wisconsin the doctoral dissertation on which this book is based. Finally, I am grateful to my wife Sally, whose professional knowledge of the English language was a substantial help, and whose gentle mixture of patience, understanding, and encouragement was a continuing support.

Lamoni, Iowa   *March, 1965*

Contents

1
'The Land of Our Exile, the State of Illinois'   1

2
'To Build Up a City': The Nauvoo Gathering   23

3
'From the Islands of the Sea': The British Mission
    and the Gathering   57

4
A Kingdom of This World: Government and the Military   92

5
A Kingdom of This World: The Land Business   115

6
A Kingdom of This World: Business, Industry, and Finance   144

7
A Dwelling for Man and a Dwelling for God: The Nauvoo
    House and the Temple   179

8
The Church Corporate as Body Politic   211

9
Conflict Within the Kingdom   242

10
The Kingdom as Empire   278

11
The Fall of the Kingdom   306

Bibliography   342

Index   351

1

'The Land of Our Exile, the State of Illinois'

Hear, O hear the . . . voice of many thousands of American citizens, who now groan in exile on Columbia's free soil. Hear, O hear the weeping and bitter lamentations of widows and orphans whose husbands and fathers have been cruelly martyred in the land where the proud eagle exulting soars!

From a memorial of the Nauvoo City Council to the United States Congress, December 21, 1843, in Joseph Smith Jr., *History of the Church of Jesus Christ of Latter-Day Saints,* B. H. Roberts, ed. (Salt Lake City, 1950), 6:130.

Early in 1839 five thousand Latter-day Saints arrived in western Illinois. They came not as ordinary settlers but as religious refugees fleeing for their lives from their former settlements in Missouri. They huddled through the winter in and around Quincy; but with the coming of spring they moved up the river some seventy miles into Hancock County and there commenced a new settlement which they named Nauvoo. Under the leadership of the young prophet Joseph Smith, the community grew from a sprawling refugee camp into a unique city, the largest in the state. But the Mormons did not really become Illinoisans, just as they had not become Missourians. They came as exiles, lived as strangers in a hostile land, and in 1846 were driven from Illinois, exiles again. They were, to use their own description, "a peculiar people."

The Church of Jesus Christ of Latter-day Saints had its origins amid the religious enthusiasm that swept western New York in the first generation of the nineteenth century. As a religion it contained many elements common to that time and place—a feeling that the millennium was imminent, a "holy" rather than a "literary" priesthood, and a tendency to expect the interposition of heavenly forces to bring about the rapid, apocalyptic triumph of the Kingdom of God on earth. Cause and effect, said Whitney Cross of the religious "ultraism" developed in western New York in the 1830's, were seen as "related to each other only by way of a supernatural connection, seldom short-circuited by any sense of coherence through the natural laws of the physical universe . . . the religious-minded of the day [were disposed] to experiment with innovations and indeed considered it a virtual necessity 'to receive the rays of truth from every quarter . . . changing our practice as often and as fast as we can obtain further information,' " [1] Piety, social idealism, millennialism, and pragmatism undergirded by faith, a sense of mission, and abundant self-confidence were woven into the fabric of early Mormonism. Recognition of these qualities might help to explain to differently endowed generations some of the spectacular achievements and equally spectacular failures of the sect in its early years. The rank and file of Latter-day Saints in 1840 were people of New England origin or ancestry, experienced in the western revivalism of their generation. Many were former Methodists, Baptists, or members of unorthodox or come-outist sects like the Campbellites and the Millerites. Sidney Rigdon, himself a Campbellite preacher at the time of his conversion to Mormonism, said in 1837 that Latter-day Saint evangelism had "puked the Campbellites effectually, no emetic could do half so well." [2] These Yankee Mormons combined a tradition of religious fervor and an ancestry rooted in the Puritan Commonwealth of New England where another generation had made a solemn attempt to bring God's Kingdom to fruition. Many Latter-day Saints had pioneered in western New York and Ohio. Orson Spencer, one of the few early Mormons who was formally educated, characterized his brethren in this way: "Our people are mostly the working class of the community, from the United States and Great Britain and her provinces [British and Canadian converts were coming in substantial numbers when Spencer wrote]. . . . Our elders are versed in religious polemics, from discussions in the pulpit, stage, barroom, canal, and steam-boat, and . . . many, very many, are from the most enlightened portion of New England . . . rocked in the cradle of orthodoxy and liberty; accustomed to fatigue, privation, and opposition. . . ." [3]

[1] Whitney Cross, *The Burned-Over District: The Social and Intellectual History of Enthusiastic Religion in Western New York, 1800–1850* (Ithaca, New York, 1950), p. 203.

[2] *Latter Day Saints' Messenger and Advocate*, January, 1837, p. 483, quoted in Raymond C. Buley, *The Old Northwest; Pioneer Period, 1815–1840* (Indianapolis, 1950), 2:483. Buley says the Baptists and Campbellites furnished "the largest percentage" of Mormon membership.

[3] Letter of Orson Spencer from Nauvoo, November 7, 1842, in Orson Spencer, *Letters Exhibiting the Most Prominent Doctrines of the Church of Jesus Christ of Latter-day Saints, by Elder Orson Spencer, A.B.* (Liverpool, 1879), p. 33.

Devotion to the Church as an institution as well as to the Faith was characteristic of Mormon converts; Smith's vision of a corporate Zionic enterprise seemed to captivate them. Being a good Mormon was a difficult challenge. One was expected to contribute time, means, and loyalty to group enterprises whenever called upon. Those who refused or grumbled too much ultimately placed their fellowship in jeopardy, and were often numbered with the "apostates" who had not kept the faith and were cast out, "turned over to the buffetings of Satan." Most male converts were ordained to the Mormon lay priesthood, often immediately after baptism, and some were "called" to go on distant missions, labor on public buildings, or perform other duties without prior notice and with no expectation of remuneration or support. The frequent conversion experiences, the common faith, the heavy investment made in corporate endeavors, and the sufferings endured from persecution created among Mormons a strong sense of group identity and loyalty, and a feeling of separation from "the World" which they felt they had to a degree renounced. They were instructed by their leaders to "gather" to the various sites where the Church was currently building its communities—in turn to Kirtland, Ohio, Independence and Far West, Missouri, and Nauvoo, Illinois. In all these places, the gentile neighbors were eventually excited to uneasiness, then to hostility toward the sect. To be sure, the Mormon religion was unorthodox, but the nation knew and tolerated many unorthodox sects. Contemporary observers did not regard individual Mormons as fanatics or find them, as individuals, very different from thousands of others of Yankee descent who spread across the upper Midwest during the first half of the nineteenth century. But Mormonism, the gentiles observed, was more than the unorthodox doctrine of ardent believers. It was a burgeoning, centralized, corporate sect committed to action upon its beliefs—and those beliefs entailed the reordering of society and the conversion of the world. It was the Mormon Church in action that aroused its neighbors. The Church was—at least in outward appearance—a tightly knit, cohesive society with strong central direction, vigorous and aggressive in operation, and, by the Nauvoo period, growing yearly by the thousands. It also developed a trend to political separatism and a kind of Mormon paranationalism that seemed subversive to outsiders. Mormonism was not infrequently referred to as America's Islam. The Church exhibited power—power enough perhaps to establish social, economic, and political dominion

3

wherever it was located by the Prophet. Such a sect invited persecution.

Joseph Smith, the founder of the Mormon religion, was also the founder and chief proprietor of Nauvoo. His was the decision to locate a city of his followers in Illinois. He chose the site, determined the name of the city and its form, and became its leading citizen and promoter. The stamp of his personality and of his vision were fixed indelibly upon Nauvoo. Its history can neither be told nor understood without particular reference to him. Superlatives whether of adoration or opprobrium fail to describe Joseph Smith adequately. He founded four cities, including Nauvoo; coincidentally he became involved in several memorable western real-estate promotions. He toyed with leading a little army, plunged into politics in Illinois, and set in motion far-flung western filibusters. Of more lasting significance than any of these, he founded a numerous religious sect, inspired a new faith in his converts, and gave them and their posterity a large body of scripture, much of which has proved of lasting religious and literary value.[4] He was an orator and preacher of great persuasion and endurance, as well as a prodigious writer. Smith's papers, correspondence, journals, and collections of Church documents fill six large volumes. The Vermont-born Mormon leader had a New Englander's sense of history. Like William Bradford he felt impelled to leave *the* history of his movement. Of his journal, Smith wrote under the entry for Saturday, December 11, 1841:

> Since I have been engaged in laying the foundation of the Church of Jesus Christ of Latter-day Saints, I have been prevented in various ways from continuing my journal and history in a manner satisfactory to myself or in justice to the cause. Long imprisonments, vexatious lawsuits,

[4] Smith has been the subject of numerous biographical writings beginning near the inception of Mormonism and continuing until the present. The accumulation is enormous, but most of it is of limited value. In the nineteenth century the common objectives of such works were to expose the Mormon prophet as a villainous fraud, and to capitalize upon popular interest in the sensational aspects of Mormonism. In the twentieth century several biographies have been written which use scholarly methodology in varying degrees but which still stand in the tradition of the sensational exposé. Such books are William A. Linn, *The Story of the Mormons* (New York and London, 1902); I. Woodbridge Riley, *The Founder of Mormonism: A Psychological Study of Joseph Smith, Jr.* (New York, 1902); Harry M. Beardsley, *Joseph Smith and His Mormon Empire* (New York, 1931); and Fawn Mackay Brodie, *No Man Knows My History: The Life of Joseph Smith the Mormon Prophet* (New York, 1945). All have serious limitations of conception and execution. For a brief, thoughtful essay on the problems of Mormon historiography see the preface to Ray B. West, *Kingdom of the Saints; The Story of Brigham Young and the Mormons* (New York, 1957).

the treachery of some of my clerks, the death of others, and the poverty of myself and brethren from continued plundering and driving, have prevented my handing down to posterity a connected memorandum of events desirable to all lovers of truth; yet I have continued to keep up a journal in the best manner my circumstances would allow . . . so that the labors and suffering of the first Elders and Saints of this last kingdom might not wholly be lost to the World.[5]

Smith was a passionate man, loving his friends and hating his enemies with equal fervor. That he should have enemies is understandable; he personified the form and substance of Mormonism to such an extent that hatred of the sect and its religion naturally centered on him. But Smith was not an easy peacemaker; he seemed to excite rather than soothe rising passions. He finally came to expect that those who were not for him must inevitably be against him. The circumstances of his life led to some bitter enmities and finally to his assassination. Not only did he find it difficult to deal harmoniously with men outside the faith but he was also sometimes a poor judge of the character of those inside the Church whom he took into his confidence. Perspicacious in matters of the spirit, he was often naive in temporal affairs and was thus an easy mark for sharp dealers and flatterers.

A person who heard Smith preach in Washington in 1840 reported by way of description: "He is not an educated man; but he is a plain, sensible, strong minded man. Everything he says, is said in a manner to leave the impression that he is sincere. There is no levity, no fanaticism, no want of dignity in his deportment. He is apparently from forty to forty-five years of age [Smith was then thirty-four], rather above the middle stature, and what the ladies would call a very good looking man. In his garb there are no peculiarities; his dress being that of a plain, unpretending citizen. He is by profession a farmer, but is evidently well read." [6] The officer of the Illinois Masonic Order who installed a lodge at Nauvoo in 1842 found

---

[5] Joseph Smith Jr., *History of the Church of Jesus Christ of Latter-day Saints, Period I*, Brigham H. Roberts, ed. (Salt Lake City, 1948–1951), 4:470. Most of Smith's writings and papers including his journal have been published by the Church of Jesus Christ of Latter-day Saints in this six-volume collection. Citations from this work will be abbreviated hereafter as "Joseph Smith's History." A seventh volume . . . *Period II—Apostolic Interregnum* (Salt Lake City, 1932), is a collection of journals of the Mormon Apostles together with miscellaneous documents from mid-1844 to mid-1848.

[6] Letter of Matthew S. Davis to his sister, February 6, 1840, quoted in Joseph Smith's History, 4:78. Smith called him a congressman, but was evidently mistaken as there was no congressman by that name.

somewhat to his surprise that Smith was a man of pleasing manner and gracious hospitality. "[Smith] appears to be much respected by those around him," said the visitor, "and has their entire confidence. . . . instead of [an] ignorant and tyrannical upstart, judge my surprise at finding him sensible, intelligent, companionable, and gentlemanly. . . . He is a fine looking man . . . and has an interesting family."[7] Another writer in the *New York Sun* of September 4, 1843, assessed the Prophet of Mormonism more in apprehension than praise: "Nothing can be more plebeian, in seeming, than this Joe Smith. Little of dignity there is in his cognomen; but few in this age have done such deeds. . . . It is no small thing in the blaze of this nineteenth century to give to men a new revelation, found a new religion, establish new forms of worship, to build a city, with new laws, institutions, and orders of architecture. . . . That Joe Smith . . . is a man of great talent—a deep thinker, an eloquent speaker, an able writer, and a man of great mental power, no one can doubt who has watched his career."

Nauvoo in the early and mid-forties was a prime attraction to the Mississippi River tourist traffic, and the Prophet and the Nauvoo Temple were objects of particular interest. Smith took time to entertain many of the visitors personally. In April, 1844, two Bostonians of some note, Josiah Quincy and Charles Francis Adams, stopped in Nauvoo. Smith responded particularly to Adams when the latter was introduced as a relative of two U.S. presidents. The visitors spent a number of hours with the Prophet, and Quincy wrote a lively if faintly sarcastic report of the encounter.

"God bless you, to begin with!" said Joseph Smith, raising his hands in the air and letting them descend upon the shoulders of Mr. Adams. The benediction, though evidently sincere, had an odd savor of what might be called official familiarity, such as a crowned head might adopt on receiving the heir presumptive of a friendly court. . . .

A *fine-looking* man is what the passer-by would instinctively have murmured upon meeting the remarkable individual who had fashioned the mould which was to shape the feelings of so many thousands of his fellow mortals. But Smith was more than this and one could not resist the impression that capacity and resource were natural to his stalwart person. . . . Of all men I have met, [Smith and Elisha R. Potter] seem best endowed with that kingly faculty which directs, by an intrinsic right, the feeble or confused souls who are looking for guidance. This is just to say with emphasis; for the reader will find so much that is puerile and even shock-

[7] From the Columbus, Illinois, *Advocate*, n.d., quoted in Joseph Smith's History, 4:565, 566, under date of March 22, 1842.

ing in the prophet's conversation that he might never suspect the impression of rugged power that was given by the man.

Smith entertained Adams and Quincy with conversation of religion and politics (he was then a candidate for President of the United States) and a tour of the city, including a visit to his mother's "museum," a collection of four mummies, some Egyptian manuscripts, and other ancient artifacts. The host discoursed knowingly on the exhibits, and then surprised the Bostonians. "The exhibition of these august relics," said Quincy, "concluded with a . . . descent into the hard modern world of fact. Monarchs, patriarchs, and parchments were very well in their way; but this was clearly the nineteenth century, when prophets must get a living and provide for their relations. 'Gentlemen,' said this *bourgeois* Mohammed, as he closed the cabinets, 'those who see these curiosities generally pay my mother a quarter of a dollar.'" Quincy offered in analysis of Smith only the following comment: "I have endeavored to give the details of my visit to the Mormon prophet with absolute accuracy. If the reader does not know what to make of Joseph Smith, I cannot help him out of the difficulty. I myself stand helpless before the puzzle." [8]

The Prophet's influence over the Latter-day Saints was extraordinary. There seemed no end to the sacrifices they would make, the journeys they would undertake, the zeal they would manifest, under his direction. One such proselyte was John Doyle Lee, a tough, rough-hewn frontiersman converted to Mormonism in 1838. Of his first impression of the Mormon leader Lee's biographer records: "He thought Joseph Smith carried an air of majesty that made him taller than his six feet as he faced the audience, and more handsome and commanding than an ordinary man. Attracting every eye and holding every heart by the sheer magnetism of his personality, he played upon the congregation as though it were a musical instrument responsive to his slightest touch. When he spoke of the beauties and mysteries of the kingdom, he brought out the melody in deep, strong tones, into which with great skill was interspersed occasional light, sparkling tones of humor." He was, said Lee, "the man who was more dear to us than all the riches and honors that could be conferred upon us by a thousand such worlds as the one we now inhabit." When news came to him of Smith's death, Lee would not at

[8] Quoted in William Mulder and A. R. Mortensen, eds., *Among the Mormons: Historic Accounts by Contemporary Observers* (New York, 1958), pp. 133, 134, 137, 142.

7

first believe it. "Of all who had lived upon the earth, Jesus Christ alone excepted, this modern prophet was greatest in the eyes of John D. Lee. . . . Never as long as he lived could . . . Lee speak of Joseph Smith without a deep emotional ring." Lee's deeds proved the sincerity of his words. He served Smith faithfully in a variety of roles, rose to a responsible rank in the Mormon priesthood, and was personally devoted to the Prophet. After Smith's martyrdom Lee transferred his fealty to Brigham Young, and in a new Mormon rite became Young's "adopted son."[9] His many-faceted career notwithstanding, Smith considered himself, and was considered by his followers, primarily a minister with superior insight into the mind and will of God. He was wounded and angered by the persecution directed against himself and his people, which he was unable to understand except in terms of devilishness contending against Godliness. Speaking of himself and his role in a sermon at Nauvoo, May 21, 1843, he said:

Many persons think a prophet must be a great deal better than anybody else. . . . I do not want you to think I am very righteous, for I am not. God judges men according to the use they make of the light which he gives them. . . .

I am like a huge, rough stone rolling down from a high mountain; and the only polishing I get is when some corner gets rubbed off by coming in contact with something else, striking . . . against religious bigotry, priestcraft, lawyer-craft, doctor-craft, lying editors, suborned judges and jurors, and the authority of perjured executives, backed by mobs, blasphemers, licentious and corrupt men and women—all hell knocking off a corner here and a corner there. Thus I will become a smooth and polished shaft in the quiver of the Almighty, who will give me dominion over all and every one of them. . . .

I am going to take up this subject [his scriptural text] by virtue of the knowledge of God in me, which I have received from heaven. The opinions of men . . . are to me as the crackling of thorns under the pot, or the whistling of the wind. I break the ground; I lead the way like Columbus. . . . I could explain a hundred fold more than I ever have of the glories of the kingdoms manifested to me in the vision, were I permitted, and were the people prepared to receive them.[10]

Smith was convinced of the imminent end of the world. His journal abounds in notations of natural calamities, wars, and unusual

[9] Juanita Brooks, *John Doyle Lee: Zealot—Pioneer Builder—Scapegoat* (Glendale, California, 1962), pp. 30, 31, 57, 60. Mrs. Brooks, a Mormon historian, wrote this biography using primarily the published and unpublished journals of Lee and such other contemporaries as Hosea Stout.

[10] Joseph Smith's History, 5:401–402.

phenomena. He saw the persecutions of himself and the Saints as particular signs of the times which heralded the Last Days. Smith's millennialism was inextricably connected in his thinking with the literal establishment of the Kingdom of God by the Mormon Church under his headship, and that work became a race against the end of time and the forces of evil. On August 10, 1841, he noted:

A shower of meteoric stones fell . . . in Hungary.

Letters from various parts of England and Scotland show that numbers are daily added to the church; while shipwrecks, floods, houses and workshops falling, great and destructive fires, sudden deaths, banks breaking, men's hearts failing them for fear, shopkeepers and manufacturers failing . . . many accidents on the railways, etc., betoken the coming of the Son of Man.

On August 22 Smith preached "on wars and desolations that await the nations." In September he noted "Another shower of flesh and blood in England" and that "Wars and rumors of wars, earthquakes, tempests, pestilence, and great fires, connected with every kind of wickedness, distress, and destruction of property are heard in almost every land and nation." During that same summer members of Smith's family together with many of his friends and associates died, and calamity weighed heavily on him. On October 30 he recorded, "I instructed the Council [of Twelve] on many principles pertaining to the gathering of the nations, the wickedness and downfall of this generation, etc." The following summer Willard Richards had a serious accident while riding the Prophet's horse, concerning which Smith wrote: "It was a trick of the devil to kill my clerk. Similar attacks have been made on myself of late, and Satan is seeking our destruction on every hand." [11] The Prophet's apocalyptic state of mind flavored the thinking of Latter-day Saints and their various enterprises, including the feverish attempt to "build up" Nauvoo.

Smith was an enigma to his own generation, unfathomed by his followers or his "enemies." He seemed in some ways simple, even superficial; in others, complex and profound. He was sometimes arrogant and sometimes contrite. He was inexperienced and frequently naive, yet the appeal of his vision could not be lightly dismissed. He was full of contradictions that sometimes bewildered him. In his thirty-ninth year he said in a sermon at Nauvoo, "You don't know me; you never knew my heart. No man knows my history. I cannot tell it: I shall never undertake it. I don't blame anyone

[11] Joseph Smith's History, 4:401, 405, 414, 415; 5:22, 23.

for not believing my history. If I had not experienced what I have, I would not believe it myself." [12] Eleven weeks later he was killed by a mob; his public career had spanned only fifteen years. In assaying the works of Joseph Smith, it is well to remember that they were done by a young man. Though in his last years he became increasingly engaged in Mormon affairs of state, Smith was fundamentally a prophet-evangelist, and his chief accomplishments were in the vision he promulgated and the people he attracted to it.

In addition to being enigmatic, Smith was a controversial figure, and he and his followers were a "peculiar people"; given their aggressive endeavors, they not surprisingly aroused antagonism on a local, then a regional, and finally a national scale. The first big eruption of anti-Mormon sentiment occurred in Missouri. The Prophet had in 1830 designated Jackson County (Independence), Missouri, as the place where Zion, the Kingdom of God, was to be established and "built up." The Church, then small and confined mostly to western New York, western Pennsylvania, and Ohio's Western Reserve, began to remove to the new place of "gathering." By 1833, however, this ambitious corporation of pious Yankees, accused of harboring unacceptable views on Negroes, but feared more particularly for their growing political power, was assaulted and driven from the county.[13]

Finding no redress in the courts or from the state government for their losses (a politician could not easily afford to espouse the cause of such a minority) they moved into a little-inhabited region of northwest Missouri and established their own county, Caldwell, and its county town, Far West. This was the first time that they had had virtual control of local government, and they formed their own county militia company. A secret organization of militant Mormons —many of dubious reputation—was also formed, vowing vengeance and retaliation on "enemies" of the faith. These "Danites," as they came to be known, were not opposed by Smith and other Mormon leaders, and may have been tacitly endorsed by some. Any such secret association committed to vigilante action and the lawless enforcement of law (and they were not uncommon on the frontiers) was certain to create a dangerous situation. "Danitism" became a front for pilfering, marauding, and other assorted forms of violence

[12] Joseph Smith's History, 6:317.
[13] See Richard L. Bushman, "Mormon Persecutions in Missouri, 1833," *Brigham Young University Studies*, 3:11–20 (1960).

both by Mormons and non-Mormons. In surrounding counties Caldwell County became an object of mounting suspicion and hostility. As the Mormon stronghold filled up with the growing stream of convert-gatherers and they spilled over into adjacent areas, troublous incidents multiplied. When some Mormons attempted to vote in a local election at Gallatin, Daviess County (just north of Caldwell), a riot resulted which precipitated a little civil war between the Saints and the gentiles. Fear of the Mormon power seized the region, and Governor Lillburn Boggs, a Jackson County man not in sympathy with the Mormons, mobilized the state militia to "expel or exterminate" them. Deciding not to resist further, the Saints gave up their arms and much personal property and made preparations to leave the state, though it was then November. After narrowly escaping summary execution at the hands of a drumhead court-martial, Smith and other Mormon leaders were thrown into prison for the winter.[14]

Various petitions and embassies to Jefferson City failed to accomplish anything concrete in the Mormons' behalf, and Boggs's expulsion order stood.[15] In January the Saints at Far West attempted to organize their evacuation, and to realize something on the sale of the land and property which they had to leave behind. With Smith and Sidney Rigdon imprisoned, Apostle David Patten killed, and Apostle Thomas B. Marsh in apostasy, Brigham Young, who had not been caught in the net thrown to capture all Mormon leaders, stood out as the ranking figure. He was at thirty-five the senior Apostle.

[14] General accounts of the Mormons in Missouri may be found in standard Mormon histories such as Brigham H. Roberts, *Comprehensive History of the Church,* Inez Smith Davis, *The Story of the Church,* and Joseph Smith III and Heman C. Smith, *History of the Reorganized Church of Jesus Christ of Latter Day Saints.* Of particular value is the chapter on Missouri in Ray B. West, *Kingdom of the Saints* (New York, 1957). See also William E. Parrish, *David Rice Atchison of Missouri, Border Politician* (Columbia, Missouri, 1961), chap. 2, and Brooks, *John Doyle Lee,* pp. 33–43. Joseph Smith's History contains extensive primary sources including the documents sent to the U.S. Congress with memorials on the Missouri persecutions. There is little published monographic writing about the Mormons in Missouri, important exceptions being Joseph A. Geddes, *The United Order Among the Mormons* (New York, 1922); and Leonard J. Arrington, "Early Mormon Communitarianism: The Law of Consecration and Stewardship," *Western Humanities Review,* 7:341–369 (Fall, 1953).

[15] The legislature appropriated $2,000 for the relief of those who were reduced to want by the "Mormon War." The Saints were intended to be the primary recipients, but the mismanagement and corruption of the administrators largely nullified any benefit. See Joseph Smith's History, 3:243.

Young was chosen president of a reorganized High Council and together with John Taylor, whom he had just ordained to the Quorum of Twelve Apostles, played an important part in directing the removal of the Saints from the state. These circumstances for the first time elevated Young to a position of prominence and made him a leading authority on matters of organized migration. He was perhaps responsible for the decision to make Quincy, Illinois, the destination of the Saints and deserves much of the credit for keeping the refugees from scattering.[16] In January, 1839, an *ad hoc* "Committee on Removal" was formed at Far West, which apparently played an important role in evacuating the Saints. A part of the function of the committee was to sell property left by the Mormons and to help obtain outfits for travel.[17] Powers of attorney were given the committee, and attempts were made to realize cash on land sales if possible, or at least settle some of the large debts against the Mormons. Joseph Smith said later that he gave $34,000 in cash, land titles, and other property to pay lawyers fees alone, and $16,000 more to settle "other vexatious suits" for which he said he "received very little in return."[18]

Historical evidence concerning the Mormon exodus from Missouri is very sketchy. Few had the time or the disposition to keep a journal; and when they wrote of the event later it was primarily to describe the persecution which preceded it and the property losses it entailed. The move began in January and continued through the rest of the winter.[19] Some of the Saints went by boat down the Missouri and up the Mississippi. The majority, lacking money, went overland by whatever means they could devise.

The Saints fled toward Quincy, Adams County, Illinois, the largest

[16] West, *Kingdom of the Saints*, pp. 87, 88, 90, 91, 96. See also Joseph Smith's History, Vol. III, chaps. 16, 17, *passim*.

[17] Joseph Smith's History, 3:249–255. The members were William Huntington, Charles Bird, Alanson Ripley, Theodore Turley, Daniel Shearer, Shadrach Roundy, Jonathan Hale, Elias Smith, Erastus Bingham, Stephen Markham, and James Newberry.

[18] *Ibid.*, 3:261, 262, 327. Smith's assessment of the value of the land involved may have been inflated. When Missouri lands could be sold, the price was modest. George W. Robinson sold six lots in the Far West plat for $25 each in October, 1839. Hancock County, Illinois, Deed Book H, p. 144. This and all deed, bond, and mortgage books subsequently referred to, unless otherwise noted, are official public records of Hancock County and are in the vault of the Circuit Clerk and Recorder, Carthage, Illinois.

[19] According to the entry in Smith's Journal for April 20, 1839, the last of the Saints left Far West on that day. Joseph Smith's History, 3:326.

town on the upper Mississippi, about 150 miles due east of Caldwell County, Missouri. Quincy authorities received the refugees kindly, said Ebenezer Robinson, a young Mormon, "recommending the citizens to give employment to those who were willing to labor, and to be careful not to say anything calculated to wound the feelings of the strangers thrown into their midst, which caution was very thoughtful and timely." [20] Nevertheless, the situation was difficult. Robinson said he arrived destitute on February 1 after walking through the snow all the way from Far West. The town was already crowded with refugee Mormons and finding work was not easy since the city "was overflowing with surplus labor." He and a companion, both printers, were fortunate enough to find employment at the *Quincy Whig* for subsistence pay. A Quincy woman describing the event said that her mother took in an old Mormon woman who was "expected to assist a little in light housework and sewing for her board." The Mormon refugees were, she said, "in such distressing condition when they arrived that the good people of the town took them in and gave them temporary relief." [21]

In addition to those who found refuge in Quincy, there were Mormons scattered for miles over the surrounding countryside. Altogether they numbered about five thousand.[22] The relief of their immediate needs by the people of Adams County was a sample of the hospitality they were to receive in the state where they had come by accident. The Mormons were prospective new settlers and as such were more than welcome. New people were considered of the greatest importance to the future prosperity of Illinois. There seemed at first to be little concern that the Mormons were a "peculiar people"; the region into which they had come was already perhaps the most cosmopolitan in the United States.

The Old Northwest—Ohio, Indiana, Illinois, Michigan, and Wisconsin—was in the first half of the nineteenth century a very ferment of promotion, settlement, and development; settlers made endless struggles to create a new life and to gain power. Civilization

[20] Ebenzer Robinson, ed., *The Return*, 2:243, April, 1890. *The Return* was a monthly paper edited by Robinson for a time for the Church of Christ (Whitmerite). See also Joseph Smith's History, 3:267, 269–271.

[21] Mrs. Paul Selby, "Recollections of a Little Girl in the Forties . . ." *Journal of the Illinois State Historical Society* (Springfield, Illinois), 16:168, 169 (1923–1924).

[22] William V. Pooley, *The Settlement of Illinois from 1830 to 1850* (Madison, 1908), p. 509; Parrish, *David Rice Atchison of Missouri*, p. 18; A. L. Fulwider, *History of Stephenson County, Illinois* (Chicago, 1910), p. 89.

was in a raw, formative state, maturing slowly in the midst of a heterogeneous population groping as usual in such circumstances with the process of forming a society in a new, vast, rich country. One observer was much exhilarated by the melting pot he saw: "The five races of both continents are present. . . . The Yankee . . . retains in full his unique identity. Men with European tongues gather here like the dispersed of the tribe of Israel. All say welcome to each other. The Frenchman shortens his mustache and becomes American. The Irishman you recognize by his hearty and native brogue. . . . Jews and Germans are here. . . . I see a respectable representation of the people of color. . . ."[23] There were in addition Englishmen, Canadians, Welsh, Scandinavians, and southerners—Kentuckians, Tennesseeans, Virginians, Carolinians—as well as immigrants from other older states and earlier settled parts of the Old Northwest itself. The flood of immigrants from whatever source was the lifeblood of the new country. Said a leading Illinois newspaper in 1838, "We welcome them. Our country is now the asylum for the oppressed of all nations." This was the official creed at least of politicians, speculators, and others dependent on the growth of population.[24] Illinois, admitted to the Union in 1818, was the third and largest of the five states formed in the Northwest Territory. It lay with its western shoulder on the Mississippi and stretched from north to south some four hundred miles. Its upper reaches pushed into the lakes and wooded country of the North and touched Lake Michigan. Its southern borders were the lower Wabash and Ohio, pointing like a great arrow into the lower Mississippi Valley, the valleys of the Cumberland and the Tennessee, and the cotton and slave empire of the Old Southwest. The geography of Illinois was the key to the pattern of its settlement and the nature of its society as a frontier state. The Great Lakes connected northern Illinois with Ohio, New York, and New England. Its southern border rivers connected it with Kentucky, Tennessee, and the South. The Mississippi and such tributaries as the Sangamon, Illinois, and Rock Rivers aided transportation along the state's enormous length.

The history of the settlement of Illinois was to a great extent the history of two frontiers—one pushed north by southerners and the other pushed south by Yankees. The settlement pattern was re-

[23] Josiah B. Grinnell, *Sketches of the West, or the Home of the Badgers* . . . (Milwaukee, 1845), p. 17, quoted in Buley, *The Old Northwest*, 2:103.
[24] Buley, *The Old Northwest*, 2:106.

flected in struggles between the two groups for political and cultural dominance. The southern migration was earlier, and southerners dominated government in early Illinois, shaping the constitution of 1818 along the lines of those of Virginia and Kentucky. The first six governors were men of southern origin, and for twenty-five years Illinois legislators were with few exceptions men born south of the Ohio.[25] In the 1830's and 1840's, however, the Yankee immigration surpassed the southern, and the struggle for power in the state took on a sectional character that made for tense, complex politics. In such a dynamic society powerful new groups were feared and resented by older settlers as a threat to their dominance. One Illinois woman of Tennessee ancestry said in 1837, "I am getting skeary about them ere Yankees; there is such a power of them coming in that they and the Injuns will squatch out the white folks." [26] Some southern Illinoisans opposed the Illinois and Michigan Canal (to connect the Illinois River with Lake Michigan) for fear it would flood the state with Yankees, whom they tended to equate with dishonest itinerant peddlers. For their part the settlers in the north sometimes viewed southerners as poor white trash log cabin squatters, and in addition resented the heavy state debt which as new settlers they inherited but from which they derived little benefit. In 1842 antagonism was so strong that a group of northern Illinois counties held a convention to secede from the state and be annexed to Wisconsin Territory.[27] The population of Illinois trebled during each decade between 1820–1840 and doubled between 1840 and 1850. The largest concentrations of settlement were in west central Illinois; in 1830 approximately half the population was in an area bounded on the north by Peoria County, on the east by Macon County (Decatur), and on the south by Marion County (Centralia). By 1840 the north was filling very fast, and Chicago and the river towns—Alton, Quincy, Jacksonville, Springfield, Peoria— where a "turbulent competitive life" was lived, were growing rapidly.[28]

[25] Lois K. (Rosenberry) Matthews, *The Expansion of New England* (Boston and New York, 1909), p. 197.
[26] Quoted in Buley, *The Old Northwest*, 2:106.
[27] Matthews, *Expansion of New England*, pp. 207–210. See also H. C. Hubbart, *The Older Middle West, 1840–1880* (New York and London, 1936), pp. 44, 45.
[28] Hubbart, *The Older Middle West*, p. 35.

ILLINOIS POPULATION, 1820–1850 [29]

Year	Population	Rate of Increase During Decennium	Number per Square Mile
1820	55,162	349.1%	1
1830	157,445	185.4%	2.8
1840	476,183	202.4%	8.5
1850	851,470	78.8%	15.2

Adams and Hancock Counties, the area into which the Mormons came, were in the Illinois Military Bounty Tract, a great wedge of country between the Illinois and Mississippi Rivers set aside by Congress to be given to veterans of the War of 1812. In 1830 the whole tract had had but thirteen thousand inhabitants, mostly in the southern tip and along the rivers. This was a mixed population from Ohio, Kentucky, Virginia, Tennessee, Pennsylvania, Indiana, Missouri, and southern Illinois. During the thirties the population increased rapidly, with settlement in the lower portion of the tract being predominantly southern, while that in the northern part was Yankee in character. Hancock County, near the middle, had ten thousand in 1840, at least double its population before the founding of Nauvoo in 1839. Adams County on the south had sixteen thousand in 1840, while McDonough County on the east had fifty-three hundred.[30] Although Mormon immigration into Hancock between 1840 and 1845 was very heavy, non-Mormon settlement virtually ceased. One historian estimated that the gentile population may even have declined.[31] Nauvoo was to be troubled by its location in a dynamic frontier country. Hancock County was in an area characterized by political and cultural tensions even before the Mormons arrived. Moreover, the city was just across the river from Lee County, Iowa Territory, an especially turbulent area of new settle-

[29] B. A. Hinsdale, *The Old Northwest* (New York, 1888), p. 395.
[30] Buley, *The Old Northwest*, 2:54; Pooley, *Settlement of Illinois*, pp. 419, 430; *Quincy Whig*, January 16, 1840; George R. Gayler, "A Social, Economic, and Political Study of the Mormons in Western Illinois, 1839–1846: A Reevaluation" (unpublished Ph.D. thesis, Department of History, Indiana University, 1955), pp. 48, 49n; *Compendium of the Sixth Census of the United States, 1840* (Washington, 1841), p. 82.
[31] Pooley, *Settlement of Illinois*, pp. 415, 416. The total population of Hancock County in 1845 was 22,559, the largest in the state. Cook County was second with 21,581. *Reports made to the Senate and the House of Representatives of the State of Illinois . . . 1846* (Springfield, 1847), p. 70.

ment, and only a few miles from the northeast corner of Missouri, where anti-Mormon feeling continued unabated.

Land sales flourished in Illinois in the 1830's. Lands were traded and retraded as rising prices encouraged speculation. The dollar volume of such sales increased from $2,500,000 in 1830 to over $25,-000,000 in 1836. The increment of land values and the continuing influx of new settlers suggested an almost limitless future of prosperity for the state and its enterprising citizens. Speculation in town lots was as attractive as that in farms. Townsites in large numbers were platted by hopeful promoters all over Illinois. Of this phenomenon Thomas Ford wrote:

In . . . 1836, the great land and town lot speculation . . . had fairly reached and spread over Illinois. It commenced . . . first at Chicago. . . . The story of the sudden fortunes made there, excited first wonder and amazement, next a gambling spirit of adventure, and lastly, an all-absorbing desire for sudden and splendid wealth. . . . The plats of towns, for a hundred miles around, were carried there to be disposed at auction. But as enough did not come to satisfy the insatiable greediness of the Chicago sharpers and speculators, they frequently consigned their wares to eastern markets . . . at less cost than a barrel of flour. In fact, lands and town lots were the staple of the country, and were the only articles of export.

The number of towns multiplied so rapidly, said Ford, and so many of them had no purpose except to make money for their promoters, "that it was waggishly remarked by many people, that the whole country was likely to be laid out in towns; and that no land would be left for farming purposes. The judgments of all our business men were unsettled. . . ."[32]

Speculation in the Military Bounty district was common as elsewhere. Though much of the land was undeveloped and unsettled, by 1837 patents had been issued for 2,831,840 acres of a total of 3,500,000 in the entire tract. Much land was still available there, presumably at the minimum federal price of $1.25 an acre, but farms were being offered and sold at much higher prices. In 1837 one Philadelphia speculator advertised 260 quarter-sections at from $5 to $40 an acre. Prices for town lots were also high. In 1836 lots in Quincy sold as high as $78 and in Peoria $100 a front foot. In 1837 Monmouth lots brought up to $1,000, whether in hard money or paper values it is impossible to know. Promoters of "paper towns"

[32] Thomas A. Ford, *A History of Illinois from Its Commencement as a State in 1818 to 1847*. . . . (Chicago and New York, 1854), pp. 181, 182.

17

where little or no settlement existed often obtained less spectacular results; but the cost of a survey was slight, and changing acres to streets and lots might also work the magic of changing small values to large ones.[33]

Promoters throughout the western country were anxious to emulate the astonishing success of the Erie Canal, which had been a means of developing New York, opening the whole Northwest to commerce and settlement, and returning a handsome profit from tolls. Architects of prosperity in Illinois were no exception. In the Prairie State an obvious proposal was to link the Great Lakes with the Mississippi and the Gulf by way of the Illinois River and a canal from its upper reaches to Lake Michigan. Such a canal would presumably do for Illinois what the Erie had done for New York. But the Illinois-Michigan Canal, as it was called, was only one part of a larger plan. Other regions of the state were anxious for their own "internal improvements," including railroads. In 1835 and 1836 the Illinois legislature granted a dozen or more charters to private corporations to build railroads, though neither the charters nor the roads yet conformed to any logical system. In 1837 the legislature approved a plan to build an interrelated system of railroads and canals all over the state at public expense. The money was to be borrowed and the work was to be carried on simultaneously so that one region would not get ahead of another. Politicians were pleased to distribute in their constituencies the patronage represented by the construction contracts. A heavy demand developed for farmlands and town lots along the new rights of way, and prices soared. The Springfield *State Register* of March 6, 1837, observed that the improvements would probably double the value of Illinois land. The Illinois internal improvement venture proved to be premature, however, because the venturers were at best inexperienced. Poor planning, mismanagement, oversanguine expectations, and local self-interests burdened the project from the beginning. The panics of 1837 and 1839 dried up the sources of finance and the entire project was brought to a halt with little accomplished but the construction of disconnected stubs of railroad tracks and canal ditches. Meantime the state debt had risen to $11,079,919, on which the interest alone was $637,800 annually. To finish the system would have required at least an additional $11,000,000.

[33] Theodore C. Pease, *Frontier State: 1818–1848*, II, *The Centennial History of Illinois* (Springfield, 1918), 175, 176.

As a result, disillusionment was as profound in 1839 as optimism had been lofty two years earlier. Said the *State Register* of December 25, "It is difficult to conceive of a worse condition of things than is now in prospect for the state of Illinois." By 1840 the *Quincy Whig* declared that the finances of the state had been in the hands of those "whose ignorance would be a disgrace to a novice." [34]

The chief hope for extricating Illinois from public bankruptcy and private ruin was the continuation of large-scale immigration into the state—a trend which had been largely unaffected by the depression. The *Peoria Register and Northwestern Gazeteer* said in 1840: "The history, present condition, and future prospect of the State of Illinois furnish a theme for contemplation which would have thrilled the bosom of an ancient historian with delight. Especially the progress of settlement . . . in the Illinois River region; and the multiplication of towns, orchards, and all the machinery of wealth and comfort, has been so unprecedentedly rapid and exuberant, that an Herodotus, a Tacitus, or a Gibbon would be astounded at the recital." Another contemporary observer agreed, "Illinois is destined to be a great state—great in her political and moral influence, as well as in her physical resources. It is to be made thus through foreign influence—the influence of immigration." The canal laborers had swelled the stream of immigrants from abroad, and the flow continued. It was expected that 1840 would bring as many as forty thousand new citizens. [35] So the Mormons, arriving in large numbers in 1839 and promising the continued immigration of their sect, were given a cordial, even enthusiastic, welcome.

Although a large Mormon settlement in Illinois seemed at the time mutually advantageous, there were dangers inherent in the situation. Group settlements were common in Illinois—whole towns moved from New England to Illinois, for example—but many "natives" continued to distrust the motives and influence of such ventures. The feeling persisted that immigration and settlement were actions that should be undertaken by individuals, not groups. When the *Boston Patriot* in 1834 carried a notice of the plans of an "association" to emigrate from Massachusetts to Illinois, the *Illinois Advocate and State Register* wished them success but advised them to come as families or individuals and hoped that they would get rid of

[34] Buley, *The Old Northwest*, 2:262 ff., 293–298; Ford, *History of Illinois*, pp. 182 ff.; Pease, *Frontier State*, pp. 194 ff.
[35] Buley, *The Old Northwest*, 2:120, 121.

certain Yankee notions. No man ought to come "if he were so strongly imbued with the peculiar manners, notions, and ways of thought of . . . home, as to be unable to shake them off and adopt those of his adopted country. . . . For one to come here determined to hold his own tastes and habits, come what will, would be . . . unwise. . . ." In a treatise titled *The Errors of Immigrants* an Illinois resident of twenty years wrote, "The idea of forming exclusive settlements of Germans, English, or Irish, is very erroneous and highly prejudicial to the interests of the settlers themselves." In 1838 a recent immigrant from Germany wrote home, "Nothing is more foolish and nothing furnishes more telling proof of the absolute ignorance of conditions in the United States, than when German Emigration Societies unite and strive to realize here a commercial plan of establishing settlements of communal interest." He predicted that such attempts would fail. James Hall, historian and promoter of the West, said in 1832 that emigrants would be best off and most welcome if they came as individuals rather than as groups, after dropping all provincial and parochial distinctions, because partisanship and dissension could grow often out of trifling matters. He observed further that too much of the spirit of reform, egotism, or arrogance would be unappreciated. The idea that group settlements mitigated the hardships while multiplying the pleasures and chances of success was, Hall believed, a delusion.

An individual knows how to make calculations for himself, and for his own household; he knows what they can do and suffer; but when he ventures into the regions of conjecture and brings many contingencies to bear on his fate, when he unites it with the uncertain fortune of others . . . the industrious member of such a society gets tired of helping his lazy neighbor, the peaceful man grows sick of the quarrels of his litigious friend, and the whole society feels degraded if one of its members falls into the hands of the sheriff for an unlucky felony. After all everyone is the best manager of his own business . . . [and should trust] to Providence, to his own exertions, and to the hospitality of those among whom his lot is cast.[36]

In the light of such thinking, the Mormon corporate pioneering enterprise was bound at least to be criticized.

Nor was the Mormon religion likely to encounter a greater tolerance than it had in Ohio or Missouri. Observers noted a strong tend-

[36] Matthews, *Expansion of New England*, pp. 211, 212, 256; Buley, *The Old Northwest*, 2:104, 105, 106. There were many societies in New England to promote emigration to Illinois.

ency against religion in Illinois and a lively prejudice in some quarters against preachers. Freedom from the constraints of religion was due partly to unchurched frontier abandon, partly to a hatred of "bigotry," and partly to feelings against an "autocratic clergy" or "puritanical" church and state restrictions, all of which was hard to distinguish from a desire to have no interference with western liberty to drink, hunt, race horses, and gamble on Sunday. Even a person like Abraham Lincoln, though personally abstemious, was said to "run smoothly in society," never addressing himself to questions of immorality, intemperance, vice, or tobacco-chewing. Though religious, he was unchurched. Mark Twain, another son of the country, was growing up just across the river to be an agnostic, neutral on theological questions and rejecting notions of salvation and damnation. The historian H. C. Hubbart said of this secularizing tendency of the forties, "Indeed, the combined influence of environment, of the tolerant, philosophical Kentuckian, the free Westerner, and the radical German was producing in many communities social attitudes far removed from the narrow Puritanism that has been described as typically midwestern." [37]

Finally, in choosing to locate on the banks of the Mississippi in Hancock and Lee Counties, the Mormons stumbled into a country already noted as the habitat of mean, rascally characters. In 1847 a traveler on the river wrote of the locale, "The captains of the steamboats seem to think that the inhabitants of Iowa, in this section of the state, are not worth much, and they give Keokuk and Montrose a bad name for thievery and all other forms of rascality. . . ." [38] All kinds of people came and went with ease in the river towns. And Governor Thomas Ford, undoubtedly jaundiced in his views by the fact that Mormon-gentile troubles had tarnished his administration, said in later years:

I had a good opportunity to know the early settlers of Hancock County. I had attended the circuit courts there as State's attorney, from 1830, when the county was organized, up to the year 1834; and to my certain knowledge the early settlers, with some honorable exceptions, were, in popular language, hard cases. In the year 1834, one Dr. Galland was a candidate for the legislature in a district composed of Hancock, Adams,

[37] Hubbart, *The Older Middle West*, p. 66. Hubbart believed the skeptical tendency to be strongest in central Illinois.

[38] J. H. Buckingham of the *Boston Courier*, "Illinois as Lincoln Knew It; A Boston Reporter's Record of a Trip in 1847," Harry E. Pratt, ed., *Illinois Papers and Transactions for the Year 1937* (Illinois State Historical Society, Springfield, 1937), p. 174.

and Pike counties. He resided in the county of Hancock, and as he had in the early part of his life been a notorious horse thief and counterfeiter, belonging to the Massac gang [desperadoes who terrorized Massac and other southern Illinois counties for years], and was then no pretender to integrity, it was useless to deny the charge. In all his speeches he freely admitted the fact, and came near obtaining a majority of the votes in his own county of Hancock. I mention this to show the character of the people for integrity.

Ford admitted that he had no contact again with the people there until after the Mormon settlement, "But having passed my whole life on the frontiers . . . I have frequently seen that a few first settlers would fix the character of a settlement for good or for bad, for many years after its commencement. . . . Rogues will find each other out, and so will honest men." The old Governor concluded that perhaps the Mormons themselves were rogues. "So it may appear that the Mormons . . . may have been induced to select Hancock as the place of their settlement, rather than many other places where they were strongly solicited to settle, by the promptings of a secret instinct, which, without much penetration, enables men to discern their fellows." [39]

[39] Ford, *History of Illinois*, pp. 406, 407.

2

'To Build Up a City':
The Nauvoo Gathering

. . . the place was literally a wilderness. The land was mostly covered with trees and bushes, and much of it so wet that it was with the utmost difficulty a footman could get through, and totally impossible for teams. Commerce was so unhealthful, very few could live there; but believing it might become a healthful place by the blessing of heaven to the Saints, and no more eligible place presenting itself, I considered it wisdom to make an attempt to build up a city.

Joseph Smith, Joseph Smith's History, 3:375, under entry of June 11, 1839.

The city of Nauvoo was built in part because of the circumstances surrounding the Mormon expulsion from Missouri. But in addition it was built because Mormon doctrine, as interpreted by Joseph Smith to his followers, required it. The Saints were to gather together in a holy city of their own. Earlier communities had failed for various reasons, but the Mormons were not daunted. Nauvoo was the result of their continuing attempt to create an ideal community, combining Smith's previously conceived city plan with the circumstances of a new time and place.

The original site for a "City of Zion" was Independence, Missouri. Smith's plat for that ill-fated Mormon community, begun in 1831, outlined a plan that influenced all successive Mormon towns, including Nauvoo. The city was to be one mile square, with streets laid out in a simple gridiron dividing the land into blocks of ten acres, each of which was subdivided into twenty equal lots. The Nauvoo version would substitute blocks of about four acres divided into four equal lots. Residents were to have space for gardens, orchard trees, and domestic animals. Smith's economic planning for the Mormon communities was primarily in terms of agriculture: the residents would have farms outside the city.[1] The design for Far West was similar.

[1] A reproduction of Smith's original plat for the City of Zion is in William E. Barrett and Alma P. Burton, eds., *Readings in L.D.S. History, from Original Manuscripts* (Salt Lake City, 1953), 1:12 facing. Smith's explanation for his design is in *ibid.*, 1:12, 13; and in Joseph Smith's History, 1:357–359. The city

Smith reminded the Saints there "on the duty of the brethren to come into cities to live, and carry on their farms out of the cities, according to the order of God." [2] There was to be a commons in the center of Independence and Far West, not for grazing, but for public buildings including a temple. No specific provision was made in early plans for the location of industrial or commercial establishments. In order to accommodate the infinite number of converts who were expected to gather, the boundaries of Smith's cities would be enlarged, and in addition satellite or associate cities would be created. These were termed "Stakes of Zion." While such a conception of urban ecology was preindustrial, oversimplified, and fraught with unforeseen or poorly understood difficulties, Mormon town building was orderly and industrious. Far West, Nauvoo, and Salt Lake City all conformed in general to the pattern laid down for Zion; all were examples of nineteenth-century American utopian thought, and reminders of seventeenth-century New England towns built by the Puritan forebears of the Mormons.[3]

When the exiled Saints gathered on the Illinois shore early in 1839 and began to consider their future, the establishment of another Mormon center was not a foregone conclusion. They were so shaken by the experience of the previous months that many doubted the wisdom of undertaking a new corporate venture which might cause a renewal of persecution. Planning was made more uncertain by the fact that the leadership structure of the Church was impaired, and the highest authorities were absent. The First Presidency were in a Liberty, Missouri, jail. Brigham Young did not leave Far West until

---

was to be a mile square, and, said Smith, "The whole plat is supposed to contain from fifteen to twenty thousand people." Perhaps his arithmetic was faulty; single dwellings on the lots proposed would have had to house more than fifteen persons each to accommodate a total of twenty thousand inhabitants.

[2] Joseph Smith's History, 3:56. "President Rigdon and Brother Hyrum Smith," said the Prophet, "spoke on the same subject."

[3] For a thoughtful consideration of historical and cultural factors that influenced the Mormon concept of a utopian agricultural community, see Lowry Nelson, *The Mormon Village* (Salt Lake City, 1952), chap. 2. A scholarly discussion of patterns of Mormon social and economic thought is Leonard J. Arrington, "Early Mormon Communitarianism: The Law of Consecration and Stewardship," 7:341–369. An extensive, though protagonistic, treatment of Joseph Smith's social and political thinking is Hyrum L. Andrus, "Joseph Smith, Social Philosopher, Theorist, and Prophet" (Doctor of Social Science dissertation, Syracuse University, 1955). The relation of Mormon theology to Mormon utopianism is exemplified in Parley P. Pratt, *A Voice of Warning and Instruction to All People* (New York, 1837). Pratt was an influential Mormon Apostle.

February 14.[4] The priesthood governing bodies were in varying degrees of disruption. In this situation Isaac Galland, a land broker of Hancock County, Illinois, and Lee County, Iowa, offered in February to sell the Mormons 20,000 acres of land in Lee County, some fifty miles up river from Quincy, at long term for $2.00 an acre. This seemingly attractive offer precipitated the first formal consideration of future plans for the Church. Sometime in February there was a meeting of the elders then in Quincy to discuss matters. William Marks, a leading High Priest, was chosen to preside. The purpose of the meeting, according to the sketchy minutes, was "to take into consideration the expediency of locating the Church in some place." Marks said that he was "altogether in favor of making the purchase, providing it was the will of the Lord that we should again gather together; but from the circumstances of being driven from the other places, he was almost led to the conclusion that it was not wisdom that we should do so. . . ." He urged the brethren to give their opinions, "the Lord would undoubtedly manifest His will by His Spirit." A debate then ensued: one brother was in favor of an immediate gathering; another thought that "it might be in consequence of not building according to the [correct] pattern, that we had been thus scattered." Bishop Edward Partridge favored the Saints scattering "to different parts," though the poor should be provided for. To regather, he said, would "not be expedient under the present circumstances." In the end the views of Marks and Partridge prevailed, and a motion was carried unanimously "that it would not be deemed advisable to locate on the lands [offered by Galland] for the present." [5] In the absence of firm leadership or a decision to undertake a group endeavor, the refugees started to make individual plans; the spring planting season was only weeks away. "This place is full of our people," wrote Partridge to Joseph Smith on March 5, "yet they are scattering off nearly all the while." [6] Smith, too, seemed bewildered and unsure of the proper course to pursue. When he wrote Partridge from prison in February, he showed interest in the idea of a large land purchase. But when Partridge informed him of the decision of the Quincy meeting, the Prophet hesitated. "Now, brethren, concerning the places for the location of the Saints, we cannot coun-

---

[4] Joseph Smith's History, 3:261.
[5] "Minutes of a Conference of the Church Held at Quincy, Illinois," in Joseph Smith's History, 3:260, 261. Partridge's letter, *ibid.*, p. 272.
[6] Partridge to Smith, in Joseph Smith's History, 3:273; Smith's "Liberty Jail Letter" of March 20–25, *ibid.*, p. 295.

sel you as we could if we were with you; as to [previous letters] we did not consider them anything very binding. . . ." He charged that the Church be directed by the decisions of a "general conference of the most faithful and respectable of the authorities of the Church" and that minutes of the meetings be sent to him. "While your humble servant remains in bondage . . . and if there should be any corrections by the word of the Lord, they shall be freely transmitted. . . . If anything should have been suggested by [me], or any names mentioned, except by commandment, or thus saith the Lord, we do not consider it binding, therefore our hearts shall not be grieved if different arrangements are entered into." He continued to counsel that in conference "everything should be discussed with a great deal of care and propriety" and that the conference should beware of "an aspiring spirit" and those who "aspire after their own aggrandizement." He feared that such men might "influence the Church to reject milder counsels," which in the past had "been the means of bringing much death and sorrow upon the Church." He suggested that the conference instruct "our brethren scattered abroad, who understand the spirit of the gathering, that they fall into the places of refuge and safety that God shall open unto them, between Kirtland [an early Mormon center near Cleveland] and Far West . . . in the most safe and quiet places they can find. . . ." Perhaps Smith thought that under the circumstances the group must necessarily separate, at least temporarily. "We further suggest," he wrote, "that there be no organizations of large bodies upon common stock principles, in property, or of large companies or firms, until the Lord shall signify it in a proper manner, as it opens such a dreadful field for the avaricious, and the corrupt hearted. . . ."[7] Such endeavors at Far West had been unsatisfactory.

Meanwhile Brigham Young arrived in Quincy and urged a reorganization of the Saints that would keep them together and perhaps be tantamount to a new communal gathering. Young proposed to a conference held March 17 that the members should settle if possible in companies or branches of the Church so as "to unite together as much as possible in extending the hand of charity for the relief of the poor, who were suffering for the Gospel's sake" and to do "what would prove for the general good of the whole Church." Otherwise, said Young, the "sheep would be scattered" whereas the need was for them to be "nourished and fed by the shepherds." The senior

[7] *Ibid.,* 3:299–301.

Apostle also served notice that though the Church might be in stringent circumstances, the hierarchy of leadership was still in force. An elder in Springfield was formally reproved for calling a conference of members there, presiding over it, and transacting his own order of business "contrary to the feelings of Elder Wilford Woodruff [an Apostle] and other official members who were present. They considered his proceedings contrary to the will and order of God." The March 17 conference at Quincy also excommunicated various members who had in some way offended the Church in Missouri, including the Danite chief Sampson Avard.[8] Brigham Young's admonition to keep the Church together focused attention again on Isaac Galland and his offer to put the Mormons in immediate possession of a large tract of land in Iowa Territory. The negotiations which ensued determined the location of Nauvoo, and determined also that the Mormons were to have persistent difficulty in obtaining proper titles to the land on which they settled.

"Doctor" Galland, as he was called, was a man of many complex interests in real estate, and, as Governor Ford later testified, a man of questionable character. His claim to the title "Doctor" was of uncertain validity; his real professions seem to have been frontier adventurer, promoter, and confidence man. According to Ford, after coming to Illinois as a young man he fell in with the "Massac Gang" of outlaws. He was once indicted for perjury in Hancock County, but was never tried. From 1835 to 1846 he edited various newspapers in Hancock County and Lee County, then Wisconsin Territory, and once ran unsuccessfully for the Illinois legislature.[9] During the land boom of the mid-thirties Galland entered the real-estate business in Hancock and Lee Counties.[10] Said a Lee County pioneer of the period, "Speculation was running high . . . and everybody we met had a town plat. There were then more towns in what was Lee County than there are now, if a paper plat constituted a town; and every man that had a town had a map of the county marked out to suit his town as county seat." A Lee County history listed fifty-five towns that were platted or named in early years. Galland had a

[8] "Minutes of the Conference at Quincy," in Joseph Smith's History, 3:283, 284.

[9] Ford, History of Illinois, p. 406; Nelson C. Roberts and Samuel W. Moorehead, History of Lee County, Iowa (Chicago, 1914), pp. 308, 1216; Dean Depew McBrien, "The Influence of the Frontier on Joseph Smith" (unpublished Ph.D. dissertation, George Washington University, 1929), p. 249; Thomas Gregg, History of Hancock County, Illinois (Chicago, 1880), pp. 240, 392.

[10] Hancock County Deed Book B, p. 137.

hand in at least two of these; he laid out a town called Nashville, on the river three miles below Montrose, and he participated in the original promotion of Keokuk.[11]

The site of Galland's speculations in Lee County was a land purchaser's nightmare called the Half-Breed Tract. In 1824 Congress had by treaty with the Sac and Fox Indians granted the region between the Mississippi and Des Moines Rivers south of the site of Ft. Madison to be a reservation for the half-breed offspring of frontier traders, trappers, soldiers, and other assorted whites who had fathered them and left them with their Indian mothers. Under the original treaty the beneficiaries had no legal right to sell or convey the land; but prompted by a desire to realize some immediate tangible gain, and encouraged by ambitious land traders, many of them petitioned Congress for the right of ownership in fee simple. When their prayer was granted in 1834, the triangular 119,000-acre tract overnight became a paradise for speculators. Said one observer of the phenomenon, "A horde of speculators rushed in to buy land of the half-breed owners, and, in many instances, a gun, a blanket, a pony, or a few quarts of whisky was sufficient for the purchase of large estates. There was a deal of sharp practice on both sides. Indians would often claim ownership of land to which they had no rightful title. On the other hand speculators often claimed land to which they had no right . . . at last things became badly mixed. There were no authorized surveys, no boundary lines to claims, and as a natural result numerous quarrels ensued." [12] The definition of the original grantees was not at all clear; and the prevailing notion of a half-breed was any person who was "part Indian and didn't wear a blanket." To rectify the omissions of the 1834 law and attempt to bring some order out of the confusion of claims and titles, the Wisconsin Territorial legislature in January, 1838, required all persons claiming purchase from half-breeds to file claims within a year in Lee County showing how and from whom title had been obtained. Commissioners were appointed to hear such claims; the ones considered unacceptable were to be voided, the land resold, and the proceeds divided among the half-breeds. The Wisconsin Claims Commission devoted the most of two years to this endeavor. Meanwhile, in June, 1838, the new Iowa Territory was created, and the Iowa legislature proceeded to repeal the Wisconsin

[11] Roberts and Moorehead, *History of Lee County*, pp. 153 ff.
[12] *Ibid.*, p. 55.

statute and invalidate the work of the Wisconsin commissioners. In lieu of pay the commissioners were afforded the right to bring suit for compensation against the Half-Breed lands, which they did. To satisfy the judgments of the court in their favor the entire tract was offered for sale. It was bought by Hugh Reid, a Keokuk attorney, for $5,773.32, or about five cents an acre.[13] This modest outlay was for Reid only an investment to establish some color of title, and was a gamble on the final outcome. Though Reid proceeded to "sell" some of the land, his claims were by 1841 tied up in litigation; and in September of that year suit was instituted in the United States District Court for Iowa Territory seeking partition by the court of the entire tract among the various claimants. Reid was a counsel for the plaintiffs, whose petition was drawn up by the New York Land Co., one of the two largest organized firms of speculators in Half-Breed lands. Isaac Galland was an agent for the company and had acquired an interest in it. The court decreed division of the tract into 101 shares of equal value, a division that formed the basis of all subsequent titles in the tract. However, at the time few believed that the titles could be thus quieted; and in 1846 the Iowa Supreme Court ruled that Reid, whose sheriff's deed had clouded all titles in the tract, was in fact owner in fee simple of the entire 119,000 acres. The whole region was thrown into an uproar by such a decree; it was reversed by decision of the United States Supreme Court in 1850, which upheld the District Court partition of 1841.[14]

Dr. Galland was an active participant in many complex land speculations in the Half-Breed Tract between 1834 and 1850.[15] For example, on January 9, 1839, he sold his interest in the New York Land Company for $21,000; then on April 27 he published notice in the *Iowa Territorial Gazette* that he proposed to dissolve his connection with the firm, but cautioned the public not to buy any of the stock issued him since it had been "fraudulently obtained."[16] How-

[13] Benjamin F. Gue, *History of Iowa* (New York, 1903), 1:170.
[14] Roberts and Moorehead, *History of Lee County*, pp. 55–59. For other discussions of the Half-Breed Tract see Jacob Van Der Zee, "The Half-Breed Tract," *Iowa Journal of History and Politics*, 13:151–164 (April, 1915); and Gue, *History of Iowa*, 1:169–172.
[15] David W. Kilbourne, *Strictures on Dr. I. Galland's Pamphlet, entitled, "Villainy Exposed," with some account of his transactions in lands in the Sac and Fox Reservations, etc., in Lee County, Iowa* (Fort Madison, Iowa, 1850), p. 5. Kilbourne, a resident of Lee County, wrote this pamphlet in rebuttal to one by Galland. All references to Lee County records are as cited by Kilbourne.
[16] *Ibid.*, p. 8; Lee County Deed Book 1, p. 434.

ever, he continued to claim membership in the firm as a basis for further manipulations. In June, 1840, Galland offered to sell the entire Half-Breed Tract, to which he was, he declared, "seized and possessed, and entitled both in law and equity." [17] Between 1839 and 1841, according to David Kilbourne, a resident of Montrose, Galland or his agents sold numerous town lots and farm lands in the tract for a total of more than $80,000 (considering the current deflation and money shortage, probably but little of it in cash). Yet in January, 1842, he again sold all his "interest" in the New York Land Company and in the Half-Breed Tract to a J. Remick of St. Louis for $50,000. Nor did he neglect sales to small purchasers; in the same month he sold one-fourth of a half-breed's share for $1,000.[18] When Remick began to sell lands he supposed he had bought from Galland, he ran afoul of other claimants. He charged Galland with fraud, but could not obtain a judgment. Kilbourne said that Remick was as culpable as Galland: "each felt confident he was cheating the other." [19] In 1845 Galland's remaining interests in the Half-Breed Tract, whatever they may have been, were sold for taxes in a sheriff's sale to a person who had earlier charged Galland with fraud in a land deal.[20]

Galland learned that the Mormons might be customers for his various wares when he met Elder Israel Barlow, an early Mormon refugee from Missouri, in the fall of 1838. Galland was living near Commerce, Illinois, a speculator's "paper town" across the river from Montrose. Commerce had few inhabitants but numerous lots for sale, lots in which Galland owned an interest. He saw the possibilities of selling both farm and town lands to such a group as the Mormons, and he began to promote his properties on both sides of the river. Joseph Smith was impressed that the connection Barlow had made with Galland was a kind of providential deliverance for the Saints: "[Barlow] was in a destitute situation; and making his wants known, found friends who assisted him, and gave him introductions to several gentlemen, among whom was Dr. Isaac Galland, to whom he communicated the situation; the relation of which enlisted Mr. Galland's sympathies, or interests, or both united, and

[17] Kilbourne pamphlet, pp. 10, 11; Lee County Deed Book 2, pp. 233, 234.
[18] Kilbourne pamphlet, p. 15; Lee County Deed Book 3, pp. 168, 178.
[19] Kilbourne pamphlet, p. 18. For an account of Joseph Smith's unhappy business dealings with Remick, see below, Chapter 5, and Joseph Smith's History, 5: 162, 334–336.
[20] *Ibid.*, p. 19; Lee County Deed Book 9, pp. 257, 261.

hence a providential introduction of the Church to Commerce . . . and its vicinity [the site of Nauvoo]. . . ."[21]

Smith concluded that Barlow had come to Commerce "either by missing his way, or by some other cause." The "other cause" might have been that among the proprietors of Commerce and the speculators in the Illinois Military District were the Brothers Hiram, Ethan, and Phineas Kimball, agents for their father, an absentee speculator in Military Tract lands. The Kimball home, where the father continued to reside, was at West Fairlee, Orange County, Vermont—a place only ten miles from Sharon, the birthplace and childhood home of the Prophet. The Kimballs were cousins of the famous Mormon Apostle Heber C. Kimball, also a Vermonter; and it is possible that their residence and interest in the Commerce area had something to do with attracting Mormon attention to the place. It might have been the Kimballs who introduced Barlow to Galland. At any rate it was Galland who first engaged the attention of the Church with his offers. While some purchases of land were subsequently made from the Kimballs, including five acres sold to cousin Heber on which he built his house, and while they generally maintained such social connections as entertaining the Twelve Apostles at Christmas of 1841 with gifts of land, their role in the founding of Nauvoo was a minor one. Although they offered a town for sale, Smith decided to plat and promote his own town.[22]

Barlow told Churchmen in Quincy that Galland was anxious to sell them land, and late in February President Sidney Rigdon, Bishop Edward Partridge, "Judge" Elias Higbee, and Barlow visited the Doctor. They concluded that "It is not wisdom to effect a trade . . . at present; possibly it may be wisdom hereafter."[23] But Galland persisted. On February 26, soon after his meeting with the group from Quincy, he wrote a persuasive, ingratiating letter to Daniel Rogers, a Mormon assigned the task of liquidating Jackson County holdings of the Church. After referring to lands both in

[21] Joseph Smith's History, 3:265, under entry for February 25, 1839.
[22] H. C. Kimball, *Journal of Heber C. Kimball* (Juvenile Instructor's Office, Salt Lake City, 1882), p. 81; Joseph Smith's History, 4:484. Information about the Kimball family was obtained in a personal interview with Mr. Preston Kimball, an attorney and life-long resident of Nauvoo. Of the Kimball brothers, Hiram joined the Mormon Church and went to Utah; Ethan returned to Vermont, and Phineas, the grandfather of Preston Kimball, remained in Nauvoo.
[23] Letter of Partridge to Joseph Smith, March 5, 1839, in Joseph Smith's History, 3:272.

Hancock County and across the river in the Half-Breed Tract that he would like to sell, Galland continued:

Since writing to Mr. Barlow, I have conversed with a friend of mine, who also conversed with Governor Lucas, of Iowa territory [who] respects [the Mormons] now as good and virtuous citizens, and feels disposed to treat them as such. . . . Isaac Van Allen, the attorney-general of Iowa territory, is a personal and tried friend of mine; and I feel fully authorized, from a conversation I have had with him on the subject, to say that I can assure you of his utmost endeavors to protect you from insult or violence. . . . I do believe that under a territorial form of government which is directly connected with the general government of the United States, your church will be better secured against the capriciousness of public opinion, than under a state government, where murder, rapine and robbery are admirable traits in the character of a demagogue; and where the greatest villains often reach the highest offices. I have written to Gov. Lucas on the subject. . . . I wish to serve your cause in any manner which Providence may afford me the opportunity of doing. . . . I feel that I am assuming a very great responsibility in this undertaking, and I wish to be governed by the dictates of wisdom and discretion. . . .[24]

Galland's alleged friendship with Van Allen and his assurance that Robert Lucas, the Territorial Governor, had spoken favorably of the Mormons was impressive, especially after the experience with government officers and agencies in Missouri. On March 9, Rogers presented Galland's letter to a kind of *ad hoc* steering committee of Church leaders in Quincy presided over by Sidney Rigdon, a member of the First Presidency who had recently escaped from Missouri. Galland's "sentiments of sympathy" were carefully noted in the meeting, and Rigdon was persuaded to think favorably about purchasing a tract from Galland. It was decided to send a group to "confer with the gentlemen who had so written, and declared themselves interested in our welfare" and to "select the land, if it can be safely occupied." Smith believed too that the Saints should do business with Galland. He wrote from prison late in March that "It still seems to weigh heavily on our minds" that the Church would do well to buy from Galland, especially since he seemed ready to work out an acceptable credit arrangement. Smith was impressed with

[24] Joseph Smith's History, 3:265–267. Neither Galland nor the Mormons are mentioned in John Carl Parish, *Robert Lucas* (Iowa City, 1907); Benjamin F. Shambaugh, ed., *The Executive Journal of Iowa as Kept by Governor Robert Lucas from July 17, 1838, to June 18, 1841* (Iowa City, 1906); or Benjamin F. Shambaugh, ed., *Messages and Proclamations of the Governors of Iowa*, Vol. I (Iowa City, 1903). The Saints probably did not communicate officially with either Lucas or Van Allen since no such correspondence is preserved in Joseph Smith's History.

what seemed to be the influential connections of Galland. The Prophet urged that "friendly feelings" be sought not only with Galland, but also with Lucas and Van Allen:

that peradventure such men may be wrought upon by the providence of God, to do good to his people. We really think that Mr. Galland's letter breathes that kind of spirit, if we may judge correctly. Governor Lucas also. We suggest the idea of praying fervently for all men who manifest any degree of sympathy for the suffering children of God. . . .

It seems to be deeply impressed on our minds that the Saints ought to lay hold of every door that shall seem to be opened unto them, to obtain foothold on the earth, and to be making all the preparation that is within their power for the terrible storms that are now gathering in the heavens. . . .[25]

On March 22 Smith wrote Galland a long letter introducing him to the Mormon religion and explaining that the Saints had been innocent victims of outrage in Missouri. In closing he wrote, "If Bishop Partridge, or if the Church have not made a purchase of your land, and if there is not anyone who feels a particular interest in making the purchase, you will hold it in reserve for us; we will purchase it of you at the proposals you made to Mr. Barlow."[26]

In February Galland had written Governor Lucas as promised asking "whether [the Mormons] could be permitted to purchase lands and settle upon them, in the territory of Iowa, and there worship Almighty God according to the dictates of their own consciences, secure from oppression. . . ." Lucas replied affirmatively in March, and on April 12 Galland sent the governor's letter to the *Quincy Argus* to be published, along with his own covering letter of explanation. He wrote the editors:

If you think the publication [of the Lucas letter] will in any way promote the cause of justice by vindicating the slandered reputation of the people called "Mormons" from the ridiculous falsehoods which the malice, cupidity, and envy of their murderers in Missouri have endeavored to heap upon them, you are respectfully solicited to publish it in the *Argus*. The testimony of Governor Lucas as to the good moral character of these people, I think will have its deserved influence upon the people of Illinois, in encouraging our citizens in their humane and benevolent exertions to relieve this distressed people, who are now wandering in our neighborhoods without comfortable food, raiment, or a shelter from the pelting storm.

The governor's letter was scarcely a "testimony . . . to the good moral character" of the Mormons. In fact Lucas said he knew little of "this peculiar people," but that he had heard no complaints of

[25] From the Liberty Jail Letter, March 20–25, *ibid.*, p. 298.
[26] *Times and Seasons*, 1:51, 52, February, 1840.

their having violated the laws of the country. With regard to their settling in Iowa, he merely affirmed that the religious liberties guaranteed by the Constitution were to be enjoyed in the territories as well as in the states. "Their religious opinions," he concluded, "have nothing to do with our political transactions." Lucas' words could scarcely be construed as an endorsement of the Mormons, but he was at least tolerant and not antagonistic.[27]

In April, 1839, Joseph Smith escaped prison. He assumed that his detention had been unlawful as well as unjust, and that once he was beyond the borders of Missouri his trouble with that state would be ended. He fled eastward unmolested and arrived in Quincy on April 22, where he was greeted with joy. His appearance was a good omen that perhaps there were further blessings in store for the distressed Saints. If five winter months in jail had affected the Prophet adversely there was no outward evidence of it. He moved with all his old energy, his mood was optimistic, and his actions were decisive.

The stage was set for the founding of a new Mormon city. Smith had all during the winter wanted the Saints to regather rather than scatter; but since Missouri, the "land of Zion," was barred to them he had been indecisive about the course to follow. Now all was changed. Illinois citizens had befriended the Mormons, and the refugees were still more or less intact as a group in the region around Quincy. Iowans also seemed friendly. So a settlement in a new region free from persecution seemed possible. The decisive factor in determining the exact location of the new gathering place was the opportunity to possess Galland's tract for no money down and long years to pay. Land for farming and for townsites was the basic Mormon economic requirement, and the river offered commercial opportunities for the future. No formal decision by a conference to effect a regathering of the Church seems to have been made, nor were plans elaborated. The planting season was upon them, and there was no time for delay. Details would be worked out as needed. The Saints looked to Smith as charismatic leader in temporal as well as spiritual affairs; the Lord and his Prophet would provide. Such were the circumstances which gave birth to Nauvoo.

Smith and other Church leaders began immediately to contract

[27] Letter of Lucas to Galland, March [?], 1839; letter of Galland to the *Quincy Argus*, April 12, 1839, in Joseph Smith's History, 3:317, 318. The Lucas letter is not in the governor's *Executive Journal.*

for the purchase of what in a few months amounted to thousands of acres, mostly in Lee County, Iowa Territory, and Hancock County, Illinois, including the site of what was to be Nauvoo. On April 25, just three days after he arrived in Quincy, Smith and members of the Committee on Removal went to look at lands in the Half-Breed Tract "to select a location for the Saints." The following week they "continued to look at the different locations which were presented in Lee County, Iowa, and about Commerce. . . ." On May 1, they agreed to purchase a farm of 135 acres about a mile south of Commerce on the Illinois bank of the river from Hugh White, a local landowner, for $5,000. They also bought 47 acres adjoining the White farm improved with what was, perhaps euphemistically, described as a "hotel," from Galland for $9,000.[28] The Mormon leaders disagreed as to how the deeds should be drawn. The majority of the committee wanted the purchases deeded to Alanson Ripley as agent for the committee, which was in turn representing the whole Church in *ad hoc* fashion. But Sidney Rigdon would not have it: "no committee should control any property he had anything to do with." So the deeds were made to George W. Robinson, Rigdon's son-in-law, "with the express understanding that he should deed it to the Church, when the Church had paid for it according to their obligations in the contract." Robinson had a month earlier taken an option on this same Galland property, plus ferry rights and some additional parcels of land, to buy at $18,000. It is impossible to know whether he was then acting as agent for the Committee on Removal, in a private capacity for the welfare of the Church, entirely in his own interests, or with a combination of interests. He may have obtained the option with his own money. Whatever the details of the affair may have been, Robinson's agency for the Church in the purchase contract was apparently a verbal one, as many Nauvoo business agreements between brethren were to be; and even though there was an "express understanding" of the responsibilities of both the agent and the Church, in the absence of a written agreement, recollections at a later time might differ as to what the verbal agreement had been. Trouble was a frequent result.[29]

Joseph Smith called a "general conference" of the Saints in the Quincy area for May 4, 5, and 6, the first such conference since the

[28] Joseph Smith's History, 3:336, 341, 342. Galland had bought the same 47 acres from White in 1837 for $2,000. Hancock County Deed Book C, p. 388.

[29] Robinson's option on the Galland property, dated April 3, 1839, is recorded in Deed Book G, p. 247.

Far West persecutions. Though many Saints were in other parts of the country and could not be represented, the conference acted for the whole Church, as did all subsequent "general conferences" held in Nauvoo. The business was begun with "some preliminary observations by Elder E. P. Greene and President Sidney Rigdon concerning a certain purchase of land in the Iowa Territory, made for the Church by the Presidency. . . ." The conference resolved unanimously to "entirely sanction" the purchase as well as "the agency thereof." On the last day of the conference William Marks was appointed to "preside over the Church at Commerce, Illinois," where settlement was also to be made. Bishop Whitney was appointed "also to go to Commerce, and there act in unison with the other Bishops of the Church." Another resolution advised the brethren "living in the Eastern States . . . to move to Kirtland [Ohio], and again settle that place as a stake of Zion, in preference to their moving farther west." [30]

The largest purchases of land were on the Iowa side of the river, despite the fact that Nauvoo was to rise on the Illinois side. Smith recorded little in his journal about the "certain purchase of land in the Iowa Territory," or about "the agency thereof." Under the entry for June 24 he wrote simply, "This day the Church purchased the town of Nashville, in Lee County, Iowa Territory, together with twenty thousand acres of land adjoining it." [31] In fact the engagements entered to purchase that princely tract were very complex, and were to school the Saints in the difficulties encountered by those who in all innocence tried to buy Half-Breed lands. According to Kilbourne, between May 13 and June 26 Galland sold to Oliver Granger and Vinson Knight, apparently acting as agents for the Church, tracts of 2,638 and 12,745 acres respectively in the Half-Breed Tract, for the sums of $6,600 and $32,342.22. Either in connection with or in addition to these contracts Galland sold the Mormons stock in something called "the Half Breed Land Company." One such stock certificate, dated May 1, 1839, read: "This is to certify that Vinson Knight is owner of five shares of stock in the Half

[30] "Minutes of a General Conference . . . held near Quincy . . . May 4th, 5th, and 6th, 1839," in Joseph Smith's History, 3:345, 347.

[31] *Ibid.*, 3:378. According to Alanson Ripley, Vinson Knight's purchases for the Church included parts of Keokuk and Montrose in addition to Nashville. He said that thirty thousand acres had been purchased, and that the "whole [Half-Breed Tract] can be purchased by a united effort of the Saints." *Times and Seasons*, 1:24, December, 1839.

Breed Land Company, and on the surrender of this certificate, which will be received at par in payment for one hundred dollars, for lands in the Sac and Fox Half Breed Reservation, the said V. Knight or his assignee, will be entitled to receive a deed to this amount of said land, to be sold at public vendue within one year from the date hereof." [32] The "Half Breed Land Company" was apparently another device by which Galland manipulated his Lee County interests. By incorporating them, whatever they may have been, Galland was able to give a customer shares of stock instead of deeds, and might be able to persuade him, at least for a time, that they were an adequate substitute. The stock was both a means of speculating in land and itself an item for speculation. If the value of the stock increased, the stockholder would benefit; if during the year the price of land should fall, he would also benefit. It is possible that the Church agents knowingly went along with such arrangements for speculative reasons; it is much more likely that they trusted Galland, took the securities that he offered, and felt that possession of the land, honorably purchased, would be nine points of the law. Galland's terms were, according to Smith, "very reasonable" and on long credit, "so that we might have the opportunity of paying for them without being distressed." The Church had received in return, said the Prophet, "clear and indisputable title" to all the land contracted for. Since there was at the time no such thing as a clear title to Half-Breed lands, the Mormons were duped. But until the inevitable reckoning time when they had to confront other claimants to the lands they thought they owned, they were grateful to Galland. He is "one of our benefactors," Smith proclaimed eighteen months later,

having under his control a large quantity of land, in the immediate vicinity of our city, and a considerable portion of the city plat, opened both his heart and his hands, and "when we were strangers, took us in," and bade us welcome to share with him in his abundance, leaving his dwelling house, the most splendid edifice in the vicinity, for our accommodation, and partook [sic] to a small, uncomfortable dwelling. . . . He is the honored instrument the Lord used to prepare a home for us, when we were driven from our inheritances, having given him control of vast bodies of land, and prepared his heart to make the use of it the Lord intended he should. Being a man of extensive information, great talents, and high literary fame, he devoted all his powers and influence to give us a standing.[33]

[32] Kilbourne pamphlet, pp. 8, 9.
[33] "A Proclamation of the First Presidency of the Church to the Saints Scattered Abroad," January 8, 1841, in Joseph Smith's History, 4:270, 271. Accord-

37

On July 2, 1839, Smith in company with other officials visited the Half-Breed purchase made by Vinson Knight "and advised that a town be built there, and called Zarahemla [the name of a city in the *Book of Mormon*]." [34]

But it was across the river on the Illinois side that the Mormons concentrated their efforts "to build up a city." Smith gave no reason why he chose the east bank of the river as his own residence or as the site of Nauvoo. "I was preparing to remove to Commerce," he recorded on May 8; and two days later, "I arrived with my family at the White purchase and took up my residence in a small log house on the bank of the river, about one mile south of Commerce City, hoping that I and my friends may here find a resting place for a little season at least." [35] A month later he put down his most extensive observation on the location of his city: "the place was literally a wilderness. The land was mostly covered with trees and bushes, and much of it so wet that it was with the utmost difficulty that a footman could get through, and totally impossible for teams. Commerce was so unhealthful very few could live there; but believing it might become a healthful place by the blessing of heaven to the Saints, and no more eligible place presenting itself, I considered it wisdom to make an attempt to build up a city." [36] It is impossible to know exactly why Smith chose to locate his new city where he did on the Illinois side. Perhaps he was attracted by the beauty of the place or by its commercial possibilities, or because there were fewer gentile settlers in the neighborhood than there were on the Iowa side. Perhaps there were other good reasons. But perhaps the location for Nauvoo was largely a matter of expediency, or even of accident. Smith knew the reputation of the place for sickness, but he disregarded it. There was need to make haste that spring; Smith moved to his new homesite less than three weeks after he arrived in Illinois. The people had to be gathered, or else they would scatter. Crops and gardens had to be planted, and stock cared for. The suffering of many refugees was acute. On June 13 Partridge wrote Smith from Quincy in distress and discouragement about the plight of the in-

---

ing to Smith, Galland subsequently took titles to lands left by the Saints in Missouri "in payment for the whole amount," and then traded with the Saints for more of their Missouri lands, which the Mormon leader claimed were worth $80,000.

[34] Joseph Smith's History, 3:382.
[35] *Ibid.*, 3:348, 349.
[36] *Ibid.*, 3:375, under entry for June 11, 1839.

digent. The time to plant garden was past, and no one seemed to have any money; the Bishop himself confessed of having only $1.44 in the world. Some were blind, many were sick, and five had recently died. "What is best for them to do," wrote Partridge, "I do not know." [37] The only thing to do was to make the best of the situation, as Smith phrased it, by entering "every door that shall seem to be opened . . . to obtain foothold on the earth. . . ." The Church had bought land on both sides of the river near Commerce and might buy more. Smith was learning how easy it was to buy on credit; there were many land dealers in the neighborhood whose sales in the summer of 1839 had been exceedingly slow and who were willing to collect later if they could sell now. Soon after moving into the log house on the swampy bottom Smith decided, as Brigham Young was to do eight years later about another unpromising location, that "this is the place."

The site of the city of Nauvoo was directly across the river from Montrose, Iowa, about 12 miles by the river north of Keokuk, 15 from Warsaw, Illinois, 53 from Quincy, and 191 from St. Louis.[38] There is at that point a bend in the river that makes a long smooth arc pointing toward the west and leaving a big bulge of bottom land on the Illinois side jutting into Iowa. Since the river flows by on the north, west, and south, the bulge is a kind of peninsula shaped like a half-ellipse, two miles long from north to south and a mile wide. A line of broken bluffs runs north and south along the east or land side of the peninsula, meeting the river on the north at the beginning of its bend and again on the south at the completion of the bend. The peninsula, which is low and flat, is separated by the bluffs from the higher prairie which stretches eastward from their top. The peninsula, the bluffs, and a considerable area on the adjacent prairie were all to be included in the City of Nauvoo. There were few inhabitants in the area before the Mormons. "When I made the purchase of White and Galland," wrote Smith, "there were one stone house, three frame houses, and two block houses, which constituted the whole city of Commerce. Between Commerce and Mr. Davison Hibbard's, there was one stone house and three log houses, including the one that I live in, and these were all the houses in this vicin-

[37] *Ibid.*, 3:376.
[38] James H. Young, *The Tourists' Pocket Map of the State of Illinois, Exhibiting Its Internal Improvements,. Roads, etc.*, 1838. Manuscript Collection of the Wisconsin State Historical Society.

ity, and the place was literally a wilderness." [39] When the Mormons arrived much of "the flat," as the peninsula was called, was an uncleared tangle of trees, vines, and other vegetation. The wetness about which Smith complained resulted not from river water but from numerous springs and streams rising in the bluffs. These had no defined drainage channel and consequently made the peninsula marshy, especially in the southern half where the Church made the first land purchases and where Smith settled. The problem was largely solved when the Mormons dug a drainage ditch along the base of the bluffs to divert the water near its source. [40]

Despite wetness and malaria the peninsula had attracted attention as a potential townsite long before the Mormons arrived. It was the only place on the Illinois side of the river for many miles in either direction where the bluffs did not come close to the riverbank. [41] It was strategically located at the head of the Des Moines Rapids of the Mississippi, a twelve-mile system of deeply submerged limestone and blue clay upcroppings that made navigation impossible for large boats and difficult for most boats when the river was low. So the head of the rapids might become a terminus for traffic on the upper Mississippi. In 1830, the Missouri legislature saw even greater potential in the area, and petitioned Congress to annex the land in southern Lee County between the Des Moines and Mississippi Rivers to their state, thus giving Missouri access to the Des Moines Rapids. "[The site] in future times," said their memorial, "will be of immense importance to the commerce of the whole western valley. Your memorialists anticipate the day when the obstructions to navigation will be overcome by a canal around those rapids; when the inexhaustible power of that mighty stream [will be applied] to almost every variety of manufacturing machinery, and when a great commercial city will spring up in that wilderness, to serve as the great entrepôt of the Upper and Lower Mississippi." [42] In 1824 a

[39] Joseph Smith's History, 3:375.
[40] Plat of the City of Nauvoo, manuscript in possession of the author; interview with Mr. Preston Kimball of Nauvoo.
[41] Perhaps the first white settler at the site was Louis Honoré, a Creole trader, around 1800. In 1805 he was joined by William Ewing, a young agricultural agent sent by the Jefferson administration to teach farming to the Sac and Fox Indians. Tradition has it that Ewing built the cabin occupied at first by Joseph Smith. A brief, lively account of the Ewing episode is Donald Jackson, "William Ewing, Agricultural Agent to the Indians," *Agricultural History*, 31:3–7 (1957).
[42] *Senate Documents*, 2nd Session, 21st Congress, No. 71, p. 4, quoted in Jacob Van Der Zee, "The Half-Breed Tract," *Iowa Journal of History and Politics*, 13:160 (April, 1915).

town was platted on the northwest bank of the peninsula and hopefully named "Commerce." The Kimballs had lots to sell in the town and made it their residence in the thirties. During the great land boom of the mid-thirties two Connecticut speculators, Horace Hotchkiss and John Gillet, bought land on the peninsula; and in 1837 they platted another more extensive town alongside Commerce which they styled "Commerce City." Neither town attracted many settlers, and after the Panic of 1837 the future of both appeared bleak.[43]

Joseph Smith assessed the site with the eye of a man who defined the future in large terms. It was a natural location for a great Mormon city which would cover the plain in the bend of the river and even the bluffs and prairies beyond with the thousands and tens of thousands of converts expected to join the faith. The city would be crowned with a great temple atop the bluffs, like those projected for Independence and Far West but never realized. The city would be called "Nauvoo," decided Smith a little later, a Hebrew word conveying the idea of "beauty and repose." During the summer of 1839 the Prophet began to purchase the entire site of his envisioned metropolis to the extent that it was for sale. In addition to the White and Galland farms he contracted the purchase of about five hundred acres from Hotchkiss and Gillet, including some of Commerce and all of Commerce City. Thus the Church would own most of the peninsula, excluding about 125 acres of the western end.[44]

The "Hotchkiss Purchase" was for Smith and the Church the greatest business venture since the Kirtland Bank.[45] Hotchkiss ap-

---

[43] Hancock County Plat Book 1, pp. 10, 11, 26, 27; in the vault of the Circuit Clerk and Recorder, Carthage, Illinois.

[44] The Hotchkiss Purchase included the northeast quarter of Section 2, the southeast fractional quarter of Section 35, the west half of the southwest quarter of Section 36, the southwest fractional quarter of Section 35, and the northeast fractional quarter of Section 35, excluding twenty-seven lots in Commerce. Deed Book 12G, pp. 399, 400. Its boundaries ran from the river at the foot of Cedar Street in Commerce east to Bain Street in Nauvoo, midway between Cutler and Young; then south on Bain to Munson; then east on Munson to Wells; then north to Macomb; then east to Barnett; then north to Brattle; then west to Wells; then north to the river. Smith, in his only description of the Hotchkiss Purchase, said, "[It] includes all the land lying north of the White purchase to the river and thence on the river south, including the best steamboat landing, but is the most sickly part of Nauvoo." Under entry of August 25, 1841, in Joseph Smith's History, 4:408.

[45] Between 1831 and 1837 Smith resided at Kirtland, in Ohio's Western Reserve, and the town attracted a sizable Mormon population. The Saints built a beautiful little temple there and launched numerous business enterprises, the

parently knew a city when he saw one coming upon his property; accordingly the price was high, considering the approaching deflation and monetary stringency. The purchase was in the form of a land contract, the Church to have possession of the property but not the deeds until the debt was paid. Apparently no money was paid down, and the terms were entailed in a series of notes. Two notes of $25,000, one maturing in ten and one in twenty years, seem to have been the principle. There were forty additional notes of $1,500 each, two of which were due every twelve months for twenty years. These were apparently the interest: eight per cent a year simple interest on $50,000. There were two additional notes of $1,250, one due in five years and the other in ten. So the Church was to pay the Hotchkiss partners $3,000 each year for twenty years, plus $1,250 the fifth year, $26,250 the tenth year, and $25,000 the twentieth year. Finally an additional $2,000 was to be paid Hugh White, who owned a small interest in the property. The total amount was $114,500.[46] Smith subsequently claimed that Hotchkiss had agreed verbally that no interest was to be charged, but the contracts do not suggest any such agreement. The obligations of the Hotchkiss Purchase forced Smith and the Church into the real-estate business on a large scale and determined that city lots in Nauvoo would not be inexpensive.

Nauvoo was platted at least as early as June 11, 1839; on that date Smith referred in his journal to a building site near his house by block and lot number. The Prophet's design for the city as revealed in the plat was a simple gridiron conforming to the lines of the established survey. There were 150 squares of about four acres, each divided into four equal lots. The streets were, with two exceptions, three rods wide (forty-nine and one-half feet) and ran north-south and east-west, regardless of the terrain. The plan of Nauvoo was

most extensive of which was a grandiose town-lot speculation. As an aid to their endeavors and as a speculation in its own right, they formed an ill-conceived bank just in time to see it swept away, along with all the rest of their ventures, by the Panic of 1837. One result was a split in the Kirtland congregation into pro- and anti-Smith factions, and a heritage of misgiving about corporate Mormon business activities. For scholarly analyses of the Kirtland period in Mormon history, see R. K. Fielding, "The Mormon Economy in Kirtland, Ohio," *Utah Historical Quarterly*, 27:331–338 (1959); and R. K. Fielding, "The Growth of the Mormon Church in Kirtland, Ohio" (Ph.D. dissertation, University of Indiana, 1957).

[46] Deed Book 12G, pp. 399, 400; Deed Book H, p. 510. The agents were Joseph and Hyrum Smith and Sidney Ridgon, the First Presidency of the Church. The price of the Hotchkiss Purchase has been frequently quoted as $53,500, but this is apparently incorrect. See for example Brigham H. Roberts, *Comprehensive History of the Church, Century I*, 2:9. The Church's further dealings with Hotchkiss are described in Chapter 5.

similar to those of Independence and Far West, except that the lots were larger and no special blocks were set aside for public buildings. There was no temple block in the original Nauvoo plat because the site Smith had in mind was on top of the bluff, land that was in the summer of 1839 still privately owned. Perhaps the Prophet also had it in mind that the other public buildings should be near the temple. According to an engraving of the city plat made by Gustavus Hills in 1842, Main Street and Water Street were to be eighty-seven and sixty-four feet wide respectively, suggesting commercial development of the two thoroughfares that intersected at the corner occupied by Smith's residence and the Nauvoo House. A ship canal was planned to run down the middle of Main Street; hence the provision for its unusual width.[47] The plats of Commerce and Commerce City did not fit the Nauvoo gridiron, and on March 1, 1841, the Nauvoo City Council moved to have them vacated. They were then entered as "Joseph Smith's Addition to Nauvoo." Subsequently Herringshaw and Thompson's addition on the prairie east of the bluffs also failed to conform to the general plan; so the two gentile proprietors, anxious that their lots not fall under any ban, hastened to correct the fault. "As Herringshaw and Thompson's addition . . . was not laid out in strict conformity to the original plan of Nauvoo," they recorded, "we do therefore declare the same vacated." It was then replatted with minor changes.[48]

Smith began at once to promote Nauvoo as a new gathering place for the Saints. He wrote letters late in May, 1839, urging his friends to come settle, reserving lots for them, and speaking of house building and the general development of the city. In July he issued a circular to all members of the Church to urge the principle of the gathering:

There will be here and there a Stake [of Zion] for the gathering of the Saints. Some may have cried peace, but the Saints and the world will have little peace from henceforth. Let this not hinder us from going to the Stakes; for God has told us to flee, not dallying, or we will be scattered, one here, and another there. There your children shall be blessed, and you in the midst of friends where you may be blessed. The Gospel net gathers in every kind.

I prophesy, that that man who tarries after he has an opportunity of going, will be afflicted by the devil. Wars are at hand; we must not delay.

[47] Joseph Smith's History, 3:375; Hancock County Plat Book 1, p. 37. The Nauvoo plat was recorded in September, 1839, by Smith, Rigdon, and G. W. Robinson.
[48] Joseph Smith's History, 4:307, 308; Plat Book 1, p. 49.

43

. . . We ought to have the building up of Zion as our greatest object. When wars come, we shall have to flee to Zion. The cry is to make haste. The last revelation says, ye shall not have time to have gone over the earth, until these things come. It will come as did the cholera, war, fires, and earthquakes; one pestilence after another, until the Ancient of Days comes, then judgment will be given to the Saints.[49]

The evidence does not indicate how many responded to Smith's invitation that first summer. Little notice was taken of the matter in the Prophet's journal. On June 13 he wrote, "About this time Elder Theodore Turley raised the first house built by the Saints in this place; it was built of logs . . . on the northeast corner of lot 4, block 147, of the White purchase." Four months later he mentioned casually, "Quite a number of families moving into Commerce."[50]

There were enough Saints who had come to the new gathering place so that the semiannual General Conference of October, 1839, was held at Nauvoo rather than at Quincy. The meeting formally ratified the Prophet's decision to build a new city: "The President . . . spoke at some length on the situation of the Church; the difficulties they have had to contend with; and the manner in which they had been led to this place; and wanted to know . . . whether they wished to appoint this a Stake of Zion or not; that he thought it was a good place, and suited for the Saints. It was then unanimously agreed upon that it should be appointed a Stake and a place of gathering for the Saints." William Marks was elected stake president, with Bishops Whitney, Partridge, and Knight to care for the three wards established in the city. A stake was also voted for the Iowa side of the river, afterward referred to as Zarahemla Stake. Sundry business was transacted, including the ordination of Robert D. Foster, a prominent local resident who had recently joined the Church, to the priesthood office of Elder. Then Lyman Wight "addressed the meeting on the subject of raising funds by contribution, towards paying for the lands which had been contracted for as a settlement for the Church, after which contributions were received for that purpose." Few of the Saints knew the extent or nature of those contracts; but now a conference had gone on record in support of them.[51]

[49] Joseph Smith's History, 3:362, 363, 390, 391.
[50] *Ibid.*, 3:375; 4:15.
[51] "Minutes of a Conference at Commerce, Illinois, October 6th, 7th, and 8th, 1839," in Joseph Smith's History, 4:12, 13. The number of Nauvoo wards was subsequently increased from three to fourteen.

From the summer of 1839 until his death in June, 1844, the Prophet urged the gathering of the Saints to Nauvoo as a religious duty and made the teaching of this doctrine a responsibility of other Church officials and of the lay ministry. The degree to which the Saints responded was intimately connected with the ability of the Church to meet its financial obligations, as well as with the general prosperity of the city. In 1841 a plan to build a temple in Nauvoo was woven into the doctrine of the gathering. More people were needed to aid in building the temple, which in turn would make possible the salvation of the Saints and of the Church.

By the autumn of 1839 it was clear that Nauvoo had become the new headquarters and center for the Church, and heavy emphasis then began to be placed upon the Nauvoo gathering. On December 8, 1839, the First Presidency and the Nauvoo High Council, a group of twelve high priests which through 1843 functioned something like a board of directors for the whole Church, issued an epistle "To the Saints scattered abroad, in the region westward from Kirtland, Ohio":

We have heard it rumored abroad, that some at least, and probably many, are making their calculations to remove back to Kirtland next season.

Now brethren . . . we advise you to abandon such an idea; yea, we warn you, in the name of the Lord, not to remove back there, unless you are counseled to do so by the First Presidency, and the High Council of Nauvoo. We do not wish by this to take your agency away from you; but we wish to be plain, and pointed in our advice . . . that your sins may not be found in our skirts. . . .[52]

At the annual General Conference held in Nauvoo in April, 1840, it became clear that the indebtedness incurred by the land purchases was likely to be a continuing concern for the whole Church. After a report of the First Presidency was read "with regard to their proceedings in purchasing lands, and securing a place of gathering for the Saints," Joseph Smith "made some observations respecting the pecuniary affairs of the Church, and requested the brethren to step forward, and assist in liquidating the debt on the town plot, so that the poor might have an inheritance." That the poor should have

[52] *Ibid.*, 4:45. Smith and others close to him obviously felt that the Kirtland church was in an unhealthy condition. On November 8, Smith had noted, "There was some division of sentiment among the Kirtland brethren." *Ibid.*, 4:20. In the epistle quoted above, it was explained that some would very probably be sent back to Kirtland "to attend to important business there," but that such should not be construed as sanctioning a regathering at Kirtland.

a literal inheritance of land in Zion and the stakes was basic Mormon doctrine, and one that had caused some difficulty in Missouri, where there seemed to be more poor to inherit than there were rich willing to provide inheritances. If the poor were to be given Nauvoo lots, the problem of "liquidating the debt on the town plot" would indeed put heavy demands on the brethren. Smith further advised the conference that the elders who went on missions should teach the gathering "as set forth in the Holy Scriptures," but that respecting those who gathered, "It had been wisdom for most of the Church to keep on this side of the river, that a foundation might be established in this place; but that now it was the privilege of the Saints to occupy the lands in Iowa, or wherever the Spirit might lead them." [53]

At the October, 1840, conference, Smith sought to answer criticisms of the magnitude of the Nauvoo undertaking by sharing with the Saints his view of the expected growth of the Church missions. New members already flowed from them in streams. "If the work rolls forward with the same rapidity that it has heretofore done," said the Mormon leader,

. . . we may soon expect to see flocking to this place, people of every land; the polished European; the degraded Hottentot, and the shivering Laplanders; persons of all languages. . . . And of every color; who shall with us worship . . . in His holy temple and offer up their orisons in his sanctuary.

It was in consideration of these things, and that a home might be provided for the Saints, that induced us to purchase the present city for a place of gathering for the Saints, and the extensive tract of land on the opposite side of the Mississippi. Although the purchases at the time . . . appeared to be large and uncalled for; yet from what we now see, it is apparent to all that we may soon have to say, "This place is too straight; give us room that we may dwell." We therefore hope that the brethren . . . will aid us in liquidating the debts which are now owing, so that the inheritances may be secured to the Church, and which eventually will be of great value.[54]

Smith was soliciting contributions to pay the debt on the land purchases; however, the method finally employed to retire that debt was the sale of lots to Saints who gathered to Nauvoo. Offerings were used primarily for other purposes. The purchase of an "inheritance" in the new city was viewed by some as a potentially profitable investment in a fast growing metropolis; speculation thus became an integral part of the whole process of the Nauvoo gathering. But the

[53] "Minutes of the General Conference of the Church," *ibid.*, 4:106, 109.
[54] "Report of the Presidency," October 5, 1840, *ibid.*, 4:213, 214.

financially irresponsible were not welcome. At the October, 1840, conference President Hyrum Smith, the Prophet's brother, stated that there were "several individuals, who on moving to this place, had no recommend from the branches of the Church where they had resided." The group then "resolved that such be disfellowshipped." [55] However, during the confused and arduous years that followed, gatherers were not always so carefully screened.

In August, 1840, Smith enlarged upon the religious consequences of the Nauvoo gathering in a general letter to the "Saints Scattered Abroad." "The work of the Lord in these last days, is one of vast magnitude, and almost beyond the comprehension of mortals. . . . The purposes of God are great," said Smith, and His goodness had been specifically manifest in "having secured a location upon which we have again commenced operations for the good of His people." The Prophet urged the Saints to

unite our energies for the upbuilding of the Kingdom, and establishing the Priesthood in their fullness and glory. . . . The work which has to be accomplished in the last days is one of vast importance, and will call into action the energy, skill, talent, and ability of the Saints, so that they may roll forth with that glory and majesty described by the prophet; and will consequently require the concentration of the Saints, to accomplish works of such magnitude and grandeur.

The work of the gathering spoken of in the Scriptures will be necessary to bring about the glories of the last dispensation. . . .

Smith then for the first time in an official communication broached the subject of building a temple at Nauvoo, "where the ordinances can be attended to agreeably to His divine will . . . to accomplish which, considerable exertion must be made, and means will be required. . . ." He told the Saints to react to these responsibilities "as though the whole labor depended on themselves alone."

To those who feel thus interested, and can assist in this great work, we say, let them come to this place; by so doing they will not only assist in the rolling on of the Kingdom, but be in a situation where they can have the advantage of instruction from the Presidency, and other authorities of the Church, and rise higher and higher in the scale of intelligence until they can "comprehend with the Saints what is the breadth and length, and depth and heighth; and to know the love of Christ which passeth knowledge." [56]

Zion in Missouri must be laid aside, at least for the present; it was in the land of enemies. The building of the Kingdom was now to be

[55] *Ibid.*, 4:205.
[56] *Ibid.*, 4:185, 186.

interpreted as the building of the city on the Mississippi. Though the idea of a general gathering of the Saints had, admitted Smith in January, 1841, been previously "associated with the most cruel and oppressing scenes, owing to our unrelenting persecutions at the hands of wicked and unjust men," he hoped that those days "of darkness and gloom" were past. The "greatest temporal and spiritual blessings" now awaited the united and concerted action of the faithful, not to be obtained by individual and scattered efforts: "there is no other way for the Saints to be saved in these last days . . . let the brethren . . . say with Nehemiah, 'We, His servants, will arise and build' . . . as watchmen to the house of Israel, as shepherds over the flock which is now scattered over a vast extent of country, [with] the anxiety we feel for their prosperity and everlasting welfare, and for the carrying out the great and glorious purposes of our God . . . we feel to urge its necessity, and say—Let the Saints come here; this is the word of the Lord. . . ." [57] This proclamation of January, 1841, was the first official commandment to the members of the Church by the Prophet, speaking *ex cathedra,* to remove to Nauvoo. Smith now linked the Nauvoo gathering and the building of a temple; the population of the faithful must increase so that the temple might be speedily completed. Furthermore Smith bade welcome to all gentile settlers. Anyone who might buy, build, and work would be welcomed to the great task of raising up the Kingdom. At the annual conference of the Church at Nauvoo in April, 1841, Joseph Smith explained an expanded vision of the gathering; it would embrace not only the city, but the whole region: "From what we now witness, we are led to look forward with pleasing anticipation to the future, and soon expect to see thousands of Israel flocking to this region in obedience to the heavenly command; numerous inhabitants—Saints—thickly studding the flowery and widespread prairies of Illinois; temples for the worship of our God erecting in various parts, and great peace resting upon Israel." The Saints must come to receive the blessings of the temple to be sure; but they must first come to build it: "We would call the attention of the Saints more particularly to the building of the temple, for on its speedy erection great blessings depend . . . those who cannot contribute labor will bring their gold and their silver, their brass and their iron, with the pine tree and the box tree, to beautify the same." [58]

[57] "A Proclamation of the First Presidency of the Church to the Saints Scattered Abroad," January 15, 1841, *ibid.,* 4:267–273.
[58] "Report of the First Presidency," *ibid.,* 4:338, 339.

Nauvoo had by 1841 become a hard taskmaster, making unrelenting demands upon the meager resources of the Mormon Church. In
May, 1841, Smith took drastic action to promote his new city, "this
corner-stone of Zion," at the expense of other Mormon settlements
and congregations: "The First Presidency . . . anxious to promote
the prosperity of [the] Church, feel it their duty to call upon the
Saints who reside out of this county [Hancock] to make preparations to come in without delay. . . . Here the Temple must be
raised, the University built, and other edifices erected which are
necessary for the great work of the last days. . . . Let it, therefore,
be understood, that all the Stakes, excepting those in this county,
and in Lee County, Iowa, are discontinued, and the Saints instructed to settle in this county as soon as circumstances will permit." [59] Such an order was bound to cause consternation in many
quarters. Since the Missouri expulsion a number of applications for
new stakes had been made by the scattered settlements of Saints,
and many had been granted. Only the previous autumn new stakes
had been approved for Springfield, for Morgan County near
Geneva, and for Quincy, Lima, Columbus, Payson, and a place
called "Mt. Ephraim" in Adams County. A literal fulfillment of the
new edict would mean abandonment of these settlements as well as
many other congregations in the East and the Middle West. Furthermore, Smith's command would mean the abandonment of Kirtland, a Mormon community of a decade, together with its lovely
and hardbought (but still debt-ridden) temple. [60]

This command of the Prophet the Saints did not, perhaps could
not, hasten to oblige. It was criticized, and created a minor crisis of
confidence. In particular Smith's willingness to forget both Kirtland
and Missouri as places for Zionic efforts, both of which he had commanded to be built up in the name of the Lord, and into which so
much suffering and treasure had been poured, in favor of yet another venture was difficult to accept. How could the Lord's will
change? How could the assurances of one day be forgotten the next?
There was also grumbling because the Prophet's leadership in spiritual matters appeared to be suffering at the expense of city building.
Smith defended himself as best he could in a meeting with the
Twelve Apostles in December, 1841. A father who could "command
his son to dig potatoes and saddle his horse, but before he had done
either . . . tell him to do something else" would not be reproved

[59] "Letter of the First Presidency to the Saints," May 24, 1841, in *ibid.*, 4:
362.
[60] *Ibid.*, 4:205, 233, 236.

for his action, "But as soon as the Lord gives a commandment and revokes that decree and commands something else, then the Prophet is considered fallen." Because the people would not meekly receive chastisement and direction "at the hand of the Prophet and Apostles, the Lord chastiseth us with sickness and death."

Some people say I am a fallen prophet because I do not bring forth more of the word of the Lord. Why do I not? Are we able to receive it? No! Not one in this room. He then chastened the congregation [sic] for their wickedness and unbelief, "for whom the Lord loveth, he chasteneth, and scourgeth every son and daughter whom he receiveth," and if we do not receive chastisements, then we are bastards and not sons. . . . The reason we do not have the secrets of the Lord revealed unto us, is because we do not keep them, but reveal [them] to the world, even to our enemies, then how would we keep the secrets of the Lord.

Heber Kimball in the same meeting discoursed on the Biblical parable of the potter and the clay in a manner designed to concur with the Prophet's views: "that when it marred in the hands of the potter it was cut off the wheel and then thrown back into the mill, to go into the next batch, and was a vessel of dishonor; but all clay that formed well in the hands of the potter, was a vessel of honor; so it was with the human family, and ever will be: all that are pliable in the hands of God and are obedient to His commands, are vessels of honor, and God will receive them." Brigham Young concluded that "one thing lay with weight on his mind; that is that we should be prepared to keep each commandment as it came from the Lord by the mouth of the prophet. . . ." Thus did the first two among the Twelve affirm their resolve to follow the Prophet no matter where and how he might lead.[61]

Evidence relating to the settlement and early growth of Nauvoo is meager. There were no newspapers for several months, no public records, and only the most casual reference to the growth of the city in the journals and recollections of the settlers themselves, including Smith. Fragments of information suggest a scene of rigorous pioneering on the townsite with pitching of tents, planting of gardens, arduous clearing and cabin building, a prevalence of sickness and privation, and a rapid increase in population. Charles C. Rich, one of the Missouri refugees at Quincy, managed to trade a deed to land in Missouri for a team, wagon and cow; he moved his family to

[61] "Minutes of a Meeting of the Twelve in the House of the Prophet," December 19, 1841, taken from the journal of Wilford Woodruff and quoted in *ibid.*, 4:478, 479.

Nauvoo during that first summer and took a timber-covered lot that provided him logs for a cabin and firewood for the coming winter. Brigham Young moved his family into an unfinished log cabin on a lot that was "so swampy that when the first attempt was made to plow it the oxen mired," but which, after the flat was drained, "became a very valuable garden spot." It remained too wet to build a cellar, however.[62] By the end of the first year Nauvoo was a big, raw, unfinished town. Hammers and axes rang on every side, and new gatherers poured in. George Miller, a Mormon settler who had a little wood yard on the Iowa side, said in the summer of 1840 that Nauvoo "was growing like a mushroom (as it were, by magic)." [63] In September he too moved to Nauvoo. In June, 1840, Smith observed that there were about 250 houses built, "mostly block [log] houses, a few framed, and many more are in course of construction." In August he wrote proudly that Nauvoo

is probably the best and most beautiful site for a city on the river . . . a situation in every respect adapted to commercial and agricultural pursuits. . . .

The number of inhabitants is nearly three thousand, and is fast increasing. If we are suffered to remain, there is every prospect of its becoming one of the largest cities on the river, if not in the western world. Numbers have moved in from the [eastern] seaboard, and a few from the islands of the sea [Great Britain].

Furthermore, he stated his intention to begin the construction of public buildings the following spring. Smith had to admit, however, in his only word of qualification about Nauvoo, "like all other places on the river, it is sickly in the summer." [64]

In January, 1841, Smith issued a kind of official prospectus of Nauvoo to "the Saints Scattered Abroad" in order to encourage them to gather. The inhabitants were numbered at about three thousand, and were "increasing with unparalleled rapidity." Various charters

[62] John H. Evans, *Charles Coulson Rich; Pioneer Builder of the West* (New York, 1936), p. 66; Brigham Young's journal in *The Latter-Day Saints' Millennial Star*, 26:88, February 6, 1864.
[63] George Miller, *Correspondence of Bishop George Miller with the Northern Islander from his first acquaintance with Mormonism up to near the end of his life, 1855* (compiled by Wingfield Watson, 1916), p. 117. Pamphlet in the library of the Wisconsin State Historical Society.
[64] Joseph Smith's History, 4:133; letter of Smith to J. C. Bennett, *ibid.*, pp. 177–178. The Federal Census for 1840 gives a population for Hancock County of 9,946, but has no figure for Nauvoo. *Compendium of the Sixth Census of the United States*, p. 82. By March, 1842, the population of Nauvoo had grown to an estimated 7,000. *Times and Seasons*, 3:750, April 1, 1842.

51

had just been obtained for the city from the Illinois legislature, and the Prophet enlarged on the great advantages of independence and legal protection they conferred on the city and the Church. He described the proposed "University of the City of Nauvoo," which, he said, "will enable us to teach our children wisdom, to instruct them in all the knowledge and learning, in the arts, sciences, and the learned professions." It was hoped that it would be "one of the great lights of the world," teaching "that kind of knowledge which will be of practicable utility, and for the public good, and also for private and individual happiness." Construction of a temple had now been started. "Let us now concentrate all our powers," said Smith, "and strive to emulate the action of the ancient covenant fathers and patriarchs" in building it. Finally, the economic advantages of the location were alluded to for the first time in an official communication: "Every facility is afforded in the city and adjacent country, in Hancock County, for the successful prosecution of the mechanical arts and the pleasing pursuits of agriculture. The waters of the Mississippi can be successfully used for manufacturing purposes to an almost unlimited extent."[65]

The Mormon city and its prophet were becoming widely known in the state. A visitor in June, 1841, was cordially entertained by Smith, and noted "the plain hospitality of the Prophet . . . to all strangers visiting the town, aided as he is . . . by his excellent wife, a woman of superior ability." The other citizens, he said,

appear to be honest and industrious, engaged in their usual vocations of building up a town, and making all things around them comfortable. On Sunday I attended one of their meetings, in front of the Temple now building, and one of the largest buildings in the state. There could not have been less than 2,500 people present, and as well appearing as this or any number that could be found in this or any state. Mr. Smith preached in the morning, and one could . . . readily learn . . . the magic by which he has built up the city, as we say in Illinois, "they believe in him," and in his honesty. It is a matter of astonishment to me . . . why so many . . . have slandered and persecuted this sect of Christians.[66]

A system of common schools for the city was in existence by 1841, when it was placed under the supervision of the Board of Regents of

[65] "A Proclamation of the First Presidency of the Church to the Saints Scattered Abroad," January 15, 1841, in Joseph Smith's History, 4:267–273.
[66] From a letter to the *Joliet Courier*, in Joseph Smith's History, 4:381, under entry of June 22, 1841.

the projected municipal university. "The school Wardens of the University for Common Schools are desired to organize the schools in their respective wards," ran a notice in the *Times and Seasons* for December 15, 1841, "in conformity to an act of the Regents in relation to that important subject—the Teachers must procure a certificate of competency from the Chancellor and the Registrar before they can be recognized by the Wardens." The following June the same paper published a standard list of textbooks for use in the schools.[67]

Nauvoo had developed sufficiently by 1842 so that there was interest in beautifying the city. Through proper landscaping, "Nauvoo in a few years may be made almost a paradise," wrote Ebenezer Robinson in the *Times and Seasons* in February, 1842: "Let each citizen fill his spare ground with fruit trees, shrubbery, vines, etc., tastefully arranged and properly cultivated, and in a short time we may each sit under his own vine and fig tree. . . . Let the division fences be lined with peach and mulberry trees, the garden walks be bordered with current, raspberry, and gooseberry bushes, and the houses surrounded with roses and prairie flowers, and their porches crowned with the grape vine, and we shall soon have formed some idea of how Eden looked. . . ." Robinson called attention to the notice of a Mr. Sayers, gardener, who advertised that he would be a fulltime horticulturist in Nauvoo specializing in "Pruning trees, laying out gardens, grafting, inoculating of trees, etc."[68]

The greatest threat to the Nauvoo gathering was the unhealthfulness of the place. Malaria was a disease endemic in the Mississippi Valley, debilitating and killing the inhabitants almost everywhere.[69] Nauvoo was on a stretch of the river bottom plagued with an especially high incidence of the disease. The Mormons were afflicted as soon as they began to settle there in the summer of 1839. "There was no meeting," wrote Smith of a sabbath in June, "on account of much rain and much sickness. . . . This week and the following were

[67] *Times and Seasons*, 3:632, 652, December 15, 1841, June 1, 1842.
[68] *Times and Seasons*, 3:678, 686, February 1, 1842.
[69] See E. H. Ackerknecht, *Malaria in the Upper Mississippi Valley, 1760–1900* (Baltimore, 1945); and Peter Harstad, "Disease and Sickness on the Wisconsin Frontier: Malaria [and] Cholera," *Wisconsin Magazine of History*, 43:83–96, 202–237, 1959–1960. "Fever" or "ague," as malaria was called, was associated at the time with wet and swampy locales, though of course not with its carrier, the anopheles mosquito. Quinine was not in general use as a remedy until later. Other diseases such as typhoid and typhus may have afflicted the Mormons in Nauvoo; the region was free from cholera, however, between 1834 and 1849.

generally spent in visiting the sick and administering to them [the sacred rite of anointing and prayer]; some had faith enough and were healed; others had not. . . . Many remain sick, and new cases are occurring daily." [70] John D. Lee called the sickness that summer a "plague," with so many ill there were hardly enough well to care for them. Morale was low, but stories of miraculous healings by the prayer of faith were told and retold. [71]

The following summer, 1840, the epidemic was worse; many died, and few escaped the ravages of the fever. Smith was worried about the situation, but hoped that things would be better in the future. In his "Proclamation" of January, 1841, advertising Nauvoo to the Church he wrote: "This place has been objected to by some on account of the sickness that has prevailed in the summer months, but it is the opinion of Dr. [John C.] Bennett that Hancock County, and all the eastern and southern portions of Nauvoo, are as healthful as any other portions of the western country, to acclimatized citizens; whilst the northwestern portion of the city has suffered much affliction from fever and ague, which, however, Dr. Bennett thinks can be easily remedied by draining the sloughs on the adjacent islands in the Mississippi." [72] But in the summer of 1841 the disease was calamitous. The dead included recent gatherers and first settlers alike. The Prophet mourned the loss of his close friend and personal secretary, Robert B. Thompson, his father, the Patriarch of the Church, and his youngest brother, twenty-six-year-old Don Carlos. So many died that Sidney Rigdon preached a "general funeral sermon" for them all. Said the Prophet sadly in a letter to Horace Hotchkiss, "As to the growth of the place, it is very rapid, and would be more so, were it not for sickness and death. There have been many deaths, which leaves a melancholy reflection, but we cannot help it." [73]

While Nauvoo continued to grow, the Mormon settlement in Lee County, Iowa, so auspiciously begun, languished. Zarahemla Stake had been reconfirmed as an official gathering place in a "revelation" made public by Smith in March, 1841; and it was the only gathering place outside Hancock County to escape Smith's interdict of May, 1841. [74] Yet it was clear that the bloom had gone from the early en-

[70] Joseph Smith's History, 4:3.
[71] Brooks, *John Doyle Lee*, pp. 47, 48.
[72] Joseph Smith's History, 4:178, 268.
[73] *Ibid.*, 4:389, 432.
[74] *Ibid.*, 4:311, 312, 362. "Let them build up a city unto my name upon the land opposite to the City of Nauvoo, and let the name of Zarahemla be named

thusiasm for settlement on the big purchase there. Nauvoo was a strong competitor for gatherers; the Nauvoo charters opened possibilities not originally foreseen for the Illinois Saints that were closed to those on the Iowa side. Furthermore, the Saints ran into trouble with the squatters and other "purchasers" of Half-Breed lands at the outset. David Kilbourne, who was antagonistic to the Mormons, described the descent of the Saints, the third layer of claimants, onto their "purchase": "Early one morning . . . the quiet citizens of Montrose were surprised by a visit from some of Joe Smith's scullions from Nauvoo, headed by Alanson Ripley, a Mormon *Bishop* . . . . With compass and chain they strided [*sic*] through gates and over fences to the very doors of the 'Gentiles,' and drove stakes for the lots of a city . . . four miles square. . . ."[75] The spectacle of the purposeful Mormons arguing over their right to drive a surveyor's stake in the dooryard of an indignant squatter may have been ludicrous, but it carried the seeds of discord and hatred. The problem of multiple claims among Galland's customers came to a head when the irate claimants aired their grievances in a public meeting, where they "fully exposed his position and operations, which stopped his sales."[76]

Another difficulty in Zarahemla Stake that augured ill for its success and stability was the development there of a kind of internal turbulence and policy of extremes. In December, 1839, the Zarahemla High Council decided that all debts contracted between brethren during the Missouri settlement were to be repudiated, and any persons pressing such obligations would be disfellowshipped. The following month it was decided to disfellowship those who went to law with a brother for any cause. In March, 1840, the Nauvoo High Council decided to take the superintendence of the Montrose ferry out of the hands of the Iowa Saints and give it to the First Presidency. The same month Joseph Smith went over the river personally to straighten out the brethren there in a number of matters. They were trying to inaugurate the "law of consecration," a kind of community of property similar to that attempted in Independence, where each was to receive an inheritance from the com-

upon it. And let all those who come from the east, and the west, and the north, and the south, that have desire to dwell therein, take up their inheritances in the same, as well as in the City of Nashville, or in the City of Nauvoo, and in all the stakes which I have appointed, saith the Lord."

[75] In the *Burlington Hawkeye and Patriot*, October, 1841, quoted in John C. Bennett, *History of the Saints* . . . (Boston, 1842), p. 101.

[76] Kilbourne pamphlet, p. 11.

mon store. Smith was not opposed to the principle of the endeavor but rather to its leadership; he feared that failure might produce an uproar that would have an ill effect on the general progress of affairs. "The law of consecration could not be kept here," the secretary reported the President as saying; "it was the will of the Lord that we should desist from trying to keep it; and if persisted in it would produce a perfect defeat of its object, and that he assumed the whole responsibility of not keeping it until proposed by himself." [77] As the resources of the Church were divided, the share of Nauvoo was large and that of the Iowa settlements was small. The situation of the Iowa Saints in the community of gentiles was insecure, their land titles were almost if not entirely worthless, and their leadership was given to extreme policies. Zarahemla Stake had attracted a membership of only about 750 by the summer of 1840.[78] It remained but a poor and wrangling relation of its powerful neighbor across the river, a doubtful return on the heavy investment made in Dr. Galland's acres.

The beginnings of Nauvoo were prompted by a need to provide a place for the Missouri refugees to regather and re-establish the Church as a corporate enterprise. But the commitments made by the land purchases and a growing complex of other vested interests, both corporate and private, caused the Mormons to make it their major community endeavor. Its growth was spectacular. The Mormons reported a population of ten thousand by late 1842; Thomas Ford in his *History of Illinois* wrote that there were by the end of that year sixteen thousand Mormons altogether in Hancock County, with several thousand more in other parts of the state. He listed Nauvoo with Chicago, Alton, Springfield, Quincy, and Galena as the Illinois towns which "had become cities before the year 1842." [79]

[77] "Extract from the Minutes of the Iowa High Council" of March 6, 1840, in *ibid.*, 4:93.

[78] *Ibid.*, 4:399.

[79] Pooley, *Settlement of Illinois*, p. 513; Ford, *History of Illinois*, pp. 229, 313.

3

'From the Islands of the Sea':
The British Mission and the Gathering

Men of Bolton—Think of mourning England and suffering Englishmen. Think of your own wretchedness and your own wrongs. Think of the iniquities which government is daily perpetrating.

> Handbill published in Bolton, England, 1839, quoted in Robert F. Wearmouth, *Methodism and the Working-Class Movements of England: 1800-1850* (London, 1837), p. 170.

Many families that have even work or part work have to live the last three days in a week on stolen turnips or on potatoes. Others, they cannot rest at night through hunger. This, my Lord, is not an exaggerated statement.

> Letter of John Skevington to Lord Normandy, 1840, quoted in Wearmouth, *Methodism and the Working-Class Movements*, p. 172.

What I might say . . . might have the tendency of encouraging my fellow Englishmen in the point of gathering. Now I would hold out to them everything that is desirable, and would say if you can get to this land, you will be better off than in England, for in this place there is a prospect of receiving every good thing both of this world and that which is to come: then be faithful, for the Lord has said that his Saints shall inherit the earth . . . the things that have been taught you are true, and Joseph Smith is a prophet of the Most High.

> Letter of Elder Francis Moon, a new migrant to Nauvoo, written November 4, 1840, to the English Saints, in *The Latter-Day Saints' Millennial Star*, 1:252–255, February, 1841.

M ormon optimism that Nauvoo would soon become a populous city resulted from faith in the success of Mormon evangelism. Anticipating a literal, imminent fulfillment of the ancient prophecy that the Kingdom of God would "roll forth unto all nations" and "fill the whole earth," Mormon expectations were high, plans were large, even grandiose, and self-assurance was limitless. Joseph Smith, Brigham Young, and many of their followers added to the native pioneering energy of their generation a dogged faith in the kingdom triumphant. When they faced a particular disappointment or failure, their discouragement was tempered by the Mormon world view. "Babylon," the wicked kingdom of men, must fall, according to prophecy; by the same token, of the increase of God's Kingdom there should be no end. Probably no single event in the first generation of Mormonism did so much to substantiate that faith as the remarkable success of the Church's mission in Great Britain.

In 1837 Smith sent Apostles Heber C. Kimball and Orson Hyde to England, together with a group of Canadian elders, to establish the first Latter-day Saint mission abroad. The British mission became the particular responsibility and triumph of the Quorum of Twelve and welded the group into a phalanx of leadership that was later to build Utah. Thousands of the first citizens of that territory were English proselytes whom the Twelve had converted and organized for immigration first to Nauvoo, then to the Great Basin; they were, in Heber C. Kimball's interpretation of the ancient Biblical metaphor, the clay on the potter's wheel.[1] Under direction of the Twelve 17,849 persons, mostly English, were baptized in the British Mission during its first decade; of these 4,733 gathered, primarily to Nauvoo.[2]

[1] The three Apostles who did not participate in the English mission work did not follow "The Twelve" under Young west to the Great Basin; William Smith, Lyman Wight, and John E. Page all became "apostates." The term "Twelve" in Mormon parlance referred to the members on the Quorum of Apostles, regardless of number. After Smith's death it came to mean the nine Apostles loyal to Brigham Young. The "Twelve" who founded Utah were the same nine men, though Young filled the positions vacated by the "apostates" with "faithful" members. The original nine were Brigham Young, Heber C. Kimball, Orson Hyde, Orson Pratt, Parley P. Pratt, Willard Richards, George Albert Smith, John Taylor, and Wilford Woodruff. Young, Taylor, and Woodruff were later to become presidents of the Church in Utah.

[2] M. Hamlin Cannon, "Migration of English Mormons to America," *American Historical Review*, 52:441 (1946–1947). About one-fourth of those baptized in the period 1837–1846 emigrated; the ratio for the period 1847–1856 was 19,538 of 57,577, or about one-third; their destination was usually Utah. Cannon lists the numbers of converts and emigrants by years as follows:

Year	Converts	Emigrants	Year	Converts	Emigrants
1837	600	0	1847	2918	0
1838	727	0	1848	6520	755
1839	190	0	1849	8602	2078
1840	2326	240	1850	8017	1612
1841	2883	1135	1851	8064	1370
1842	3216	1614	1852	6665	732
1843	1195	769	1853	4603	2312
1844	1762	623	1854	4530	2534
1845	2505	302	1855	3711	4225
1846	2354	50	1856	3974	5000

Joseph Smith had repeatedly prophesied that "the field is white, already to harvest; therefore whoso desireth to reap, let him thrust in his sickle with his might, and reap while the day lasts. . . ." [3] The missionary success of Mormon elders had proven the prophecy, but nowhere perhaps in such spectacular fashion as in the British Isles. Nor was there in American or Canadian missions a more direct relation between conversions and the gathering. [4] The Twelve organized carefully the means and resources for telling in Britain the good news of the Kingdom of God and directed emigration of converts to Nauvoo, the land of their inheritances. The apparently limitless success of the English Mission and the English migration to Nauvoo supported notions of a great kingdom on the Mississippi, and after that in the Great Basin.

In the eighteen-thirties and forties England was a fertile soil for the gospel of Mormonism. The forms of government and society had not evolved rapidly enough to match the demands of a new urban industrial nation. "A great mass of our unskilled and but little skilled labourers, and a very considerable number of our skilled labourers," wrote an English commentator, "are in poverty and great deprivation all their lives, [but] they are neither ignorant of their condition nor reconciled to it; they are amongst others who are better off than themselves, with whom they compare themselves and they cannot understand why there should be so great a difference. . . ." [5] Under such circumstances a depression with its widespread unemployment meant tragedy and disaster for the industrial population; and such a condition existed when Heber Kimball first arrived in England.

In 1836 there was a depression which, says a modern historian, "In intensity and duration . . . competes with later rivals for the title of 'the Great Depression.' " [6] In Birmingham, where the already minimal wages were reduced one-third to one-half and many were unemployed, a speaker at a protest meeting in 1838 declared, "there [are] thousands of mothers and children crying for bread and [can] not obtain it," and another such meeting resolved "that the present

[3] *The Book of Doctrine and Covenants*, various editions, Section 2 and *passim*.
[4] For a treatment of domestic evangelism see S. George Ellsworth, "A History of Mormon Missions in the United States and Canada, 1830–1860" (Ph.D. dissertation, University of California at Berkeley, 1951).
[5] Quoted in Wearmouth, *Methodism and the Working-Class Movements*, p. 169.
[6] Herbert Heaton, "Economic Change and Growth," *The New Cambridge Modern History* (Cambridge, England, 1960), 10:47.

sufferings of the industrious classes [in Birmingham] are general and extreme. . . ." From Manchester came a report in 1839 of "a very large unemployed population thrown out of work by the total or partial stoppage of the mills to an unusual extent." A petition of 1842 compared the archbishop's salary of £52 a day [*sic*] with that of "thousands [who] have to maintain their families upon an income, not exceeding two pence per head per day." The same year a petition of the power loom weavers of Manchester stated they were "at this moment suffering under circumstances which are beyond human endurance . . . perishing for lack of the necessities of life." Officials were apprehensive. A report to the Home Office from Burnley in 1842 said, "The state of distress experienced by the lower orders in this densely populous manufacturing district from an almost total want of employment is alarming [and] it is almost impossible to alleviate that distress." Another report to the Home Office from Manchester in 1839 had warned, "Want of employment and consequent distress among the labouring population . . . may, I fear, lead to disturbances during the winter." In conservative England, still ruled by an oligarchy based on land, wealth, and the Church (the Reform Act of 1832 had only admitted industrialists and similarly powerful new elements to the oligarchy), the distressed urban proletariat had only a few nonrevolutionary outlets for their protest: modest reform movements, emigration, and religion.[7]

English proletarians were angry over the high prices of food, which they ascribed mainly to the import duties, or "Corn Laws." Closely related in their thinking were conservative fiscal policies to protect the pound sterling. "Nearly the whole of . . . the present sufferings of the industrious classes," said an 1837 resolution of protest, "are undoubtedly to be attributed to the cruel and oppressive laws which have made food . . . and money dear and scarce." The Manchester Working Man's Association said, "We are compelled by the government to purchase coffee at two shillings per pound instead of sixpence . . . sugar at sevenpence or eightpence per pound instead of threepence, tea at four or five shillings . . . instead of one shilling or one shilling and threepence."[8] The Anti-Corn Law League, established in 1838, Robert Owen's "Christian Socialists," and in the forties consumer cooperatives, all suggested panaceas and had their adherents. They emphasized the fact that the basic

[7] Wearmouth, *Methodism and the Working-Class Movements*, pp. 169–173.
[8] *Ibid.*, pp. 169, 170.

concern of many Englishmen was not to prosper but to keep from starving.

The reform which attracted the distressed masses more than any other was the People's Charter movement, or "Chartism." Chartism was explicitly political in aim, a relatively mild proposal for more representative government. But its implicit promise was of a reformed society and economy which would provide a better situation for the poverty stricken and the insecure. It was this implication that made Chartism for a few years a mass movement. When it was discredited in 1842 and 1843, its followers tended to look elsewhere for leadership.[9]

Many fled England to escape social and economic distress. An "emigration of desperation" took place between 1815 and 1845, especially during times of depression. The government encouraged it by such devices as the Commission of Emigration established in 1831 to give information and advice to prospective emigrants. While the natural increase of population of ten industrial counties was 16 per cent between 1831 and 1841, emigration depleted the population by an equal number.[10] An example of such refugees from the urban and industrial revolutions was Edwin Bottomly, a midlands textile worker who left in 1842 to become a farmer on the Wisconsin frontier. He was a skilled laborer commanding higher wages and better job security than ordinary mill hands; but he feared that his children had no future in England. He wrote from his new home sentiments perhaps common to others like himself:

Dear friends and fellow workmen you may wish to know how I like this country for myself I like [it] very well and the more I Persever I shall like [it] Better you must be aware that a new Settler in this cuntry as to struggle with Difficulties but hopes of future reward (*which can not be realized in a cuntry wher Labour the source of all Real Wealth is troden under foot By Monopoly Taxation and Oppression*) gives him strength to Persever I do not expect to realize a great fortune here But I do hope to place myself in circumstances on[e] day . . . so that I can see my children smileing around me in contentment and be able to assist theire parents in theire Declining years . . . which is worth all that I can do and no more than I desire. and with no other object In View Did I emigrate to this cuntry. . . .[11]

[9] Carlton J. H. Hayes, *A Political and Cultural History of Modern Europe* (London, 1954), p. 405.

[10] Milton Briggs and Percy Jordan, *An Economic History of England* (London, 1954), p. 405; Heaton, "Economic Change and Growth," p. 45.

[11] Milo M. Quaife, ed., *An English Settler in Wisconsin: The Letters of Edwin Bottomly, 1842–1850* (Madison, 1918), p. 39.

Methodism paved the way for successful Mormon evangelism among the English laboring classes. The long series of events which increased the social and economic difficulties of the lower classes had served also to disturb their traditional religious life. As a consequence new religious modes arose to meet new needs. Methodism was the most important of these. The Wesleys and their associates preached an imminent God and the hope of salvation, at least in the world to come, to a proletariat considerably estranged from the established church. The new method broke with ecclesiastic traditions and organized the people for religious experience wherever they were. Methodism grew in England with the industrial and urban revolutions, drawing its followers largely from the working classes; between 1800 and 1850 its membership increased six times, a figure unmatched by any other social movement of the time in England.[12]

But the Methodist Church was autocratic in leadership and conservative in social and economic outlook. It did not share the reform spirit which animated so many of its members. So while Chartism numbered many Methodists among its leaders and perhaps the mass of Methodists among its sympathizers, and though the enemies of Chartism and Methodism were identical, the Methodist Church officially disapproved the Peoples' Charter movement and even expelled some members for activity in it.[13] When Mormon elders first began preaching in the dingy halls of Liverpool and Preston the Methodist Church was in ferment. There were repeated revolts and schisms, noteworthy splits occurring in 1828, 1834, 1835, 1836, and 1849. Except for the schism of 1835, all were for political rather than doctrinal reasons. In 1841 Joseph Barker, a prominent Chartist, left the Wesleyan Church for the "New Connexion," a splinter sect; when he was expelled even from that, twenty-nine churches and 4,348 members went with him. The Primitive Methodists, an unlettered sect of schismatic proletarians, doubled their numbers during the Chartist agitation. Various English and European reform impulses, not excluding the Revolution of 1848, were reflected in rumblings and dissatisfactions in the Methodist Church.

The Mormon gospel and the Mormon missionaries seemed tai-

---

[12] Wearmouth, *Methodism and the Working-Class Movements*, p. 271. This was in spite of repeated schisms in the sect.

[13] Maldyn Edwards, *After Wesley: A Study of the Social and Political Influence of Methodism in the Middle Period: 1791–1849* (London, 1935), p. 93; *ibid.*, p. 273; Harold Underwood Faulkner, *Chartism and the Churches* (New York, 1916), pp. 81, 82, 93.

lored to the occasion. They spoke of a new heaven and a new earth, of nonviolent, Christian revolution, of brotherhood and equality, and of emigration to the Kingdom of God.[14] A new life for the body and the spirit was offered to converts. Zion in America was a sanctuary from the desolation sure to visit the earth. Land and gainful employment were available, offering opportunities equal to those enjoyed by the "best people." The decline of Chartism coincided with the rising tide of Mormon conversions and of their gatherings to America.[15] The English reform impulse eased the Mormon task in a number of ways. Willard Richards wrote:

Some year's previously [to 1837], the principles of the Temperance Society (originally established in America) were introduced into England, and Preston was the first town to receive them. Among the many valuable items held forth by the Temperance people, it was often remarked . . . that Temperance was the fore-runner of the Gospel, which prophecy proved true; for when the fullness of the Gospel came from America to England, it was first preached in Preston, and through the influence of the Temperance Society, the Latter-day Saints procured the use of the Temperance Hall . . . (a commodious building, originally erected for cockfighting) . . . and continued until they were ejected by others. . . . Similar favors have been received from several other Temperance Societies in England, for which the Lord reward them.[16]

Methodists, perhaps schismatics in particular, found Mormonism congenial and appealing. It offered "kingdom building" not only as a social philosophy but a social operation actually in process. Its missionary preaching declared the apocalyptic fulfillment of Bible prophecies. Its modified congregationalism satisfied some democratic longings, while its "called" priesthood and its hierarchy of "leaders" were not dissimilar to the system of lay leadership Methodists were accustomed to. Mormonism was also a layman's church; every convert was a steward, called to win his neighbor to the new truth. But lay leadership in the Mormon Church, even at the top, was not separated by class distinctions from the rank and file as it was in the Methodist Church. Brigham Young was a farmer and carpenter; Heber Kimball was a potter by trade.[17] Young, discours-

---

[14] Joseph Smith had sent Apostles Kimball and Hyde from Kirtland in 1837 to open a British mission as a counterpoise to the disastrous troubles the Church was experiencing in that Ohio town. "God revealed to me," wrote Smith of the inception of the project, "that something new must be done for the salvation of this church." Joseph Smith's History, 2:489.

[15] Cannon, "Migration of English Mormons," pp. 436 ff.

[16] "History of the British Mission," under entry for March 23, 1841, in Joseph Smith's History, 4:319.

[17] Larson, Prelude to the Kingdom, p. 57.

ing in later years on the proper and effective missionary method, paid tribute to Kimball's common touch:

> Brother Kimball would say [to an inquirer] "Come my friend, sit down; do not be in a hurry;" and he would begin and preach the Gospel in a plain, familiar manner, and make his hearers believe everything he said, and make them testify of its truth, whether they believed it or not, asking them, "Now you believe this? You see how plain the Gospel is? Come along now;" and he would lead them into the waters of baptism. The people would want to come and see him early in the morning, and stay with him until noon, and from that until night; and he would put his arm around their necks, and say, "Come, let us go down to the water."

Speaking of his own work in England, Young said he would go to a house and, without identifying himself at first, ask for something to eat.

> The reply was invariably "Yes." And we would sit, and talk and sing, and make ourselves familiar and agreeable; and . . . after they had learned who we were, they would frequently ask, "Will you not stay and preach for us?" and proffer to gather in the members of their family and their neighbors; and the feeling would be, "Well, if this is 'Mormonism,' then I will feed all the 'Mormon' Elders that come." [18]

In the first three years of the English Mission, 1837, 1838, and 1839, 1,417 were baptized, mostly in the western midlands. Liverpool and Preston were early mission centers; Joseph Smith noted in his journal for March 10, 1839, "The work continues to spread in Manchester and vicinity, among the Staffordshire potteries, and other places in England." [19] After the contingent of eight Apostles began their labors in the fall of 1839, the Church grew rapidly. The number of new members recorded in 1840, 1841, and 1842 was 8,425, six times the number for the preceding three years. Heber Kimball wrote from Preston, April 17, 1840: "The work of the Lord is progressing here. . . . The Gospel is spreading, the devils are roaring. As nigh as I can learn, the priests are howling, the tares are binding up, the wheat is gathering, nations are trembling, and kingdoms are tottering; 'men's hearts failing them for fear, and for looking for those things that are coming on the earth.' The poor among men are rejoicing in the Lord, and the meek do increase their joy. The hearts of the wicked do wax worse and worse, deceiving and

---

[18] "Remarks, by President Brigham Young, delivered at the opening of the Conference, Great Salt Lake City, April 6, 1857," in *The Journal of Discourses* (Liverpool and London, 1857), 4:305.

[19] Cannon, "Migration of English Mormons," p. 441; Joseph Smith's History, 3:277.

being deceived." Brigham Young wrote from Herefordshire in May, "If we could go four ways at a time, we could not fill all the calls we have for preaching."[20] Wilford Woodruff's journal chronicles the labors of that Apostle during 1840: he traveled 4,469 miles, "visited or labored in" Liverpool, Preston, Manchester, Newcastle, Tunstall, Burslem, Hanley, Stoke, Longton, Stafford, Wolverhampton, Birmingham, Worcester, Hereford, Ledbury, Malvern Hill, Gloucester, Cheltenham, Oxford, and London; he held 230 meetings, established fifty-three places for preaching, "planted" and organized forty-seven "branches"; was personally involved in the conversion of nearly 1,600, mostly in Herefordshire; and he baptized fifty-seven lay preachers of the "United Brethren," a schismatic Methodist sect.[21] The baptism and almost certain ordination of such lay leaders to the Mormon priesthood could mean the exchange of a Methodist for a Mormon cap with but little interruption in the convert's relation to his former Methodist class or society, many members of which he would baptize into his new faith.

Mormon missionaries shook the Methodist tree vigorously on the Isle of Man. "A staunch Wesleyan" wrote to the *Manx Liberal,* with tongue ever-so-slightly in cheek:

Sir—I feel rather surprised and chagrined that the modern delusion . . . "Mormonism," should have made such rapid strides in this town. . . . I had thought that the powerful and argumentative addresses of the dissenting ministers would have checked such a gross piece of imposition in its infance. . . . But, sir, alas! alas! the case is quite the reverse. . . . The members of our society . . . seem to be the most conspicuous in sanctioning and promoting this vile and abominable doctrine.

Oh, sir, the result to our connection will be dreadful. . . . just think of the majority of our *leading* and intelligent men aiding and abetting a cause of this description! Oh, sir, lamentable and heartrending to witness the beaming countenances, and smiles of approbation displayed recently at [Apostle John] Taylor's meeting! . . . I will mention . . . the names of a few who attended one of the last meetings . . . such a wholesale conversion to Mormonism was never before witnessed in any town or country. What will become of our society? . . . what makes the case worse is . . . that all these men [class leaders and ministers] are to be baptized! That is duly immersed in the salt water of Douglas Bay. . . . Immersion! (my hand shakes while I write) and in winter too! . . . surely this American dipper intends to drown them; he can have no other object in view, therefore, brethren of the Methodist society, beware! Drowning

[20] Joseph Smith's History, 4:115, 127.
[21] Matthias F. Cowley, *Wilford Woodruff* (Salt Lake City, 1909), p. 134.

is not to be envied, and that too in your sins. . . . What would the vener-
able John Wesley . . . say . . . ? What will the conference say? And
what will the world say? . . . listen no longer to the follies of man.[22]

Kimball, Woodruff, and George Albert Smith wrote the editors of
Times and Seasons from Manchester, October 12, 1840, detailing
some of their labors; their excitement was but thinly veiled. Of a
meeting held in Leigh, Gloucestershire, they related: "We had an
interesting time; we baptized fifteen, and ordained one Elder and
two Priests. Two Methodist priests came twelve miles to hear; we
baptized them after the first sermon, and confirmed and ordained
them at the same time, and sent them to preach the Gospel." [23]
They reported conferences in Herefordshire representing 1,007
members, 113 priesthood, and 40 branches, "the whole of whom
had received the fullness of the Everlasting Gospel, and been baptized in less than seven months . . . and the work is still progressing very rapidly throughout that region. . . ." A conference in the
"Staffordshire Potteries" reported 231 members and 59 priesthood.
In the whole Mission the gain of members between April and
October, 1840, had been more than two thousand. "Thus you see,"
they concluded, "the Lord hath given us an increase, and blessed the
labors of the servants of God universally in this land, for which we
feel thankful; and our constant prayer is . . . that His kingdom
may roll forth. . . ." [24] Said Brigham Young of the astonishing
number of conversions: "The people are very different in this country from what the Americans are. They say it cannot be possible that
men should leave their homes and come so far, unless they be truly
the servants of the Lord; they do not seem to understand argument;
simply testimony is enough for them; they beg and plead for the
Book of Mormon, and were it not for the priests, the people would
follow after [us] and inquire what they should do to be saved. . . .
Almost without exception it is the poor that receive the Gospel." [25]

The implications for the growth of Nauvoo soon appeared as the

---

[22] Quoted in Joseph Smith's History, 4:234–236. The debates between Taylor
and the Manx ministers were reprinted from the *Manx Liberal* in the *Millennial
Star*, 1:178 ff., November, 1840.

[23] With such a meager grounding in the gospel of Mormonism for new converts it is not remarkable that Young reported in 1849, "We need help very
much in this country. One American can do more here than a number of Elders
who are raised up here by the preaching of the Gospel." Letter of May 7, 1840,
in *ibid.*, p. 127. Time diminished the disparity between native and American
leadership.

[24] *Ibid.*, pp. 221, 222, 224.

[25] Letter of May 7, 1840, in *ibid.*, pp. 125–127.

new English Saints began to inquire about gathering to America. No specific plans had been made by the Church for a gathering, especially of such proportions as now seemed in prospect, and Young was uncertain what advice to give. "The brethren here are very anxious to emigrate to that country," he wrote the Prophet in May, 1840. "Where shall they go? Their customs are different from ours, and it would be more pleasant for them to settle by themselves. . . . I think there will be some over this fall. My counsel to such as intend to go is, that they go to the western states, where they can live among the farmers and wait for orders from the authorities of the Church, and all will be well." [26] With faith to compensate for a lack of plans and arrangements, forty English Saints under an Elder John Moon sailed for New York from Liverpool on June 6, 1840, "being the first Saints," said Joseph Smith, "that have sailed from England to America." They carried a "recommend" from Kimball to the Church in Nauvoo, which read in part:

> To the Presidency, High Council and Bishop . . . at Commerce [Nauvoo]. We commend to your notice the brethren and sisters that have the commendatory letters from us of this date, that you will do all that you consistently can for them, for I verily believe they have the utmost confidence in you and submit to the rules and regulations of the Church. They have our blessings, and we trust their subsequent conduct will entitle them to your blessings also. . . . We have witnessed the flowing of the Saints towards Zion; the stream has begun, and we expect to see it continue running until it shall have drained the salt, or the light, from Babylon, when we hope to shout hosanna home.[27]

Because the Apostles were still feeling their way toward a policy for the gathering from England, their official attitude continued until the fall of 1840 to be one of tacit encouragement only. An editorial in *The Latter-Day Saints' Millennial Star*, the official Church organ then in its first year of publication, expressed mock horror at the charges made against the Church:

1. The Latter-Day Saints have purchased land in America!
2. The Latter-Day Saints are about to cultivate that land!
3. The Latter-Day Saints emigrate to America!!
4. The Latter-Day Saints are so deluded that they even pay their own passage to America!!!

All the above charges are set down in the *North Wales Chronicle*, together with many expressions of surprise that men can be so far gone in delusion. . . .

[26] *Ibid.*
[27] *Ibid.*, pp. 132, 134.

That emigrating to America is a delusion, or a new doctrine, must be a new discovery! We had supposed that all denominations of Christians were in the habit of emigrating there more or less.

If this emigation plan had been discovered to be a delusion two hundred years ago, America would still be an unsettled wilderness.

We see men out of employ—they come to us for advice, our pity is moved—we tell them to emigrate to a country where there is plenty of labour, where provisions are cheap; we advise the rich to impart to the poor, &c., and while we do this, we are said to be deluding the people. The Lord be judge between us.[28]

On October 19, 1840, Joseph Smith replied to Brigham Young's query about gathering the English Saints with specific instructions which related to the economic development of Nauvoo:

Inasmuch as [Nauvoo] has been appointed for the gathering of the Saints, it is necessary that it be attended to in the order that the Lord intends . . . there are great numbers of the Saints in England who are extremely poor, and not accustomed to the farming business, who must have certain preparations made for them before they can support themselves in this country, therefore, to prevent disappointment and confusion when they arrive here, let those men who are accustomed to make machinery, and those who can command capital, though it be small, come here as soon as convenient, and put up machinery, and make such other preparations as may be necessary, so that when the poor come, they may have employment to come to. This place has advantages for manufacturing and commercial purposes, which but very few can boast of; and the establishing of cotton factories, foundaries, potteries, etc., would be the means of bringing in wealth, and raising it to a very important elevation.

The theory of the Prophet's planning was sound; the means and technique of implementation, however, were difficult to come by. Smith and Young were to grapple for the rest of their lives with the problem of how to industrialize the Kingdom.

In the same letter Smith told the Twelve to come home the following spring. United States–British relations were clouded; furthermore there might be revolution in England: "There have been whisperings of the spirit that there will be some agitation, excitements, and trouble in the land where you are now laboring." In addition Smith needed help in Nauvoo. Parley Pratt alone was to remain in England, but the Church was to be organized "so that those who cannot come with you in the spring, may not be left as sheep without a shepherd." [29]

[28] *Millennial Star*, 1:191, 192, November, 1840. The monthly periodical was then edited by Apostle Parley Parker Pratt.

[29] Joseph Smith's History, 4:227, 228.

The *Millennial Star* served to acquaint the English Saints with the current and past history of the Mormon Church, especially the Missouri persecutions and Nauvoo developments. Addresses by John C. Bennett added fire and drama to the episodes in Missouri, or "western Egypt," as he called it.[30] Under "Highly Interesting to the Emigrating Saints" was a description of the country in Iowa Territory for ninety miles up the Des Moines River from its mouth, and suggestions by a committee concerning sites there for Mormon settlements.[31]

During the 1840 season, only 240 Saints left England for America, a small fraction of the English Church where a total of 4,743 had been baptized. This pioneer band, however, paved the way for a host which followed. An Elder Francis Moon, one of the first party to emigrate, wrote home from Nauvoo, November 4, 1840, to encourage his brethren to gather. "I know what it is to bid farewell to my native land," said Moon, "but . . . the Lord has helped me, and brought me safely through; and now I have the privilege of being acquainted with the mysteries of the kingdom of God. . . ." Moon reported economic conditions in some detail as they would affect immigrants: a dollar a day wage for farm work, a dollar and a half for making a pair of boots, as well as the relatively small cost of provisions. He did not mention the cost of land or housing; perhaps the former he considered out of the reach of most English immigrants, or perhaps so expensive as to be discouraging. "If one is disposed to keep a cow," he said, "(and but few are without two or three) they may keep them free of expense, by sending them out to graze on the neighboring plains, and for the winter's keep they are at liberty to cut as much grass as they please." Moon considered the hegira of the English Saints as a re-enactment of the movements of ancient Israel. "The gathering of the people of God," he began, "has been a subject of great importance in all ages of the world." He rehearsed the miraculous deliverance of Israel from the Egyptian bondage and compared it with the purpose of God at present:

Now it appears that we live in a time in which the Lord is going to gather his people, to that land that was promised to Joseph and his seed [Amer-

[30] See for example *ibid.*, 1:231, 233, and Bennett's address reprinted from *Times and Seasons*, which the editor Pratt described as having been written by "one of the highest military officers of the State of Illinois" and breathing "a spirit of partriotism, justice, and equity worthy to be imitated by all the 'Saints of Light.'" Bennett signed himself "JOAB. General in Israel."
[31] *Ibid.*, p. 231.

ical which is a choice land above all lands . . . there are two important things in the gathering . . . first it is the design of the Lord to deliver his people from the troubles that are coming upon the earth, for it is far from him to destroy the righteous with the wicked; and for the benefit of his people he has prepared an hiding place from the tempest. . . . Another reason for the gathering of the people of God is . . . that they may build a sanctuary to the name of the Most High . . . and attend to such ordinances and receive such blessings as they could not while scattered upon the face of the whole earth.

Even since he had come, said Moon, the Prophet had "revealed a most glorious principle, which has been hid from the children of men for many generations, but has now been made known," a reference probably to baptism for the dead. But the Saints must remember that "those who desire to receive these blessings must be tried even as Abraham," and only the faithful would be inheritors of the promise. "You will be tried by the reports of those who . . . will speak evil of . . . the good land . . . and all that appertain to it." Was it not so in the days of Joshua, where ten of twelve brought back evil report of the land of Canaan? But now as then faith must prevail over doubt.

The Lord has said, it is a good land, and . . . I will give it you: who then . . . would not join Joshua in saying, let us go up and possess the good land, for we are well able! And when you bid your native land farewell . . . and set your face towards the land that the Lord has blessed, may the same principles that bore up the mind of Moses in his afflictions yield comfort to you. . . . And what would be the feelings in his heart when he with such emotion says . . . "We are journeying to the land that the Lord our God hath said he will give us!" . . . Now I would hold out to [you] everything that is desirable, and . . . if you can get to this land, you will be better off than in England. . . . As respects the land it is extremely good. . . . The plan in which this town . . . is laid out is very good. . . . Then let those who have the means delay no longer but come and unite with us in building the house of the Lord. My fellow Englishmen and brethren, you may rely on what I say . . . in this place there is a prospect of receiving every good thing both of this world and that which is to come: then be faithful, for the Lord has said his saints shall inherit the earth. . . .[32]

Such letters written by the first emigrants encouraged the large number that soon followed, though repeated warnings against naysayers suggest that not all letters were favorable. On another page of

[32] *Millennial Star*, 1:252–255, February, 1841. Pratt headlined the letter "IMPORTANT FROM AMERICA—Interesting letter from Elder Moon, who lately emigrated from England to America."

the *Millennial Star* that carried Moon's letter, the editor observed: "The news from the emigrants who sailed . . . last season, is so very encouraging that it will give a new impulse to the spirit of emigration, and put to shame those who have published falsehoods concerning this plan of deliverance." In the summer of 1841 a Sister Melling, recently arrived in Nauvoo, wrote home to England:

We are all in good spirits, and more convinced than ever that this is the work of the Lord. . . .

In gathering to this land many shake out by the way, and others after they arrive. . . . Do not persuade any barren souls to come here—we want men of faith who can sacrifice their all for Christ's sake and the Gospel's.

There are many fallen that came from England, and some will return, and spread all manner of evil. The reason is because they know neither the Father nor the Son. But verily, saith the Lord, they shall have their reward, and God will do his own work in spite of apostates or devils. . . . Our strength does not lie in numbers, but in the power of God; this is true and faithful. Even so, Amen.[33]

When the Twelve returned to America in 1841 they had been in England a year and a half. They had organized the burgeoning mission into branches, districts, and conferences, and ordained all ranks of priesthood from Deacons to High Priests. The new local leadership received little instruction, but such was the early Mormon manner. To augment their own extensive labors the Twelve had published 2,500 copies of the *Millennial Star*, 3,000 hymnals, and, of particular importance, 5,000 copies of the *Book of Mormon*, a basic canon of Latter-day Saint scripture hitherto virtually unobtainable in England.[34] They had "laid a foundation"; and the stage was set to implement the gathering of the English Saints to Nauvoo. In 1841 and 1842 no fewer than 2,749 were to emigrate, more than half the total who emigrated from Britain during the entire Nauvoo period. The February, 1841, *Millennial Star* contained news of emigrating Saints, together with editorial encouragement:

EMIGRATION—We feel truly thankful that amidst the general distress, poverty, and famine which prevails throughout this country, several hundred of our brothers and sisters have just been enabled to embark for the country which God has provided for a refuge for all nations. Upwards of two hundred and forty . . . from Preston, Manchester, and . . . other towns . . . were to sail from Liverpool, for New Orleans on Sunday last . . . [and] another ship company . . . from Bristol [made up of Saints]

[33] *Ibid.*, 1:263, February, 1841; 2:96, October, 1841.
[34] Cannon, "Migration of English Mormons," p. 441.

from Herefordshire and the surrounding country . . . destined for the colonies of the Saints in the State of Illinois and the Territory of Iowa.

Among this company was a large proportion of the industrious poor, who were upon the point of starvation in this land, or who were working like slaves to procure a very scanty subsistence. By the kindness of their brethren they were enabled to escape from worse than Egyptian bondage, and go to a country where they can by their industry obtain an inheritance. . . .

We sincerely hope that the Saints will continue to cultivate that spirit of love and union which will work a full and complete deliverance of the rich and poor of his people, that they may all be gathered in *one;* that *"there may be one fold and one shepherd."* [35]

On April 2, 1841, the Twelve appointed Elder Amos Fielding "to superintend fitting out the Saints from Liverpool to America," [36] and in the current issue of the *Millennial Star* they addressed a pastoral letter to the British Saints which contained an elaborate code of instructions for emigration. The preamble recalled that the "spirit of emigration" peopled the plains of Shinar as well as England and America and was the historic means of civilizing "the loneliness of an empty earth." "In short," they wrote, "it is emigration that is the only effectual remedy for the evils which now confront the over-populated countries of Europe . . . the Saints, as well as thousands of others, seem to be actuated with the spirit of enterprise and imigration. . . ."

While their language suggested that each of the migrating Saints would emigrate on his own responsibility, the Twelve wished to "impart a few words of counsel" on the subject.

It will be necessary in the first place for men of capital to go first and make large purchases of land, and erect mills, machinery, manufactories, etc., so that the poor . . . can find employment. Therefore, it is not wisdom

[35] *Millennial Star,* 1:263, February, 1841.

[36] "Minutes of a Council Meeting of the Twelve," in Joseph Smith's History, 4:325. On April 6 an assembled conference of the Mission was surprised with an unusual and symbolic feast, the significance of which was duly noted:

"A very richly ornamented cake, a present from New York, from Elder George J. Adams' wife to the Twelve, was then exhibited to the meeting. This was blessed by them and then distributed to all the officers and members, consisting, perhaps, of seven hundred people; a large fragment was still preserved for some who were not present. During the distribution several appropriate hymns were sung, and a powerful general feeling of delight universally pervaded the meeting. . . .

"Elder Fielding remarked [of] the rich cake . . . that he considered it a type of the good things of that land whence it came. . . ."

Conference minutes, in *ibid.,* 4:335.

for the poor to flock to that place extensively, until the necessary preparations are made. Neither is it wisdom for all who feel a spirit of benevolence to expend all their means in helping others to emigrate, and thus all arrive in a new country empty-handed. In all settlements there must be capital and labor united, in order to flourish. The brethren will recollect that they are not going to enter cities already built up, but are going to "build cities and inhabit them."

None were to go "in haste, nor by flight," but after careful preparation. Pains were to be taken to leave no debts, at least not without sincere arrangements to pay them at first opportunity, "that the cause of truth be not evil spoken of." All were to go to Liverpool to see Elder Amos Fielding at once; he would make the arrangements. "There are some brethren who have felt themselves competent to do their own business in these matters and, rather despising the counsel of their friends, have been cheated out of nearly all they had." [37]

Going in companies rather than individually would be highly advantageous, the Saints were advised. A vessel could be chartered, thus reducing the unit cost of passage. Provisions could be purchased wholesale; in New Orleans the charter of a riverboat would reduce the fare almost by half, saving some hundreds of pounds on each shipload. A "man of experience who will know how to avoid rogues and knaves" should head each company. Finally, going with companies of Saints would "avoid bad company on the passage." Gold was "more profitable than silver," and the brethren were cautioned against American money. "Let them not venture to take paper money of that country . . . banks are breaking almost daily." While the route through New Orleans was "much cheaper" than that through New York, "it will never do for emigrants to go by New Orleans in the summer, on account of the heat and sickness of the climate. It is, therefore, advisable for the Saints to emigrate in autumn, winter, or spring." Finally all were enjoined to "obtain a letter of recommendation from the Elders where they are acquainted, to the brethren where they are going, certifying their membership; and let the Elders be careful not to recommend any who do not conduct themselves as Saints; and especially those who would go with a design to defraud their creditors." [38]

[37] Brigham Young characteristically portrayed the evil consequences that came to those who despised "counsel," especially when they forsook the group enterprise for individual endeavors.
[38] "An Epistle from the Twelve Apostles to the Church . . . in England, Scotland, Ireland, Wales, and the Isle of Man" in the *Millennial Star*, 1:310, 311, April, 1841; the letter is reprinted in Joseph Smith's History, 4:345–347.

Young's counsel to the emigrants served them well; Mormon emigrant companies soon became famous for their careful preparation,
efficiency, and good order. The August, 1841, edition of the *Millennial Star* carried further detailed instruction to emigrants. They were
to take no furniture except beds, bedding, and cooking utensils. "Do
not be encumbered with old bedsteads, chairs, tables, stands, drawers, broken boxes, worn-out bedding, soiled clothing, rusty tools,
etc." They were also to take plenty of good stout clothing and bedding as well as "every necessary article of manufactured goods . . .
because these things are much dearer in Western America than in
England and no duties will be charged . . . on clothing already
made up. . . ." They were advised how to pack, and what to expect
in freight charges. Fielding needed names, ages, and money for the
fare ten days in advance. The passengers and goods would not need
to arrive till two or three days before the time of sailing, at which
time the passengers might go directly on board to avoid the cost of
lodgings in Liverpool. It was estimated that the total cost from
Liverpool to New Orleans would be approximately £5 for adults, £3
for those under fourteen years. Infants up to one year might go free.
"However, be it more or less, the passage will be obtained by
Brother Fielding on the lowest terms, and provisions purchased to
the best advantage . . . with a strict account of all these matters,
and no other profit or charge on the part of Brother Fielding, except
a reasonable remuneration for his time. . . ." In New Orleans the
company was to charter a steamer to St. Louis or Nauvoo, "which
will probably be from 15s. to 25s. per head, and provisions to be
purchased for about two weeks." The total cost from Liverpool to
Nauvoo was estimated to be £5 to £7. "It will be much dearer to go
individually; and even in companies the utmost prudence will be
necessary, in order to go through on the amount above named."
Emigrants were advised that they might expect many inconven-
iences in Nauvoo. "They cannot expect to rent houses and enter at
once on a comfortable living, but must pitch their tents, and build
themselves temporary cottages. About 30 or 40 yards of calico will
make a very good tent. . . ." A small cottage could be built in four
to six weeks "with little or no expense . . . which the settlers in that
country consider both comfortable and respectable." Money was
"very scarce" and even a few pounds in hand would "go very far in
supplying . . . home and provision; but if a man had nothing but his
hands he is far better off in that country than in England." Pratt detailed the cost of provisions in Nauvoo, adding that "Pigs, poultry,

etc., are very cheap, and may be reared in great abundance by the poorest inhabitants." They were told that fuel would cost little or nothing "except the trouble of obtaining it from the wilderness." Saintly conduct and hard work was to provide emigrants the opportunity for home and happiness, "surrounded with the unspeakable blessings of free institutions." [39] "Pratt & Fielding, Agents" entered notice in the *Millennial Star*, September through November, 1841, of ship sailings for companies of emigrants, prices, and other pertinent information. The notices were in the nature of promotional advertising, not religious instruction. Once chartered, the ships had to be filled. Pratt wrote Joseph Smith in October that chartering the ship *Tyrean*, which sailed September 20 with "upwards of two hundred Saints," had saved the company five or six hundred dollars. Another charter was scheduled to sail November 5 with an equal number aboard.[40]

On January 29, 1842, a brother G. Walker wrote from Manchester to the Twelve, now returned to Nauvoo, of the worsening economic situation in England: "There is very great distress among the operatives and the poor generally, and great excitement respecting the agitation of the repeal of the corn laws. . . . There is great depression in almost every branch of manufactures, and great perplexity; and I am more and more convinced that the time is not far distant when Babylon the great will be fallen and become a desolation, and the kings and the merchants of the earth weep and mourn over her. . . ." [41] The deepening depression in England increased the fever for gathering. Letters received from Illinois had appetizing grocery lists attached. "Provisions are very cheap here," wrote Thomas Brotherton, recently of Manchester, on December 7, 1841: "good beef, 1½ d . . . Last Saturday I bought 9½ lbs. good standing rib beef, for 1s. 3d. . . . I have now a ham in salt 10 lbs. for 1s. . . . pork 1¼ d.; new butter 6d. per lb.; flour, 19s. per barrel; Indian Corn, 1s. per bushel." "Rent and labour," he added, "are high." [42]

[39] *Millennial Star*, 2:60, 61, August, 1841. The foregoing is appended to an extract from *Chambers' Information for the People*, No. 18, describing the United States in general and the Mississippi Valley region in particular, which Pratt included in the *Star*.

[40] *Ibid.*, 2:80, 96, 112, September, October, and November, 1841; Joseph Smith's History, 4:441.

[41] Joseph Smith's History, 4:507, 508.

[42] *Millennial Star*, 2:156, January, 1842. Pratt commended the writer as "a man of intelligence, sound judgment, and integrity, being an old resident of

Editor Pratt wrote in the January *Millennial Star* an editorial re-
flecting his roles both as spiritual shepherd and emigration agent:
"In the midst of the general distress which prevails in this country
on account of the want of employment, the high price of provisions,
the oppression, priestcraft, and iniquity . . . it is pleasing . . . to
think that thousands of the Saints have already made their escape
from this country and all its abuses and distress. . . ." Not two
years had elapsed, continued Pratt, since the first brethren had left
the native shore; despite the warnings and falsehoods put forward
by enemies to frighten them from going, the land they had actually
encountered was flowing with milk and honey. After entering a list
of Nauvoo food prices ("The expense of living is about ⅛ of what it
costs in this country"), Pratt pictured the Land of Zion for his English brethren:

Millions on millions of acres lie before them unoccupied, with a soil as rich
as Eden, and a surface as smooth, clear, and ready for the plow as the
park scenery of Engand.
   Instead of a lonely swamp or dense forest filled with savages, wild
beasts, and serpents, large cities and villages are springing up in their
midst, with schools, colleges, and temples. The mingled noises of mecha-
nism, the bustle of trade, the song of devotion, are heard in the distance,
while thousands of flocks and herds are seen grazing peacefully on the
plains, and the fields and gardens smile with plenty, and the wild red men
of the forest are only seen as they come on a friendly visit to the Saints,
and to learn the way of the Lord. . . .
   Ye children of Zion, once more we say . . . arise, break off your
shackles, loose yourselves from the bonds of your neck, and go forth to inherit the earth, and to build up the waste places of many generations. . . .
In this way we shall not only bring about the deliverance of tens of thousands who must otherwise suffer in this country, but we shall add to the
strength of Zion . . . the young men and the middle aged will serve to
increase her legions . . . that the enemies of law and order, who have
sought her destruction may stand afar off and tremble, and her banners
become terrible to the wicked.

Pratt further exhorted emigrants to deal with the Church agents
for their passage. He said the cost to New Orleans "at no time this
season" had exceeded £4, and had usually been as low as £3 15s.
"This is remarkable. . . . But it is obtained . . . by the union of

this place." Brotherton's letter would confound "the foolish, ignorant, falsehoods" of the *Manchester Courier* in which the Mormons had been accused of
cheating, tricking and swindling immigrants "by obtaining immense sums of
money from [them] and then shipping them to perish in the pestilential swamps
of New Orleans; and all for the sake of selling them uninhabitable land, etc."

effort among the Saints, and by the faithful and persevering exertions of their agents." As soon as the emigrant gatherers sailed "they hoist the *Flag of Liberty*—the ensign of Zion—the stars and stripes of the American union; and under its protection they completely and practically NULIFY [*sic*] THE BREAD TAX. They eat free bread, free tea, free sugar, free everything, and thus accomplish a journey of five thousand miles [for what] it would cost to feed them for the same length of time in England." The New Orleans route, said Pratt, was less than half as expensive as going by New York or Quebec. A company arriving at New Orleans in November, 1842, paid $2.50 a person "for one of the largest and best [river] steamboats in this port." Each person was allowed a hundred pounds of luggage, with 25¢ charged for each additional hundred pounds.[43] He said that none should sail by the southern route after March 10 because of the climate; but

If thousands wish to go between this time [January, 1842] and the 10th of March, they have only to furnish us with their names and about £4 per head [for adults] . . . . We do not wish to confine the benefit of our emigration plan to the Saints, but are willing to [accommodate] all industrious, honest, and well-disposed persons . . . there being abundant room for more than a hundred million inhabitants.
Thousands have gone, and millions
more must go,
The Gentiles as a stream to Zion flow.[44]

The economic extremity that prompted Saints to emigrate immediately also made it much more difficult for them to acquire the relatively few pounds sterling required to do so. The Twelve, writing to the English Church on November 15, 1841, said, "He that believeth shall not make haste, but let all the Saints who desire to keep the commandments of heaven and work righteousness, come to the place of gathering as soon as circumstances will permit." But, they continued, "We are not altogether ignorant of the increase of difficulty among the laboring classes in England since our departure. . . . We would not press the subject of gathering on you . . . for in due time you will be delivered." [45]

To help the hard-pressed Saints to emigrate, early in 1842 an ingenious plan was devised in Nauvoo to weave a sort of import-

[43] Joseph Smith's History, 5:185.
[44] *Millennial Star*, 2:153 ff., January, 1842. Also in Joseph Smith's History, 4:510–513.
[45] Joseph Smith's History, 4:450.

export business into the process of gathering the indigent. Perhaps a little profit might be turned besides. A brother John Snyder was "called" to go from Nauvoo to England to collect money from the Saints for building the Temple and Nauvoo House. In addition he was to collect all the cotton, woolen, and silken goods he could, together with hardware, cutlery, and "all the varieties of [manufactured] goods which might be useful in [America]." Such products were as good as gold in Illinois; and the emigrating Saints were to be paid for them in provisions needed for the sea voyage and in lands, houses, and livestock when they arrived. Each group of emigrants was to continue to bring such English goods. Cheap American provisions were to be shipped back to supply the next group coming over, and so a circular trade would be established to the mutual benefit of the Saints. This trade would also aid in the building of "manufacturing establishments ready for the brethren when they arrive in our midst." The plan was justified on the grounds that during "the great depression of the moneyed institutions . . . and while the gold and silver are secreted by the hands of unprincipled speculators," it was necessary to resort to "all laudable measures" to effect emigration "from one kingdom to another," as well as for payment of debts and to get started in America. "And thus thousands and tens of thousands may . . . rejoice in this land of plenty while, were it not for a concert of action, they might remain where they are for years, or never [appear] . . . among us . . . until the morning of the first resurrection." [46]

Evidence is lacking to indicate whether the proposed barter of goods between Nauvoo and Liverpool was ever carried on extensively. The *Millennial Star* did not promote it; apparently it did not become organized or institutionalized until 1845. In a letter of May, 1844, to the president of the British Mission, Brigham Young made a single reference to the matter: "We have proposed to Brother Clark to return to your assistance in the shipping business soon; also to enter into exchange of goods and produce." [47] However, the important idea of a circular financial arrangement for the gathering of Saints from abroad was born. It was to mature in Utah as the Perpetual

[46] "An Epistle of the Twelve to the Church . . . in its various branches and conferences in Europe," March 20, 1842, in Joseph Smith's History, 4:561–563. The Apostles ascribed this scheme to spiritual guidance and the Prophet's instructions.

[47] Letter of Brigham Young to Reuben Hedlock, May 3, 1844, in Joseph Smith's History, 4:353.

Emigrating Company, one of the Church's greatest economic enterprises of the nineteenth century. The Perpetual Emigration Fund was a body of revolving capital supplemented from tithing and other Church sources which financed directly or indirectly the gathering of more than one hundred thousand persons at a cost of $12,-500,000.[48]

From 1840 through 1846 a total of 4,733 Saints emigrated from Great Britain. As the number grew from hundreds to thousands, their organization and outfitting became an extensive business. For some reason there was in 1842 official displeasure with Amos Fielding, the first agent. Smith and the Twelve in Council on June 14, "Voted that Hiram Clark go immediately to England . . . and take charge of the emigration . . . instead of Amos Fielding. . . . Voted that Brother Fielding come immediately to [Nauvoo]. . . ." Clark went as instructed; but Fielding did not leave Liverpool that year.[49] An Elder Reuben Hedlock, newly appointed Mission President, was sent the following year with similar instructions regarding Fielding. Hedlock wrote from Liverpool, October 4, 1843: "I found Elders Hyrum Clark, Thomas Ward [then editor of the *Millennial Star*] and Amos Fielding in Liverpool. . . . Elder Fielding wept when I showed him your decision concerning him and his coming to Nauvoo by the first ship to see you face to face. The brethren say . . . that he has been too hasty in some things, and has given some offense. . . ."[50]

By 1844 the emigration business of the British Mission had grown to the point where it might perhaps do more for the Church than gather the Saints to America. On May 3, 1844, Brigham Young wrote Hedlock a significant letter indicating that circumstances in Nauvoo demanded that a new complexion be placed upon the affairs of the British Mission. From then on, wrote Young, Hedlock was to make as much money as possible:

The whisperings of the Spirit to us are that you do well to content yourself awhile longer in old England. . . . We hope the Temple may be completed, say one year from this spring, when in many respects changes

[48] See Leonard J. Arrington, *Great Basin Kingdom: An Economic History of the Mormons: 1830–1900* (Cambridge, Massachusetts, 1950), p. 382 and *passim*. Arrington says that the total is an equivalent figure, since much was in goods and services rather than money. Had the immigrants used regular commercial channels rather than those of the "P. E. Company" the cost to them would have approximated $25.000.000.
[49] Joseph Smith's History, 5:26.
[50] *Ibid.*, 6:44.

will take place. Until then, who can do better in England than yourself!
. . . print as many *Stars,* pamphlets, hymn books, tracts, cards, etc., as
you can sell; and make all the money you can in righteousness. . . . Sell
the Books of Mormon the first opportunity, if it be at reduced prices, and
forward the money by the first safe conveyance to Brigham Young. . . .

We also wish you to unfurl your flag on your shipping office, and send
all the Saints you can to New York, or Boston, or Philadelphia or any other
port in the United States, but not at our expense any longer. . . . Tell
the Saints, when they arrive in America, to . . . not be overanxious if
they cannot come to Nauvoo. They will find Elders in all the States . . .
and if they can gather something by the way by their industry to assist
themselves, when they arrive here, it will be well for them. . . . We have
need of something to sustain us in our labors . . . make enough to support yourself and help us a bit. You will doubtless find it necessary to
employ Brother Ward. We will send Elders to your assistance. . . .

Ship everybody to America you can get money for—Saint and sinner—
a general shipping-office. And we would like to have our shipping agent
in Liverpool sleep on as good a bed, eat at as respectable a house, keep
as genteel an office, and have his boots shine as bright, and blacked as
often as any other office keeper. Yes, sir; make you money enough to wear
a good broadcloth, and show the world that you represent gentlemen of
worth, character, and respectability. . . . What will hinder your doing
a good business in shipping this season? Good? Yes, in competing with
the first offices in the city, and by next season taking the lead, if not
this. . . .

We will by-and-by have offices from the rivers to the ends of the earth,
and we will begin at Liverpool . . . and increase and increase and *increase* the business. . . . Employ a runner, if necessary, and show the
world you can do a better and more honorable business than anybody else,
and more of it. Don't be afraid to blow your trumpet. . . .

Send no more emigrants [on credit] or *Star* money. . . . Keep all your
books straight, so that in the end we can know every particular. . . .

Let nobody know your business but the underwriters. Our wives
know not all our business, neither does any wise man's wife . . . for the
secret of the Lord is with those who fear Him and do His business . . .
keep our business from your wife and from everybody else. . . .

Brother Hedlock, a word with you privately. Joseph said, last Conference [April, 1844], that Zion included all North and South America;
and after the Temple was done, and the Elders endowed, they would
spread and build up cities all over the United States; but at present we are
not to teach this doctrine. Nay, hold your tongue. But by this you can
see why it is wisdom for the Saints to get into the United States—anywhere rather than stay in England and starve.

The specific purpose behind Young's unusual instructions to Hedlock is perhaps revealed in the following paragraph of his letter:
"The prophet has a charter for a dam from the lower line of the city
to the island opposite Montrose, and from thence to the sand bar

above. . . . Could five, six, or seven thousand dollars be raised to commence the dam at the lower extremity, and erect a building, any machinery might be propelled by water. The value of a steam engine would nearly build the dam sufficient for a cotton factory, which we much need. Start some capitalists, if you can: 'tis the greatest speculation in the world: a world of cotton and woolen goods are wanted here." [51]

Hedlock needed financial sustenance in his own labors. His position as president of the Mission, agent for the now extensive publishing operation, and agent for emigrants had left him in straitened rather than enlarged circumstances. In the March, 1844, *Millennial Star* he appealed to the "liberality of the Saints generally, on behalf of the presidency in England, owing to the great demand made upon us by the authorities in Nauvoo, to send over as many families, free of expense [*sic*]." He was further "very circumscribed in . . . pecuniary means" by £40 costs incurred to defend two elders charged with manslaughter in the accidental drowning of a woman they were attempting to baptize. At the April Mission Conference he again spoke of "so many demands made . . . by the authorities of Nauvoo." The traveling elders often asked him for funds; and he was obliged to maintain an office in Liverpool costing £70 a year. Finally he had to support himself and his family.[52] By 1844 the rate of emigration from the English Mission was declining. Whereas in 1841 and 1842 it had totaled 2,749, in 1843 and 1844 the figure was 1,392, and in 1845 it fell to 302. Slackening emigration was perhaps due in part to a slight improvement of conditions in Britain and in part to the Bennett scandal and other related troubles in Nauvoo (see below, Chapter 9). So Young's plans for a grandiose and lucrative "general shipping-office" faced a diminishing market as far as emigrating Saints were concerned.

Furthermore, Young's injunction that Hedlock take only cash customers was difficult to apply in practice. In the March, 1845, *Millennial Star,* Hedlock complained that he had "shipped over one hundred adult passengers to New Orleans . . . who have not paid me one penny." His arrears were almost £400.[53]

Hedlock had a scheme of his own for supplying the economic

[51] Joseph Smith's History, 6:351–353.
[52] *Millennial Star,* 4:176, March, 1844; 4:199, April, 1844; 5:154, March, 1845.
[53] *Ibid.,* 5:154, March, 1845.

needs of Nauvoo and the British Mission as well that had a wider scope than that of Young. He combined the Apostle's proposal for a general shipping office with the 1842 plan for the forwarding of British manufactured goods to Nauvoo in a scheme for a great joint-stock corporation to gather money, goods, and labor to invest in Nauvoo manufactures. In April, 1844, even before he received Young's instructions, he wrote in the *Millennial Star:*

Manufacturers of various kinds are the great desideratum required at Nauvoo, in order to give employment to multitudes of poor . . . and also to preserve amongst themselves that money which they are at present compelled to spend elsewhere. It is in contemplation at no distant period and we throw out this hint to the Church generally, to form a sort of company on both sides of the Atlantic [to] supply building materials and raise factories, while others in this land prepare sufficient machinery for the same . . . we only want the Saints to be imbued with the true principle of building up Zion, and we are fully persuaded that many things which now appear . . . unsurmountable . . . will be speedily overcome.[54]

The kind of enterprise Hedlock had in mind was one not inconsistent with the economic philosophy then current in Nauvoo—self-sufficiency, cooperation of laborers and artisans, and pooling of capital. In July he spoke of "eight thousand Saints in Britain, and one united effort would place manufactories in Nauvoo. . . ." He requested all those mechanics favorably disposed to the proposition, "in the Church, or out of it," to write him what machinery they could build to send to Nauvoo by September, 1845, at latest, as well as "the amount of stock which they would take." He called for a formal joint-stock corporation, shares to be purchased "in money, machinery, material, or labor. . . ."[55] By March, 1845, the plan was ready for formal endorsement by the spring Mission conference. The Saints were called upon in the *Star* to send delegates "prepared, as far as possible, to state what amount of capital in money, machinery, or other goods could be employed in taking shares in said company. . . ." The shares were to have a face value of £5 each.[56]

The April Conference convened in Manchester, with the joint-stock company its major consideration. Hedlock took the lead in promoting it, utilizing both the principle of gathering, this time of

[54] *Ibid.*, 4:205, April, 1844.
[55] *Ibid.*, 5:31, July, 1844.
[56] The conference prospectus was published over the names of Wilford Woodruff, now back in England as Mission President, and Hedlock and Ward as his counselors. *Ibid.*, 5:157, March, 1845.

capital goods and skills, and the building up of Zion. Moreover Hedlock did not fail to state "that the shareholders would be benefited by the adoption of such a plan, inasmuch as the capital so employed, by judicious management, would in a few years double its capital." The anticipated scope of the company activities included a general export business, both of freight and people, and the import of "provisions . . . from our brethren in the West [Nauvoo], which, placed in bond in this country, would be a great advantage in the supply of sea stores to those that emigrated." He planned to have emigration agents "in all parts of the country." The corporation needed "men of business to enter into this work" and should "afford a fair return for labour on business-like principles." The conference adopted forty-five articles for governing "The Mutual Benefit Association." It would be a private corporation controlled by fifteen directors chosen by the conference from among the shareholders. Thomas Ward of the Mission Presidency was appointed president, and Hedlock was included on the board of seven operating directors who would run the business in Liverpool. The capital was to consist "of not less than thirty thousand pounds"; but since few people could afford the five pound share originally proposed, the price was reduced to ten shillings, with subscriptions made easy and attractive. One shilling down was sufficient, and payment of that could be deferred for two months. The remaining nine shillings might be paid in weekly or monthly installments covering eighteen months. Sixty thousand of such shares were to be marketed. An integral part of the plan was to use the ecclesiastical organization of the Church to subscribe the stock and handle the proceeds: each branch was to have a "Committee of management" over which was a similar committee for each district: these in turn dealt with the company directors. While the articles of authorization display a knowledge of business law, they also reveal oversanguine expectations for the concern. Its objectives were primarily Zionic, but they also included "the greatest amount of profit, requiring . . . the least amount of capital. . . ." The company should import "food and provisions from America, that the members may have abundance of those things both cheap and good" at a price low enough to effect "a saving far exceeding the weekly payment for one share." If the Saints subscribed the stock themselves, each man, woman, and child needed to purchase more than seven shares; nevertheless, provision was made for the next conference to issue sixty thousand additional shares if necessary.

At last Hedlock seemed situated to do what Brigham Young had ordered. The Kingdom would be built up, the poor gathered to Zion, and God's servants would be profited and strengthened for their labors. Hedlock continued as chief agent for the concern and early sought connections outside the Church to enlarge the business. He formed a partnership with a man who had extensive interests in Ireland, hoping thereby to tap the large Irish famine emigration. He had other gentile associates as well in Liverpool. But Hedlock gave in to the temptation to believe literally Brigham Young's expansive exhortation about good food, good lodgings, and well-shined boots. He was also trapped into thinking that his chief article of merchandise was shares of stock rather than goods and services. His staff was large, his agents everywhere, and there was even talk of buying ships and opening a general merchandise store in Liverpool. As he became more deeply involved he loaned himself funds from the company on an informal and unsecured basis.[57] While such a practice was not uncommon for Mormon leaders handling temporal enterprises, it was most hazardous should those enterprises fail. After Wilford Woodruff returned to America early in 1846, Hedlock again became Mission President, and rumblings began in the Church. Thomas Ward finally wrote the Twelve complaining of Hedlock's mismanagement, his connections with "the rascally brokers of Liverpool," and the threat of scandal overhanging the whole business.[58]

The Twelve, occupied in the summer of 1846 with the exodus from Nauvoo, disfellowshipped both Hedlock and Ward "until they shall appear before the council [Council of Fifty?] and make satisfaction for their repeated disregard of counsel." [59] A delegation of Apostles Orson Hyde, Parley Pratt, and John Taylor was sent to straighten matters; they left Council Bluffs on July 31 and arrived in England in October. They immediately dissociated the Church from the Mutual Benefit Association and advised the Saints to patronize it "no more for the present." One way to pursue business, they said,

[57] Cannon, "Migration of English Mormons," pp. 442–444; and Brigham H. Roberts, *Comprehensive History of the Church* (Salt Lake City, 1930), 3:122–128.
[58] Letter of Thomas Ward to Brigham Young and the Twelve, from the *History of Brigham Young, Ms.*, quoted in Roberts, *Comprehensive History*, 3:124. No date is given.
[59] Roberts, *Comprehensive History*, 3:127n. The date of the action was July 16, 1846.

was with "prudence and economy," and the other was with "wasteful prodigality." The Saints were promised "proper instructions . . . upon all these matters" at the next conference. An audit of the books revealed that £1644 had been subscribed from sale of stock, of which £1418 had been consumed in organizational and overhead expenses. Hedlock had retired from both his Church and business positions in face of the anticipated apostolic wrath. He was excommunicated at the October conference. Thomas Ward faced the situation and attempted an accounting, but, according to the historian Brigham H. Roberts, "He did not long survive the shock his errors brought upon him . . . as he died . . . five months later." On October 17 and 19 the directors dissolved the company and paid the receivers only one shilling and three pence on the pound sterling. Said Orson Hyde, who was temporarily editing the *Millennial Star*, of the remaining officers, "let the yoke be taken from their necks, and let them go free, with the fellowship of the Church, and let them make their calling and election sure, if they will." [60] Their work accomplished, the apostolic commission returned to America early in 1847. Elder Orson Spencer was sent "from the Camp of Israel in the Wilderness" to be the new Mission President.

Morman emigration from the British Isles was only fifty persons in 1846; and none were recorded in 1847. This pause was due primarily to the great transmigration of Saints taking place in America, but perhaps also in part to a reaction against the Mutual Benefit Association. The establishment of the Church in the Salt Lake Valley and the renewal of depression in England, as well as the revolutionary disturbances on the European continent, set the stage for record-breaking baptisms and emigrations from the British mission in the years just ahead. In the three years 1848–1850, 23,139 persons became Mormons and 4,445 went to America. When the Perpetual Emigrating Company was established in 1849 to handle the European gathering, its headquarters were in Utah and its direction was in the hands of Brigham Young. [61] Brigham H. Roberts in his official account of the Mutual Benefit Association carefully avoided implicating the Twelve in the disastrous venture. Of Young's letter to Hedlock in May, 1844, he said only that "president Hedlock had

---

[60] *Millennial Star*, 9:22, January 15, 1847; Roberts, *Comprehensive History*, 3:125–127.

[61] Leonard J. Arrington, *Great Basin Kingdom*, p. 77; Roberts, *Comprehensive History*, 3:128. The Perpetual Emigrating Company was also concerned with gathering American Saints to Utah.

been instructed to enlarge [the emigration business] into a general emigration agency," open a general shipping office, and show the world he could do a deal of honorable business. Though Woodruff was Mission President when the scheme was formalized and launched, Roberts implicitly absolved him from any fault. Hedlock undoubtedly mismanaged the firm; but Young and Woodruff had a share in its original malconception. However, they confessed no blame, and were apparently accorded none.

The British Saints who gathered to Nauvoo played an important role both in terms of enlarging the population of the city and forming its character. At least thirty-two companies of British emigrants totaling nearly five thousand persons gathered to Nauvoo and comprised perhaps a quarter of its citizens by 1845.[62] Most of them came up the river from New Orleans; the Church's little steamer *Maid of Iowa*, captained by a Welsh convert named Dan Jones, carried many of them. Though Mormon sources give abundant evidence that the poor bulked large among the immigrants, gentile observers did not consider them mean or degraded in appearance. The *Madison City Express* for April 25, 1844, called them respectable-looking mechanics and farmers "who would make good settlers if they were free of the infatuation of Mormonism."[63] The *Quincy Whig* for April 14, 1841, noted a company from Lancashire with "an honest and healthy look." The group included "many comely woman . . . handsome and delicate," as well as ninety children under the age of fourteen; "we hope," the writer added, "where they go . . . they will preserve their health and their morals." The *Ft. Madison Courier* for November 13, 1841, said of a company that came from Gloucestershire by the St. Lawrence, "They appear to be quite inoffensive people and possessed of some means."[64] An English paper also observed that Mormon emigrants were "in appearance and worldly circumstances above the ordinary run of steerage passengers."[65] A Scots minister, traveling on the Mississippi in the sum-

[62] Larsen, *Prelude to the Kingdom*, p. 50. They seemed an even larger proportion to some. One traveler said, "of the 16,000 followers assembled at Nauvoo, 10,000 are said to be from England." G. Lewis, *Impressions of America and the American Churches* (Edinburgh, 1845), p. 265.

[63] Quoted in Pooley, *Settlement of Illinois*, p. 515.

[64] Quoted in Cecil A. Snider, "Development of Attitudes in Sectarian Conflict: A Study of Mormonism in Illinois in Contemporary Newspaper Sources" (unpublished M.A. thesis, State University of Iowa), 1933, pp. 22, 23.

[65] The *Liverpool Albion*, September, 1842, quoted in Henry Caswall, *Prophet of the Nineteenth Century* (London, 1843), p. 137.

mer of 1844, was especially interested in the Mormon immigrants he observed since the British churches were much shaken by the impact of Mormonism. He described one Latter-day Saint woman with whom he conversed as "intelligent on all other points but the Mormonite delusion, on which she seemed crazed. She conceived Nauvoo to be the Paradise from which our first parents were expelled." He concluded that "Nauvoo, at this extremity of the world, acts as a kind of receptacle for all the odd and fantastic minds, not only of America, but of Great Britain. There their enthusiasm works less dangerously than in the crowded cities." [66]

At home in Britain the Mormon gathering to an American Zion fomented a storm of abuse and dire predictions in the churches and press. Mormonism was new, and untried by experience; its adherents were motivated mainly by faith, hope, and in some cases desperation, to leave hearth and home forever. It is not surprising therefore that there was apprehension among the British Saints as to what Nauvoo would be like, and how the emigrants would react to it. Such emotions were unspoken and reflected only in the flood of answers written back to satisfy the unasked questions. Were the latter-day Zion, the latter-day Prophet, the inheritances for Latter-day Saints really as promised? Some answered yes, and some answered no. The answers finally became a test of faith and fellowship, with the yea-sayers warning their brethren at home to beware of the nay-sayers, who were "apostates." Almost every testimonial letter in the *Millennial Star,* and there were dozens of them, treated the theme of those who had "shaken out by the way" and had become critical of the Kingdom. In contrast were the fervent affirmations that all was well in Zion. Nevertheless it was a novel place and excited the wonder of many when they saw it for the first time. Joseph Fielding, who emigrated in the autumn of 1841, described his first impressions of Nauvoo:

Late in the evening . . . we came in sight of some neat cottages fenced in with pickets, manifesting to us that the hand of industry was there different from anything we had seen since leaving England, even by the light of the moon; this was the first we saw of the city of the Saints . . . and we were then told that we had two miles to go to that part of the city where we were going. We soon passed the temple, went from street to street, as in some large city, till we came near the river. . . . I can truly say that the place, in general, exceeds my expectations; in short, one could hardly believe it possible that a town of such extent,

[66] Lewis, *Impressions of America and the American Churches,* pp. 265, 266.

could have been built in so short a time, especially by a people generally poor—there are many log, many frame, and many brick houses. . . .

Of the Temple, then built up to the first floor level, Fielding wrote:

It would be vain to attempt to describe my feelings on beholding this interesting sight; but if you have the same faith as myself in the great work of God, and consider that the things on earth are patterns of things in heaven, at the same time look back on the form of the temple and font, you may judge of my feelings. Many have been baptized therein for their deceased relatives, and also for the healing of their own afflicted bodies.[67]

In 1843 a brother John Needham had written a long letter to his family near Warrington, and editor Pratt requested it for publication in the *Star*. Needham's enthusiastic letter sought to allay the anxiety of his relatives at home:

When within five or six miles of this place, we heard the agreeable cry, "Nauvoo to be seen," the long-looked-for place; every eye was stretched toward the place, as you may be sure our eyes gazed with delight, but astonishment, to see the great extent of it. The city seemed to rise gradually from the sea, with the houses much scattered, but over a great extent of ground; it has without any mistake, more so than any place we had seen before, a grand appearance. It looked very pretty from the river. . . . The extent of the city is four miles, laid out in lots and streets in nice order; I mean that each house has a piece of land attached to it, either a quarter, half, or whole acre . . . and some more, which makes the houses appear scattered. For two miles square the city is covered that way, but in the center, near the temple, they are quite close like other towns. If all the houses were put together like other places, they would make a large place; I should think twice or thrice the size of Warrington. . . .[68]

Yet emigration brought dissatisfaction and disgust to many English Saints. Some came with vague or mixed motives. Many came primarily to escape conditions in England, with faith insufficient to face the difficulties of Nauvoo. But immigrants other than Mormons also had difficulties of adjustment. Edwin Bottomly wrote back to his father in England: "Some people form expectations of this country before they come which would be impossible to realize in any country in the world . . . some imagine that when they get to this country they will find fish in every pool . . . fruit on every tree and that wild fowl will come to them to be shot, furnished houses on every plot of land they want to purchase and that they will have

[67] Letter of Joseph Fielding to Parley Pratt, January, 1842, in the *Millennial Star*, 3:77, 78, August, 1842.
[68] *Millennial Star*, 4:87, 88, October, 1843.

nothing to do but sit them down in ease and plenty when they get here. I must say there is plenty of Fruit and fish and fowl but they are the same in this country as in any other, *no catch no eat.*" [69] An English traveler across Illinois compared his emigrant countrymen unfavorably with the Germans, Scots, Irish, and French: "Of all emigrants, the Englishman experiences the most difficulty in settling down in a new country, and making up his mind to yield to circumstances. . . . He comes in general with his mind hampered by prejudice in favor of the customs and habits of his own country, and deeming customary gratifications an absolute necessity of life." [70]

Though Mormon preaching to English proselytes about Zion dealt in sanguine generalities, specific instructions to emigrants admonished them repeatedly to keep their expectations realistic. In Joseph Smith's proclamation of January 15, 1841, which proclaimed a general gathering to Nauvoo, the Prophet warned the Saints to anticipate some difficulties:

We would wish the Saints to understand that, when they come here, they must not expect perfection, or that all will be harmony, peace, and love; if they indulge these ideas, they will undoubtedly be deceived, for here there are persons, not only from different states, but from different nations, who, although they feel a great attachment to the cause of truth, have their prejudices of education, and consequently, it requires some time before these things can be overcome. Again, there are many that creep in unawares, and endeavor to sow discord, strife, and animosity in our midst, and in so doing, bring evil upon the Saints. These things we have to bear with, and these things will prevail either to a greater or less extent until "the floor be thoroughly purged" and "the chaff be burnt up." [71]

Said John Needham in 1843 of the difficulties of building a saintly city: "People that come to Nauvoo have to learn a great deal by experience that they cannot be taught away from here: and be assured that all that come here must not expect perfection nor a perfect place. . . . I tell you what, *if wheat and tares grow together anywhere, it is here;* but a day of sifting will come, and our trials are only to see what we will bear for the truth." [72]

Even the Illinois press commented early on the dissatisfaction of Englishmen in Nauvoo. On May 19, 1841, the *Quincy Whig* reported that many of them were opposed to the government of the

[69] Quaife, ed., *The Bottomly Letters*, pp. 90, 91.
[70] Charles Joseph Latrobe, *The Rambler in North America* (London, 1836), 2:222.
[71] Joseph Smith's History, 4:272, 273.
[72] *Millennial Star*, 4:89, October, 1843.

city, disbelieved in Smith's prophetic power, and had left both the city and the Church. President Sidney Rigdon was quoted in defense as saying that "in general," the newcomers were "well satisfied." [73] William Clayton, Smith's scribe, wrote home to the English brethren on March 30, 1842, a frank confession of the problem of those who were "shaking out" and cited the instance of "brother B" [Brotherton?]:

Old Mr. B. — and daughter, like many others, were assailed by the apostate crews [those previously "shaken out"], who lay along the banks of the river; and all manner of evil reports were sounded in their ears, until they became discouraged; and finally, almost denied the faith before they reached Nauvoo. . . . The B—ton family . . . were something like spies, afraid to be spoken to by anyone lest they should be ensnared, and especially afraid to meet Joseph Smith, lest he should want their money. After remaining a short time here, they went back to Warsaw, where some of the greatest enemies reside, and . . . have joined in the general clamor and business of circulating evil reports, some of which I, MYSELF, KNOW POSITIVELY TO BE FALSE.[74]

A brother Boscow wrote to England in May, 1842: "the reports here . . . and coming up the river, are sufficient to stagger any who are not of strong mind and firmly grounded in the faith." [75] Even Smith was nettled that so many were becoming disaffected, as was illustrated by his remarks to newly arrived immigrants on October 29, 1842:

I spoke to them at considerable length, showing them the proper course to pursue, and how to act in regard to making purchases of land, etc.
I showed them it was generally in consequence of the brethren disregarding or disobeying counsel that they became dissatisfied and murmured; and many . . . were dissatisfied with the conduct of the Saints, because everything was not done perfectly right, and they get angry, and thus the devil gets advantage over them to destroy them. I told them I was but a man, and they must not expect me to be perfect . . . if they would bear with my infirmities and the infirmities of the brethren, I would likewise bear with their infirmities.[76]

Much attention was given to the "counselling" of immigrants, and attempts were made to protect their interests. When the Twelve returned to Nauvoo in 1841 they were charged to "attend to the set-

---

[73] Quoted in Snider, "Attitudes in Sectarian Conflict," p. 178.
[74] *Millennial Star*, 3:75, August, 1842. Clayton may have been referring to the family of Martha Brotherton, who accused Smith and Young of urging her to become a plural wife.
[75] *Ibid.*
[76] Joseph Smith's History, 5:181.

tling of emigrants [sic]." Anyone who should try "to influence any emigrants belonging to the Church, either to buy of them (except provisions) or sell to them (except the Church agents) shall be immediately tried for fellowship . . . and unless they repent be cut off from the Church. President Rigdon then made some appropriate remarks on speculation." [77] But even the Apostles were unable to solve all problems. Their new Mormon faith was a strength to many English gatherers, helping them to endure the hardships met in Nauvoo and Utah; for some it was a hindrance. But the matter of faith aside, bringing so many indigent immigrants with inflated expectations to such an economically immature city as Nauvoo must inevitably create problems.

[77] "Minutes of a Special Conference at Nauvoo," August 16, 1841, in *ibid.*, 4:403, 404. The action may have been in part an attempt to create a Church monoply over the immigrant trade.

4

A Kingdom of This World:
Government and the Military

We are laying the foundation of a kingdom that will last forever—that shall bloom in time, and blossom in eternity. We are engaged in a greater work than ever occupied the attention of mortals. We live in a day that prophets and kings desire to see, but died without the sight.

Sermon of John Taylor at Nauvoo, April 6, 1844, in "The History of Joseph Smith," *The Latter-Day Saints' Millennial Star*, 23:215, March 30, 1861.

The firm heart of the Sage and the Patriot is warm'd
By the grand "Nauvoo Legion:" the Legion is form'd
To oppose vile oppression, and nobly to stand
In defense of the honor, and laws of the land.
Base, illegal proscribers may tremble—'tis right
That the lawless aggressor should shrink with affright,
From a band that's united fell mobbers to chase,
And protect our lov'd country from utter disgrace. . . .

Eliza R. Snow

M. R. Werner, *Brigham Young* (New York, 1925), p. 121.

This [Nauvoo] city charter . . . gave them power to pass . . . ordinances . . . not repugnant to the Constitution . . . of this State. This seemed to give them power to pass ordinances in violation of the laws of the State, and to erect a system of government for themselves.

Ford, *History of Illinois*, pp. 263, 264.

The first generation of Mormons attempted the formation of their own semi-independent and quasi-sovereign governments within the general framework of the American federal system. The creation in 1838 of a "Mormon county" (Caldwell County, Missouri) with a Mormon population, government, and militia, began a process which ended with the attempt to form a Mormon empire in the Great Basin. The government of Nauvoo was an important intermediate step. Joseph Smith's plan, embodied in a charter to incorporate the city, was for a comprehensive system of local government, with its own military establishment, that would be largely free from outside interference, even by the state that authorized it. The city charter was written by Smith and John C. Bennett, a somewhat mysterious man who appeared suddenly on the scene in 1840 and played a brief but dramatic role in Mormon history. The charter was enacted by the Illinois legislature in February, 1841, and provided the legal basis of government for Nauvoo until it was repealed in January, 1845.

In 1839 Smith was inexperienced in the affairs of government and politics; and there were few among the Saints who could help him, especially since nine members of the Quorum of Twelve were in England. Faced with the necessity of making his and the Church's way in a new state and, above all, of protecting the Saints from a repetition of the Missouri disaster, the Prophet sought to make powerful and influential friends outside the Church. He was always the careful host, the prolific letter writer, the cultivator of important people, and soon he numbered men of some standing as friends and benefactors of the Saints. In a proclamation to the Church, January, 1841, he singled out several such men, including Isaac Galland, the land broker; Sangamon County Judge of Probate General James Adams; Sidney Knowlton of Hancock County; a Dr. Green of Shelby County, and Robert D. Foster of Nauvoo. "We make mention of them," said Smith, "that the Saints may be encouraged, and also that they may see that the persecutions we suffered in Missouri were but the prelude to a far more glorious display of the power of truth, of the religion we have espoused." Several persons of "eminence and distinction in society," said Smith, even "several of the principal men of Illinois" had heard the gospel, obeyed it, "and are rejoicing in the same." [1]

It seemed not to occur to Smith that some men might wish to cultivate him for their own purposes. Mormonism, like any growing enterprise, attracted the ambitious and the clever. Some were men of integrity and some were not; Dr. John C. Bennett, M.D., Quartermaster General of Illinois, was apparently one of the latter, but Smith was at the outset of their relationship a less able judge of character than of talent and charm. Little is known of Bennett either before or after his affair with the Mormons. He was an officer of the "Invincible Dragoons," a militia company of Edwards, White, and Wabash Counties in southeastern Illinois, and was living at Fairfield

---

[1] Joseph Smith's History, 4:270, 271.

in neighboring Wayne County in 1840.[2] Despite the medical title, Bennett presented the image of a military man. Politics and the pursuit of influence were the professions he sought when he approached the Mormons and offered his services. Two letters written July 25 and 27, 1840, from "Quartermaster General's Office" at Fairfield reveal something of the man's style: "Reverend and Dear Friends Smith and Rigdon: The last time I wrote you was during the pendency of your difficulties with the Missourians. You are aware that at the time I held the office of 'Brigadier-General of the Invincible Dragoons' of this state, and profered you my entire energies for your deliverance from a ruthless and savage, but cowardly foe . . . and had not the conflict terminated so speedily, I should have been with you then . . . but the Lord came to your rescue, and saved you with a powerful arm. I am happy to find that you are now in a Civilized land. . . ." Bennett appreciated the political and economic potential of the gathering. "It would be my deliberate advice to you," he continued, "to concentrate all of your Church at one point. If Hancock County, with Commerce as its commercial emporium, is to be that point, well; fix upon it. Let us cooperate with a general concerted action. . . . Be so good as to inform me substantially of the population of Commerce and Hancock County, the fare of the country, the climate, soil, health, etc. How many of your people are concentrated there? Please to write me in full immediately. . . ." Bennett in his letter conveyed the air of a busy man of affairs with obligations and responsibilities of moment. Yet he seemed to be one of those noblemen of the earth who had condescended to believe God's truth with humility, and with meekness to obey the command of His Prophet:

At the last District and Circuit Court of the United States, holden at Springfield . . . I had the honor of being on the grand inquest [jury?] of the United State for the District of Illinois . . . I propose to meet you in Springfield on the first Monday in December next, as I shall be then . . . on state and United States business.

I hope . . . to remove to Commerce, and unite with your church next spring. . . . You can rely on me in any event. I am with you in spirit, and will be in person as soon as circumstances permit and immediately if

[2] "An Act to Incorporate the Invincible Dragoons of the second division of Illinois militia," *Laws of Incorporation of the State of Illinois passed by the Eleventh General Assembly*, 1839, p. 45. Bennett's name is listed first among the commissioned officers. There were Bennetts prominent in Wayne County, but a search of the histories of Wayne, Edwards, White, and Wabash Counties has failed to reveal any reference to John C. Bennett.

it is your desire. Wealth is no material object with me. I desire to be happy, and am fully satisfied that I can enjoy myself better with your people . . . than with any other. I hope that in time your people will become my people, and your God my God. . . .

I do not expect to resign my office of "Quartermaster-General of Illinois" unless you advise otherwise. I shall expect to practice my profession; but at the same time your people shall have all the benefits of my speaking powers, and my untiring energies in behalf of the good and holy faith. *Un necessariis unitas, in non necessariis libertas, in omnibus charitas,* shall be my motto, with—*Suaviter in modo, fortiter in re.*[3]

Bennett was serious about moving to Nauvoo and joining the Church, and he arrived in August or September of 1840. He was there, however, not as an ordinary convert, but in the seat of power at the Prophet's right hand. The Mormon leader felt himself in need of a man such as Bennett seemed to be as an adviser, confidant, and executive lieutenant. Sidney Rigdon was proving a slender reed in the demanding business of kingdom building. Brigham Young and Heber Kimball were in England. Smith was young, without knowledge of the ways of the world in which he was now committed to promote the Kingdom, and he was standing virtually alone at the head of his people. Bennett seemed to be a man of ambition, force, energy, and intelligence—qualities that had already won him preferment in the world. They were attributes which Smith possessed himself and admired in others, and he expected this prestigious new aid-de-camp to "open doors" for the advancement of Nauvoo. Bennett played a conspicuous role in developing two of the most characteristic and important Nauvoo institutions: the city government and the Legion. He took up residence in Nauvoo in time to avail the benefits of his "speaking powers" to the semiannual conference in October, 1840, which took official action concerning these institutions. The minutes of October 4 took the first public cognizance of the man:

John C. Bennett, M.D., then spoke at some length, on the oppression to which the Church had been subjected, and remarked that it was necessary for the brethren to stand by each other, and resist every unlawful attempt at persecution.[4]

Bennett was, recalled Ebenezer Robinson, "a man of rather pleasing address, calculated to make a favorable impression on the minds of

---

[3] Joseph Smith's History, 4:168–170. The earlier letter or letters of Bennett to the Mormon leaders is not in Joseph Smith's History and presumably is not extant.
[4] Joseph Smith's History, 4:205.

most people." [5] On October 5 the agenda of business included a motion to appoint a committee responsible for drafting "a bill for the incorporation of the town of Nauvoo, and for other purposes." Smith, Bennett, and Robert B. Thompson were designated as the committee, presumably by Smith as presiding officer. Smith and Bennett had already been at work on the charter and probably had it completed before the conference met. On the same afternoon that the committee was authorized Bennett reported to the assembly "the outlines" of the city charter. The conference endorsed the committee's work, apparently with little or no debate. Bennett was now an officially recognized and endorsed architect of the city's future.[6]

When the state legislature convened in December, 1840, General Bennett was in Springfield as lobbyist for the proposed city and associated charters.[7] The circumstances of the legislative session were propitious for their passage. The lawmakers were preoccupied with the state fiscal crisis caused by the depression and the collapse of the heavily indebted internal improvements programs. Furthermore, they were deluged with requests to enact charters for incorporation of every conceivable sort, of which the Nauvoo City bill was only one. Forty-seven acts of incorporation were finally passed by the Twelfth General Assembly including seven other city charters. But the legislators did not overlook the fact that the Mormons represented a powerful political bloc, which they were at that time disposed to serve. The young Stephen A. Douglas, then Secretary of State and already a power in the Illinois Democracy, lent his support to Bennett's measure; so did Whig Senator Sidney H. Little of McDonough County, which adjoined Hancock on the east. A biographer of Douglas wrote, "That Douglas and Little are entitled to all the doubtful credit for the enactment of these laws, there is little room for doubt." [8]

On December 27 the Nauvoo charter bill was introduced in the Upper House by Senator Little, whose only comment was that it contained "an extraordinary militia clause" which he considered "harmless." Under a suspension of the rules, the bill was read the

[5] *The Return*, 2:285, June, 1890.
[6] "Minutes of the General Conference . . . Beginning October 3, 1840," in Joseph Smith's History, 4:205, 206.
[7] Two other charters were introduced, one to incorporate an "Agricultural and Manufacturing Association," and the other a "Nauvoo House [hotel] Association." See below, Chapters 6 and 7.
[8] Frank E. Stevens, "Life of Stephen A. Douglas," *Journal of the Illinois State Historical Society*, 16:340, 341 (1923–1924).

first and second times and referred to the Judiciary Committee; on December 5 it was reported back with an unspecified amendment; and on December 9 it was read the third time and passed, in company with other miscellaneous bills. In the House of Representatives the procedure was similar. Introduced from the Senate on December 10 it was read twice by title and referred to committee; two days later it was reported back without amendment, read again by title, and shouted through without calling for ayes and nays. It next went to the Council of Revision, a review body with amending powers made up of Democratic Governor Thomas Carlin and the four supreme court Justices, three Whigs and one Democrat. This group passed it without change on December 18.[9]

The hurried passage of the ill-examined charter owed much to political expediency—Ford and the historian Frank Stevens sardonically assigned this as the only reason—as well as to the inexperience and legal incapacity of many legislators and the press of other business. But beyond these circumstances, its routine enactment seems natural considering the high optimism that prevailed in the state. Illinois was growing and society was moving ahead. New counties, new cities and towns, new institutions, new groups of every sort were springing up across the state, clamoring for recognition, for legal status, for power and political preferment. The tendency was to welcome them and to help them; there was presumably room for all and a need for all. The Mormons were desirable as an especially populous new group. The years 1839–1840 were something of an "Era of Good Feeling" between Mormons and Illinoisans.

Bennett's role in promoting the enactment of the charter is not clear; Ford accorded him considerable credit. "He flattered both sides with the hope of Mormon favor," wrote the old governor, "and both sides expected to receive their votes." While the charter might have passed without his presence, Bennett was accorded both status and prestige by his new Mormon brethren in thanks for the achievement.[10] However, Joseph Smith wrote in his journal, "The City Charter of Nauvoo is my own plan and device; I concocted it for the

[9] Pease, *Frontier State*, p. 344; Ford, *History of Illinois*, p. 264; *Journal of the Senate of the Twelfth General Assembly of the State of Illinois*, 1840–1841, pp. 23, 45, 61, 89; *Journal of the House of Representatives of the Twelfth General Assembly of the State of Illinois*, 1840–1841, pp. 101, 110; *Laws of the State of Illinois, the Twelfth General Assembly, passim.*

[10] Ford, *History of Illinois*, p. 264. See also Bennett's exultant letter to Nauvoo, December 16, 1840, announcing the victory, and specifically naming those to whom political thanks was due, in Joseph Smith's History, 4:248.

salvation of the Church, and on principles so broad, that every honest man might dwell secure under its protective influence without distinction of sect or party." [11]

That the Nauvoo City Charter excited so little interest in the legislature when it was passed and so much a short time later (it was a major political issue in Illinois from 1842 until its repeal in 1845) is not surprising. The charter itself seemed harmless; what the Mormons accomplished under its provisions did not. The document was frankly based on the Springfield Charter, enacted in 1839. Many sections of the two laws, including some singled out as examples of subversive Mormon intentions, are identical. Section 13 of the Nauvoo Charter, enumerating the privileges of the city council, concludes that "in fine [they are] to exercise such other legislative powers as are conferred on the city council of the city of Springfield. . . ." [12] In practice, however, the Mormons created a quasi-sovereign government tailored to suit what were thought to be the unique requirements of the Latter-day Saints' community and church. The oligarchic flavor of Mormon church organization was evident in the relative absence of a real separation of powers between the branches and the functions of government. The mayor was an active member of the city council and was at the same time chief justice of the municipal court. Four aldermen, who with nine "Councillors" formed the city council, were associate justices. Section 17 of the charter begins, "The mayor shall have exclusive jurisdiction in all cases arising under the ordinances of the corporation, and shall issue such process as may be necessary to carry such ordinances into execution and effect." Any decision of the mayor or aldermen acting as justices of the peace might be appealed to the same men sitting as the municipal court, of which the mayor was chief justice. Further appeals to the circuit court of the county were lawful, but frowned upon by the Church as "lawing before the world." Since most of the men holding city offices were Mormon "leaders," with Smith as mayor after the spring of 1842, the civil

[11] Under date of December 16, 1840, in Joseph Smith's History, 4:249.

[12] See for example Article I, Sections 4, 5; Article II, Sections 1, 2, 12; Article V, Section 36; Article VI, Section 8, of the Springfield Charter and Sections 2, 3, 4, 5, 13, and 17 of the Nauvoo Charter. *Laws of the State of Illinois passed by the Eleventh General Assembly, Special Session of 1839*, pp. 6–15; and *Laws . . . Twelfth General Assembly*, pp. 52–57. See also Therald Jensen, "Mormon Theory of Church and State" (Ph.D. dissertation, University of Chicago, 1938), pp. 59–68, for an extensive discussion of the Nauvoo Charter.

government was in effect an adjunct to the well-articulated Church government, in Nauvoo further refined in ward organizations, forming an amalgam extensive in powers and scope.

The charter had an unusual feature empowering the municipal court to grant writs of habeas corpus "in all cases arising under the ordinances of the City Council." The court was in the future to issue such writs to free arrested persons, in particular Joseph Smith, regardless of the jurisdiction under which they were arrested. The City Council of Nauvoo could and did define the jurisdiction of the municipal court in any way it wished; the council was limited only by the provision that such definitions be "not repugnant to the constitution of the United States or of this State" (Nauvoo Charter Section 8; Springfield Charter Article V, Section 36). The habeas corpus provision was designed to make Nauvoo an island of legal safety in which Mormons arrested by "outside" civil officers could be freed by legal process. The net result was not only to help protect the Mormons from legal persecution, real or imagined, but also to make "outside" law enforceable in Nauvoo only if the city government concurred. The frequent inability of county and state law enforcement officers to arrest accused persons in Nauvoo aroused the opposition of the gentile citizens around the city. "I cannot describe to you the many iniquities they did commit," recalled a Carthage citizen. "They murdered many of our best citizens, and there was nothing (eight ox team [or] a diaper) that they would not steal. . . . The law could not reach them . . . our lives and property was at the mercy of the worst set of outlaws that ever congregated together. The result was war to the knife and knife to the hilt." [13] The habeas corpus clause of the charter and the cavalier fashion in which the Mormons used it generated much popular fear and hatred, and were the points upon which legal attacks on the whole charter finally focused. Smith's riddled body at Carthage jail and the dissolution of the city corporation marked the conclusion of the issue.

The charter also provided that the boundaries of Nauvoo, generous to begin with, could be easily enlarged. The city limits contained the peninsula on which the first settlement took place and a large tract to the north, south, and east as well, comprising in all

[13] Letter of Dr. Thomas L. Barnes, n.d., in the manuscript collection of the Illinois State Historical Library. Barnes attended the wounded Taylor after the Smith murders.

more than six square miles. The corporation limits also included about five miles of river frontage (Sections 1, 2).[14] The provision was not unique, however. It was copied verbatim from the Springfield Charter (Article I, Section 4).

The crowning provision of the charter gave the city its own little army, the famous Nauvoo Legion. Section 25 ordained that

> The City Council may organize the inhabitants of said city subject to military duty, into a body of independant militarymen, to be called the "Nauvoo Legion," the Court Martial of which shall be composed of the commissioned officers . . . and constitute the law making department, with full power and authority to make . . . and execute . . . such laws . . . as may be . . . necessary for the . . . regulation of said Legion, provided said Court Martial shall pass no law or act, repugnant to, or inconsistent with, the Constitution of the United States, or of this State; and provided . . . that the officers . . . shall be commissioned by the governor of the State.[15]

In a sense the Legion was related to the system of Illinois militia: it issued commissions to its officers, it received state arms, its terms of service were to be the same "as is now or may hereafter be required of the regular militia of the state," and it was to be at the disposal of the governor for "the public defense." [16] But at the same time, it partook of the special separate, independent character of Nauvoo, to which independence it was designed to make a major contribution. Its officers, elected by the Legion, were to constitute a court martial empowered "to establish and execute" all laws and ordinances it considered discretionary, being limited only by the provision that such ordinances not be repugnant to state or federal constitutions. The Legion was therefore independent of and not subject to the military laws of Illinois. Finally, to make it clear that the Legion was intended to be an instrument of power rather than a mere chowder and marching society, it was specified that "said Legion . . . shall be at the disposal of the mayor in executing the laws and ordinances of the city corporation, and the laws of the State. . . ." The unusual provisions that the military was to be a police force and that the

[14] Section 2 of the charter reads: "Whenever any tract of land adjoining . . . shall have been laid into town lots, and duly recorded . . . the same shall form a part of the 'City of Nauvoo.' " The Mormons seemed to expect and the citizens of Hancock to fear that the city would be enlarged indefinitely; thus the gentiles came to oppose this provision.

[15] Joseph Smith's History, 4:244.

[16] See "An Act organizing the Militia of this State," *Laws passed by the First General Assembly of the State of Illinois, Second Session, Kaskaskia,* 1819, pp. 270–296.

mayor of Nauvoo might choose to interpret and "enforce the laws of the State" became portentous as fear and hatred of corporate Mormonism grew in Illinois.[17] But Joseph Smith, obsessed by fear of arrests, raids, kidnappings, and general "mobbing," sought to hedge the Nauvoo kingdom about with as many security devices as possible. The Legion was the product of a defensive rather than an aggressive psychology.[18]

The first municipal election was held February 1, 1841, the day the charter officially became state law. Dr. Bennett received his reward when he was elected the first mayor. The four aldermen were Stake President William Marks, Bishop Newel K. Whitney, Samuel H. Smith, a high priest and younger brother of the Prophet, and Daniel H. Wells, a gentile. (Wells was a local farmer who later joined and rose to power in the Church.) The nine city councilors included the three members of the First Presidency as well as Charles C. Rich, Wilson Law, Don Carlos Smith, and Bishop Vinson Knight. There seems to have been no opposing slate of candidates, and it is likely that the new city officers were nominees of the Church authorities and ran unopposed. Bennett said that his election was by the "unanimous suffrage of all parties and interests." [19] The following month the new city council added to the machinery of government a "collector of the city," a "weigher and sealer," a "market master," a surveyor and engineer, an assessor, a supervisor of streets, and four high constables for each of the city's wards. In order to insure an orderly and morally upright community and one secure against "mobbers," statutes were enacted to impose a fine of up to five hundred dollars for inciting to riot, disturbing the peace, interrupting public meetings, disobeying a civil officer, or refusing to obey the law. There were also ordinances against vagrant and "disorderly" persons, mad dogs, naked swimming, and "in relation to

[17] The principle is suggested in the Springfield Charter, Article VI, Section 4: "[The Mayor] is . . . authorized to call on any male inhabitant of said city over the age of eighteen years to aid in enforcing the laws and ordinances; and in case of riot, to call out the militia. . . ." Of course there was no city militia force as in Nauvoo.

[18] The Nauvoo City Charter is in Joseph Smith's History, 4:239–249, and *Laws . . . Twelfth General Assembly*, pp. 52–57. It served as a model for many Utah towns and cities. See Jensen, "Mormon Theory of Church and State," p. 68.

[19] Smith said that the victorious candidates "were elected by majorities varying from 330 to 337 votes," probably an indication of the total vote cast for each candidate rather than the normal implication of "majority" in an election between two candidates. Joseph Smith's History, 4:287, 288.

Hawkers, Pedlars, Public Shows and Exhibitions, in order to prevent any immoral or obscene exhibition." There was another ordinance imposing fine or imprisonment for violating the religious rights of gentiles in the city.[20]

In 1842 Smith sought to expand the prerogatives of the city to include a Nauvoo Registry of Deeds, a function normally of the county government. There was reason to make such a move for the sake of convenience; the buying and selling of real property was reaching a large volume of business, and the county seat was twenty-five miles away. But opposition to Smith's proposal arose in the city council. Was it not a presumptuous encroachment on county government? Would it not excite feelings in Carthage? Perhaps such a statute, if tested in the courts, would be disallowed as illegal. Smith quieted such timidity: "I attended an adjourned meeting of the City Council February 18, 1842, and spoke at considerable length . . . on the great privileges of the Nauvoo Charter, and especially on the registry of deeds, and prophesied in the name of the Lord God, that Judge Douglas and no other [nor any other?] judge of the circuit court will ever set aside a law of the City Council, establishing a registry of deeds in the City of Nauvoo." It was an election year, and the Prophet had grasped the relation between politics and the dispensation of justice. He urged the matter again the following month, when at last the council relented. Smith was appointed recorder with William Clayton, one of his scribes, as deputy. As might have been expected, a desultory feud resulted between the Nauvoo and Hancock County recorders.[21] But the registry of deeds seemed to be in jeopardy by 1844, along with the whole city government. After the Prophet's death an avalanche of deeds, many dated years earlier, were recorded in Carthage by Mormon property owners who feared the possible invalidity of titles not recorded in the county records.

[20] *Ibid.*, 4:306–308, 447, 461; the *Nauvoo Neighbor* of June 27, 1843; *Sangamo Journal* (Springfield) of March 1, 1841, quoted in Gayler, "The Mormons in Western Illinois," p. 127. The several laws controlling the sale of spirits will be discussed in Chapter 9.

[21] In January, 1844, John Taylor reprinted in the *Nauvoo Neighbor* the city ordinance exempting those married in Nauvoo from the necessity of obtaining a license from the county seat. "It would be well," Taylor commented, "for some people in our city to ask the county clerk whether it is lawful to eat butter or go without; and to enquire which of the two is lawful, to feed their horses corn or oats?" Joseph Smith's History, 4:516, 543; *The Nauvoo Neighbor*, January 3, 1844. One of the deeds recorded in Nauvoo by Smith as Recorder is in the possession of Mr. Preston Kimball of Nauvoo.

Ebenezer Robinson later observed, "This office of registry of deeds for Nauvoo proved a mistake, as I have been credibly informed the courts *did not* recognize those records. . . . Thus that prophecy failed." [22]

Though Bennett was mayor, Smith chose to retain the main policy-making initiative in city government. Perhaps Bennett proved less able as a Mormon leader than expected; perhaps Smith felt that a twin executive was undesirable. At any rate his relations with Bennett were strained before the year 1841 ended. The Prophet continued to act, as he had before the creation of a formal city government, as though there were no real differences between the direction of the city and the direction of the Church. In January, 1842, when Bennett was indisposed for some reason, Smith was elected mayor *pro tem* by the city council. The following May, when Bennett broke with Smith and left Nauvoo, the council elected the Prophet mayor to fill the vacancy. He continued in the office until his death two years later. Smith apparently controlled the council from the beginning, and its major decisions were in accord with his wishes. It was but another instrument of his will. Even as the balloting on May 19 which elected him mayor was progressing, he delivered himself of an imperious gesture suggestive of his use of the tools of power.

While the election was going on, I received and wrote the following revelation:

"Verily thus saith the Lord . . . Hiram Kimball has been insinuating evil, and forming evil opinions against you, with others; and if he continue in them, he and they will be accursed, for I am the Lord thy God, and will stand by thee and bless thee. Amen."

This I threw across the room to Hiram Kimball, one of the councillors. After the election I spoke at some length concerning the evil reports abroad in the city concerning myself, and the necessity of counteracting the designs of our enemies, establishing a night watch, etc., whereupon the council resolved that the mayor be authorized to establish a night watch, and control the same.[23]

Just as the office of mayor was an adjunct to Smith's position as president and prophet, so was the city government a legal and constitutional apparatus of the whole Mormon sacerdotal structure of leadership. The civil officials were an oligarchy of Mormon leaders headed by the Prophet; the government was conceived and operated not as an expression of the popular will but as an instrument of

---

[22] Deed Book M, pp. 397 ff.; *The Return*, 3:13, January, 1891.
[23] Under entry of May 19, 1842, in Joseph Smith's History, 5:12, 13.

Church policy. That such a result could and did proceed from the Nauvoo Charter was what made the charter in effect so extraordinary, and after a while so objectionable to Illinoisans. On its face it was just another city charter with some novel clauses; in operation it was a charter to create a Mormon kingdom in the sovereign state of Illinois. Smith conceived Nauvoo to be federated with Illinois somewhat as Illinois was federated with the United States, with strong legal and patriotic ties, to be sure, but also with guaranteed immunities and rights of its own. When the citizens of Illinois became aware of this Mormon view, as they did in practical experience with the way government was carried on in Nauvoo, there was sentiment to revoke or at least amend the charter.

That the Saints held a very different notion of their rights under the charter from that which prevailed in the state was illustrated by the Prophet's resistance to the attempts of Missouri to extradite him through the agency of the Illinois executive in August, 1842. The charge was complicity in the attempted assassination of ex-Governor Boggs. Boggs, who as governor of Missouri in 1838 had issued the infamous "Extermination Order" against the Mormons, was in May, 1843, shot and nearly killed in his Independence home by an unknown assassin. The assailant was never apprehended, but Missourians were convinced that the man was the Mormon Orrin Porter Rockwell and that he had acted on direct orders of Joseph Smith. Consequently, Smith was charged with the conspiracy and an attempt was made to have him extradited. Nauvooans believed that his ultimate safety depended on the habeas corpus power of their municipal court, which could free him from any arrest. But, it was feared, Illinois Governor Thomas Carlin might make the attempt anyway. Emma Smith, Joseph's spirited wife, engaged in correspondence with Carlin in defense of her husband. He could not be guilty of the crime, she urged, since he had been in Illinois at the time. Why did the governor thus threaten to overrule the right of Nauvoo to keep him free under the habeas corpus provision of the charter? "These powers are positively granted in the charter over your own signature," said Emma Smith. "And now, dear sir, where can be the justice of depriving us of these rights which are lawfully ours . . . ?" Governor Carlin replied in part:

I have examined both the Charters and the city ordinances on the subject and must express my surprise at the extraordinary assumption of power by the board of aldermen as contained in the ordinance! From my recollection of the Charter it authorizes the municipal court to issue writs of habeas corpus in all cases of imprisonment or custody arising from the authority of the ordinances of said city; but that the power was granted, or intended to be granted, to release persons held in custody under the authority of writs issued by the courts or executive of the state, is most absurd and ridiculous; and to attempt to exercise it is a gross usurpation of power that cannot be tolerated.

I have always expected and desired that Mr. Smith should avail himself of the benefits of the laws of this state, and that he would be entitled to a writ of habeas corpus issued by the Circuit Court, and entitled to a hearing before said court; but to claim the right of a hearing before the municipal court of the City of Nauvoo is a burlesque upon the city Charter itself.[24]

But the attempts of Missouri to get Smith for trial became an annual summer event, and the governor's view of the limited habeas corpus power of the municipal court could not be tolerated in Nauvoo. In June, 1843, the Prophet was surprised and arrested in Lee County, Illinois, by Missouri officers bound to return him for trial on the old 1838 charge of treason. He managed to get Illinois officers to take him to Nauvoo, where he was again freed by a writ of habeas corpus. On June 30, soon after his entrance into the city, Smith addressed a crowd of thousands with a strident estimate of the power and sovereignty of Nauvoo:

Relative to our city charter, courts, right of habeas corpus, etc., I wish to know and publish that we have all power; and if any man from this time forth says anything to the contrary, cast it into his teeth.

There is a secret in this. If there is not power in our charter and courts, then there is not power in the state of Illinois, nor in the Congress or Constitution of the United States; for the United States gave unto Illinois her constitution or charter, and Illinois gave unto Nauvoo her charters, ceding unto us our vested rights, which she has no power or right to take from us. All the power there was in Illinois, she gave to Nauvoo; and any man that says to the contrary is a fool. . . .

I wish the lawyer who says we have no powers in Nauvoo may be choked to death on his own words. Don't employ lawyers, or pay them money for their knowledge, as I have learned that they don't know anything. I know more than they all.

Go ye into all the world and preach the gospel. He that believeth in

[24] Letter of Emma Smith to Carlin, August 27, 1842, and Carlin's reply, September 7, 1842, are in Joseph Smith's History, 5:132, 133, 154. The ordinance to which Emma Smith referred, enacted July 5, 1842, stated in part: "no citizen of this city may be taken out of the city by any writs, without the privilege of investigation before the municipal court, and the benefit of a writ of habeas corpus . . . that they may have the right of trial in this city, and not be subjected to illegal process by their enemies." *Ibid.*, 5:57.

our chartered rights may come here and be saved. . . . I have converted this candidate for congress [indicating Cyrus Walker, his defense attorney!] that the right of habeas corpus is included in our charter. If he continues converted, I will vote for him. . . .

If any citizens of Illinois say we shall not have our rights, treat them as strangers and not friends, and let them all go to hell and be damned! Some say they will mob us. Let them mob and be damned! If we have to give up our chartered rights, privileges, and freedom, which our fathers fought, bled, and died for . . . we will do it only at the point of the sword and bayonet. . . .

I want you to hear and learn, O Israel, this day, what is for the happiness and peace of this city and people. If our enemies are determined to oppress us . . . and the authorities that are on the earth will not sustain us in our rights . . . then we will claim them from a higher power—from heaven—yea, from God almighty.[25]

In Smith's view the constitution of the Kingdom of God might have to be wrested from and defended against earthly powers, but it was authored and pledged by divinity. The notion was a prototype of that proclaimed only a few years later by Brigham Young for an independent Mormon State of Deseret.

Government as well as less formal means of social control in the Mormon Church was intimately related to the institution of the priesthood. It was an important belief of the Latter-day Saints that God had restored to earth His Holy Priesthood, the same as instituted and held by Christ but due to wickedness removed from the earth. Joseph Smith and an associate were the original recipients of the priesthood authority. The unction also conferred on them the right to discern the Divine Will as to which other men should receive the same authority. While many, perhaps most, male converts received the "call" and were ordained, the fraternity thus formed was not just a simple equalitarian lay priesthood. As developed it was hierarchical in structure, a vertical rather than a horizontal organization. Priesthood was articulated into two large orders, the Aaronic, or "lesser" order and the Melchisedek, or "higher" order. The Aaronic was made up of the three offices of priest, teacher, and deacon; the Melchisedek, while all its members were technically "elders," had two main divisions, the Elders and the High Priests.

[25] From Joseph Smith's speech at Nauvoo, June 30, 1843, in Joseph Smith's *History*, 5:466–468. What Smith called "a brief synopsis" of the address, taken from the reports of Willard Richards and Wilford Woodruff, occupies six and one-half pages of small print in his published journal. Compare this address with that of Sidney Rigdon, July 4, 1838, in Far West, in Mulder and Mortensen, eds., *Among the Mormons*, pp. 94, 95.

The High Priests were the spiritual and executive leaders of the Church. All stake high council members, all patriarchs, bishops, and apostles were high priests, as were stake presidents and members of the First President's quorum. Joseph Smith as President of the High Priesthood was regarded by Mormons as charismatic, a fact basic to his power and authority in the sect. Major charismatic functions also were inherent in his priesthood as "Prophet, Seer, and Revelator," including the power to understand and translate unknown languages. Smith's charisma was the basis of the sect's apprehension of the "restored gospel," the *Book of Mormon*, the Inspired Version of the Scriptures (his own revision of the Authorized Version), as well as the whole concept and execution of the literal divine kingdom on earth. Many of Smith's "revelations" were collected at various times and published as the third Mormon Canon of scripture, *The Book of Doctrine and Covenants*. Minor charismatic functions were exercised by all orders of the priesthood, especially the Melchisedek order, and included prophecy and other Pauline spiritual gifts. Especially important was healing the sick through an ordinance known as "administration," which consisted of anointing with oil and laying on of hands with prayer. There was considerable expectancy among the people that guidance and a continual flow of blessings would be theirs through charismatic priesthood ministrations, and accordingly deference was given the priesthood.[26]

Although the Church stressed that the "lowest" priesthood office was as great in the eyes of God as was the "highest," in reality a distinction was made between grades of authority and power. The priesthood formed a sort of pyramid of organized influence, with the "higher" orders expecting fealty of the "lower." There seems not to have been, however, any accepted sense of class or caste distinction attaching to the hierarchy. When special social or material privileges appeared, grumbles developed in the ranks. Coupled with the equalitarianism of Mormon culture was a genuine sense of fraternity: all were "brethren." Brother Joseph, Brother Brigham, Brother Heber C., and others were powerful and exalted, but they were also men of the people, among them, like them, and intimate with them. The priesthood performed religious ordinances which were con-

---

[26] Thomas O'Dea, *The Mormons* (Chicago, 1957), pp. 155–160, is an analysis of Joseph Smith's handling of charisma. For a sensitive discussion of the priesthood in the matrix of Mormon religious life from the viewpoint of the Reorganized Church, see R. D. Zinser, "Sectarian Commitment and Withdrawal" (unpublished Ph.D. dissertation, University of Chicago, 1963), chap. 3 *passim.*

sidered essential for personal and group salvation. They conducted divine worship and instruction in a mode not dissimilar to that of the Protestant churches from which most Mormons had come. Coupled with public functions was a close concern for the welfare and activities of every member; a private life which varied to any extent from the group mores was difficult to pursue as it would almost surely bring priesthood censure or "counsel." A priesthood function was to urge and promote righteousness and to unearth unrighteousness. Everyone's business was legitimate priesthood business. Such an arrangement was not necessarily onerous or oppressive, though it could be so, depending on the tastes and values of different members and the manner of the priestly action. The Mormon priesthood was, however, a structure organically related to the Church institution and permeating it for the control and direction of group and individual life. In times of crisis where group life was threatened, priesthood power was enhanced, and since the history of Mormonism from its founding for at least sixty years was one of successive crises, the role of priesthood was enlarged and its techniques of control refined. Many devout Mormons, believers in doctrines of the Church but rebels against some of its institutional expressions, became "apostates" in opposition to what they considered a growing "priestcraft." [27]

In Joseph Smith's thinking priesthood was the foundation of the Kingdom. It was to be the means of "accomplishing all things." He was concerned about preparing and equipping priesthood for kingdom building. His term for such preparation was "to order," that is to organize, instruct, direct, and endow with special blessings of authority and spiritual power. As highest in the hierarchy of priests, it was the First President's function to "order" the Twelve Apostles. They, in turn, "ordered" the lesser priesthood, and so on down through the sacerdotal chain of authority. The priesthood as a whole "ordered" the Church and Kingdom, that is the rank and file of the membership.[28] After the death of Joseph Smith, Brigham Young

[27] Many Mormon splinter sects had in succeeding years the rejection of priestly authoritarianism as a characteristic of their particular identity. The Whitmerites and Hedrickites, for example, rejected the doctrine of High Priesthood, contending that Smith became a "fallen prophet" when he introduced it.

[28] An example of the importance which Smith attached to the symbolism of priesthood order is the curious instruction written in his journal on the occasion of the laying of the Nauvoo Temple's four great cornerstones:

"If the strict order of the Priesthood were carried out in the building of temples, the first stone would be laid at the south-east corner, by the First

forged the priesthood into an even stronger instrument by which he sought to accomplish "all things," in particular to replace the repealed city government, to gain control of the recalcitrant elements in the Church, to effect the move west, and to build the Great Basin Kingdom. As purposed by Smith and fashioned by Young the Mormon priesthood was at once the ministry of consolation and the arm of power.[29]

The symbol of the quasi-sovereignty of Nauvoo was the Legion. The idea of a military force for the Church and Kingdom was born easily. Universal manhood militia service was a commonplace in western America, though in peace time it often amounted to little more than roistering on muster days. Militia companies were usually formed when a new county was organized; such companies elected their own officers, who were then commissioned by the state. The state also armed the militia at least nominally. The first Mormon militia had come into being with the creation of Caldwell County, Missouri, and was an important factor in anti-Mormon feeling there. In Illinois, the Nauvoo Charter granted the sect not a county but a new kind of governmental entity. The "extraordinary militia clause" in the charter provided for a military force to be semi-independent, like the city, and to have relations to county and state militia which were ill-defined and ambiguous. The Legion took its character from Smith's definition of Nauvoo as a federated rather than a subordinate government in the state of Illinois. Said the Prophet on January 8, 1841, "The 'Nauvoo Legion' . . . will enable us to perform our military [militia] duty by ourselves, and thus afford us the power and privilege of avoiding one of the most fruitful sources of strife, oppression, and collision with the world." But it was not to be a hostile force: "It will enable us to show our attachment to the state and nation, as a people, whenever the public serv-

---

Presidency of the Church. (The others should be laid in order, proceeding clockwise). The First Presidency should dictate who were the proper persons to lay the other corner stones.

"If a Temple is built at a distance, and the First Presidency is not present, then the Quorum of Twelve Apostles are the persons to dictate the order . . . in their absence, then the Presidency of the Stake will lay the south-east corner stone; the Melchisidek Priesthood laying those on the east side . . . and the Lesser Priesthood those on the west side."

Under entry of April 6, 1841, in Joseph Smith's History, 4:331.

[29] The relation of priesthood to the structure and function of the church is extensively and skillfully treated in S. George Ellsworth, "A History of Mormon Missions in the United States and Canada, 1830–1860," *passim.*

ice requires our aid, thus proving ourselves obedient to the paramount laws of the land, and ready at all times to sustain and execute
them." [30]

Whether the Legion was originally Smith's or Bennett's idea is
difficult to know; it was enthusiastically favored by both. In his in-
augural address as mayor, Bennett said:

> I would recommend the immediate organization of the Legion. Com-
> prising, as it does, the entire military power of our city . . . early
> facilities should be afforded the court martial for perfecting their plans of
> drill, rules, and regulations. Nothing is more necessary to the preservation
> of order and the supremacy of the laws. . . . The Legion should be all-
> powerful, panoplied with justice and equity, to consummate the designs
> of its projectors. . . . *Sicut patribus sit Deus nobis;* "as God was with our
> fathers, so may he be with us"—to fight the battles of our country, as
> victors, and as freemen; the justice of the uva [*sic*] and the spirit of insub-
> ordination should never enter our camp—but we should stand, ever stand,
> as a united people—one and indivisible.[31]

Bennett contributed his knowledge of military organization, manners, and parade-ground tactics, and as he conceived and organized
it, the Nauvoo Legion appeared grand indeed. It was to consist of
two cohorts, one of foot and one of mounted troops, to be formed
from the adult male population of the city and "such citizens of
Hancock County as may be enrolled by voluntary enlistment," either
gentiles or Mormons not residing in Nauvoo. It was to be commanded by a lieutenant general (a rank not otherwise extant in the
United States from George Washington to Ulysses Grant) with a
major general, the adjutant and inspector general, second in command.[32] Smith was the lieutenant general, and Bennett the major
general. Smith's staff would consist of three colonels and twelve captains; Bennett's, of an adjutant, a surgeon in chief, a cornet, a quartermaster, a paymaster, a commissary, and a chaplain, all colonels,
as well as a surgeon for each cohort, a quartermaster sergeant, sergeant major, chief musician and two other musicians, all captains.
Each cohort was commanded by a brigadier general with appropriate staff. The troops might elect their officers of lesser rank only
upon nomination of the court-martial.[33]

[30] "A Proclamation of the First Presidency of the Church to the Saints Scattered
Abroad," in Joseph Smith's History, 4:269.
[31] Under entry of February 3, 1841, in *ibid.*, 4:288.
[32] When the post of lieutenant general was proposed to be resurrected and
bestowed on Thomas Hart Benton during the Mexican War, a storm of protest
arose and the proposal was defeated. See William N. Chambers, *Old Bullion
Benton; Senator from the New West* (Boston and Toronto, 1956), pp. 311, 312.
[33] Joseph Smith's History, 4:294.

The officers comprising the first Legion court-martial were men already holding state commissions as members of Hancock County militia companies. Since the Mormons had been in the county almost two years, there were a number of them, including Don Carlos Smith (a lieutenant colonel), C. C. Rich, William and Wilson Law, A. P. Rockwood, Francis and Chauncey Higbee, Amos Davis, and Hosea Stout. Partly as a result of their service in the Legion many officers finally rose to power in the hierarchy of the Church. The Legion became the training ground and prototype of the paramilitary priesthood organization of Utah, where high military and high canonical rank tended to be synonymous.[34]

The Legion from its beginning played a major part in the social and ceremonial life of Nauvoo. At the conference of April, 1841, it took a conspicuous part in the ceremonies of laying the Temple cornerstones, framing the proceedings in a large square of troops. The ladies of the city presented a silk flag, which was reviewed by the commander in chief. All was accompanied by the booming of the new cannon. Smith recorded the excitement in his journal: "The appearance, order, and movements of the Legion were chaste, grand, and imposing, and reflected great credit on the taste, skill, and tact of the men comprising said Legion. We doubt whether the like can be presented in any other city in the western country." [35] When the Legion celebrated Independence Day, 1841, it was again "reviewed by Lieutenant-General Joseph Smith, who made an eloquent and patriotic speech to the troops . . . and closed with these remarkable words. 'I would ask no greater boon, than to lay down my life for my country.'" [36] On September 11, Hosea Stout, the Legion clerk, reported that the cohorts totaled 1,490 men, and that at a special review the Lieutenant General "delivered a military speech to the troops in his usual energetic style." [37] The following April 28, 1842, the Prophet issued an invitation which was sure to cement his leadership of Nauvoo "society":

General Joseph Smith and lady, present their compliments to the officers (and their respective ladies) of the consolidated General Staff of the Nauvoo Legion . . . and respectfully solicit their company at a *Repast Militaire*, at his quarters on the 7th day of May *proximo*, at one o'clock p.m.

General Bennett has been ordered to issue a programme of the operations and field exercises of the day. . . .

[34] *Ibid.*, 4:295.
[35] *Ibid.*, 4:326, 327.
[36] Legion minutes for Saturday, July 3, 1841, in *ibid.*, 4:382.
[37] *Ibid.*, 4:415.

On the appointed May 7 about two thousand troops participated in day-long ceremonies, including "an animated sham battle." Smith "commanded through the day" and delivered "a most animated and appropriate address in which he remarked 'that his soul was never better satisfied than on this occasion.'" The General Staff ate a "sumptuous dinner" at the house of the commander in chief together with some distinguished gentile visitors. "Such was the curious and interesting excitement which prevailed at the time, in the surrounding country, about the Legion," the clerk wrote, "that Judge [Stephen A.] Douglas adjourned the circuit court, then in session in Carthage, and came with some of the principal lawyers, to see the splendid military parade of the Legion, upon notice of which . . . General Smith . . . immediately invited them to partake of the repast prepared. . . ."[38]

In the 1840's, particularly in the West, military titles, connections, and exploits were much in vogue in America. Social status and political careers were thought to depend on military prestige. Militia officers, though by hardly any stretch of the imagination could they be considered anything but civilians, preferred the use of their militia rank as titles in everyday as well as formal intercourse. In thirty years in the United States Senate, Thomas Hart Benton, according to one biographer, was never referred to as Senator, always as "Colonel" and then "General." Andrew Jackson was called "General" rather than "President."[39] The Nauvoo Legionnaires were no exception to the rule, and "Colonel," "Captain," or "General" came to replace "Brother," "Elder," or "President" in the address of the Saints. Military trappings were for them a particular symbol of status, prestige, and reassurance in a life so beset with insecurities and deprivations. The record clearly reveals that Lieutenant General (he preferred the full title) Smith set great store by his military role. Josiah Quincy reported a conversation overheard between the Prophet and a visiting Protestant minister. The gentile divine, said Quincy, "having occasion to allude to some erroneous doctrine which I forget, suddenly exclaimed, 'Why I told my congregation the other Sunday they might as well believe Joe Smith as such theology as that.' 'Did you say Joe Smith in a sermon?' inquired the person to whom that title had been applied. 'Of course I did. Why not?' The prophet's reply was given with a quiet superiority that was over-

[38] *Ibid.*, 4:601; 5:3.
[39] Chambers, *Old Bullion Benton*, pp. 311, 312.

whelming: 'Considering only the day and the place, it would have been more respectful to have said Lieutenant-General Joseph Smith.' " [40]

As the city grew, so did the Legion, exciting apprehension among gentiles in the vicinity concerning the nature and intent of the Mormon kingdom. The *Warsaw Signal* for July 21, 1842, stated "Everything they say or do seems to breathe the spirit of military tactics. . . . Truly *fighting* must be the creed of these Saints." On the third of the previous month, the *Sangamo Journal* had queried, "What would be thought if the Baptists, Methodists, Presbyterians, or Episcopalians of this state had military organizations . . . ?" In 1843, one observer who had seen the Legion drill wrote in the *St. Louis Reporter* that its cohorts numbered some "four or five thousand" thoroughly disciplined and "well acquainted with the use of artillery. Apprehensions exist that the frequent drilling of the Legion forbodes no good purpose on the part of the Mormon prophet." [41] Brave and militant language was bandied about in Nauvoo, though generally breathing no spirit more seditious than that of florid patriotism and righteous indignation at iniquity.

Early in 1842 a passage of words was reported in the widely circulated official Church periodical *Times and Seasons* that proved inflammatory to sectional and antiabolitionist sentiments in Illinois and especially in Missouri. Dr. Bennett had in January, 1842, exchanged letters with a Dr. Dyer of Chicago, apparently an anti-slavery minister, in which the outrages committed against the Mormons in Missouri were equated with the treatment of returned runaway slaves. Bennett's flights of oratorical bombast excited a response from Joseph Smith who was still sensitive about Missouri and just beginning to formulate firm opinions on the injustice of slavery. He wrote Bennett: "I have just been perusing your correspondence with Dr. Dyer, on the subject of American slavery . . . and it makes my blood boil. . . . When will these things cease to be . . . ? I fear for my beloved country—mob violence, injustice, and cruelty appear to be the darling attributes of Missouri, and no man taketh it to heart! *O Tempora! O Mores!* What think you should be done?" Bennett's reply was doubtless well noted by the "enemies" of the Saints, in Illinois as well as in Missouri:

[40] Quoted in Mulder and Mortensen, eds., *Among the Mormons*, p. 140.
[41] *Warsaw Signal* and *Sangamon Journal* quoted in Gayler, "The Mormons in Western Illinois," p. 94; *St. Louis Reporter* quoted in the *Niles National Register*, 65:229, December 9, 1843.

The master spirits of the age must rise . . . then will the present minions of power hide their faces in the dust . . . for the time is at hand—and if man will not do the work, the thunderings of Sinai will wind up the scene—the blood of the murdered Mormons cries aloud for help, and the restoration of the inheritances of the Saints; and God has heard the cry . . . he who answers by fire will cause the sword and flame to do their office . . . and I swear by the Lord God of Israel, that the sword shall not depart from my thigh, nor the buckler from my arm, until . . . the hydra-headed, fiery dragon is slain. This done the proud southron will no longer boast of ill-gotten gain, or wash his hands in the blood of the innocent, or immure the freemen of the prairie State [Illinois] within Missouri's sullied, poisoned, deathly prison walls. . . . The day of vengeance will assuredly come when the Omnipotent hand of the Great God will effect the restitution of the trophies of the brigand victories of Missouri, and again place the Saints on high.[42]

The idea of a holy war against Missouri as hinted at in Bennett's letter now seems and should then have seemed wholly absurd. Furthermore, Bennett did not speak for the Church, though Smith freely published his views in the official organ. Yet, as the gentile reaction against the militant stance and strident tone of the Nauvoo Mormons grew more pronounced anything might have been believed. Perhaps in their more sanguine moments some of the Saints thought themselves capable of any "righteous" action.

But not all Mormons shared the general enthusiasm for the Legion and what it seemed to stand for. In 1890 Elder Ebenezer Robinson added a dissenting footnote to the history of the kingdom on the Mississippi: "I never mustered a day or a time in the Legion, always believing the church of Christ had no use for such an organization, and really feeling that that part of the charter business was of the devil. The officers of the Legion threatened to courtmartial and fine me." But still he refused military service and, he claimed, never paid a fine. "I am fully persuaded, after these years of experience, that the church and military organizations, or church and state, cannot be united and enjoy prosperity. . . . Let the history and downfall of Nauvoo be a solemn warning to the members of the church of Christ, and let us be content with the plain and simple teachings of the gospel. . . ."[43] As Major General Bennett might have phrased it, *sic transit gloria*.

[42] Smith's letter to Bennett, and Bennett's reply are in Joseph Smith's History, 4:544, 547, 548, and the Bennett-Dyer correspondence, pp. 544–547.
[43] *The Return*, 2:301, July, 1890.

5

A Kingdom of This World:
The Land Business

The place was alive with business, much more so than any I have visited since the hard times commenced . . . I could see no loungers about the streets, or drunkards about the taverns . . . I heard not an oath in the place, saw not a gloomy countenance; all were cheerful, polite and industrious.

> The Reverend Samuel A. Prior, visiting Nauvoo in 1843, quoted in Larson, *Prelude to the Kingdom*, p. 48.

After Council, I worked in my garden, walked out in the city, and borrowed two sovereigns to make a payment.

> Joseph Smith under entry for May 14, 1842, in Joseph Smith's History, 5:8.

It will scarcely be denied that defective and worthless titles to real property, are among the greatest misfortunes met with in civilized society. Millions . . . are annually expended in losses and litigations connected therewith, and thousands of families reduced to poverty and want, by hasty and inconsiderate purchases of real property.
These examples should admonish all concerned in such purchases to careful inquiry, and the use of diligence in matters of such absorbing importance.

> Dr. Isaac Galland, from a pamphlet of Isaac Galland, quoted in David W. Kilbourne, *Strictures on Dr. I. Galland's Pamphlet*, entitled, *"Villainy Exposed"* with some account of his transactions in lands in the Sac and Fox Reservations, etc., in Lee County, Iowa (Ft. Madison, Iowa), 1850, pp. 14, 15.

The economy of Nauvoo was different from that of other flourishing western towns. It was not a center for marketing, manufacture, transportation, or government, though all of those activities were carried on to some degree. Nauvoo was primarily a religious center, but one in which the pilgrims who gathered there intended to remain. As a result, the business of trading and improving land, important in any fast-growing town, took on especial significance. In lieu of other goods or services, land and buildings were the town's chief stock-in-trade, and trading them was the most lucrative business. The Church and the leading Churchmen naturally were prominent in the profession and played a leading role in this aspect of the Nauvoo economy.

Nauvoo at the outset had neither industry nor commerce. The town existed to realize the vision of the good and righteous life of the Kingdom of God on earth. The economy of the city was a secondary matter, something that would take care of itself somehow when the primary response to God's will had been made and the Saints had gathered together in a "holy city." With regard to the economy of the Kingdom, Joseph Smith's experience had all too little to offer him. He saw prophetically a vision of a stable society of Saints with their own "inheritances" in Zion—each, as it were, under his own vine and fig tree. But as to the process whereby the inheritances were to be obtained the vision was blurred. Smith's experience was rural and agricultural, not urban and industrial. He was schooled in the America of abundant land, of speculation, and of wealth obtained by the unearned increment of rising land values. "The rich" among the Saints, thought Smith in the early 1830's, should purchase "inheritances," defined as farms and town lots, which would then be divided among all according to need; but there were far more of the poor to claim "inheritances" than brethren of means willing to provide them. The Saints who gathered to Independence, Kirtland, Far West, and Nauvoo did not wait until such problems were solved; and as the number of gatherers increased, Zion's economic difficulties multiplied. Since most of the Saints were farmers, a successful agriculture for the Kingdom was a goal obvious to all. But Zion was primarily an urban design; if city dwellers in numbers tried to follow Smith's injunction to live in town and farm outside, there would be an intense competition for accessible acres. Kirtland and Nauvoo, the two towns of size where the Saints were "suffered to remain" for any length of time, provided a short-range solution to this dilemma: the basis of economic life was to be the "building up" of the cities themselves. Such economies might remain viable as long as the towns continued to grow at an ever increasing rate. New settlers might provide a continuing inflow of money in sufficient quantities to pay for the importation of goods and services which the population did not supply for itself. Deficits might be met by borrowing, by the investments of new citizens, by the export of goods, and by the increment both earned and unearned of real-estate values. In the event, borrowing proved a temporary and expensive measure, but one frequently resorted to by the Mormons. Investment made by new arrivals was helpful but insufficient. For various reasons exporting was not accomplished; and the rise of land values, though for a while suggesting the flush of prosperity, was illusory, since it only slightly increased the real wealth of community and Church. Lots and houses, regardless of their market value, were but part of the necessities of life. Furthermore, as the price of urban real estate rose, land purchase absorbed more and more of the inflow of capital, leaving little for more productive forms of investment.

In Nauvoo the economic problem was further complicated by the fact that the land was not cheap when the Church bought it in the first place. The five thousand or so Saints who were the first settlers had after the Missouri persecution little capital to invest, and a heavy debt with high rates of interest was the result. They expected to pay the debt and recoup their own lost fortunes out of the antici- pated growth and prosperity of the Kingdom. The Nauvoo land purchase was intended to serve the purposes of the gathering; but soon the gathering had to be made to serve the unrelenting demands of the land purchase indebtedness and the necessity to maintain an expanding economy.

The twenty-five thousand Mormons who finally came to Hancock County found that Dr. Galland's pious warning about questionable land titles was apropos to their situation as well as to that of the brethren across the river in Iowa. Hancock was one of several coun- ties between the Illinois and Mississippi rivers that lay in the Illinois Military Bounty Tract, a region set aside by the Congress after the War of 1812 to provide land grants for war veterans in lieu of pay. The Tract had a long history of speculation in lands, with frequent and complex transfers of titles that were ever more difficult to clear. After the War of 1812, small speculators had purchased most of the original land warrants from veterans. The prices paid had been sub- stantial, and the Panic of 1819 occasioned a flood of distressed sell- ing. The lands were bought up by large speculators and companies that expected to wait until the anticipated wave of settlers would drive the prices up again. But the wait proved too long for many; between 1827 and 1833 more than sixteen thousand quarter-sections were sold for taxes. The land boom of the thirties stimulated prices, but the number of land parcels offered again at tax sales in 1837 ran into the thousands. Aside from the volume of sales and the ques- tionable record keeping, a problem of clouded titles arose from the fact that the courts failed to settle the hotly contested question of whether a tax title obtained from the state completely superseded other kinds of titles or merely gave "color of title." More and more claimants appeared, including the original veteran patentees, flooding the courts with litigation. The state legislature passed "Quieting Titles" acts in 1835 and 1837, which seemed to give clear title to an owner who had paid taxes on the property for seven years. However, in 1842 the U.S. Supreme Court rendered a decision which largely negated the Illinois legislation and cast the whole title problem back into uncertainty.[1]

The buying and selling of land in the Military Tract frequently involved only buying and selling the promise of title. Such a promise might be hedged about with conditions of great complexity, dependent both on the purchaser's good faith and ability to pay, and the ability of the seller to obtain the title himself, for which he might be depending on a similar arrangement with a previous owner. Bonds were usually given to insure delivery of title; these might then be negotiated and circulated as commercial paper in the currency-starved economy, thus involving third, fourth, and fifth parties in the original transaction. The Saints, with their complicated and unrefined corporate structure and their need to buy on credit, were caught up in some monumental financial tangles. For example, on October 18, 1841, George W. Robinson, who in the early Nauvoo years was active in private and Church land trading, deeded a quarter-section in northeast Hancock County to a Samuel James for $4,400. However, the transaction depended on other dealings: James, together with Robinson and Robinson's father-in-law Sidney Rigdon, had, by request of Robinson, entered into a bond of $9,000 to a firm of Witter *et al.* of Warsaw, Illinois. The bond was security on a mortgage made by a Benjamin R. to a Charles Ivins of New Jersey. Ivins had sold and given a bond for the assignment of this mortgage to Robinson, which the latter had in turn assigned to Witter *et al.* on February 6, 1841, "guaranteeing . . . that said mortgage . . . is good and sufficient security for the face of said security and interest thereon from the first of April next [1842] . . . and that the same is ample security for the payment of [$4,414] which is the face of said mortgage." If the value of the mortgage proved not to be as stated and if Witter and company should collect bond of James Ivins in consequence, then "this obligation shall be in *Tennor*

[1] Theodore L. Carlson, *The Illinois Military Tract; A Study of Land Occupation, Utilization, and Tenure* (Urbana, Illinois, 1951), pp. 40 ff.

1. The Nauvoo Temple. Daguerrotype probably taken in 1845. Note the inverted star stones and the outsized window.

2. Joseph Smith, from a daguerrotype.

3. Brigham Young, from a daguerrotype.

Utah State Historical Society.

4. Hyrum Smith, brother of the Prophet, member of the First Presidency, and Presiding Patriarch.

Church of Jesus Christ of Latter-Day Saints.

5. Parley Parker Pratt, Apostle, editor of the *Millennial Star.*

Utah State Historical Society.

6. Heber C. Kimball, Apostle.

Church of Jesus Christ of Latter-Day Saints.

7. John Taylor, Apostle, editor of *Times and Seasons* and *Nauvoo Neighbor.*

8. Orson Hyde, Apostle.

9. Willard Richards, Apostle.

10. Orson Pratt, Apostle.

11. Wilford Woodruff, Apostle.

12. Ebenezer Robinson, founder and first editor of *Times and Seasons.* Photo taken late in life.

13. William Marks, Nauvoo Stake President.

14. Sidney Rigdon, member of the First Presidency.

15. John C. Bennett, first mayor of Nauvoo, organizer and Major General of the Nauvoo Legion.

Samuel Strange, the Nauvoo Independent.

16. Nauvoo as seen from Montrose, Iowa. Photograph probably taken late nineteenth century, before the Keokuk dam downstream raised the river to its modern level. View is northeast, showing the "flat" at center and left, and the "hill" in center distance. The church spire is at the approximate site of the Temple. The foot of Main Street is at lower right.

Illinois State Historical Society.

17. Photograph probably taken in 1845 or 1846, looking northeastward from the "flat" toward the "hill." Large structures near the Temple are commercial buildings on Mulholland Street.

18. The Seventy's Hall.

19. Home of Joseph Young.

20. The "Homestead," residence of Joseph Smith from 1839 to 1843.

Audio-Visual Department, the Reorganized Church of Jesus Christ of Latter Day Saints.

21. Modern view of Main Street looking south by southeast. The restored Nauvoo Mansion, residence of the Prophet after 1842, is in the foreground; the site of the Nauvoo House is at right of photo, across Water Street. River in the background.

22. Keeping room of the Homestead (restored).

23. Joseph Smith's parlor, the Nauvoo Mansion (restored).

Illinois State Historical Society.

24. Nauvoo Temple ruins.

25. Temple sun stone, typical of all the pilaster capitals. On the grounds of the Quincy, Illinois, Historical Sociey.

Reorganized Church of Jesus Christ of Latter Day Saints.

26. The Nauvoo House as it was left by the Mormons. Painting made by David H. Smith, youngest son of the Prophet, looking northeast from near the riverbank. The main entrance faced Main Street.

Photographs by the author.

27-28. Three residences on Parley Street as they appear today. The finely chiseled limestone inset above the arched porch in the upper photograph reads "P. Mix-1846."

and *effect* to secure payment to said James . . . of whatsoever he shall pay or loose [*sic*] in consequence of signing and becoming security in said bond executed to Witter *et al.*, and provided that James should not be called upon to pay . . . moneys in consequence of said bond . . . then this obligation shall be void." On August 11, 1842, Robinson obtained a quitclaim to void the mortgage "for a valuable consideration."[2] When for any reason such tangled business arrangements broke down the result among brethren was often bitterness and rancor, and for the defaulter a reputation for shady dealings that was not always deserved. "I hereby warn the public," ran a newspaper notice, "against purchasing or receiving certain notes which I James Huddleston gave to Josiah Ells . . . for a certain piece of land which has been paid for in part. The payment on the above notes will not be made until the said Ells will secure unto me a good and sufficient title to the land. . . ."[3]

Since the Church was the largest purchaser of land in Nauvoo, it became also the biggest land jobber. In the beginning there were a variety of *ad hoc* agencies dealing for the Church—bishops, various officials, and individuals, including of course Joseph Smith himself.[4] The Church did not envision any real separation of powers between spiritual and temporal executives. As the volume of business and the press of financial matters increased, a move was made to regularize the Church's business affairs. The course to be taken was obvious: on October 20, 1839, the Nauvoo High Council made Joseph Smith treasurer of the Church, empowered to set prices and to sell lots as well as to discharge other business functions. James Mulholland and Henry G. Sherwood were to assist and be responsible to him. The Council suggested that lots average $500 each, with none to sell for less than $200 nor more than $800.[5]

To comply with state law respecting the business transactions of religious corporations Smith was elected Trustee-in-Trust for the Church of Jesus Christ of Latter-day Saints on January 30, 1841.[6]

[2] Hancock County Bond and Mortgage Book 1, pp. 161, 162, 354.

[3] *Nauvoo Wasp*, March 8, 1843.

[4] Joseph Smith's History, 3:367. Stephen Markham was appointed "financial agent" for the Church, May 27, 1839. George Robinson, Galland, the Prophet's brothers Hyrum and William, and others served in varying and sometimes ambiguous fiscal capacities.

[5] *Ibid.*, 4:16, 17.

[6] *Ibid.*, pp. 286, 287. Smith was empowered "to receive, acquire, manage or convey property, real, personal, or mixed, for the sole use and benefit of said church, agreeably to the provisions of an Act entitled 'An Act Concerning Religious Societies,' approved February 6, 1835."

Smith used the office to combine corporate and personal affairs in an intricate manner never entirely unraveled after his death.[7] The Prophet became the busiest land jobber in Nauvoo and perhaps in the state. A large proportion of his time was given over to this business, and though he had assistance, he liked to attend to its detail himself. He sold city lots to whomever he could and at good prices if the buyer had means. Despite the proposed $800 ceiling, $1,000 was asked and obtained for many unimproved one-acre lots. Smith was most willing to job town lots in quantities; Edward Hunter, a new convert from Pennsylvania, bought in September, 1841, lots and farm acres worth $4,500, on which he paid $2,000 in hard cash—a rare kind of customer indeed. Smith was also willing to compromise the city plan by selling fractions of lots, either because of the demand for them or in hope of increasing the per acre value.

The Prophet continued to purchase land. In October, 1840, he bought eighty acres of farmland twelve miles south of the city for $2,000; in March, 1842, he offered $2,000 for twenty acres in Nauvoo yet unowned by the Church. In March, 1841, he purchased from his secretary, Robert Thompson, fifty lots in Nauvoo for $10,000. The following July, Thompson sold Emma Smith 123 acres in the south edge of Nauvoo for $4,000. Mrs. Smith might have been proxy or agent for her husband in this transaction. To what extent Smith was acting as a private entrepreneur in these purchases it is impossible to know. At least at first he considered his fortunes intimately connected with those of the Church; the device of Trustee was only a necessary legal convention. The county records are not a reliable guide to the extent of his dealings; many transactions were not recorded there until after his death, and many were never recorded there at all.[8] Smith's most extensive holdings were in the neighborhood of his own residence, near the river bank at the corner of Main and Water Streets on the south side of the flat. His general merchandise store, which also housed his office, was nearby, as well as the Nauvoo House hotel, the *Times and Seasons* office, the houses of several Apostles, and, in 1843, his Nauvoo Mansion hotel. Lots in

[7] In Utah Brigham Young as Trustee-in-Trust was to do the same, though on a greatly expanded scale. See Leonard J. Arrington, *Great Basin Kingdom*, pp. 129–142, 200, and *passim;* and Arrington, "The Settlement of the Brigham Young Estate," *Pacific Historical Review*, 21:1–20 (1952).

[8] Smith bought four lots in April, 1840, for $600 from Oliver Granger and sold them in October for $3,000. Deed Book H, pp. 409, 410 and Deed Book I, p. 195. See also Deed Book H, pp. 557, 575; Deed Book I, pp. 238–330, 254, 379, 445; and Joseph Smith's History, 4:416, 543.

the area were in demand, and it was the earliest and most completely developed part of the lower town. "On the south," said an observer late in 1841, "the lots are mostly taken, and a great share of the improvements seem to be bestowed on this part of the city." [9]

There were strong feelings in the Church against speculators and speculation, a common American antagonism heightened in the case of the Mormons because so many had been hurt by the bursting of the Kirtland bubble. Yet it is impossible to conceive of the Nauvoo land business as being free of speculation. Nauvoo was by definition a speculation, if not for private, then for community gain. Professional speculators would have slipped past armed patrols to reach Nauvoo. Attracted by its spectacular growth, many of these professional speculators joined the Church, and some were accorded the honors of successful businessmen. Smith justified his own trading in land as profiting the common good: "Suppose I sell some land for ten dollars an acre, and I gave three, four, or five dollars per acre; then some persons may cry out 'you are speculating;' Yes, I will tell them: I buy other lands and give them to the widow and the fatherless. If the speculators run against me, they run against the buckles of Jehovah." [10]

On June 18, 1840, the Prophet asked the High Council to relieve him from his responsibility as chief land agent because the burden was heavy and he needed more time for other activities. He rehearsed the necessity for the original purchase of Hancock and Lee County lands, for which "your Memorialist had to become responsible for the payment of the same, and had to use considerable exertion in order to commence a settlement. . . . Under the then existing circumstances your memorialist had necessarily to engage in the temporalities of the Church. . . ." But the spiritual needs of the Church were now pressing. He wanted to pursue his inspired revision of the Bible and to translate some Egyptian parchments he considered of import. Furthermore he wished to be free to "wait upon the Lord for such revelations as may be suited to the conditions and circumstances of the Church."

And in order that he may be enabled to attend to those things, he prays your honorable body will relieve him from the anxiety and trouble necessarily attendant on business transactions, by appointing someone to take charge of the city plot. . . .

[9] *Times and Seasons,* 3:605, November 15, 1841.
[10] "Remarks of the Prophet to the Saints Newly Arrived from England," April 13, 1843, from a report of Willard Richards in Joseph Smith's History, 5:356.

The High Council considered his request but failed to do more than to give him another salesman. The Prophet responded with an irritated veto of the action. The Council, though chastened, remained insistent that Smith not resign the temporal responsibilities since no one else was willing or able to assume them. They were in perfect accord with the spirit and intent of his request. They thought it "wise" and "appropriate," and they would try to give him more help; but, they said, "as he is held responsible for the payment of the city plot, and knowing no way to relieve him from the responsibility at present, we would request of him to act as treasurer for the city plot and to whom those persons whom we may appoint to make sales of lots and attend to the business affairs of the Church may be at all times responsible. . . ." [11]

As Smith had been supporting himself in whole or in part by profits taken in the land business, he asked the High Council to provide other remuneration if he were to be divested of that income. The Mormon convention respecting pay for the ministry was that there should be none, as each minister was expected to support himself. The case of the Prophet was different since presumably he engaged his full time in the service of the Church. But the provisions for his emoluments were irregular and haphazard. The resulting situation made for inevitable conflicts of interest; he and other Church authorities were tempted or even forced on occasion to seek profit from their high positions, both as spiritual leaders and as directors of various economic enterprises.[12] The High Council of Nauvoo agreed with the Prophet that sources of support for him other than profits taken from land sales should be found. Not only was Smith supporting himself from land sales, but the proceeds constituted a kind of general fund from which the Church's various operating expenses were met. It was a situation which augured ill for an orderly retirement of the debt on the land purchase; and the High Council resolved "That the funds of the city plot shall not be taken to pro-

[11] Joseph Smith's History, 4:136, 137, 140, 141, 144. Brigham H. Roberts, editing Joseph Smith's History, commented on the veto as follows: "it is evident that the Council failed to grasp the importance of the subjects presented to them, and made such disposition of them as was neither in keeping with the dignity of the Prophet or the weight of the matters on which they acted . . ." p. 141n.

[12] In Utah Brigham Young was accorded such special favors as using the capital resources of the Church without interest to finance his private business operations, in lieu of other more formal (and costly) remuneration. Yet he claimed that he was a self-supporting minister. See for example Leonard J. Arrington, "The Settlement of the Brigham Young Estate," 21:4n, 13–15, 20.

vide for the presidency or clerks, but that the Bishops be instructed to raise funds from other sources . . . and monies received for lots shall be deposited in the hands of the Treasurer to liquidate the debts of the city plot." [13]

In the summer of 1841 the Prophet, still seeking more time for his work on the Egyptian parchments [the "Book of Abraham"], asked the Twelve Apostles "to take the burthen of the business of the Church at Nauvoo, and respecially as pertaining to the selling of Church lands." These brethren, returned from their English mission with heightened prestige and with Brigham Young ensconced as their leader and spokesman, accepted willingly. While assuming none of the debt, they did take a major part in promoting and managing the gathering. Such a position made their assumption of control over the Nauvoo Church the easier after Smith's death. It also afforded Brigham Young an opportunity to develop and display his remarkable powers as organizer and manager. [14]

The Apostles urged that the legal person of Trustee-in-Trust be made responsible for the Church's obligations, and be separated from the affairs of Joseph Smith, entrepreneur. They wanted all properties and obligations to be transferred to the Trustee, and may have attempted in other ways to untangle financial affairs. Their actions reflected a general uneasiness about the state of the Prophet's finances and business dealings. Smith had been authorized by the conference to deed himself Church properties for his support; this the Twelve reaffirmed, but wished that such transactions

[13] Joseph Smith's History, 4:144, 145. Formal public financial accountings were not made in Nauvoo since they were considered the business only of the authorities. While "temporal affairs" were reported to conferences, the purpose was more often to exhort than to account; the people's role was to ratify the decisions of the "leaders" and meet the obligations to which the Church was committed. In Utah as in Nauvoo only the Councils of the Church were privy to its financial affairs. A primary characteristic of the Reorganized Church as the chief dissenting sect of Mormonism in later years was to make a complete financial accounting part of the business of every General Conference, which body controlled the purse strings of the Church.

[14] A special conference of August 16, 1841, was to ratify such a temporal role for the Twelve. Smith told the conference: "the times had come when the Twelve should . . . stand in their place next to the First Presidency, and attend to the settling of emigrants and the business of the Church at the stakes, and assist to bear off the Kingdom victoriously to the nations, and as they had been faithful, and had borne the burden in the heat of the day, that it was right they should have an opportunity of providing something for themselves and families [in the land business?], and at the same time relieve him, so that he might attend to the business of translating." *Ibid.*, 4:402, 403.

be unmixed with the main business of selling the lots and paying the debts.[15] While the desired separation between public and private business was not completed, the county records show an extensive transfer of properties and obligations to Smith as Trustee-in-Trust in 1841 and early 1842.

The Prophet had bought a great deal of land in the name of the Church and he urged the newly arrived Saints to buy their lots and farms from the Church. Smith went so far as to say in private conversation "that those brethren who come here having money, and purchased without the Church and without counsel, must be cut off." After hearing this and "other observations," a recent gatherer from Massachusetts who was present "appeared in great wrath." [16] The Church pressed its real estate upon the Saints with a combination of advertising and exhortation. William Clayton, one of Smith's agents, ran the following in the *Nauvoo Neighbor* during the winter of 1843–1844:

To Emigrants and Latter-Day Saints Generally:
I feel it my duty to say . . . that there is in the hands of the trustee in trust, a large quantity of lands, both in the city and adjoining townships in this county, which is for sale, some of which belongs to the Church and is designed for the benefit of the poor, and also to liquidate debts owing to the Church, for which the trustee in trust is responsible. Some, also, is land which has been consecrated for the building of the Temple and the Nauvoo House.

If the brethren who move in here and want an inheritance, will buy their lands of the trustee in trust, they will thereby benefit the poor, the Temple, and the Nauvoo House, and even then only will be doing that which is their duty, and which I know, by considerable experience, will be vastly for their benefit and satisfaction in days to come. Let all the brethren, therefore, when they move into Nauvoo, consult President Joseph Smith, the trustee in trust, and purchase their lands of him; and I am bold to say that God will bless them. . . .

We hold ourselves ready at any time to wait upon the brethren and show them the lands . . . and can be found any day, either at President Joseph Smith's bar-room, or the Temple Recorder's office at the Temple.
Nauvoo, December 16, 1843 [17]

Yet there remained a place for private dealers, including Joseph and Hyrum Smith and Brigham Young. Hyrum Smith bought forty acres on the northeast edge of Nauvoo from Robert Thompson in January, 1840, for $3,100 which he platted and offered for sale. He

[15] *Ibid.*, 4:400, 401, 413.
[16] Under entry of February 13, 1843, in Joseph Smith's History, 5:272, 273.
[17] *Nauvoo Neighbor*, December 20, 1843.

purchased additional property for an unspecified sum, and platted a second addition of seven lots. Nauvoo did not develop in the direction of his location, however, and he seems to have sold only a few lots averaging $105 apiece. Hyrum Smith also traded modestly in lots in the original Nauvoo plat and in farm lands both in Hancock and Adams Counties. Brigham Young ran notices in the *Neighbor* in the spring of 1843 advertising his lands:

> *Look Here*
>
> I would say to emigrants, and all the brethren, that I have a few lots on hand, that I will sell very cheap, as I am going on my mission soon. . . . Also I have lots with buildings on them. If anyone wishes for a good store building near the Temple, I can accommodate them.

Ethan Kimball as agent for his father platted three additions to Nauvoo, including one of eighty acres that was divided into outsized lots of four acres each. Other proprietors of additions to the Nauvoo plat were Davison Hibbard (two), George W. Robinson, the James Robinson heirs, Benjamin Warrington, Herringshaw and Thompson, Daniel H. Wells, one Barnett, and Spears and Worthington. All but two of the additions were platted before or during 1842.[18] Exemplary, if not entirely typical, of such private dealers was Daniel H. Wells, a Whig farmer of New York nativity and Connecticut forebears, who came west to Commerce in 1827 and welcomed the Mormons in 1839. He became an alderman and a friend of the Saints. During the exodus of 1846, he was baptized a Mormon. Wells owned an eighty-acre farm in a particularly desirable location atop the Nauvoo bluff, a level tract just centering the flat below. A semi-official biographical sketch of Wells written in Utah said of him, "[his farm] he platted into city lots, which he let the poor and persecuted refugees have at very low prices and on long time for payment. This endeared him to the people. . . ." Perhaps this was so, but "squire" Wells also mixed a deal of Yankee business with his philanthropy. He sold part of his land too early, in June, 1839, for only $200. But in February, 1840, he bought it back for $1,000, platted the whole eighty in April, and more than recouped his loss, for the Temple was located in his addition. The four-acre Temple block he deeded to the Trustee-in-Trust for $1,100, a modest sum. However, the Temple made the neighborhood more desirable, and

[18] Hancock County Plat Book 1, pp. 40, 57, 66, 67; Deed Book H, p. 408; Deed Book I, pp. 34, 299, 402; Bond and Mortgage Book 1, pp. 110, 111; and the Hyrum Smith Estate Papers, in the vault of the Hancock County Clerk.

many of Wells's lots brought as much as $1,000.[19] It is impossible to ascertain how much cash Wells was able to collect from his sales. The story of the Nauvoo land, however, is not simply one of buying and selling; land was alienated in other ways and served many purposes. Town lots and farm lands owned by the Church were given to "the poor." Some who had lost property in Far West were recompensed in this way. In January, 1840, the High Council voted to give lots to "Father" Joseph Knight, an aged brother, and to James Hendrix, an indigent shot and wounded in Missouri; they also promised to build houses on the lots. Nor were these isolated instances. In August, 1841, Brigham Young, speaking for the Twelve, formally endorsed such policy and urged that it be continued, "either by land or goods, as the properties of the Church will admit," and as the wisdom of the Prophet should dictate, "so that no one shall be denied the privilege of remaining in our midst and enjoying the necessaries of life, who has been faithful in his duties to God and the Church." [20] If brethren possessed negotiable titles to Missouri lands they might be received in lieu of other payment in exchange for Nauvoo properties. Such deeds were given to Galland in payment for the Iowa lands.[21] Furthermore, lands were given as gratuities to Smith as already noted; evidence is lacking to indicate for certain whether the same policy was applied to other leading officials.

Nauvoo had no banks or other formal lending institutions, a remarkable lack in a city of such proportions. There was of course but

[19] Andrew Jensen, *Latter-Day Saint Biographical Encyclopedia* (Salt Lake City, 1901), 1:62. Wells's land dealings are recorded in Deed Book 12G, pp. 137, 367; Deed Book M, p. 397; Deed Book K, pp. 189, 367; Deed Book L, pp. 222, 311; Bond and Mortgage Book 1, pp. 403, 521. Wells, like most Nauvoo land dealers, also traded out-of-city farm lands.

[20] Brooks, *John Doyle Lee*, p. 48; Joseph Smith's History, 4:76, 413. The belief that the worthy poor, members "in good standing," had a claim on the resources of the community was characteristic of Brigham Young's social philosophy and of the Utah Mormon commonwealth.

[21] In the Joseph Smith Estate Papers, Hancock County Clerk's vault, there is a voucher for such property, apparently never redeemed and made as a claim against the Prophet's estate:

"Nauvoo, Sept. [?] 1840

"Received of Israel Duty-lands lying in the state of Missouri amounting to $150 . . . this receipt shall apply in the payment of lands in Lee County Iowa Territory or Town lots in Nauvoo.

Joseph Smith Jr.
P—RB Thompson"

little money; and although banks had often been begun under similar disabilities and by those more anxious to borrow than to lend, the Mormon experience with such a bank in Kirtland had been disastrous and was not repeated. Instead, the land served as a fund of capital on which to float credit without benefit of other institutional arrangements. It was as easy to borrow against the land as to obtain land on credit in the first place. Of course there were hazards whenever land not yet paid for was mortgaged, as was evidenced by the large bonds often pledged as security. Nevertheless, risks were considered necessary if the Saints' depleted fortunes were to be augmented. Joseph Smith repeatedly mortgaged real estate, either his own or that of the Church. He also lent money secured by land mortgages, and thus performed a kind of banking service for many. Another kind of credit device used was making a down payment on a piece of land, obtaining a substantial bond for deed, and then negotiating the bond.[22] Such arrangements were complex and left much for the future to work out, but they raised money as long as the economy inspired confidence and optimism. The land was also the basis of an informal currency of vouchers which circulated among the brethren. Once when in Springfield Smith needed money, he dashed off such a note on a scrap of paper:

> Springfield November 7th 1839
> Mr. Henry G. Sherwood [one of Smith's agents]
> You will please pay to John A. Hicks fifty Dollars and charge the same to me Yours etc
> Joseph Smith Jr
> The above order is for money to bear our expenses [sic] on the road he will take a lot of [?] land if you have any to please him if not you can sell the lot that Br Jonathan Hampton was to have I have seen him he paid the damages etc etc
> Joseph Smith [23]

There were exigencies of economic life in Nauvoo for which such induced credit would not suffice, and Joseph Smith was harried to meet them. On May 27, 1839, he began his fiscal career in Nauvoo

[22] Deed Book F, pp. 409, 416; Bond and Mortgage Book A, p. 111; Bond and Mortgage Book 1, pp. 148, 228, 265, 270. Joseph Smith in April, 1842, agreed to buy from one Eric Rhodes a piece of land for $1,535. He paid $100 down and received a $3,000 bond for deed which the following October he sold to William Clayton for $1,500. The bond is in the Joseph Smith Estate Papers.

[23] Document in the Joseph Smith Estate Papers. The voucher was probaby not redeemed, but circulated as commercial paper and was finally filed as a claim against the Smith estate.

by borrowing money: "Now as money seems to come in too slowly, in order that we may meet our engagements, we have determined to call upon the liberality of Father Bigler [for the sum of] five or six hundred dollars, for which he will have the security of said committee on removal . . . and the thanks of the church besides."[24] Real money could be, when obtainable, very dear. After considerable exertion Ebenezer Robinson in May, 1840, was able to borrow $145 from a brother for a year to finance a new printing of the *Book of Mormon*. The rate of interest charged was thirty-five per cent.[25] The need to raise hard cash prompted another novel expedient. Smith recorded in his journal on July 17, 1840: "By my suggestion, High Council voted that Samuel Bent and George W. Harris go on a mission to procure money for printing certain books . . . and also to procure loans in behalf of the Church." Those brethren dutifully headed east, armed with letters of recommendation. But the best they could report was notes for $83 from various Illinois brethren, a horse, harness, and carriage for the Prophet from Ohio Saints and the intelligence that "We found the brethren very anxious and willing to assist the Church in the great and glorious cause, but I am sorry to say I found them destitute of means to relieve our present necessity."[26]

Perhaps of all the perplexities of temporal affairs, none made Joseph Smith more anxious to return to the responsibilities of the spirit than the Hotchkiss indebtedness. The correspondence between the Church and the Connecticut land dealer from whom the Church had purchased the large tract on "the flat" on land contract in 1839 chronicles the fiscal problems of Nauvoo and the tortured attempts made to solve them. Hotchkiss was delicate but persistent about his interest in the Saints' pecuniary affairs and their ability to retire the $3,000 in notes due to mature each twelvemonth. He wrote on March 17, 1840, to inquire after the progress of the Church's memorials then before Congress asking redress for the Missouri losses. The Saints entertained great expectations that there would be some substantial settlement made; indeed, that was the implicit object of the petitions.[27] Hotchkiss had been assured that the success of this project would underwrite the Nauvoo land purchase. He wanted to know "whether you have any friends in the House and Senate, who

[24] Joseph Smith's History, 3:366.
[25] *The Return*, 2:258, May, 1890.
[26] Joseph Smith's History, 4:161, 164, 199, 200.
[27] For a discussion of these memorials see Chapter 10.

will bring forward your case, and advocate it in sincerity, and perse-
vere in your behalf with skill and ability until something is accomplished. Milk and water friends in Congress are good for nothing."
Two weeks later he was satisfied that the Congress would not give
any money to the Church, and since the first payment was due in a
few months he enjoined the Saints to gird up their loins and prepare
to rely on their own resources. "The greatest reliance you have for
regaining your wealth is in the honorable conduct of your people—
their pure morals—their correct habits—their indefatigable industry
—their untiring perseverance—and their well directed enterprise.
These constitute a capital which can never be shaken by man." His
confidence was sufficient to offer them an additional twelve thousand
acres in Sangamon, Mercer, and Henry Counties.[28]

On July 28, 1840, Smith replied in a fashion characteristic of his
correspondence with the Church's creditors:

It would afford me great pleasure indeed, could I hold out any prospect
of the two notes [for $1,500 each] due next month being met at maturity,
or even this fall. Having had considerable difficulty (necessarily consequent on a new settlement) to contend with, as well as poverty and considerable sickness, our first payment will be probably somewhat delayed,
until we again get a good start in the world . . . the prospect is indeed
favorable. However, every exertion on our part shall be made to meet
the demands against us, so that if we cannot accomplish all we wish to,
it is our misfortune, and not our fault.

Smith alluded to the awkwardness resulting from the fact that the
Church still had no title to most of the Hotchkiss purchase.[29] Many
prospective buyers would "make an effort to raise money, for the
sake of getting a deed; which effort they would not be so likely to
make if we could only give them a bond [for deed]." With some
actual titles to work with, said Smith, "I . . . hope that we shall be
able by and by to make some cash sales." While he did not say it in
so many words, he implied a *quid pro quo.* If Hotchkiss would give
him title to the rest of the purchase *before* the lands were paid for,

[28] Hotchkiss letters in *ibid.,* 4:98, 100–102.
[29] William White, who had a joint interest with Hotchkiss in ninety acres
of the purchase and who had the title in his possession, gave it to Smith for
a cash settlement of his interest. "I hope," wrote the Prophet to Hotchkiss, "this
arrangement will meet your approbation, although it is a departure from the common rules of business, but I was induced to do so from the advantages which
will result from it, which I hope will be mutual." Those advantages would
be, he explained, in being able to offer a title to prospective purchasers who
might not buy from the Church otherwise.

the prospect of making those payments would be much enhanced. But the shrewd Connecticut man would have none of that.[30] The first notes apparently were paid; but the following summer, 1841, the problem of meeting the second payment would again be acute. So Smith and his brethren hit upon a new device which would meet the Hotchkiss obligation, promote the gathering to Nauvoo, and perhaps even raise extra money. The technique was to send agents among the Saints in the East to convince them to move to Nauvoo, and to give them bills of exchange for the titles to their property. These bills could be cashed in Nauvoo for lots or farm lands of comparable value. The agents would give the titles to eastern lands thus acquired to Hotchkiss in an amount sufficient to pay the notes due him, and if possible sell the rest. Hotchkiss agreed to this arrangement. The Mormon agents who went east in the spring of 1841 were the Smith brothers, Hyrum and William, and Dr. Isaac Galland. The title-trading business seemed at first a success. William Smith wrote from Chester County, Pennsylvania, a fertile field of missionary endeavor, "the cause in these eastern lands is flourishing, and we want more laborers; fifty doors opened for preaching where there is but one laborer. I wish you would send us more." [31] Joseph Smith recorded one such exchange of land on February 28, 1842: "Paid Brother Robert Pierce $2,700, the balance due him for a farm Dr. Galland bought . . . in Brandywine Township, Chester County, Pennsylvania, for $5,000, namely [three Nauvoo lots, valued at $1,100, $800, and $806], the remainder having been previously paid . . . and Brother Pierce expressed his satisfaction of the whole. . . ." Pierce communicated that satisfaction to the *Times and Seasons:* "many supposed . . . that I would get nothing in return [for my farm], but I wish to say to all my old friends and enemies in Pennsylvania . . . that I have received my pay in full from the Church . . . through you, sir, as trustee-in-trust, according to the original contract. . . ." [32] The need for a testimonial suggests some suspicion of such land barters.

But in August Joseph Smith received supplementary intelligence from his brothers and a letter from Hotchkiss that must have caused him consternation. Hotchkiss wrote that Galland was leaving for the West without coming to see him, as he had expected, "to make

[30] Smith's letter to Hotchkiss in *ibid.*, 4:170–172.
[31] Letter of William Smith to Joseph Smith, August 5, 1841, in *ibid.*, 4:391, 392.
[32] *Ibid.*, 4:519.

some arrangement . . . respecting the interest due to myself, Mr. Tuttle, and Mr. Gillet . . . I and Mr. Tuttle think that we have much reason to be dissatisfied with the silence and apparent neglect. Permit me to ask if this is a proper return for the confidence we have bestowed, or the indulgence we have extended?" It was his "urgent wish" that Hyrum Smith should come to see him, and he charged the Prophet to "write him [Hyrum] immediately. . . ." [33] The Prophet was surprised and distressed that Hotchkiss expected a separate interest payment and that he was, according to Galland and Hyrum Smith, threatening to repudiate the arrangement to receive land instead of cash. "If you have forgotten," Joseph Smith replied, "I will here remind you [that] you verbally agreed . . . that you would not exact the payment of the interest . . . under five years, and that you would not coerce the payment even then; to all this you pledged your honor." Hotchkiss had but recently agreed to accept eastern lands in lieu of a cash settlement, Smith reminded him, so that the Church could "pay you off for the whole purchase that we made of you." But now according to Smith's agents Hotchkiss would receive land titles only in payment of the interest, and not the principal. Smith concluded his letter to Hotchkiss with a threat of his own to repudiate the contract between them:

I presume you are no stranger to the part of the city plot we bought of you being a sickly hole, and that we have not been able in consequence to realize any valuable consideration from it, athough we have been keeping up appearances, and holding out inducements to encourage immigration, that we scarcely think justifiable in consequence of the mortality that almost invariably awaits those who come from far distant parts (and that with a view to enable us to meet our engagements), and now to be goaded by you, for a breach of good faith, and neglect and dishonorable conduct, seems to me to be almost beyond endurance.

You are aware that we came from Missouri destitute of everything but physical force, had nothing but our energies and perseverance to rely upon to meet the payment of the extortionate sum that you exacted for the land we had of you. Have you no feelings of Commiseration? Or is it your design to crush us with a ponderous load before we can walk? Or can you better dispose of the property than we are doing for your interest? If so, to the alternative.

I therefore propose . . . that you come and take the premises, and make the best you can of it, or stand off and give us an opportunity that we may manage the concern, and enable us to meet our engagements, as was originally contemplated. . . . We have been making every exertion, and used all the means at our command to lay a foundation that will

[33] Hotchkiss' letter of July 24, 1841, to Joseph Smith, *ibid.,* 4:406.

enable us now to begin to meet our pecuniary engagements, and no doubt in our minds to the entire satisfaction of all those concerned, if they will but exercise a small degree of patience, and stay a resort to coercive measures which would kill us in the germ, even before we can (by reason of the season) begin to bud and blossom in order to bring forth a plentiful yield of fruit.[34]

Smith hoped by pleas, threats, exaggerations, and repeated assurances to avoid being pressed too closely or brought to a reckoning by "coercive measures" that would be embarrassing if not disastrous. But he was upset just then by another matter to which he did not allude in the letter to Hotchkiss—the disappearance of Galland with money and land titles in his possession.

Dr. Galland had furthered his relations with the Church by becoming a baptized member on July 3, 1839; and two hours later Joseph Smith ordained him an elder. The following September Galland was in Kirtland on Church business, probably as an agent of some kind.[35] He had the confidence of Smith and was a natural choice to be one of the agents to trade for eastern lands and handle the Hotchkiss payments. But it was partly if not primarily his malfeasance that caused the sharp exchange of letters between Hotchkiss and the Prophet. Smith Tuttle, one of the Hotchkiss partners, wrote the Mormon leader in September a soothing letter which detailed Galland's failure to follow through on his promises. In light of Tuttle's explanation, replied Smith, "my feelings are changed, and I think that you all had cause for complaining." Brother Hyrum had been forced by ill health to return to Nauvoo, leaving the whole of the business in Galland's hands. "Why he has not done according to my instructions," wrote Smith, "God only knows. . . ." The Prophet, though worried, was not yet ready to admit that the esteemed Doctor might have absconded with the funds. But nothing occurred in the succeeding weeks to suggest the contrary. In a letter to Hotchkiss on December 10 Smith referred to "the inefficiency, neglect, or sickness of Dr. Galland" as a cause of their difficulty.[36] When Galland finally returned to the vicinity of Nauvoo, apparently in December or January, bringing him to account proved difficult. On January 17 and 18, Smith and Galland exchanged letters, neither of

[34] Letter of Smith to Hotchkiss, August 25, 1841, in *ibid.*, 4:406, 407.

[35] *Ibid.*, 3:393; Smith to Galland, September 11, 1839, 4:8, 9.

[36] Tuttle's letter is not in Smith's journal and is probably not extant. Smith's letters to Tuttle on October 9, 1841, and to Hotchkiss December 10 are in Joseph Smith's History, 4:430–432, 469.

which is extant. Galland's language apparently served to warn Smith that if Galland were pressed for a close accounting of his agency he might in return call for debts due him from the Church. He was certainly in a position to cause an uproar and a scandal over the complex credit arrangements within the Church; perhaps he threatened foreclosure on Iowa lands as well. Smith wrote him on January 19:

Dear Sir:—By your reply of the 18th instant to my note of the 17th, I . . . conclude that you received [it] in a manner altogether unintended by me, and that there may be no misunderstanding between us, and that you may be satisfied that I did not intend . . . anything, only upon the principles of the strictest integrity and uprightness before God, and to do as I would be done unto, I will state I have become embarrassed in my operations to a certain extent, and partly from a presentation of notes, which you, as my agent, had given for lands purchased in the eastern states, they having been sent to me. I have been obliged to cash them, and having no returns from you to meet those demands, or even the trifling expenses of your outfit, it has placed me in rather an unpleasant situation, and having a considerable quantity of your scrip on hand [Half Breed Land Company scrip?] enough as I suppose, to counterbalance the debts due you [to which Galland had apparently called attention], and leave a balance in my favor, even if it were small; and as I was pressed for funds, from the causes above mentioned, as well as others, I had hoped it would be convenient for you to lend me some assistance at the present time and this was the reason I sent a messenger to you as I did.

And now, sir, that we may have no misunderstanding in this matter, I think we had better have a settlement, and if I am owing you, I will pay as soon as I can, and if you owe me, I shall only expect the same in return, for . . . short reckonings make long friends. . . .[37]

Despite the attempted conciliation on January 18, Smith published a notice of the revocation of Galland's agency and power-of-attorney in the *Times and Seasons.* Two days later he called a special conference of the Saints to ratify his actions; and the body "instructed the trustee-in-trust to proceed with Dr. Galland's affairs . . . as he shall judge most expedient." On January 26 Smith borrowed money "to refund for money borrowed of John Benbow, as outfit for Dr. Galland in his agency." The next day Brigham Young and James Ivins, returned from a visit with Galland, "gave a favorable report" of the Doctor, which suggests that an accommodation had been reached. On February 2 Smith and Galland "councilled" together, and on February 4 Smith "instructed that an invoice of Dr. Galland's scrip be made." [38] This was the last time Smith mentioned

[37] *Ibid.*, pp. 499, 500.
[38] *Ibid.*, 4:500, 502, 503, 513.

the affair in his journal. The conclusion of Galland's relations with the Church are left to conjecture. It is scarcely accurate to say that he "fell from favor"; rather he seems to have been dropped from official cognizance. At the same time there was increasing though still private attention being given to the problem of General Bennett, whose "fall" was to be spectacular and soon; and trouble with Galland was to be avoided. Probably the Saints' dealings with him, and the heavy costs they entailed, were charged to experience. Perhaps Galland had been recognized from the beginning as a "temporal" Latter-day Saint, to be concerned with business rather than religious matters. Perhaps likewise his eldership was a "temporal" priesthood; certainly "spiritual" elders were not financed in their "missions" as he was. Galland soon withdrew his fellowship and boasted his conviction that Joseph Smith was a fraud.[39]

The Prophet aired the entire Hotchkiss business before the semi-annual conference on October 2, 1841. Brigham Young reacted to the matter with vigor, expressing "his earnest desire that the business might be speedily adjusted, and a proper title obtained by the church." Smith moved and the Conference assented "that the Twelve write an epistle to the Saints abroad, to use their influence and exertions to secure by exchange, purchase, donation, etc., a title to the Hotchkiss purchase." That such a matter as five years of interest on notes totaling more than $50,000 could have been the subject of a verbal agreement was incredible; but now the trouble thus aroused suggested caution. Smith was doubtless counseled by the Twelve and perhaps others that the Church could not afford the pugnacious attitude he displayed in his letter to Hotchkiss of August 25. For the eastern creditors to foreclose their mortgage would be catastrophic. In the sober mood of the conference Smith wrote Tuttle, the Hotchkiss partner, as conciliatory and reassuring a letter as he knew how to do. Their misunderstanding had been most unfortunate; he himself had acted in the best of faith. "I must plead innocent," he said, "I have done all that I could . . . I will still do all that I can. I will not leave one stone unturned." The matter had been "Fairly presented before our general conference . . . of ten thousand people for the wisest and best course in relation to meeting your demands." The Twelve were now employed to help procure eastern lands for the creditors. When Smith now mentioned interest he reversed himself and spoke as though there had never been

[39] Roberts and Moorehead, *History of Lee County*, p. 308.

any question about paying it. Galland had been instructed, he wrote, to pay the accrued interest and the sum that would accrue through 1842 "so as to be in advance of our indebtedness"; the default was therefore Galland's. The Church had every intention of discharging its obligations in full, but Tuttle must realize the difficulties under which the Saints labored. He had, Smith continued, been unjustly imprisoned during the summer and had endured "some ten or eleven hundred dollars' expense and trouble, such as lawyers' fees, witnesses, etc., etc., before I could be redeemed. . . ." He had been sick that autumn, and now "cold weather is rolling in upon us [October 9]." In conclusion Smith made another characteristic appeal:

> And now in contemplating the face of the whole subject, I find that I am under the necessity of asking a little further indulgence—say, till next spring, so that I may be able to recover myself, and then, if God spares my life . . . I will come in person to your country, and will never cease my labors until the whole matter is completely adjusted to the full satisfaction of all of you. . . . We intend to struggle with all our misfortunes in life, and shoulder them up handsomely, like men. . . . We are the sons of Adam. We are free born sons of America, and having been trampled upon, and our rights taken from us—even our constitutional rights, by a good many who boast themselves of being valiant in freedom's cause, while their hearts possess not a spark of its benign and enlightening influence—will afford a sufficient excuse, we hope, for any harsh remarks which may have been dropped by us, when we thought there was an assumption of superiority designed to gall our feelings.
>
> We are very sensitive as a people—we confess it; but we want to be pardoned for our sins, if any we have committed.

In closing his long and diplomatic letter to Tuttle, Smith could not resist saying, "It is still, however, my firm conviction that my understanding concerning the interest was correct." [40] The willingness of the creditors to go along with the Saints was abetted by John Gillet, the Illinois partner, whom Tuttle had been urging to "visit our Mormon friends." This Gillet had not been able to do, having "no money to bear my expenses and no possible chance of getting any." However, he wrote Tuttle on November 14, "from all I can learn, they are making large improvements and accumulating in numbers rapidly. . . . My belief is that they want to pay but their means are limited." [41]

The same week that Smith wrote Tuttle, the Twelve were com-

[40] Smith's letter to Tuttle, in Joseph Smith's History, 4:430–433.
[41] John Gillet to Smith Tuttle, Gillett Family Papers, Case 9, Drawer 5, Folder 1. Manuscript Collection of the Illinois State Historical Library.

posing an epistle to the eastern Saints. They urged gathering to Nauvoo in forceful language, frankly linking its necessity to the Hotchkiss debt embarrassment. Six thousand dollars in accrued interest had not been paid, and they wrote, "it is necessary that the notes should be taken up, the interest stopped and a warrantee title secured immediately. . . ." The means of accomplishing these things was simply for the eastern Saints to trade their real estate for Nauvoo lots or farms. "Thus your property will prove to you as good as money, inasmuch as you desire to emigrate; and you will no longer be obliged to tarry afar off because that money is so scarce you cannot sell to get your pay." [42] To dispel rumors that the Prophet was enriching himself as middleman in the barter of land, the Apostles declared:

Let us not for a moment lend an ear to evil and designing men who would subvert the truth and blacken the character of the servant of the most high God by publishing abroad that the Prophet is enriching himself on the spoils of the brethren.

When Brother Joseph stated to the general conference the amount and situation of the property of the Church, of which he is trustee-in-trust by the united voice of the Church [at Nauvoo], he also stated the amount of his own possessions on earth; and what do you think it was? We will tell you: his old Charley (a horse) given him in Kirtland, two pet deer, two old turkeys and four young ones, the old cow given him by a brother in Missouri, his old Major (a dog) his wife, children, and a little household furniture; and this is the amount of the great estates, the splendid mansions and noble living of him who has spent a life of toil and suffering, of privation and hardships, of imprisonments and chains, of dungeons and vexatious lawsuits, and every kind of contumely and contempt ungodly men could heap upon him, and last of all report him as rolling in wealth and luxury which he had plundered from the spoils of those for whose good he has thus toiled and suffered.

The Twelve in their new capacity as promoters and managers of the Kingdom, further expounded in their letter the philosophy of gathering as an inescapable principle of the Mormon religion. While

[42] Joseph Smith's History, 5:435. The Twelve stated that the Hotchkiss contract was for "the specified sum of fifty-three thousand, five hundred dollars . . . in two notes of equal amount, one payable in ten years, and one in twenty. . . ." The contract as recorded in the county record entailed two notes of $25,000 each, maturing in ten and twenty years respectively, and forty additional notes of $1,500 each, two of which were to mature each twelve months for twenty years. The Apostles failed to mention the latter, perhaps because in accord with Smith's contention, they refused to recognize interest charges on the principal. General histories have used the $53,500 figure as the total price of the Hotchkiss purchase, presumably based upon this letter of the Twelve. See for example, Roberts, *Comprehensive History*, 2:9, 10.

careful not to call Nauvoo "Zion," they portrayed it as a "resting place . . . within the peaceful bosom of Illinois—a state whose citizens are inspired with a love of liberty, whose souls are endowed with . . . charity and benevolence" and the soil of which "is vieing with its citizens in all that is good and lovely." Here the Saints were "beginning to realize the fulfillment of the ancient prophets—'They shall build houses and inhabit them, plant vineyards and eat the fruit thereof, having none to molest or make afraid.'" The Apostles compared the Latter-day Saints with the children of Israel, and Nauvoo with the Land of Promise. The city lots, "a part of which have been sold, a part has been distributed to the widow and orphan, and a part remains for sale . . . are for the inheritance of the Saints, a resting place for the Church, a habitation for the God of Jacob, for here He has commanded a house to be built unto this name where He may manifest Himself to His people as in former times. . . ." Like the ancient Covenant People, the Saints were uprooted and caused to wander in order to establish the Kingdom:

The journeyings, the gatherings, and buildings of the Saints are nothing new, and as they are expecting, looking, and praying for the completion of the dispensation of the fullness of times, they must also expect that their progress will be onward, or they will be of no avail, for what is not faith is sin, and can you believe that God will hear your prayers and bring you on your journey, gather you and build your houses, and you not put forth your hand . . . to help yourself? No. Therefore, inasmuch as the Saints believe that Father Abraham journed [*sic*] to a distant land at the command of the Highest, where himself and household (whose household we are if we keep his commandments) might enjoy the fruits of their labors unmolested, and worship the God of heaven according to the dictates of their own conscience and His law; that his seed afterwards gathered to Canaan, the land of promise; that the people of God were commanded to build a house where the Son of Man might have a place to lay his head, and the disciples be endowed with power from on high, and were with one accord in one place; they must also believe that this [present] dispensation comprehends all the great works of all former dispensations; and that the children must gather as did the fathers, must build a house where they may be endowed, and be found together worshipping and doing as their fathers did when Jehovah spake, and the angels of heaven ministering unto them; and if these things are not in this generation, then we have not arrived at the dispensation of the fullness of times . . . and our faith and prayers are vain.

Realizing that some brethren with money to invest in Nauvoo might recall the fate of similar investments in Zionic enterprises at Independence, Kirtland, and Far West and consequently hesitate to invest in new ventures, the Apostles pointed out that such fears were groundless: "Is it possible that we labor for naught, and that we shall be disappointed at the last? No! We know assuredly that the set time to favor Zion has come, and her sons and daughters shall rejoice in her glory." They noted further that the timid, the doubters, the vacillating had no place in the Kingdom of God, that the need to "build it up" was urgent, that the promises of success were sure, and that the consummation would be glorious. "Brethren," concluded Brigham Young's quorum in characteristic spirit, "in view of all these things, let us be up and doing." [43]

Despite the pressure of creditors, the Prophet's expanding vision of the kingdom of righteousness on the Mississippi could not be dimmed. He foresaw that Nauvoo was not the only city to be "built up" under the direction of the Twelve. In giving them their commission at the special conference of August 16, 1841, Smith specified that Zarahemla, Warren, Nashville, and Ramus "should now be built up." [44] Zarahemla and Nashville were the settlements across the river in Iowa, in the Galland purchase. Warren, twenty miles down river, was really an addition to the town of Warsaw though it was platted as a separate town. Laid out as a speculation by Warsaw promoters, Warren engaged the interest of the Church in August, 1841, as a means of raising money for the Hotchkiss payment, at which time the Mormon leaders made a contract with the proprietors to promote it as a Mormon town. [45]

Ramus was a community of Saints in Fountain Green Township, about ten miles northeast of Carthage and twenty miles east by southeast across the prairie from Nauvoo. It was platted for the Church in August, 1840, by William Wightman, later a bishop, into twenty-four blocks totaling eighty-six lots; the following February, fifty-four additional lots were platted. The lots were the same size as those in Nauvoo, and the streets the same three rods wide. In the center of town a block was reserved for public buildings. [46] Ramus was organized ecclesiastically as a stake, with a church government like that of Nauvoo. In March, 1843, it was incorporated as a town by the state legislature which authorized an ordinary civil government and changed its name from Ramus to Macedonia. [47] In the

[43] "An Epistle of the Twelve Apostles, to the Brethren Scattered Abroad on the Continent of America," October 12, 1841, in Joseph Smith's History, 4:433–438.
[44] *Ibid.*, 4:404.
[45] *Ibid.*, 4:405.
[46] Hancock County Plat Book 1, p. 45.
[47] *Laws of the State of Illinois, the 13th General Assembly*, 1842–1843, pp. 305–307. The village is now called Webster.

summer of 1843, a gentile traveler visited the town and noted the contrast between its apparent busyness and the depression he had seen in other Illinois villages. The population, he was told, totaled about five hundred, and "The buildings, yards, barns, etc. seemed well constructed and tastefully arranged. Macedonia is . . . surrounded by numerous mills and good farming lands. . . . The place seemed much unlike any in my knowledge. Mechanics of most kinds seemed plenty and busily employed. Every house seemed occupied. A beautiful square lay near the centre of town, on which we were informed a house for literary and religious purposes was to be erected." [48] By 1845 Macedonia (Ramus) had become the third largest community in the county, only Nauvoo and Warsaw being larger. The state census of that year indicated a population of 382, probably closer to its optimum size than the figure of five hundred given the traveler. It apparently enjoyed modest prosperity as the hamlet for an agricultural neighborhood. In December, 1841, the Twelve had held a local conference there and returned to Nauvoo with nearly a thousand dollars' worth of goods solicited for the Temple—"horses, wagons, provisions, clothing, etc." [49] But Warren and Nauvoo were promoted too vigorously by Church leaders to permit Ramus to prosper from any extensive immigration. There was a good deal of trading by Nauvooans in Macedonia lots; but the ordinary price for an unimproved lot was only $50. In December, 1841, Wightman, who had originally acted as proprietor and agent of Ramus, deeded all the "unsold and bonded lots" as well as notes taken on sales of lots to the Trustee-in-Trust "for the benefit of the whole Church." The action served further to centralize all Church finance in Nauvoo. In his journal Smith described the transfer as gratuitous, or as a transfer of Church property from local to central management; but the county record of the deed shows that Wightman received $5,000 from the Trustee-in-Trust. It is likely that Wightman underwrote the original land purchase on which the town was platted, and that the arrangement was that peculiar Mormon mixture of public and private enterprise in which personal profit was taken from investments made to advance the common cause. [50]

On February 10, 1843, a possibility for further expansion opened when the Prophet was visited by a Mr. Cowan, emissary from the

---

[48] From a letter in the *Nauvoo Neighbor,* September 20, 1843.

[49] Joseph Smith's History, 4:469.

[50] *Ibid.,* 4:468, 477; Deed Book K, pp. 19, 20. The transaction was recorded December 8, 1841. Four days later Wightman sold Joseph Smith a single lot, probably improved, for $400.

citizens of Shokoquon [or Shokokon], a place twenty miles up river in Henderson County. They wanted Smith to send "a talented Mormon preacher" to reside among them; they would provide him a good house and support, and "accord him liberty" to invite as many Saints there as he would. A brother John Bear was dispatched to preach, and Smith began to consider the possibilities of a new Mormon town there, especially when "Mr. Cowan proposed to give me one-fourth of the city lots in Shokoquon." Six days later Smith, Orson Hyde, and others visited the place and "found it a very desirable location for a city." [51] However, it failed to develop.

The following month, March, 1843, Smith was again concerned with affairs in the satellite towns. He likened the Mormon kingdom on the Mississippi to a wheel: "Nauvoo is the hub: we will drive the first spoke in Ramus, second in LaHarpe, third Shokoquon, fourth in Lima: that is half the wheel. The other half is over the river: we will let that alone at present. We will call the Saints from Iowa to these [Illinois] spokes, then send elders over to convert the whole people." [52] Although LaHarpe was a gentile village in the northeast corner of the county a few miles north of Ramus, it was "town" to an undetermined but considerable number of Mormon farmers in the township. In Adams County, twenty-five miles south of Nauvoo and seventeen north of Quincy, was Lima, an agricultural community of Mormons spread upon the prairie a few miles from the river. It was frequently referred to as "the Morley Settlement" after a "Patriarch Morley" who had moved there from Missouri with a few families over whom he presided. The neighborhood gradually attracted more Saints, was given a stake organization, and attained importance as a "gathering place" for farmers. In October, 1841, congregations totaling 424 members were represented at a conference of Lima Stake.[53]

Although most of the Mormon promotional language dealt with Nauvoo, the "regions round about" were in demand by gatherers who wanted farms rather than, or in addition to, city lots. Consequently the Church and its agents as well as gentile dealers, such as Wells and the Kimballs, were actively trading in farm lands. The volume of

[51] Joseph Smith's History, 5:268, 278, 279.
[52] *Ibid.*, 5:296. In response to an inquiry about using the Church lands in Ramos-Macedonia to finance a meeting house there, Smith said: "I told them the property of the Church should be disposed of by the direction of the Trustee-in-Trust, appointed by the voice of the whole Church. . . ."
[53] Eliza Roxey Snow, *Biography and Family Records of Lorenzo Snow* (Salt Lake City, 1884), p. 75; Brigham Young's journal in *The Millennial Star*, 26: 104, February 13, 1864.

this trade suggests a distinct speculative trend.[54] The tracts were generally small, seldom more than 160 acres and often 80, 40, or even 20 and 10. The records of deeds do not indicate either the quality or improvement of the land, so the prices paid are not a reliable indication of its relative expensiveness; however, it was not cheap. Ten to fifteen times the minimum federal price, or even more, was not uncommon.[55]

In Smith's analogy of the gathering as a wheel with hub and spokes, he omitted Warren, where severe difficulties with the citizens of Warsaw had developed. He suggested further that the Iowa development should be "let . . . alone at present," with its people being brought over to the Illinois side. At the annual conference in April, 1843, Smith made his meaning more explicit. The governor of Iowa Territory had issued a writ for his extradition on request of the Missouri governor, and he was thus subject to arrest in Iowa. "It is now held in Iowa," said Smith,

as a cudgel over my head. . . . I will therefore advise you to serve them a trick that the devil never did,—i.e., come away and leave them, come into Illinois, and let the Iowegians take their own course. I don't care whether you come away or not. I do not wish to control you; but if you wish for my advice, I would say, let every man, as soon as he conveniently can, come over here; for you can live in peace with us. We are all green mountain boys—Southerners, Northerners, Westerners, and every other kind of "ers," and will treat you well: and let that governor [Chambers] know that we don't like to be imposed upon.[56]

[54] In June, 1842, Samuel Marshall sold Ethan Kimball the southeast quarter of section twenty-five in Appanoose Township, five miles east of Nauvoo, for $200. Ethan Kimball resold it the same month to Joseph Smith for $1,500. The author was kindly shown an abstract to title to this tract by Mr. Preston Kimball of Nauvoo.

[55] As examples the following sales are cited:

G. W. Robinson to S. James—160 acres for $4400, October, 1841.
Eric Rhodes to Joseph Smith—153½ acres for $1535; April, 1842.
Francis Church to Joseph Smith—80 acres for $2000; October, 1840.
Joseph Smith as Trustee to Isaac Chase—80 acres for $1200; Jan., 1843.
Joseph Smith as Trustee to Asahel Perry—80 acres for $800; March, 1843.
William Blackhurst to the children of Joseph Smith—15 acres for $225; August, 1843.
Samuel Rolfe to Joseph Smith as Trustee—80 acres for $300; March, 1842.
William Weeks to Joseph Smith as Trustee—10 acres for $50; April, 1842.
Joseph Smith as Trustee to Nancy Allred—80 acres for $800; Feb., 1843.
Joseph Smith as Trustee to Sally Murdock—25 acres for $500; Nov., 1843.

The above transactions are recorded in Bond and Mortgage Book 1, pp. 161, 228; and Deed Books H, p. 623; L, pp. 173, 245; and M, pp. 5, 10, 11, 13, 48, 115.

[56] Joseph Smith's History, 5:334.

Smith had further reason for discomfiture about his Iowa involvement. Galland's imposition had by then become clear, and in trying to salvage something from it, the Prophet was taken in by another confidence man. James Remick, who had dealt with Galland in what David Kilbourne called a mutual swindle, came to Smith and represented himself as Galland's agent and as being in possession of the Church's notes of indebtedness to the Doctor. His proposal was to give Smith a quitclaim deed for all the Galland purchase, as well as half of "my right to all my land in Iowa Territory." Furthermore the Galland notes would be handed over. "You paid Galland the notes," Smith reported Remick as saying, "and [you] ought to have them: they are in my hands as his agent, and I will give them up." What Remick wanted in return was for Smith to promote Keokuk as a Mormon settlement. However, Remick also wanted "loans," and Smith obliged him in the amount of $1,100. "I have since found that he is swindling," said Smith to the conference, "and . . . there is no prospect of getting anything from him." [57] Smith then admitted that the whole Mormon development in Iowa was a failure, and said, "I ask forgiveness of all whom I advised to go there."

I am not so much a "Christian" as many suppose I am. When a man undertakes to ride me for a horse, I feel disposed to kick up and throw him off, and ride him. David did so, and so did Joshua. My only weapon is my tongue. I would not buy property in Iowa territory: I consider it stooping to accept it as a gift.

In relation to the half-breed land, it is best described by its name—it is half-breed land; and every wise and judicious person as soon as he can dispose of his effects, if he is not a half-breed, will come away. I wish we could exchange some half-breeds and let them go over the river. If there are any that are not good citizens, they will be finding fault tomorrow with my remarks, and that is the keyword whereby you may know them. There is a chance in that place for every abomination to be practiced on the innocent, if they go. . . . The men who have possession have the best title; all the rest are forms for swindling. I do not wish for the Saints to have a quarrel there.[58]

The acquiring, promoting, dividing, and selling of land were necessary ingredients in the gathering of "modern Israel" to their latter-day land of promise. But the purity of Christian motive, where it existed in the endeavor, was tarnished by swindlers, speculation, in-

[57] In September, 1842, seven months earlier, Smith recorded, "Mr. Remmick gave me a deed to one half his landed property in Keokuk, though it will be a long time, if ever, before it will be any benefit to me." *Ibid.*, 5:162.
[58] *Ibid.*, 5:334–336.

experience, bad management, and the heavy wear and tear of "temporal" affairs to which the "spiritual" kingdom-building endeavor at Nauvoo seemed especially prone. The land distribution was not a failure, but neither was it an unqualified success, bringing as it did oversanguine expectations, high costs, frequent losses, and individual and corporate disappointments. Doubt was bound to arise in the minds of some about the process by which the Kingdom of God should be "built up" on the earth.

6

A Kingdom of This World:
Business, Industry, and Finance

Business begins to assume a cheering aspect in our city. Everywhere we see men of industry with countenances beaming with cheerful content hurrying to their various occupations and scenes of labour. The sound of the axe, the hammer, and the saw, greet your ear in every direction. . . . Habitations are reared for miles in every direction, and others are springing up, and, ere we are aware of their existence, are filled with happy occupants. . . . Though emigrants are flocking in in multitudes, and have their homes and their wants to be supplied, yet all things move in their accustomed order and with accelerating force. Hundreds of houses, shops, mills, etc., are expected to go up in the course of the summer, when our city will present a scene of industry, beauty, and comfort, hardly equalled . . . in our country. The Saints have a great and arduous work before them, but persevering industry and diligence, stimulated by a zeal for God and his cause, will surely accomplish it, and they will reap the full reward of their toil.

Times and Seasons, 2:363, April 1, 1841.

Nauvoo did not have an economy that was able adequately to support its population, and signs of economic immaturity were readily apparent, especially in the early years. The first concerns of settlers were to get a roof over the family and find something to do in order to live. For those Saints who chose to farm outside Nauvoo it was pioneering in the ordinary manner; but pioneering in the city presented special problems. To be sure, the acquisition of a one-acre lot meant that a cow or two, poultry, and a large garden could be kept; whether or not swine should be allowed in the city was a contested issue. The small competence provided by a city lot might keep a family from want. Orson Spencer observed in 1842, "though they had nothing but . . . a little bundle on their back when they came, they have now in many instances a comfortable cottage, a flourishing garden, and a good cow." [1] But the "inheritance" represented by a city lot was expensive and it did not provide the means to make a living. Despite all the cooperation, shar-

[1] Spencer, *Letters*, pp. 31, 32.

144

ing, and barter that went on to help ease the financial squeeze there was no adequate substitute for jobs and money. It was expected that an increasing population would bring prosperity to Nauvoo, but the opposite tended to be the case. Large numbers of poor English immigrants, as well as those from the states little better off, drove the per capita wealth of the city down. The heavy demand for goods and services which had been expected to invigorate the economy tended to depress it instead, since the capital to finance both production and consumption was inadequate.

George Miller, a harassed bishop responsible for the care of the destitute, wrote in 1841 of trying conditions:

Early this spring the English emigrants . . . began to come in, in apparent poverty. . . . Besides these, [others] were crowding in from the States, all poor, as the rich did not generally respond to the proclamation of the prophet to come with their effects, and assist in building the Temple and Nauvoo House. The poor had to be cared for, and labor created . . . there not being one in ten persons who could set themselves to work. . . . My Brethren of the Committee of the Nauvoo House Association, and the Committee of the Temple, all bore a part in the employment of labourers, and . . . providing food for them. . . . The poor, the blind, the lame, the widow, and the fatherless all looked to me for their daily wants; and but for the fact of some private property I had on hand they must have starved.

Miller said that no tithe funds were available to help, since all went to build the Temple. Contributions were difficult to obtain even for burying the pauper dead, let alone to feed the living. "The rich among us," he complained, "pretended to be too poor to barely feed themselves and nurse their speculations which they were more or less engaged in." During the summer "sickly season" his burden increased. "My days were filled with toil and care," said Miller, "and my nights in sleepless anxiety in waiting on the suffering poor and sick of the city . . . and hundreds of mouths to feed." [2] At the special conference of August 16, 1841, where the Twelve were given their managerial responsibilities to "assist to bear off the kingdom

[2] Miller, *Correspondence*, p. 8. These letters were written in 1855 to the Strangite newspaper on Beaver Island, Michigan. They were compiled and printed privately by Wingfield Watson of Burlington, Wisconsin, in 1916. A copy of the pamphlet is in the library of the Wisconsin State Historical Society. Miller kept a journal in the fashion of Mormon elders, which he used in writing the historical passages of his letters. The journal and copies of the letters were taken by his family to California where they were reproduced in part in H. W. Mills, "De Tal Palo Tal Astilla," *Publications of the Historical Society of Southern California*, 10:3:86–174 (1915–1917).

victoriously to the nations," Bishop Miller and Vinson Knight "presented . . . the situation of the poor of Nauvoo City . . . and a collection was taken for their benefit."[3] On June 13, 1842, Smith noted in his journal: "Attended a general council . . . to devise ways and means to furnish the poor with labor. Many of the English Saints have gathered to Nauvoo, most of whom are unacquainted with any kind of labor, except spinning, weaving, etc.; and having no factories in this place, they are troubled to know what to do. Those who have funds have more generally neglected to gather, and left the poor to build up the city and the kingdom of God in these last days."[4] Two weeks later Brigham Young recorded in his journal: "I addressed the Saints on the principle of union in building up the city, and sustaining the poor by providing employment for them. . . . [Later, in Council] we spent a season in prayer that the Lord would deliver us from our enemies, and provide means for us to build [the Temple and the Nauvoo House] as he had commanded his people."[5] Caring for the destitute was accepted as a Church responsibility and was organized by city wards, a practice later followed in Salt Lake City. In January, 1844, an Elder Carn, Bishop of the Sixth Ward, ran the following notice in the newspaper:

I take this opportunity of notifying all those that feel an interest in getting Wood for the Poor of the 6th ward, that on Monday, the 5th of February, I shall meet all these at the Upper Steam Mill, to conduct them to the Big Island, as I have permission of Messrs Law, to get all the Wood I want for the Poor.

Come on neighbors, with your axes and teams, for the ice is good and the weather is cold, and many of the poor are without wood; come on brethren, and don't neglect the poor.[6]

There was employment, but few had money to pay out in wages, and the laborer was often required to take produce or goods. An English convert reported in 1840 that farm labor brought a dollar a day "or something equal to it"; a man digging potatoes would receive one-fifth of what he dug; if he cut corn, he received one-eighth. In 1843 another immigrant wrote: "We can't get money for labour, at least in a general way . . . a man gets work for land, bricks, wood, or stone, provisions, etc.; well, in a year or two, or say

[3] Joseph Smith's History, 4:403.
[4] *Ibid.*, 5:25.
[5] Brigham Young's journal, entry for June 26, 1842, in the *Millennial Star*, 26:134, February 27, 1864.
[6] *Nauvoo Neighbor*, January 13, 1844.

more, he may pay for his land, get bricks enough for a house and other things. He cultivates his own land and is then his own master, but not without many pinches in the time if he has a family. He then begins to see better days. This is the way the poor have to act here." [7]

Nauvoo needed industry; almost everyone who commented on the economy or was responsible for its welfare agreed upon the need. However, industrializing Nauvoo was more typically the concern of the laborer seeking employment, the Church official worried about jobs for the poor, or the consumer anxious about the high cost of imported manufactures than it was of the profit-seeking capitalist-entrepreneur, of whom there were relatively few. The kind of workers' cooperative, self-sufficient, moneyless economy that budded in Nauvoo and blossomed in Utah was a natural result. "Those who have funds," Smith said, "have more generally neglected to gather, and left the poor to build up . . . the kingdom of God. . . ." The idea of the Church itself as an investment corporation utilizing tithes and offerings was experimented with in Nauvoo; as refined in Utah it helped build a viable economy in the Great Basin.

Many English immigrants were experienced factory workers, including weavers and other textile laborers, bootmakers, potters, and carriage-makers. They naturally urged the creation of manufactories in Nauvoo. Francis Moon wrote home in 1840: "we have no factory as yet, but we want means to build corn mills, and not having much machinery we have to do at home what would be done at factories if we had them. What we want is some persons with property for to raise these places . . . and then the clothing would be at a less rate, and we English would feel more at home. . . . But after all this . . . is a new country. . . ." [8] Joseph Fielding wrote early in 1842 that the Church wanted industries established. "Some of the brethren might put their money together and accomplish this. . . ." But until such a thing were done, "a man with a small capital would do well to set up some hand looms; he may get the cotton thread or cops at St. Louis. . . . Sheep are increasing here, and of course the wool will too." Weaving enterprises would keep in Nauvoo the money spent for clothing and "also furnish many with employment who are better acquainted with weaving than any other work." Fielding noted in addition that "several have done well at shop-

---

[7] *Millennial Star*, 1:255, February, 1841; and 4:88, October, 1843.
[8] *Millennial Star*, 1:255, February, 1841.

keeping, and it is likely to be a good business. Farming is also important, as all we get out of the earth . . . has not to be purchased from the world." [9] John Needham wrote in the summer of 1843: "With regard to the labouring people here, we want some one with money to raise a manufactory or more; we then could employ many idle hands, and many who go to the neighboring towns and states. This is caused by the often flush of emigrants, both from the Eastern States and from England. It would be a great thing for this place to have manufactories of different kinds, but time and perseverance and faithfulness before the Lord, will bring [about] a good deal. . . ." [10] No one was more anxious for industry or enthusiastic about its benefit than Joseph Smith. In December, 1841, he wrote to Edward Hunter, a Pennsylvania convert of means who was about to gather to Nauvoo:

As respects steam engines and mills . . . we cannot have too many. . . . This place has suffered exceedingly from the want of such mills . . . and neither one or two can do the business of this place another season. We have no good grain or board mill . . . and most of our flour and lumber has to be brought twenty miles. . . .

The city is rapidly advancing, many new buildings have been erected . . . and many more would have arisen, if brick and lumber could have been obtained. There is scarcely any limits which can be imagined to the mills and machinery and manufacturing of all kinds which might be put into profitable operation in this city, and even if others should raise a mill before you get here, it need be no discouragement to either you or Brother Buckwalter, for it will be difficult for the mills to keep pace with the growth of the place, and you will do well to bring the engine. If you can persuade any of the brethren who are manufacturers of woolens or cottons to come on and establish their business, do so.[11]

The legislature that granted the city government also chartered a joint-stock corporation called "The Nauvoo Agricultural and Mechanical Association." It was to raise money through the sale of stock "to promote agriculture and husbandry in all its branches, and for the manufacture of flour, lumber, and such other useful articles as are necessary for the ordinary purposes of life." The promoters were sanguine in their expectations of the money it would attract: capitalization was set at $100,000 with the privilege of increases to $300,000. Shares of the firm were $50 each. Joseph Smith, Sidney Rigdon, and William Law, the First Presidency of the Church, were

[9] *Ibid.*, 3:79, August, 1842.
[10] *Ibid.*, 4:89, July, 1843.
[11] Joseph Smith's History, 4:482.

appointed commissioners for the sale of stock. The concern was to be governed by twenty trustees, elected annually by the shareholders.[12] The history of the Agricultural and Manufacturing Association is obscure, but apparently in the rigorous competition for capital in Nauvoo it did not fare well. Wilford Woodruff reported of a public meeting on June 18, 1842, "The main part of the day was taken up by the business of the Agricultural and Manufacturing Society. Arrangements were entered into to commence operations immediately, under the charter granted by the legislature." [13] The Association planned to build and operate a pottery factory in Nauvoo. But a year later the building was still unfinished and the making of pottery was not yet begun. In May, 1843, Apostle John Taylor wrote an editorial in the *Nauvoo Neighbor* criticizing the slow progress of the enterprise. "We would ask of the agricultural and manufacturing society . . . why it is that the building of the pottery is not progressing this spring? A great deal of money has already been expended in building . . . we have as good potters as can be found elsewhere, and why is it that when money is so *scarce* we have to send it away for articles we can make ourselves?" [14] Sidney Rigdon, the president of the Agricultural and Manufacturing Association, replied that the "first great object" of the company was to build the pottery to produce "the various kinds of pottery in common use in the country." A search had been made for suitable clays by persons "such as had been employed all their lives in the business," and they

[12] Joseph Smith's History, 4:303–305; *Laws . . . the Twelfth General Assembly*, pp. 139–141. Thirty-four associates were named in the act, including the first board of trustees.

The twenty trustees were:

Allred, James	Knight, Vinson	Robinson, George W.
Barrett, John	Law, William	Smith, Don Carlos
Bennett, John C.	Law, Wilson	Smith, Hyrum
Haws, John	Marks, William	Thompson, Robert B.
Haws, Peter	Miller, George	Turley, Theodore
Huntington, William	Rigdon, Sidney	Wells, Daniel H.
James, Samuel	Robinson, Ebenezer	

The other fourteen associates were:

Barlow, Israel	Higbee, Isaac	Smith, Joseph
Cutler, Alpheas	Kelly, James	Snyder, John
Foster, Robert D.	Knowlton, Sidney	Soby, Leonard
Green, John P.	Olney, John F.	Weld, John F.
Higbee, Elias	Pratt, Orson	

[13] Joseph Smith's History, 5:35.
[14] *Nauvoo Neighbor*, May 13, 1843.

reported soils in the immediate vicinity as good as those used in England. Land had then been purchased and a stone building begun to house the works. The association planned also to "supply all their workmen with all their necessaries as far as could be," perhaps partly in lieu of pay. "A considerable amount of land . . . for agricultural purposes . . . was obtained in order to supply such provisions," and "arrangements were making" to stock it. The building "had progressed . . . with much rapidity . . . up to the height of one story. . . . Persons possessing means felt desirable of investing . . . in the business. All was prosperous and all flattering." But then political developments, said Rigdon, had paralyzed the whole operation. A number of candidates for the state legislature to convene in December, 1842, had campaigned on platforms promising the repeal of Nauvoo's charters, including that of the Agricultural and Mechanical Association. Though the legislature when it met had not repealed the charters, such bills had been introduced, and many legislators were disposed to see them enacted. "Not that the company supposed that there was any such power vested in the legislature," said Ridgon, "either in the constitution or in common sense; but they did not know how far a reckless spirit might lead men in the violation of both." The old Mormon fear of outside legal interference in their ventures had reasserted itself. "As the matter now stands," continued Rigdon, "those having capital are at a loss whether to invest it that way or not, lest the same reckless spirit may inevitably carry the design into effect." Rigdon vigorously defended the integrity and capability of the company: "Work has not stopped for want of means," he said; "means, material, and workmen of the first order are all at hand. But where is the safety, while such doctrines are boldly maintained by our legislature?" [15]

There was the prospect that Nauvoo might even have a railroad. "A charter has been obtained from the legislature," wrote Smith in August, 1840, "for a railroad from Warsaw, being immediately below the rapids of the Mississippi, to this place—a distance of about twenty miles, which if carried into operation will be of incalculable advantage . . . as steamboats can only ascend the rapids at a high stage of water." The proposed Des Moines Rapids Railroad would link Nauvoo with a proposed Warsaw, Peoria, and Wabash Railroad running from Warsaw on the Mississippi through Carthage, Macomb, Peoria, and Bloomington, on to the Indiana border where it would connect with the Lake Erie and Wabash Canal. When the

[15] *Nauvoo Neighbor,* June 21, 1843, and Joseph Smith's History, 5:436–438.

Des Moines Rapids road was not built within the time limit set by the original charter, extensions were granted. But apparently construction was never begun.[16]

Wherever there was a fall of a few feet in a stream of water, there was a potential location for a water-driven mill. Before the era of the steam engine such millsites were valued also as townsites. Nauvoo was located at a millsite, but one of enormous proportions, since the millstream was the Mississippi River. The city lay along the upper reaches of the Des Moines Rapids, and as the river swept around the Nauvoo peninsula it fell enough to provide an adequate head of water to drive machinery. Undaunted by the magnitude of the project, the Mormons sought repeatedly to harness the great stream. Perhaps the first and most spectacular proposal was made by John C. Bennett early in 1841. Main Street in Nauvoo ran south to north across the flat, intersecting the river at both ends. At the north end of the street there was a ravine paralleling the street and forming a narrow inlet of the river. Bennett proposed a wing dam beginning at the mouth of the ravine and extending north into the river, and the excavation of a ship canal from near the inlet south right down the middle of Main Street until it regained the river on the lower side of the peninsula, "Terminating in a grand reservoir on the bank of [the] river, east of the foot of said street." Sheltered wharfage, said Bennett, "and the best harbor for steamboats, for winter quarters, on this magnificent stream," would thus be provided. The canal would be about two miles long. But the chief benefit would be water power: a millrace running straight through the heart of the city would be ample, said Bennett, "for propelling any amount of machinery for mill and manufacturing purposes, so essentially necessary to the building up of a great commercial city in the heart of one of the most productive and delightful countries on earth." Smith obtained authorization from the city council for a survey of the canal, but investigation proved the scheme impracticable. The northern end of the proposed cut lay across a stratum of solid limestone. Instead of a canal site it became a quarry for Temple stone.[17]

Two years later, in 1843, Smith turned his attention again to har-

[16] Joseph Smith's History, 4:178; *Laws of the Ninth General Assembly of the State of Illinois*, 1835–1836, p. 76; *Laws . . . the Twelfth General Assembly*, p. 197. The act to incorporate the Des Moines Rapids Railroad Company does not appear in the legislative record, but is alluded to in supplementary legislation.
[17] Joseph Smith's History, 4:291, 292, 297.

nessing the river. On November 22 he recorded in his journal, "walked down to the river to look at the stream, rocks, etc. . . . Suggested the idea of petitioning congress for a grant to make a canal over the falls, or a dam to turn the water to the city, so that we might erect mills and other machinery." There were several petitions to Congress in the following months, but none of them concerned damming the river. Apparently Smith had decided to promote that development himself. The city council on December 8 passed an ordinance granting Joseph Smith "and his successors for the term of perpetual succession" authority to build extensive wing dams in the river. He was to have "full liberty to use the said dam and water for the purpose of propelling mills and machinery" to use the catch basin as a harbor for riverboats "for which [he] may construct docks, wharfs, and landings," and to receive tolls collected for the use of a road along the top of the dam. His compensation in tolls, wharfage, and water power use was to be set and regulated by the city council. The plan was to build a wing dam from a point "below the Nauvoo House" (the foot of Main Street) in a general westerly direction to an island that lay between Nauvoo and Montrose, Iowa. A "dam, pier, or breakwater" would then be built from the island north to a sandbar, creating a basin that utilized the fall of the river. Such an arrangement would obviate the necessity for damming the whole river and blocking the channel with the subsequent necessity to construct a bypass canal and locks.[18] During the winter and spring of 1844 politics and persecution preoccupied the Mormon leaders, and events were to climax in June with the lynching of the Prophet. But interest in the dam continued nevertheless. "'Tis the greatest speculation in the world," wrote Brigham Young to Reuben Hedlock, President of British Mission, in May, 1844. "Could five, six, or seven thousand dollars be raised to commence the dam . . . any machinery [even] a cotton factory . . . might be propelled by water. . . . A world of cotton and woolen goods are wanted here." [19] After a degree of confidence had been re-established following the excitement and fear caused by Smith's death, interest in the dam reawakened. In the winter of 1844–1845 an association of artisans tried to finance a factory for themselves. At one of the "Trades Meetings," as they were called, Alanson Ripley, who had surveyed

[18] *Ibid.*, 6:80, 106. The island and sandbar were inundated when the Keokuk Dam was built and are now under water.
[19] Letter of Young to Hedlock, *ibid.*, 6:353.

the damsite for Smith, suggested that the association raise its sights to include the dam. The Prophet had estimated the cost at $250,000, recalled Ripley; "This sounds large, but may be accomplished by the citizens in a short space of time." He estimated that ten mills might be powered at the dam. In the discussion that followed considerable enthusiasm was aroused, and a committee was appointed to talk to the trustees-in-trust to ascertain the Church's position on the matter. "No doubt," said a brother (Edward?) Hunter, "we shall [eventually] make some use of the rapids for manufacturing." It was then January 2, 1845. Trades Meetings on January 7 and 15 were given over to discussion of the venture; interest grew and a course of action was decided upon. A "large assemblage" subscribed $1,550, moved to acquire the land at the site where the dam would join the shore, and inquired about stone and machinery. By the end of January the officers of the Agricultural and Manufacturing Association asked to join the enterprise, and on February 5 Ripley was ready with a detailed report of what might be accomplished. He estimated a three-foot head of water and thought that three wheels might be put into operation for $7,500. There would be room for fifty-three wheels in all. Suddenly there was widespread interest and excitement in Nauvoo about the dam. Perhaps at last it might actually be possible to get it built, and thus open the long-blocked door to the industrialization of Nauvoo. A "Nauvoo Water Power Company" was formed, with Apostle John E. Page president. Shares of stock were to be sold for labor or goods as well as cash. [20] But it was too late to float any more large-scale capital ventures in Nauvoo. The city charter had just been repealed by the state legislature; and though Brigham Young expressed optimism about the future of the city in June, in September he was to order the city abandoned. Work on the dam was scarcely begun.[21]

The industries planned for Nauvoo were large and extensive; those actually developed were for the most part small craft and home enterprises. The Prophet recognized the necessity, under the

---

[20] *The Nauvoo Neighbor*, January 8, 15, 29, February 5, March 5, 1845. "The Nauvoo Water Power Company" was not incorporated by state law.

[21] For Young's outlook in June, 1845, see his letter to Wilford Woodruff, June 27, in Roberts, ed., *History of the Church, Period II: Apostolic Interregnum*, 7:431. This is the final volume of the set of Joseph Smith's History. In 1848 the citizens of Keokuk, at the foot of the Des Moines Rapids twelve miles below Nauvoo, began to agitate for a dam across the river; and in 1877 the Federal Government finally began the construction of such a dam. Roberts and Moorehead, *History of Lee County*, p. 243.

circumstances, of such a trend. "Instead of going abroad to buy goods," he said in October, 1843, ". . . buy grain, cattle, flax, wool, and work it up yourselves. . . . Set our women to work, and stop their spinning street yarns and talking about spiritual wives."[22] Lacking capital, large-scale power sources, and machinery, Nauvoo's economy remained mostly pre-industrial. There were at least two steam sawmills, one equipped with a grist mill.[23] There was a "match factory," a "leather manufactory," a tanyard, a rope and cord maker, a lime kiln, several brickyards, a glove and strawbonnet shop, a brewery, a bakery and confectionery, a pottery, a "tool factory," a carpenter's and joiner's shop, a water grist mill, a blacksmithy, a "cast-iron foundry" owned by Hiram Kimball and George W. Robinson, a jeweler, gilder, and watchmaker, a "comb manufactory," a spinning-wheel maker, a cabinet maker, a printing office and book bindery, and several tailors, weavers, cobblers, cordwainers, and wagoners. The record does not indicate whether the products of the city were sold in outside markets to any extent.[24]

The conditions of the Nauvoo society and economy were propitious for the formation of laborers' cooperative industries. There was little capital but there were many skilled artisans willing and anxious for industrial employment. The bond of fellowship in the Church made cooperation a natural practice. Furthermore the cooperation movement was creating great enthusiasm among the working classes in England in the early forties. In 1843 a guild of boot and shoemakers was formed in Nauvoo; but it was criticized, misunderstood, and even feared by those who thought that the purpose was to monopolize local cobbling in order to force the already high price of footwear even higher. The guild members sought to quiet apprehension by explaining their true objectives in the *Nauvoo Neighbor:* the combination was a concerted effort to bring the cost of cobbling down sufficiently to enable Nauvoo-made boots to compete with the products of eastern factories, "and consequently giving

[22] Joseph Smith's History, 6:58.
[23] The mills were owned by the Law brothers and Edward Hunter. Joseph Smith sold land to the former for their mill, and bought ninety acres of nearby timberland to supply the latter. He was active in both enterprises. See Joseph Smith's History, 4:482, 501.
[24] This list of businesses was compiled from an article on Nauvoo building enterprises in the *Nauvoo Wasp*, October 29, 1842, and from advertisements in the *Wasp* and *Nauvoo Neighbor*, 1842–1845. Kimball and Robinson advertised almost continuously for "stone coal" for the foundry, suggesting that they lacked a ready supply of good fuel.

employment to about two hundred boot and shoemakers . . . who
have come hither in accordance with the commands of God. . . .
All that is wanting is a little capital. . . ." Their plan was a producers' cooperative for buying raw materials and then manufacturing
and selling a finished product. They would barter when necessary,
even taking raw hides from farmers in payment for boots. "To conclude," said the bootmakers' guild, ". . . we would quote the language of the celebrated Glasgow spinners: that 'the working man's
only protection . . . is Union . . .

> 'Union walls are high and grand
> Union walls, if nobly manned,
> Union walls are made to stand,
> Against the strongest foe.' [25]

In March, 1844, the citizens of the Tenth Ward established a producers' and consumers' cooperative. Smith, who attended the organizational meeting, said that the benefits of a cooperative store were
"clearly pointed out." It would furnish employment for mechanics,
and "furnish the necessaries and comforts of life on the lowest possible terms." [26] In the autumn of 1844, when the Twelve were trying
to restore confidence in Nauvoo after the Prophet's assassination,
there was an attempt made to begin a general producers' and consumers' cooperative, to "manufacture rather than import" the city's
needs. Apostle John Taylor presided at a meeting called to promote
the idea, and he and other Church leaders spoke to the assembly.
They said that "we possessed the power of workmen—(the efficient
capital, *labor*) to produce all the dry goods, hardware, cutlery,
crockery, or any other commodity. . . ." Taylor discussed "the best
method of carrying on business for the good of the whole, without
creating monopolies." Another meeting held in November was addressed by Brigham Young and Taylor. "The drift of their discourses," said the report of the occasion, "were [*sic*] to go ahead and
carry out the project of building up Nauvoo by its own mechanical
and manual labor." "There is no speculation in it," Taylor assured
the group. "We can eventually carry it out on matter of fact principles." Young said, "We can eventually produce a reaction and bring
back some of the money that has been going away from us all the
time." Mayor Spencer concluded: "it [is] in the interest of every
Latter-day Saint to use their [*sic*] influence (both pecuniary and in

[25] *Nauvoo Neighbor*, September 13, 27, 1843.
[26] Joseph Smith's History, 6:263.

labor,) and to come forward and assist to build us all up as one.
. . . We are identified as one and ought to feel the interest of all
—we must support one another." A cooperative carriage works was
organized January 15, 1845, as a result; but the cooperative movement as a whole merged with and gave added impetus to the dam
and water power industries promotion.[27]

The one industry which employed more labor and capital probably than all others in Nauvoo combined was the building industry.
Most descriptions of Nauvoo speak of the continuous raising of
houses and public buildings. The population of thousands had not
only to be housed but in many instances rehoused, since the original
shelter was often a hastily constructed log or frame hut. Even Joseph Smith and Brigham Young had humble dwellings for several
years. Smith lived in a two-story log and frame house until 1842
when he moved into his new "Nauvoo Mansion"; Young moved his
family out of a damp log cabin and into a twenty-two-by-sixteen-
foot, story-and-a-half brick house in April, 1843, "thankful to God for
the privilege of having a comfortable, though small habitation." [28]
In October, 1842, a raft of pine timbers, lumber, and shingles "covering an acre" arrived in the river from the Mormon lumbering
camp on the Black River in Wisconsin territory. Said the *Wasp*, reporting the event, "The rapid increase of our city is almost incredi-
ble. . . . Every day is seen, phoenix-like, the ponderous fronts of
new and extensive buildings starting into existence, peering themselves above the roofs of the more humble ones that surround them,
and where lots [in a short time] smile under the products of cultiva-
tion to be crowned with residences. . . ." [29] John Needham wrote:

We have a good many brick houses, and others are frame-wood and log
houses. Some . . . appear strange to the person who has been accustomed to live in a fine-built place, *but a great many are quite smart large
brick houses,* which would look well in any city. I was quite surprised to
find so many good brick-built houses. Brick houses, stone, and others, are

[27] *Nauvoo Neighbor,* October 9, 16, November 13, 1844, January 15, 1845.

[28] Joseph Smith's History, 6:33; Brigham Young's journal in the *Millennial
Star,* 26:184, March 19, 1864. An idea of the cost of such a house as Young's
may be gained from Edwin Bottomly's experience in building a comparable
dwelling in southern Wisconsin in 1842. His fifteen-by-thirty-foot, story-and-a-
half brick house cost an estimated £50, or $242. He used 23,000 bricks at $3.50
a thousand; lime for the mortar was ten cents a bushel. See Quaife, *The
Bottomly Letters,* pp. 59, 87. Prices in Nauvoo may have been higher.

[29] *Nauvoo Wasp,* October 29, 1842. Joseph Smith said that the raft contained
90,000 feet of lumber and 24,000 feet of timber. Under entry for October 13,
1842, in Joseph Smith's History, 5:169, 170.

building as fast as they can, and I see a great difference in the short time I have been here. It is a saying in Nauvoo, "they spring up like mushrooms. . . ." In a general way the houses have one good room below and a bed room. Some have more. . . . I did not know but that I might have had to live gipsy fashion, but I soon got a home. . . . Two or three areas in the city have a very business-like appearance with having different kinds of shops.[30]

The demand for housing and land improvements made speculative building attractive to both capital and labor. John Taylor editorialized in the *Neighbor* in May, 1843, that the lag in manufacturing activity might be traced to this diversion of effort. "Our mechanics . . . our merchants . . . and all our neighbors have been wondering why we have not paid more attention to manufactures. . . ." wrote Taylor. "We do not mean . . . that the Saints are idlers. . . . The difficulty is that men are not employed at what they ought to be. Men that have been accustomed to manufacturing cotton goods are making ditches on the prairie, woolen manufacturers are carrying the hod, and working at day labor . . . and potters have been metamorphosed into builders and wood choppers."[31] In the spring of 1842 Ebenezer Robinson took the money he had received from sale of the *Times and Seasons* printing shop and built a "brick row of eleven tenements" for rentals. The following January Hiram Kimball, who had interests in many Nauvoo enterprises, was advertising to let a contract for the making of a million bricks— enough to build thirty to forty brick houses. He also wanted bids for the building of "twelve hundred rods of ditch and turf fence." In February, 1844, "A Builder" advertised for a half-million bricks. The result was that as time passed newly arrived citizens with money or sound credit found houses ready for occupancy.[32] Even as early as July, 1841, a wagon train of seventy Saints from Chester County, Pennsylvania, and another with an unspecified number from Canada all found a place to live "in two or three days."[33] Domestic building was sufficiently attractive to divert men and materials even

[30] *Millennial Star*, 4:88, September, 1843. Needham added, "The streets not yet paved, but are in the rough, in dry weather pleasant, except for a little dust, but in wet weather unpleasant: some are better than others."

[31] *Nauvoo Neighbor*, May 31, 1843.

[32] *The Return*, 3:13, January, 1890; *Nauvoo Wasp*, January 4, 1843; *Nauvoo Neighbor*, February 21, 1844. In April, 1842, the city council had standardized the size of brick molds used in the city by law. *Nauvoo Wasp*, April 30, 1842.

[33] From a letter of Heber C. Kimball, July 15, 1841, quoted in Larsen, *Prelude to the Kingdom*, p. 49.

from the Temple and the Nauvoo House hotel, the two most cherished public building projects.

A sizable lumbering camp in Wisconsin had been established in 1842 specifically to provide for the construction of the Temple and the Nauvoo House; [34] but in the fall of 1843 Bishop George Miller, who was in charge of the "pineries" as they were called, was surprised to discover a different arrangement:

when I took down the last rafts in the fall season . . . I found a great deal of the lumber that we had (the last two seasons of toil and sacrifice) made for the temple and Nauvoo House had, to my great mortification, been used for other purposes than those intended. The Temple Committee said that the workmen must needs have houses, and they had to pay their men. But the truth of the case was, that that committee had become house builders; they were not alone content to have fresh eggs to set themselves, but they wanted eggs to set all their numerous brood of chickens, and that it was really convenient to use the material provided for the Nauvoo House (as its operations were temporarily suspended,) as in like manner the Temple materials also, as we had in common such productive mills in the pinery.

Miller remonstrated with Joseph Smith about what he considered a breach of faith; but "Joseph told me to be content, and that he would see by and by that all would be made right. . . ." [35] However, the Prophet himself did not take such a purist's view as Miller. "Tell the Temple committee," he had ordered the previous April, "to put hands enough on that house (on the diagonal corner from the brick store), and finish it right off. The Lord hath need of other houses as well as the Temple." [36] The Black River lumber was in great demand, and the price was high; but it was hoped, said the *Wasp* in August, 1842, that there would be a sufficient quantity sent down from Wisconsin to "eventually level the price of lumber to other commodities." During the 1843 season the pineries rafted 600,000 board feet of lumber to Nauvoo including a "large amount of hewed timbers . . . shingles, and a raft of barn boards." [37]

When John D. Lee returned from a mission in August, 1843, he found Nauvoo "full of new homes and public buildings." The Temple walls were up to the second story, a new Masonic Temple was

[34] See below, Chapter 7.
[35] Miller, *Correspondence*, p. 15. Smith added that "it was most likely his persecutors would let him alone since his find discharge by Judge Pope, and he would in future have more leisure."
[36] Joseph Smith's History, 5:368.
[37] *Navooo Wasp*, August 4, 1842; Miller, *Correspondence*, p. 14.

almost ready for dedication, and a large armory, built on the bluff near the Temple "for the security of the public arms" of the Nauvoo Legion, was completed and in use. There were new meeting houses for the Seventies and High Priests under construction, and the Prophet's "Nauvoo Mansion" hotel would soon be open for business.[38]

The erection of numerous public buildings and the bureaucratization of the corporate life of Church and Kingdom provided a kind of patronage which was apparently divided among favored and deserving Churchmen. Lee was employed after his return as a laborer and then as supervisor of the construction of the Seventies' Hall and additionally as a "special policeman," jobs which he found, according to his biographer, "both enjoyable and remunerative." "In the meanwhile," wrote Lee in his journal, "I had an opportunity of teaching of the broadsword exercise . . . by which I was enable [*sic*] to help myself to about $5,000 in tithing labor for which I was enable together with the avails of my own labor otherwise to build quite a house about 50 feet in length—breadth 23 feet 2½ storys above ground—." [39] The Temple provided fulltime employment for some laborers and for supervisors and tithe collectors. The construction of the Nauvoo House required the services of Apostle Wilford Woodruff in 1841 and 1842 to operate its "provision store." There were in addition numerous paying positions in the Church bureaucracy and the Nauvoo Legion with its salaried officer corps and elaborate staffs.[40]

Joseph Smith's position as Prophet, director of public enterprises, and private entrepreneur made him liable to charges that he enriched himself at the expense of his followers. But he seemed oblivious of any "conflict of interests"; he repeated that his affairs and those of the Church were inseparable, an untenable position for the Trustee-in-Trust of the corporation to take. Smith's business activities typified the Mormon mixture of public and private enterprise. He had been accorded the right to deed Church property to himself and his relatives by the October, 1839, Conference. He was to take

[38] Brooks, *John Doyle Lee*, p. 57; Gayler, "The Mormons in Western Illinois," p. 122.
[39] Brooks, *John Doyle Lee*, pp. 59, 65.
[40] Cowley, *Wilford Woodruff*, p. 155; Gayler, "The Mormons in Western Illinois," p. 122; letter of an "Irish High Priest" from Nauvoo, March 27, 1842, quoted in the *Journal of the Illinois State Historical Society*, 46:313–315 (1953). The writer said he was appointed "Secretary of War" under John C. Bennett.

such property "as in his wisdom he shall judge expedient, till his own, and his father's household, shall have an inheritance secured to them in our midst. . . ." The Twelve resolved in August, 1841, "that we for ourselves, and the Church we represent, approve of the proceedings of President Smith, so far as he has gone, in making over certain properties to his wife, children, and friends for their support, and that he continue . . . agreeably to the vote of the General Conference . . . in October, 1839." [41] The Prophet benefited from other emoluments and gifts from time to time. In 1841 the Twelve, arranging the finances of the new five-thousand-copy English edition of the *Book of Mormon*, resolved that "said committee settle the financial or business matters thereof with Joseph Smith, to whom the profits rightly belong." [42] When Smith was acquitted in January, 1843, from the attempts of Missouri to extradite him, the Twelve commended "to the consideration of the brethren the situation of our President, who has long had his business affairs deranged, and has been . . . obliged to expend large sums of money in procuring his release from unjust persecution, leaving him destitute of the necessaries. . . . We therefore recommend that collections be taken at the various meetings for his benefit . . . provisions will be an excellent substitute . . . for the laborer is worthy of his hire." The city council acted that same month to pay Smith $500 annually as mayor, and $3 a day when he sat as justice of the Municipal Court.[43] The Twelve continued to be solicitous of the Prophet's welfare. In January, 1844, they invited the brethren to cut wood for him. According to Young two hundred loads were cut and a hundred hauled to his Nauvoo Mansion hotel.[44]

Since Smith was apparently penniless when he arrived in Illinois in 1839 and seemed always short or devoid of money, the capital base from which he launched his various business enterprises was the gratuity in lands he deeded himself, and whatever credit he was able to obtain. The Prophet's trade in real estate was his most absorbing business interest. In addition he owned stock in the Nauvoo House Association (see Chapter 7) and probably in the Agricultural and Manufacturing Association. In the summer of 1840 he pur-

[41] Joseph Smith's History, 4:412, 413. No such action appears in the minutes of the October, 1839, conference as recorded in Smith's journal, but the Twelve alluded specifically to such a conference resolution.
[42] Joseph Smith's History, 4:325.
[43] *Nauvoo Wasp*, January 28, 1843.
[44] Brigham Young's journal, in the *Millennial Star*, 26:326, May 21, 1864.

chased a steamboat from the federal government, named it *Nauvoo*, and entered it in the upper river trade. It may be that Smith did not pay for the boat, however, since the government obtained a judgment against him for $5,184.31 in the U.S. District Court for Illinois on July 11, 1842. The details are unavailable, but the steamboat purchase seems to have been the only reason for such a judgment.[45] In 1842 two citizens of Nauvoo, Dan Jones and Levi Moffatt, built a little steamer, *Maid of Iowa*, which during the immigration season each year brought Mormon convert-gatherers from New Orleans to Nauvoo. Jones, himself a Welsh convert, captained the boat until the spring of 1843 when the Twelve ordered him on a mission back to Wales. Smith then purchased a half-interest in the *Maid of Iowa* for $1,375 (in notes, not cash). Early in June the city council awarded the Prophet exclusive rights to operate a ferry boat at Nauvoo; competitors would have their boats confiscated. Smith then put *Maid of Iowa* into ferry service between Nauvoo and Montrose. Despite the monopoly, the venture failed to prosper, and in April, 1844, it was in debt $1,700. "After much conversation and deliberation," wrote Smith in his journal, "I agreed to buy out Jones, by giving him property in the city worth $1,321, and assuming the debts." In less than two months the Prophet was dead and the *Maid of Iowa* became a part of the tangled affairs of his estate.[46]

In the autumn of 1841 Smith built a two-story brick building a short distance west on Water Street from his house for a general store. The upstairs contained his office and a room for conferences and small assemblies. In November Bishop Newel Whitney bought $5,000 worth of merchandise for Smith in the East, and in December Edward Hunter purchased a stock of goods which Smith accepted "as payment on your debt, so far as it goes . . . as you propose. . . ." Hunter owed Smith at least $3,500 for land purchased in September. Three days before Christmas thirteen wagons of goods bought in St. Louis arrived from Warsaw with "sugar, molasses, glass, salt, tea, coffee, etc." "The original stock purchased in

[45] Miller, *Correspondence*, p. 7; Hancock County Deed Book B, pp. 31, 592. This judgment was entered in the county records with no details given; the records of the U.S. District Court for Illinois for the year 1842 are not extant. The judgment was not collected and was brought as a claim against Smith's estate after his death.

[46] Joseph Smith's History, 5:386, 417–418, 6:334; Inez Smith Davis, *Story of the Church* (Independence, Missouri, 1955), pp. 261, 262; *Nauvoo Neighbor*, June 7, 1843. Davis says that the Church owned the *Maid of Iowa* in 1842 after it was built, but this is apparently incorrect.

New Orleans," said Smith, "[had] been detained at St. Louis by one Holbrook, inkeeper, under false pretenses."[47] On January 5, 1842, the Prophet opened his store to the public with evident pride. "The . . . building is somewhat spacious . . . for a country store," he wrote:

The painting of the store has been executed by . . . one of our English brethren; and the counters, drawers, and pillars present a very respectable representation of oak, mahogany and marble for a backwoods establishment.

The Lord has blessed our exertions in a wonderful manner . . . [and] we have been enabled to secure goods to a considerable amount . . . sufficient to fill all the shelves as soon as they were completed, and have some in reserve, both in loft and cellar.

Our assortment is tolerably good—very good considering the different purchases made by different individuals at different times . . . the hearts of many of the poor brethren and sisters will be made glad with those comforts which are now within their reach.

The store has been filled to overflowing [on opening day] and I have stood behind the counter all day, dealing out goods as steady as any clerk you ever saw, to oblige those who were compelled to go without their usual Christmas or New Year's dinners, for want of a little sugar, molasses, raisins, etc., etc.; and to please myself also, for I love to wait upon the Saints, and be a servant to all, hoping that I may be exalted in the due time of the Lord.[48]

The trouble with the store was the trouble with the whole Nauvoo economy; business was brisk, but there was too much credit and too little cash. The steady flow of goods from the shelves and bins suggested that the enterprise was prospering, when in fact it was approaching insolvency. The record suggests that Smith was perhaps more interested in supplying the citizens of Nauvoo with much needed goods than with profits or with the financial integrity of the business. All debts were to be paid eventually out of the increment of the Kingdom. Smith depended increasingly on Edward Hunter, a propertied convert, to finance his store operations and to handle credit for him; in return the Prophet apparently gave land, his own or the Church's, and was agent for Hunter's growing interests in

[47] The Church had given two notes to a "Holbrook and Firm" in 1837 in Ohio, one for $287 and the other for an undetermined amount; apparently neither was retired. It may be that the Holbrook who detained Smith's goods "under false pretenses" was trying to collect a bad debt. Joseph Smith's History, 4:447, 482, 483; Joseph Smith Estate Papers, Office of the Hancock County Clerk.

[48] Smith to Edward Hunter, January 5, 1842, in Joseph Smith's History, 4:491, 492.

Nauvoo. "I have purchased the lands you desired," Smith wrote Hunter on March 8, 1842, "and will use my influence to have the improvements made which you wish." The need to replenish stock at the store caused Smith to divert contributions intended for his cherished Temple and Nauvoo House—an extraordinary move for him. "The eight hundred dollars for the Temple and Nauvoo House, I wish you to bring in goods," he instructed Hunter, "for which I will give you stock and credit as soon as received."[49] However, much more was needed to continue the operation, and Smith began to realize that he had neither the time nor the money to be a merchant.

In the spring of 1842 the Prophet added to his other duties those of Mayor, Chief Magistrate, and Register of Deeds of Nauvoo. The Temple and Nauvoo House were under construction, and though each had a building committee, Smith attended closely to their affairs. He was writing the *Book of Abraham,* the troubles with Galland, Bennett, and Hotchkiss were brewing, and the land business, on which all other operations seemed ultimately to depend, was a constant, absorbing concern. The money problem was acute; specie had practically disappeared, and commercial and bank paper was even less dependable than usual. "The State Bank is down," Smith wrote Hunter, "and we cannot tell you what bank would be safe a month hence . . . gold and silver is the only safe money a man can keep these times. . . ." Hunter should bring specie to Nauvoo if he could. It would command a premium in excess of bank deposit rates; besides, "The bank you deposit in might fall before you had time to draw it out again." Smith hoped in March, 1842, to be able to shift the responsibility of the store to Hunter and to other men of means. The Prophet wrote Hunter to bring as large a stock of goods as possible to Nauvoo; eight or ten thousand dollars' worth would be advantageous. "I will purchase them of you . . . if we agree to terms," said Smith, "or you can have my new brick store to rent . . . it is a very fine house, and cost me a handsome sum."[50] After March of 1842 Smith dropped the store business from the cognizance of his journal, and evidence is lacking to suggest the course of its affairs. He never devoted himself to the day by day operation; whether or not it remained in continuous business is uncertain. More than two years later, in May, 1844, Hiram Kimball added it to his

[49] Smith to Hunter, March 9, 1842, in *ibid.,* 4:548, 549.
[50] *Ibid.,* 5:548, 549.

numerous business interests in Nauvoo, advertising a "general dry goods store" in Joseph Smith's store building.[51] Brigham Young offered a reflection upon Smith's merchandising operations in Nauvoo and elsewhere when in the 1850's he refused to allow the Church in Utah to engage in similar enterprises. "Why does not our church keep a store here?" he asked. "Many can answer that question who have lived . . . in Nauvoo, in Missouri, [and] in Kirtland. . . . Let me just give you a few reasons why Joseph could not keep a store, and be a merchant. . . .'" If Smith demanded cash, said Young, the brethren would leave in a huff and say, " 'Brother Joseph is no Prophet; I have found *that* out, and I am glad of it.' " But if credit were extended, the response was, " 'He is a first-rate man, and I fully believe he is a Prophet. See here, he has trusted me this shawl.' " Smith's response to such behavior, said Young, was " 'These goods make the people apostatize; so over they go, they are of less value than the people.' " Young concluded that the Saints would "lie awake nights" pondering ways to pay debts owed gentiles; but they expected indefinite credit of the brethren, especially of the Prophet, as a natural right. "Joseph was a first rate fellow with them all the time," said Young, "provided he never would ask them to pay him." [52]

Private and public finances were becoming so much overextended, and the prospect of retiring debts so remote, that the Mormons resorted finally to cancellation, repudiation, and bankruptcy to extricate themselves.

Many debts incurred at Kirtland before 1838 still remained unpaid, and the temple there was mortgaged. In Nauvoo the unhappy Kirtland experience with its bankruptcies and recriminations seemed long ago and far away; but the outstanding notes of the Church persisted, to the annoyance of brethren engaged in the building of another city with its own complex debts. Smith had sent Oliver Granger, a trusted and propertied brother, to Kirtland as Church agent to settle affairs if possible. The Prophet learned that Granger had been very sick, and wrote him in May, 1841, to urge that Dr. Galland, then in the East trading lands, be made a party to Kirtland matters. The judgment against the Kirtland Temple must be removed, even if Granger had to use his own money to do it. "I will settle with you," wrote Smith, "the same as if you held [the mort-

[51] *Nauvoo Neighbor,* May 15, 1844.
[52] Sermons of Brigham Young on October 9, 1852, and October 8, 1855, quoted in Leonard J. Arrington, *Great Basin Kingdom,* pp. 83, 84.

gage] yourself." If debts could not be retired, they might at least be brought within the fellowship. "This I must beg leave to urge upon you to do, for delays are dangerous, your health is precarious and if anything should occur—so that you were to bid adieu to mortality . . . I should again be involved in difficulties from which it would be impossible for me to extricate myself. . . . I am very anxious indeed to have the matters which concern the First Presidency settled as soon as possible, for until they are I have to labor under a load that is impossible to bear." [53] Galland did nothing to help the Kirtland situation; and Smith's fears about his agent's health were justified. Granger died within a few months, though not before he freed the Temple from encumbrance. Smith had finally to settle not with Granger, but with his heirs. The month after Smith wrote Granger he was at Monmouth, Illinois, when a man rushed up and said, "Which is Jo Smith? I have got a five dollar Kirtland bill, and I'll be damned if he don't pay it back I'll sue him, for his name is to it." The Prophet said he paid the man in specie, "which he took very reluctantly, being anxious to kick up a fuss." [54] But there were far too many Kirtland claims for that kind of redemption; at least $6,992 in unpaid notes from Kirtland were left in 1844 to be claims against Smith's estate. [55]

The policy which emerged regarding old debts was to repudiate them. The October, 1841, General Conference resolved that "the trustee-in-trust be instructed not to appropriate Church property to liquidate old claims that may be brought forward from Kirtland and Missouri." Hyrum Smith called attention of the Conference to "some embarrassment growing out of his signing, as security, a certain obligation in Kirtland in favor of Mr. Eaton." A resolution was then adopted "that Church property here not be appropriated to liquidate such claim." [56] Early in 1843 a brother Abel Owen came to

[53] Smith to Oliver Granger, May 4, 1841, in *Journal of the Illinois State Historical Society,* 40:85–86 (1947). The "Bro Carlos" discussed in p. 86n. was evidently Carlos Granger, not Don Carlos Smith.

[54] Joseph Smith's History, 4:368.

[55] Joseph Smith Estate Papers.

[56] "Minutes of the General Conference of the Church—held at Nauvoo, October, 1841," in Joseph Smith's History, 4:427, 428. "Elder Lyman Wight spoke at some length . . . on the old debts and obligations that are so frequently brought up from Kirtland and Missouri; one of which, in the form of a $50 note, he held in his hand, and proclaimed it his text. . . . President Brigham Young made some appropriate and weighty remarks on the importance of more liberal consecrations and more energetic efforts to forward the work of building the Temple and the Nauvoo House; and after purchasing Elder Wight's text [for] fifty cents, tore it in pieces and gave it to the winds, saying, 'Go ye and do likewise, with all old claims against the Church.' "

Smith with a Kirtland claim "of considerable amount" and some of Oliver Granger's notes against the Church. He hoped to redeem them for something, "as he was poor and unable to labor and wanted something to live on." Smith told him to burn the notes, and then he would be helped. "He gave me the papers," wrote Smith, "and I gave him an order on Mr. Cowan for fifteen dollars worth of provisions. This was a gift, as the Church was not obligated to pay those debts." [57] Smith said of the notes issued by the Kirtland Safety Society, the Church's ill-fated bank, "I again caution all persons against receiving or trading in . . . currency called 'Kirtland Safety Society' . . . as all that was issued as genuine was redeemed." He said that the vault had been robbed "of several hundred thousand dollars," signatures forged, and the spurious bills circulated. Anyway, added Smith with unconscious irony, "the bills are not collectable by law in an unchartered institution." The Ohio legislature had refused to charter the bank, but the Mormons had operated it anyway as an "Anti-Banking Society." [58] Creditors who were ignored, however, had a way of becoming more insistent in their demands. On September 1, 1837, Hyrum Smith, Jared Carter, and Reynolds Cahoon had, as principals for the Church, signed a note to borrow $2,251.77 for one year from a firm of Halstead and Haines at Painesville, Ohio.[59] It was never paid and in the fall of 1841 Halstead and Haines gave it to agents for collection. "I must inform you," Smith replied to their demands,

that I am not in possession of means, belonging to me individually to liquidate those notes at present; I need not relate to you the persecution I have suffered, and the loss and confiscation of all my effects at various times as a reason of my inability . . . if [Halstead and Haines] will give me time (and no more than I must necessarily have), they shall have their pay in some way or other. I have means at command in the East, which . . . will enable me to pay them every whit. . . . All I ask of those gentlemen and this generation is that they should not tie up my hands, nor thwart me in my operations. If this is granted me, I pledge my word, yea, my sacred honor, that all that can in fairness be demanded at my hands . . . shall ultimately be adjusted to the satisfaction of all concerned.[60]

[57] Joseph Smith's History, 5:287.
[58] *Ibid.*, 6:429. See also Fielding, "The Mormon Economy in Kirtland, Ohio," 27:331 ff.
[59] Joseph Smith Estate Papers, FB3, 4. There were thirty-one co-signers of the note, including Joseph Smith, Brigham Young, Sidney Rigdon, Oliver Cowdery, Oliver Olney, Oliver Granger, Reuben Hedlock, and Vinson Knight.
[60] Smith to Browning and Bushnell, December 7, 1841, in Joseph Smith's History, 4:468.

The Halstead and Haines note was only one of many financial problems trying the Prophet just then. Smith was beginning his store business in the winter of 1841–1842. He managed in March, 1842, to repay William Marks, the Nauvoo Stake President, "who had loaned money and property to the Church at various times." Smith recorded with evident satisfaction, "Closed a settlement with William Marks . . . and paid him off, principal and interest to the last farthing for all that myself or the Church had had of him." The following day he recorded simply, "Settled with Brother Niswanger." But he was unable to retire his obligation to the estate of Oliver Granger. "Finally failed to effect anything," he complained. "[Gilbert] Granger refused to give up the papers to me, which he had received of his father, although I presented him deeds, mortgages and paper to the amount of some thousands against his father, more than he had against the Church." [61] It was in March that Smith advised Edward Hunter to bring specie to Nauvoo and offered him the store; the Prophet's financial condition was by then critical. Yet he did not suspend his land-buying operations. On March 2 he offered a New York land speculator $100 an acre for twenty acres in the city not yet owned by the Church, "or to take an agency to sell the same," and a month later he bought a farm for $1,150. [62]

General economic conditions in the state were at that time near a state of collapse. The whole country had remained depressed following 1839; and in Illinois the chronic fiscal crisis stemming from the enormous state debt incurred by the plan of works had further hindered recovery. Public and private credit had long been strained, and early in 1842 the Bank of Illinois at Shawneetown and the Illinois State Bank at Springfield failed. With the collapse of the two largest banks financial ruin spread throughout the state. What commerce there was was on a near barter basis. [63]

On April 12 the Quorum of Twelve initiated a program of debt forgiveness within the Church. Many Saints had borrowed from their brethren over a period of years, and the Presidency and Bishopric had done likewise to relieve the destitute from the Missouri expulsion and to build up Nauvoo. "Many of these claims have already been settled," said the Apostles, "many have been given up as

[61] *Ibid.*, 4:542, 565, 582. Smith itemized debts owed him by Oliver Granger amounting to $5883.50. Document in the Joseph Smith Papers, Illinois State Historical Library.

[62] *Ibid.*, 4:542, 582.

[63] Pease, *Frontier State*, pp. 232, 233, 312–314. The liquidation of these two banks extended into 1843.

cancelled by those who held them, and many remain unsettled." Now the Twelve urged a general cancellation of all such claims "which have arisen out of the difficulties and calamities of the Church . . . that when the Temple is completed, there will be nothing from this source to produce jars, and discords, strifes, and animosities, so as to prevent the blessings of heaven descending upon us as a people. . . . While things remain as they are, and men remain subject to the temptations of evil as they now are, the day of release, and year of jubilee cannot be. . . ." How were the Saints to prosper when the Church, the Presidency, the bishops, and "those who have sacrificed everything but life . . . for our salvation, are thus encumbered? It cannot be." They advised that all such "old accounts, notes, bonds, etc." be consecrated to the Temple; if they could be negotiated, the proceeds would advance the building; if not, after the Temple was finished, "we will make a burnt-offering of them . . . which shall bind the brethren together in the bonds of eternal peace, and love, and union . . . and you shall rejoice . . . that [you] have hearkened unto counsel, and set our brethren free. . . ." The Twelve concluded their admonition with a paradoxical reminder that the decision was up to the creditor, not the debtor: "Let nothing in this epistle be so construed as to destroy the validity of contracts, or give anyone license not to pay his debts. The commandment is to pay every man his dues, and no man can get to heaven who justly owes his brother or his neighbor, who has or can get the means and will not pay it; it is dishonest, and no dishonest man can enter where God is." [64]

Having repudiated debts owed to gentiles and urged the forgiveness of debt owed to brethren, the next step was not surprising: Smith and a number of other Mormon leaders filed petitions of bankruptcy. The legal firm of Ralston, Warren, and Wheat of Quincy advertised in the April, 1842, *Nauvoo Wasp* that they were "prepared to attend to all application for discharge under the Bankrupt Law. . . . One member of the firm will be at Carthage and Nauvoo about the 14th inst. . . ." [65] Calvin Warren was engaged by Smith on April 14 to commence "an investigation of the principles of general insolvency in my behalf according to the statutes. . . ." Bankruptcy was apparently a novel idea to the Prophet, and he explained the principle carefully in his journal. Although

[64] Joseph Smith's History, 4:592, 593.
[65] *Nauvoo Wasp*, April, 1842.

one's property might pay "but the least percentage, or none at all" of one's debts, "the individual was at liberty to start anew in the world, and was not subject to . . . any claims . . . held against him previous to his insolvency. . . ." The prospect of a new start financially was appealing. "The justice or injustice of such a principle in law," Smith said,

I leave for them who made it, the United States. Suffice it to say, the law was as good for the Saints as for the Gentiles and whether I would or not, I was forced into the measure by having been robbed, mobbed, plundered, and wasted of all my property, time after time, in various places, by the very ones who made the law, namely the people of the United States, thereby having been obliged to contract heavy debts to prevent the utter destruction of myself, family and friends, and by those who were justly and legally owing me, taking advantage of the same act of bankruptcy, so that I could not collect my just dues, thus leaving me no alternative but to become subject again to stripping, wasting, and destitution, by vexations writs, and law suits, and imprisonments, or take that course to extricate myself, which the law has pointed out.[66]

Joseph Smith and his brothers Hyrum and Samuel declared themselves insolvent before the county commissioner's court on April 18, 1842, and filed petitions to be certified bankrupt by the United States District Court for Illinois. Concurrently other leading Mormons filed similar petitions, including President Sidney Rigdon, Bishop Vinson Knight, "Judge" Elias Higbee, Reynolds Cahoon, Henry G. Sherwood, John P. Green, Arthur Morrison, George Morey, Jared Carter, Amos Davis, Charles Warner, William P. Lyon, William Niswanger, and John Fullmer. They were joined by at least one prominent gentile businessman of Nauvoo, Hiram Kimball.[67]

The federal Bankruptcy Act was passed by Congress in August, 1841, to become effective February 1, 1842. It provided that an inventory of assets and creditors be provided the court, which then decided whether to grant a decree and certificate of bankruptcy. Household and personal effects to a value of $300 were exempt. Smith chose to ignore the provision of the law that no trustee-in-trust was eligible for bankruptcy.[68]

[66] Joseph Smith's History, 4:594, 595.
[67] Joseph Smith's History, 4:600; *Nauvoo Wasp*, May 7, 14, and June 18.
[68] *The Public Statutes at Large of the United States of America, 1789–1845* (Boston, 1848), 5:440–449. The law provided that "the proceedings in all cases shall be deemed matters of record; but . . . shall not be required to be recorded at large, but shall be carefully filed, kept, and numbered, in the office

After Smith initiated bankruptcy proceedings, he recorded few additional details of the matter. David Kilbourne, an unfriendly neighbor of the Saints in Montrose, claimed that the commissioner of bankruptcy for Hancock County, a Mr. Catlin, told him that Joseph and Hyrum Smith included seventy to eighty thousand dollars' worth of Galland's worthless Half-Breed land scrip in their inventory of assets.[69] John C. Bennett, who in May, 1842, broke with the Church, included in his spectacular attack on Smith the charge that the Prophet was attempting to use the bankruptcy law to perpetrate a huge swindle of his creditors. Bennett claimed that when Smith was in Carthage in April to begin his bankruptcy proceedings, he recorded in the county deed book the transfer of a block of Nauvoo property from Smith to the Trustee-in-Trust dated October 5, 1841. The date, said Bennett, was fictitious; no such transfer was made until Smith decided to undertake bankruptcy.[70]

It is true that on April 18, 1842, the day Smith was in Carthage declaring insolvency, the deed to which Bennett referred was entered in the county deed book. It recorded the transfer of 239 Nauvoo city lots, almost three hundred acres, from Joseph and Emma Smith to Joseph Smith as Trustee-in-Trust "in consideration of one dollar on a just and lawful settlement" with the Church. The land included all of the city plat south of Ripley and west of Wells Streets, or most of the south half of the lower town. Only 31 of the 270 blocks in the area were excluded.[71] The coincidence of the bankruptcy with the recording of this deed is not extraordinary, and there seems to be nothing to substantiate Bennett's charge. The October 5, 1841, date was acknowledged on the deed by Ebenezer Robinson as Justice of the Peace. It was the last day of a semiannual General Conference that had concerned itself with the Hotchkiss debt and the land problems of the Church in general. The Twelve had been urging Smith to get the Church properties deeded to the Trustee-in-Trust, and it is reasonable to assume that the transfer in question was made at that time. The transaction was probably recorded in the Nauvoo Registry of Deeds; but when Smith undertook

of the court, and a docket only or short memorandum, with the numbers thereof, kept in a book by the clerk of the court." Since the 1842 records of the United States District Court for the District of Illinois are not extant, no details of the Smith bankruptcy are available from that source.

[69] Kilbourne pamphlet, p. 10.

[70] Snider, "Attitudes in Sectarian Conflict," pp. 117 ff.

[71] Deed Book K, pp. 159–161. Smith's home was included in the transfer, but not the Nauvoo House or his store.

bankruptcy, he doubtless saw the necessity of having the deed recorded in the county registry as well.

The declaration of insolvency was quickly and easily made, but obtaining a court decree was, in Smith's case at least, a protracted and ultimately futile affair. On December 5, seven and one-half months after the procedure was begun, the Prophet wrote, "Attended in council with Brothers Hyrum and others on bankruptcy, making an inventory of our property, and schedule of our liabilities, that we might be prepared to avail ourselves of the laws of the land as did others." Ten days later he wrote: "My delegates at Springfield continued to prosecute my discharge. On the 16th, Brother Hyrum received his discharge in case of bankruptcy; every arrangement was made with Mr. Butterfield [Smith's attorney], whereby I was equally entitled to a discharge, but was put off with a plea that he must write to the office in Washington before it could be granted." [72] If Smith was ever granted the coveted decree, he failed to record it in his journal—an unlikely omission in a matter of such importance. It is probable that the Prophet's private affairs and corporate obligations were too badly mixed for the court to untangle.

Smith expected that his bankruptcy would relieve him of the responsibility for the Hotchkiss debt or at least postpone it. He wrote Hotchkiss on May 13, 1842: "you will probably be apprised of the failure of myself and brethren to execute our designs in paying off our contracts, or in other words, that we have been compelled to pay our debts by the most popular method; that is by petitioning for the privilege of general bankruptcy, a principle so popular at the present . . . throughout the United States." He repeated the persecutions to which the Church had been subjected, the "influence of mobs and designing men," as well as the pressure of debts "absolutely unjust in themselves." He and his brethren had waited until the last moment, "hoping that something would turn in our favor, so that we might be saved the painful necessity of resorting to such measures, to accomplish which, justice demanded a very different course from those who are justly our debtors, but demanded in vain." Hotchkiss was aware, said Smith, "that all [creditors] have to share alike in such cases."

But, sir, you have one, yea, two things to comfort you; our faith, intention, and good feeling remain the same to all our creditors, and to none more than yourself; and secondly there is property in the inventory sufficient to pay every debt, and some to spare, according to the testimony of

[72] Joseph Smith's History, 5:200, 205.

our solicitors, and the good judgment of others; and if the court will allow us someone for assignee, who will do justice to the cause, we confidently believe that yourself and all others will get their compensation in full, and we have enough left for one loaf more for each of our families. . . . I have no doubt you will . . . have your pay in full, in the way I have before proposed, or some other equally advantageous, but money is out of sight, it might as well be out of mind, for it cannot be had.

Rest assured, dear sir, that no influence or exertion I can yet make shall be wanting to give you satisfaction, and liquidate your claims, but for a little season you are aware that all proceedings are staid; but I will seek the earliest moment to acquaint you with anything new in this matter.[73]

Hotchkiss replied on May 27 that he regretted "very much the step you have taken, as I am fearful it will have a most disastrous influence upon your society, both commercially and religiously." He was sure however that Smith had "weighed the subject with sufficient care to arrive at a correct decision." As for his own affairs with the Church, he wanted them made clear at once.

You will oblige me by stating, immediately upon receipt of this letter, your precise meaning, in saying, that "all your creditors would fare alike. . . ."

You have my bond for certain lands, or rather you have my bond that you shall have a deed to certain lands upon the payment of notes specified in said bond. I wish to know exactly how this bond stands in your inventory. Of course, it cannot stand as a title to the property; but I want to know the disposition which is to be made of it.

Possibly some arrangement might be made between us at once; still I do not know how Mr. Tuttle and Mr. Gillet will view the subject.[74]

Smith replied on June 30, the same day he received the Hotchkiss letter. "Your papers are inventoried along with all the other property," he said, suggesting that the Hotchkiss bonds for deed had been listed with Smith's assets, though the original contract had been made with Smith and others as agents for the Church. "The influence this step may have upon our society," added the Prophet, "is a matter we cannot stop to consult, as we had no alternative left."[75] Hotchkiss seems to have thought it unusual, upon reflection, that his land contract with the Church should have figured in

[73] Joseph Smith's History, 5:6, 7.
[74] *Ibid.*, 5:51.
[75] *Ibid.*, 5:52. When the contract was made with Hotchkiss in 1839, Joseph and Hyrum Smith and Sidney Rigdon signed as presidents for the Church. The trusteeship-in-trust was not established until 1841. The record of the original agreement was overwritten with a quitclaim dated July 7, 1843, assigning the title to Smith as Trustee-in-Trust. Deed Book 12G, p. 339.

Smith's bankruptcy at all. During the summer he wrote Smith again, but according to the Mormon leader the letter failed to reach him. Receiving no reply, on November 8, Hotchkiss wrote Sidney Rigdon. Smith answered on November 26. The Prophet explained somewhat lamely that "When I found it necessary to avail myself of the benefits of the bankruptcy law, I knew not but what the law required of me to include you amongst the list of my creditors, notwithstanding the nature of the contract between us." He had learned subsequently that he was wrong, and now considered the contract in force, "provided you will not press the payments." He reminded Hotchkiss of "the extreme hardness of the times" and "the great scarcity of money," and said that if his creditors would "offer a lenity equivalent to the state of the times . . . I shall yet endeavor to make the payments as fast as possible." [76]

The Hotchkiss partners faced a dilemma. Their Nauvoo property was returning them virtually nothing, but they were still legally obligated to pay the taxes since they held the deeds. All land speculators had the problem; but this particular case was different in that the property was being improved and its taxable valuation was increasing. Furthermore, their financial condition was apparently as delicate as that of the Mormons, and there were many tax arrears in Nauvoo. The situation was detailed in a letter of John Gillet to Smith Tuttle, September 18, 1842:

I know of no way that I can raise the money to pay the taxes. . . . The property had ought to be got into some kind of shape that we shall not be compelled to pay [them]. . . . The city taxes . . . if they have not been paid . . . will be another large amount. . . . I did not think it best to see [Joseph] Smith on the subject as I should not have placed any confidence in anything he might have told me. What course it will be best to take with them I do not know—but I think if we have to pay the taxes on the property we had better have possession of it if we can get it. . . . It will be a troublesome piece of business to ascertain what portion of the property sold as Nauvoo Lots [was] on our property. I think it will require the surveyor a good deal of labor—if one or both of you came out I think some arrangement might possibly be made with them to make our debt secure without this endless trouble and expense of having the taxes to attend to—if the place improved for ten years as the appearance now warrants it will take all and probably a good deal more than the interest on the property to pay them—and as it now stands we have them to pay or lose the property—even admitting they were

<hr>

[76] Joseph Smith's History, 5:195. Hotchkiss' letter to Rigdon is not in Smith's History and apparently is not extant.

compelled to pay the taxes but fail to do so and they are sold we are left without any remedy.[77]

On February 23, 1843, Smith wrote in his journal, "Gave my clerk instructions not to pay any more taxes on the Hotchkiss purchase." On April 7 Hotchkiss again wrote Smith:

I received on Saturday last a letter from Mr. Catlin [County Commissioner of Bankruptcy], notifying me that the equity of redemption in my Nauvoo property would be sold on the 12th instant [tax sale?] and asking me whether I wished it to be purchased for me. I suppose it is quite immaterial whether I or you hold the right of redeeming; for if it should again come into my possession, I wish it understood distinctly by them who have built upon it that I shall not attempt to take their buildings from them, but shall be ready at any time to give them a lease of their lots for a very long period, at a reasonable rent. My wish, as well as my interest, leads me to conciliate and make them my friends, instead of . . . enemies.[78]

On the following September 27, Hotchkiss wrote again in some anxiety. He had read of the rising tide of gentile opposition in Hancock County, evidenced by "several severe resolutions passed condemning the conduct of the Mormons." Was this indeed the case? He hoped the Prophet would keep him informed as to the true state of affairs. "Of course I feel an interest in the prosperity of Nauvoo, and . . . in the success of the Mormon enterprise, and a deep interest in the welfare of your people; and the more so certainly, as their pecuniary interest is identified with my own." He added, however, that he would be as anxious "had I not one dollar invested in Nauvoo, because the complete triumph of energetic exertions is always gratifying to business men." Smith replied that the Carthage resolutions against the Mormons were the work of "Unprincipled men and disappointed demagogues," but that "patriots and honest men generally frown upon such audacious proceedings as beneath the dignity of freemen." He assured Hotchkiss that "With the smiling prospects around us at present, success seems certain; and, with the blessings of Jehovah, we shall reap the reward of virtue and goodness." [79] As had often been the case before, Smith's letter to Hotchkiss was more sanguine than circumstances justified. On the same day he recorded in his journal: "I sent William Clayton to Lathrop, to borrow $50, that I might be able to redeem $5,000 worth of property, which was published to be sold today [for taxes?] at Rhodes';

---

[77] Gillet to Tuttle, September 18, 1842, Gillett Family Papers, Illinois State Historical Library.
[78] Joseph Smith's History, 5:288, 382, 383.
[79] Ibid., 6:55, 56.

but Lathrop refused. He also went to Eli Chase's, but was refused by him. I was grieved that the brethren felt so penurious in their spirit, although they professed to be guided by the revelations which the Lord gives through me. On my afterwards giving a pledge that I would repay the $50 in forty-eight hours, Lathrop lent me the money and enabled me to redeem the land." [80]

The affairs of the Hotchkiss purchase appear to have remained in the condition of stalemate they had reached by the fall of 1843. Hotchkiss was on the defensive; he was ready to accept if necessary the position of landlord granting long-term leases, or perhaps any condition that offered possibilities for a financial return upon his Nauvoo investment, which had been a speculation in the first place. For his part, the Prophet recorded no other reference to his obligations to Hotchkiss, which he apparently considered to be suspended. Besides, in September, 1843, he was absorbed in the opening of his new hotel.

The log and frame house where Smith lived from 1839 to 1842 was on the west side of Main Street just south of the intersection of Main and Water Streets. The site of the Nauvoo House was directly across Main Street, and the riverbank was a long stone's throw to the south. The "Homestead" was inadequate to house a family of six and the constant stream of guests. It was, wrote the Prophet's eldest son, "generally overrun with visitors. There was scarcely a Sunday in ordinary weather that the house and yard were not crowded—the yard with teams and the house with callers. This made a heavy burden of added toil for Mother and unnecessary expense for Father." [81] In 1842, according to the recollection of "Young Joseph," his father built the family a new and much larger house on the northeast corner of Main and Water Streets. It was a graceful two-story frame structure designed somewhat in the Federal style. Inasmuch as the Smith home continued to be crowded with guests and completing the Nauvoo House had become a forlorn hope, friends suggested that the Prophet make a virtue of necessity and convert his house into an inn. So in the summer of 1843 Smith built an extensive two-story wing behind the house with a large dining room and kitchen on the ground floor, six single and four double sleeping rooms upstairs, and a cooking range and space for storing provisions in the

[80] *Ibid.*, 6:54, 55.

[81] Mary A. Smith Anderson and Bertha A. Anderson Hulmes, eds., *Joseph Smith III and the Restoration* (Independence, Missouri, 1952), p. 73. This is a condensed version of the memories of Joseph Smith III (1832–1914), the eldest son of the Prophet, cited hereafter as Memoirs of Joseph Smith III.

cellar underneath. The dining room was used for dancing, though "it was barely large enough," said young Joseph, "for four sets of dancers in the old fashioned square dances. . . ." Emma Smith was to be the proprietress, and she went to St. Louis to buy furniture, bed and table linen, curtains, china, and utensils "as were needed to properly equip and operate a hostlery of its kind." [82] On September 15 Smith posted the following public notice:

"Nauvoo Mansion"
In consequence of my house being constantly crowded with strangers and other persons wishing to see me, or who had business in the city, I found myself unable to support so much company free of charge, which I have done from the foundation of the Church. My house has been a home and resting place for thousands, and my family many times obliged to do without food, after having fed all they had to visitors; and I could have continued the same liberal course, had it not been for the cruel and untiring persecution of my relentless enemies. I have been reduced to the necessity of opening "The Mansion" as a hotel. I have provided the best table accommodations in the city; and the Mansion, being large and convenient, renders travelers more comfortable than any other place on the upper Mississippi. I have erected a large and commodious brick stable, and it is capable of accomodating seventy-five horses at one time, and storing the requisite amount of forage, and is unsurpassed by any similar establishment in the State.[83]

Smith opened the Mansion to the public on October 3, 1843, with a memorable dinner party for "more than one hundred couple [*sic*]." To be proprietor of such an establishment and to provide such lavish entertainment seemed not inappropriate to a man of his position; considering, however, the chronic difficulty of his circumstances in the past and his declaration of bankruptcy in 1842 it did suggest a certain fluidity of fortune. Notices of the occasion prepared for publication in the *Nauvoo Neighbor* reported that "General Joseph Smith, the proprietor of said house, provided a luxurious feast for a pleasure party; and all having partaken of the luxuries of a well spread board, the cloth was removed, and a committee appointed to draft resolutions suitable to the occasion." After a hymn and prayer resolutions were adopted honoring the Legion, the charter, Governor Ford, and the city of Nauvoo, "the great emporium of the West, the center of all centers . . . a population of 15,000 souls congre-

[82] *Ibid.*, pp. 73, 74; Joseph Smith's History, 5:556. In the years following her husband's death Emma Smith continued to operate the inn in order to support her family. See Flanders, "The Mormons Who Did Not Go West: A Study of the Emergence of the Reorganized Church of Jesus Christ of Latter Day Saints" (Master's thesis, University of Wisconsin, 1954), pp. 109, 112.
[83] Joseph Smith's History, 6:33.

gated from the four quarters of the globe, embracing the intelligence of all nations, with industry, frugality, economy, virtue, and brotherly love, unsurpassed by any age in the world—a suitable home for the Saints." The main resolution was for the host: "General Joseph Smith, whether we view him as Prophet at the head of the Church, a General at the head of the Legion, a mayor at the head of the City Council, or as a landlord at the head of his table, if he has equals, he has no superiors." After speeches by Colonel Francis M. Higbee, Professor Orson Spencer, and Apostle John Taylor, Smith offered his thanks to the company "in a very touching and suitable manner." He recited again the woes and persecutions he had suffered, but thought that after he, like Job, "had suffered and drank the very drop of affliction, the Lord had remembered him in mercy, and was about to bless him abundantly." [84]

But the Prophet did not stay in the tavern business very long; in January, 1844, he leased the Nauvoo Mansion and stables to Ebenezer Robinson for $1,000 a year, plus three rooms reserved for the Smith family, together with board and stabling for Smith's horses. [85] Apparently the Mormon leader was in financial straits again; on the same day that he concluded the lease with Robinson he sold the *Times and Seasons* print shop, press, bindery, and foundry to John Taylor for $2,832. In addition Taylor "was to assume the responsibility of the Lawrence estate." In June, 1841, Smith had been appointed guardian of the minor heirs of Edward Lawrence and trustee for them of an estate of $3,831. He had apparently incurred debts to this estate which Taylor was to assume. [86] Though the price agreed upon for the printing establishment was determined by his friends W. W. Phelps, Apostle Richards, and Bishop Whitney, Smith thought "the appraised valuation . . . rather too low." [87] He had bought it, he said, from Ebenezer Robinson in March, 1842, for "between seven and eight thousand dollars." [88]

The progress of Smith's many enterprises was not unlike that of the whole Nauvoo economy. The Prophet pursued his interests with energy, made optimistic plans, and had an air of building for the future. But his creditors were an evil he could not seem to escape, as he could not escape the insecurity and instability of Nauvoo itself.

[84] Joseph Smith's History, 6:42, 43.
[85] *Ibid.*, 6:185.
[86] Joseph Smith Estate Papers.
[87] Joseph Smith's History, 4:513, 514, 6:185. The print shop was at the corner of Bain and Water Streets, two blocks west of the Mansion.
[88] See below, Chapter 9.

Smith's estate was found after his death to be burdened with debt; and his assets to cover them were of uncertain value. Despite the urgent desire of the Nauvoo Mormons to diversify their precarious economy, particularly to include manufactures, the odds against success within so short a period of time proved insurmountable. Too much capital was consumed in procuring land and buildings, and too little was left for more productive investment. Although there was an abundance of experienced laborers there were few with managerial knowledge. Furthermore, the peculiarities and exclusiveness of the Mormon kingdom were unattractive to gentile capital, while the insecurity caused by persecution, internal conflicts, and the undependability of Church leadership caused Mormon investors to hesitate. Though home and craft industries were employed in Nauvoo, the goods they produced could not compete with the manufactured goods that were for sale in the national market.

Moving the Saints from Nauvoo to the Great Basin provided a fortuitous solution to some of the Mormon economic dilemmas. In the West the economy was nurtured in semi-isolation by an absolutist church-state. The land was poor, but it cost the Mormon squatters nothing; speculation was forbidden and land was alotted by the Church officials according to need. The Saints were for a time beyond the national market, with its tempting goods that took away from a meager store of capital. Circumstances there were more propitious for experimentation with what one historian has termed the "imaginative [Mormon] mixture of individualism and collectivism."[89] The emphasis in Utah was on a simple, domestic economy that stressed isolation, independence, cooperation, and self-sufficiency. Brigham Young made a conscious effort to avoid some of the economic difficulties encountered in Nauvoo.[90]

[89] Leonard J. Arrington, "Early Mormon Communitarianism: The Law of Consecration and Stewardship," 7:341.

[90] For a discussion of the Utah land system and a comprehensive and perceptive treatment of various Mormon cooperative movements see Leonard J. Arrington, *Great Basin Kingdom*, pp. 51, 52, 94, 127, 293 ff., 301, 302, 311, and *passim*. There were many disappointments and near disastrous failures in Church-directed economic ventures in Utah. In 1860, Young was so discouraged with the experience of recent years that he officially opposed a contemplated merchandising cooperative. "That kind of business [is] not for us," he said, "the Kingdom is for us." *Great Basin Kingdom*, pp. 294, 295. On the Utah land system see also Gustive O. Larson, "Land Contest in Early Utah," *Utah Historical Quarterly*, 29:309–325 (October, 1961). For other detailed treatments of Mormon cooperative movements see E. J. Allen, *The Second United Order Among the Mormons* (New York, 1936), and Leonard J. Arrington, *Orderville, Utah: A Pioneer Mormon Experiment in Economic Organization* (Logan, Utah, 1954).

7

A Dwelling for Man
and a Dwelling for God:
The Nauvoo House and the Temple

The first great object before us, and the saints generally, is to help forward the completion of the Temple and Nauvoo House—buildings which are now in progress according to the revelations, and which must be completed to secure the salvation of the Church in the last days; for God requires . . . a house wherein his servants may be instructed, and endowed with power from on high, to prepare them to . . . proclaim the fullness of the Gospel for the last time, and bind up the law, and seal up the testimony, leaving this generation without excuse, and the earth prepared for the judgements which will follow. . . .

The set time to favor the stakes of Zion is at hand, and soon the kings and queens, the princes and the nobles, the rich and the honorable of the earth, will come up hither to visit the Temple of our God, and to inquire concerning his strange works; and as kings are to become nursing fathers, and queens nursing mothers in the habitations of the righteous, it is right that . . . such, as well as the saints should have a comfortable house for boarding and lodging when they come hither, and it is according to the revelations that such a house should be built.

> Epistle of the Twelve Apostles to the English Saints, November 15, 1841, in Joseph Smith's History, 4:449.

The largest and most expensive of Nauvoo building projects were the Temple and the Nauvoo House. With spasmodic delays of varying duration they were under construction continuously from the spring of 1841; the Temple was complete by 1846 except for finishing the interior, but the hotel was never roofed. These buildings came to symbolize the process and the progress of "building up" the Kingdom. They were initiated together by Joseph Smith's *ex cathedra* revelatory command; each had religious significance, and each was a particular interest and concern of the Prophet. They were fundamentally different, however, in that one was a business venture backed by a joint-stock corporation while the other was to be a labor of love on which the salvation of all Latter-day Saints depended.

At the time Smith proclaimed the revelation commanding that the temple and hotel be built, a bill was already pending in the state legislature to incorporate a "Nauvoo House Association" to build the hotel envisioned in his revelation. The measure was enacted on February 23, 1841, the third and last of the Nauvoo charters granted by the Twelfth General Assembly. George Miller, Peter Haws, Lyman Wight, and John Snyder were named trustees "to erect and furnish a public house of entertainment to be called the 'Nauvoo House.' Spiritous liquors shall never be vended as a beverage or introduced into common use in said house." The law provided further that "whereas Joseph Smith has furnished the . . . ground whereon to erect said house [he] and his heirs shall hold by perpetual succession a suite of rooms . . . to be set apart and conveyed in due form of law. . . ." [1]

The preamble of Smith's revelation of January 19, 1841, spoke of "this stake of which I (the Lord) have planted to be a cornerstone of Zion, which shall be polished with the refinement which is after the similitude of a palace." In pursuance of this objective a hotel was to be built:

My servant George [Miller], and my servant Lyman [Wight], and my servant John Snyder, and others, build a house unto my name, such a one as my servant Joseph shall show unto them; upon the place which he shall show unto them also.

And it shall be for a house of boarding, a house that strangers may come from afar to dwell therein; therefore let it be a good house, worthy of all acceptation, that the weary traveler may find health and safety while he shall contemplate the word of the Lord, and the cornerstone I have appointed for Zion.

This house shall be a healthy habitation if it be built unto my name, and if the governor which shall be appointed unto it shall suffer any pollution to come upon it [*sic*]. It shall be holy, or the Lord your God will not dwell therein. . . . Let it be built unto my name, and let my name be named upon it, and let my servant Joseph, and his house have place therein, from generation to generation.

For this annointing have I put upon his head, that his blessing shall also be upon the head of his posterity after him.

And as I said unto Abraham concerning the kindreds of the earth, even so I say unto my servant Joseph, in thee and in thy seed, shall the kindred of the earth be blessed.

Therefore let my servant Joseph and his seed after him have place in that house, from generation to generation, for ever and ever, saith the Lord.

And let the name of that house be called the Nauvoo House, and let

---

[1] *Laws . . . the Twelfth General Assembly*, pp. 131, 132. Also in Joseph Smith's History, 4:301, 302.

it be a delightful habitation for man, and a resting place for the weary traveler, that he may contemplate the glory of Zion, and the glory of this, the corner-stone thereof; that he may receive counsel from those whom I have set as plants of renown, and as watchmen upon her walls.

The revelation contained specific instructions as to how the corporation was to be formed and by whom; Miller, Wight, Snyder, and Peter Haws were to "organize themselves, and appoint one of them to be president over their quorum for the purpose of building that house. And they shall form a constitution whereby they may receive stock for the building of that house." Shares were to be sold for $50 each, but no one might purchase more than $15,000 worth. The money received from sale of stock was not to be appropriated for any other purpose; if the managers did so "without the consent of the stockholder, and do not repay fourfold . . . they shall be accursed, and shall be moved out of their place, saith the Lord God, for I, the Lord, am God and cannot be mocked in any of these things." Hyrum Smith, Vinson Knight, Isaac Galland, William Marks, Henry G. Sherwood, William Law, and Amos Davis were commanded to buy stock; and each was given a personal word of counsel or commendation, such as, "concerning my servant Vinson Knight, if he will do my will, let him put stock into that house for himself, and for his generation after him, from generation to generation, and let him lift up his voice long and loud . . . to plead the cause of the poor and needy. . . ." and "Let my servant Isaac Galland put stock into that house for I, the Lord, love him for the work he hath done, and will forgive all his sins. . . ." Even Joseph Smith was commanded to buy stock "as seemeth him good; but my servant Joseph cannot pay over fifteen thousand dollars stock in that house . . . neither can any man, saith the Lord." Miller, Wight, Snyder and Haws were to have "a just recompense of wages for all their labors . . . in building the Nauvoo House . . . as shall be accounted unto them as stock in that house." Finally, all stockholders were to be believers in the *Book of Mormon* "and the revelations which I have given you. . . . For that which is more or less than this cometh of evil, and shall be attended with cursings, and not blessings, saith the Lord your God. Even so Amen." [2]

A supplemental revelation on March 20, 1841, commanded Presi-

[2] Joseph Smith's History, 4:274–286. The document is included as Section 124 of the *Doctrine and Covenants* of the Church of Jesus Christ of Latter-day Saints, and as Section 107 of the *Doctrine and Covenants* of the Reorganized Church of Jesus Christ of Latter Day Saints.

dent Henry W. Miller of Freedom Stake and Bishop James Allred of Pleasant Vale Stake, two outlying Mormon neighborhoods, to be agents for selling Nauvoo House stock and to join the four associates charged with the project; "and for this purpose let them devote all their properties, saith the Lord." In addition this revelation suggested another purpose for the venture: "That the poor of my people may have employment."³ Both the Temple and the Nauvoo House were to become significant public works relief projects.

According to Smith's instruction, the hotel was located on the east side of Main Street between Water Street and the river, which was but a stone's throw to the south of the building. The land was given the association by Smith, whose chief city holdings were in that neighborhood. "For magnitude and splendor of workmanship," said the *Times and Seasons*, "[the Nauvoo House] will stand unrivalled in the western country. . . ." The architect was Lucian Woodworth, a gentile who apparently resided in Nauvoo and supervised the construction. The building was to be in an L shape with the two wings, each 120 feet long and 40 feet deep, facing Main Street and the river. A stone basement story was to be topped by three upper stories of brick, all with cut limestone sills and lintels apparently imported from St. Louis. The quality of workmanship on the walls was indeed exceptionally fine. A portion of the original structure is still standing, and the bricks and joints have weathered a century and a quarter with little wear. The entrance was to be on Main Street, with a spacious lobby running the depth of the building and opening onto an elevated veranda which was to overlook spacious grounds in the rear. The arrangement of the interior foundation walls suggests that the plan might have been for about seventy-five rooms; but the interior was never begun. When work was stopped in 1843 the walls were built up only to the level of the second floor.⁴

The operations of the Nauvoo House Association remain a shadow illuminated by fragments of information supplied mostly by Bishop George Miller, one of the trustees. According to Miller he and Lyman Wight were chiefly responsible during the summer and fall of 1841 for raising the initial capital to purchase materials and pay workers. The following winter, work had to be suspended; but the association continued to feed and house the laborers, "They hav-

³ Joseph Smith's History, 4:311.
⁴ *Times and Seasons*, 2:369, April 1, 1841; Joseph Smith's History, 5:283; correspondence with Mr. Kenneth Stobaugh of Nauvoo, official guide of the Reorganized Church of Jesus Christ of Latter Day Saints.

ing no means without our aid." Joseph Smith advised Miller to sell some personal property in order to finance operations the following spring, and along with Wight, to take a mission east "to visit those who could not gather up to Nauvoo, get what [we] could, and sell what stock [we] could, and return early in the spring." Miller went among the Saints in Kentucky and returned with "a hundred head of cattle, some horses and other effects." Wight continued soliciting in the East through the summer and obtained "a good deal" for the Temple; but, said Miller, "All of our lumbering operations having proved nearly abortive Lyman's labors produced very little for the Nauvoo House." [5]

The "lumbering operations" to which Miller referred consisted of sawmills on the Black River in Wisconsin. The meager resources of the Nauvoo House Association were being used in part to finance this "pinery," as it was called, an enterprise which proved in the end to be the most important activity of the Association. Church leaders thought that sawmills to furnish the great timbers and other lumber for the hotel and the Temple might be operated in the Winnebago Indian preserve at no cost other than for outfit and equipment. Lumber was to be made also for the Nauvoo trade, a profitable business which would help finance both buildings. Costs were to be divided equally between the Nauvoo House Association and the Temple Committee. On September 22, 1841, a company left Nauvoo for Wisconsin with provisions for nine months, a little money, and but small knowledge of lumbering. They were captained by Peter Haws of the Association and Alpheus Cutler, Temple master mason and member of the Temple Committee. They bought a decrepit mill near the falls of the Black River for $1,500 and suffered through the winter trying to rebuild it to an operational condition. Progress was slow, however. Among other difficulties, they encountered an irate lumberman who accused them of poaching on his claim and who drove them off with an armed band. It was weeks before they dared return to work.[6] By October, 1842, said Miller, the company had returned to Nauvoo, and the project was $3,000 in debt "with so little lumber made, our work was almost brought to a stand." The work of

[5] Miller, *Correspondence*, pp. 8 ff.; *Times and Seasons*, 3:664, January 15, 1842.

[6] Abner Dexter Polleys, *Stories of Pioneer Days in the Black River Valley* (Black River Falls, Wisconsin, 1948), pp. 46, 49. The country was not surveyed until 1846 and no titles to land could be secured. "Men cut timber at will," said Polleys, "only respecting the rights of others."

the first season was not so futile as Miller remembered it, however. Smith noted on October 13 the arrival of a raft of 90,000 feet of boards and 24,000 cubic feet of timbers.[7] That same fall of 1842, Miller recruited another company and returned to Wisconsin, still hoping to make the operation productive and debt free. Haws and Wight remained in Nauvoo to "drive the work at home."

According to Miller's account the difficulties of the second company were scarcely less trying than those of the first. On the way north some members did not meet the scheduled rendezvous at Prairie du Chien, ice closed the rivers, and the party could get no farther than the mouth of the Black where they were forced to leave all their freight, 120 miles from the mill. The overland journey had to be made through deep snow, which exhausted them; it was all they could do to keep man and beast from freezing or starving. When they did get to the mill, they began to have trouble with the Indians. The Winnebagos, also starving, demanded provisions under threat of burning the mill; they claimed further that the timber was rightly theirs. But they were put off with a little food. Again in the winter of 1843–1844 the Indians threatened to make trouble, this time by putting the government on the Mormons for poaching. If, on the other hand, the Indians received food, they offered to intercede with the Indian agent to allow the Mormons to cut above the falls where the best timber was, an area which had been closed to lumbering while that below the falls apparently was not. As it turned out, the Indians had no influence with the agent; but that official offered privately to "cooperate" with the Mormons in return for a partnership in the concern. Negotiations with him were then broken off.[8] At last, however, the various difficulties were surmounted. Miller arrived in Nauvoo on July 18, 1843, with about 170,000 feet of timbers, lumber, and sawed shingles, enough to provide for the Temple and Nauvoo House and in addition help liquidate some debts of the Association. He had contracted to buy all claims to the mills for $12,000, he reported, payable in lumber in three years; a third had already been paid. More mills could be built and the quantities of lumber that might be sawed were unlimited; "All that is wanting," said the bishop, "is hands." [9]

[7] Joseph Smith's History, 4:417, 418; 5:169, 170; Miller, *Correspondence*, p. 9.

[8] Miller, *Correspondence*, pp. 10 ff.

[9] Quoted in a letter of Willard Richards to Brigham Young, July 18, 1843, in Joseph Smith's History, 5:512.

In the meantime, according to Miller, Lyman Wight had brought the Association to the brink of disaster. He had been sidetracked by "other speculative business ventures," namely, house building in Nauvoo. Then, taking a mission east in the interests of the Association, he had lost a trunk containing a quantity of Nauvoo House stock certificates which were never recovered. "Lyman had become wholly disqualified for business of any kind, in consequence of his indulgence in a habit he was occasionally addicted to [drinking], his face and body very much bloated or swollen. . . . He had accomplished nothing for the Nauvoo House." Miller's assertion that the Nauvoo House Association had been poorly managed in his absence seems to be corroborated by a cryptic remark of Willard Richards. "No investigation of Nauvoo House books yet," he wrote Brigham Young in July; "Joseph says little about it." [10] Joseph and Hyrum Smith advised Miller privately to take Wight back to the pineries, since he was better suited to that kind of work and would be more "free from temptation." Wight readily agreed to go to the mills and raised a large company including many widows and children whom he thought could find labor and support there, and who would be the nucleus for a Mormon colony in Wisconsin. Miller feared that they would only burden the lumbering operation. Though houses were built for the party at the mills and fifty acres of land cleared and planted in wheat, the winter of 1843–1844 was one of great hardship. By February, 1844, the leaders proposed to abandon the pineries altogether and use their company in a grand colonizing and missionary scheme in the Southwest. Their proposal became a part of the plan for a western Mormon empire that was beginning to mature in 1844.[11]

Joseph Smith promoted the Nauvoo House with ardor and persistence. His revelation had initiated the venture, and the brethren had invested a great deal of their time and money at his command. The Prophet felt the need for a hotel more keenly than did anyone else, since the task of entertaining the stream of visitors and guests in Nauvoo devolved chiefly upon his household. At least the numer-

[10] *Ibid.*
[11] Miller, *Correspondence*, pp. 9–20. Miller wrote his letters to the *Northern Islander* in 1855, soon after returning from Texas and a bitterly unhappy experience with Lyman Wight and the colony of Mormons he had planted there. Furthermore, Wight had been made the Twelfth Apostle by Joseph Smith while Miller had not advanced in priesthood, and the old bishop may have been jealous. His evaluation of Wight must be considered subject to prejudice.

ous transients augured well for the success of the hotel business when the building was completed. When that time should come, Smith would be able to abandon his old log and frame house for commodious and gratuitous residence in the fine new hostelry, where, in gracious surroundings, he would continue to be the host to paying guests. Finally, Smith owned stock in the Association, the more reason to reinforce his endorsement of its prosperity.

But the Nauvoo House faced the problems characteristic of kingdom building in Nauvoo. Being a private profit-making venture, invested with the public interest, backed by Smith, and possessed of the priority of revelatory sanction, it naturally excited jealousy among entrepreneurs lacking such support. Its uneven management and progress gave rise to apprehensions of speculation in high places. Furthermore, it had to compete not only with other private ventures, particularly housebuilding, for capital, labor, and materials, but also with its great sister project, the Temple.

Months before Miller had complained to Smith about the diversion of Temple and hotel lumber into housebuilding, the Prophet was angrily denouncing that and other impediments to the completion of the hotel. He exerted himself in a variety of ways to keep the project going. On February 21, 1843, Smith recorded, "At eleven I went to the Temple and found a large assembly, and Brother Haws preaching about the Nauvoo House; after which, Mr. Lucian Woodworth, the architect of the house, continued the subject. . . ." The Nauvoo House Committee was trying apparently to stir up some enthusiasm for the hotel down on "the flat" where the pay for laborers was less certain than in housebuilding in the Temple neighborhood up on "the hill." "When I have had a pound of meat or a quart of meal," Smith reported Woodworth as saying, "I have divided with the workmen. We have had about three hundred men on the job, and some of the best men in the world. Those that have not complained I want to continue with me; and those that hate 'Mormonism' and everything else that's good, I want them to get their pay and run away as quickly as possible." Then Smith took up the subject with a will. If stores and houses were to be built, "it will curse the place." He chastised those who speculated in buildings on "the hill," and called attention to unfinished buildings all over town "such as grog-shops, and card-shops, and counterfeit-shops, etc., got up . . . for speculation, while the Nauvoo House is neglected."

There may be some speculations about the Nauvoo House, say some . . . that the people on the flats are aggrandizing themselves by the Nauvoo

House. . . . How the Nauvoo House cheats this man and that man, say the speculators. Those who report such things ought to hide their heads in hollow pumpkins, and never take them out again. . . . Some think [aggrandizement] unlawful . . . [but] everything that God does is to aggrandize this kingdom. And how does he lay the foundation? "Build a temple to my great name, and call the attention of the great, the rich, and the noble." But where shall we lay our heads? In an old log cabin [referring perhaps to his own house] . . . when men have done what they can or will do for the Temple, let them do what they can for the Nauvoo House. We never can accomplish one work at the expense of the other. There is a great deal of murmuring in the Church about me; but I don't care . . . the growling dog gets the sorest head. . . . Who laid the foundation of the Temple? Brother Joseph, in the name of the Lord, not for his own aggrandizement, but for the good of the whole of the Saints. . . . The building of the Nauvoo House is just as sacred in my view as the Temple. I want the Nauvoo House built. It *must* be built. Our salvation depends upon it.[12]

Smith went on to urge a continuing effort, which, he promised, if persevered in would bring success and profit. "You will then be on Pisgah's top," he said, "and the great men will come from the four quarters of the earth—will pile the gold and silver into it till you are weary of receiving them . . . and they will cover up and hide all your former sins and, according to scripture, will hide a multitude of sins; and you will shine forth fair as the sun, clear as the moon, and you will become terrible, as an army with banners." He promised that those laborers on the hotel that had been unable to get their wage could, if they were hungry, be fed from the Prophet's own table. "Don't take away the brick, lumber and materials that belong to that house, but come and tell me, and I will divide with them to the last morsel; and then if a man is not satisfied, I will kick his backside." Since Smith was trying to inspire greater confidence in the Nauvoo House, he probably did not intend to express the displeasure he felt at the mismanagement of the Association's affairs. But when he wandered onto the topic of money and currency problems, he gave himself away. Counseling his auditors to avoid currency, or "rag money," in favor of specie, he said by way of illustration: "I would not do as the Nauvoo House committee have done— sell stock for an old store-house, where all the people who tried to live in it died, [or] put that stock into a man's hands to go east and

---

[12] Joseph Smith's History, 5:283–287. The editor interpolated a phrase to make the above statement read: "Our salvation [as a city] depends upon it." However the original was apparently as quoted above. See "Joseph Smith's History" for February 21, 1843, in the *Millennial Star*, 20:582, September 11, 1858.

purchase rags [sell stock for paper currency] to come here and build mammoth bones with. . . . I command the Nauvoo House Committee not to sell stock . . . without the gold or silver."

Smith was annoyed that the neighborhood of his cherished Temple was becoming the focus of rival real-estate promotions by both Mormon and gentile entrepreneurs, including William and Wilson Law, Robert D. Foster, the Higbees, the Kimball brothers, Daniel H. Wells, and Augustine Spencer. Main Street on the "flat" was intended by Smith to be the commercial center of the city, and indeed the southern portion of it finally became built up with business properties for more than a mile. Main Street frontage was divided into lots as small as fifteen feet wide, suggesting its desirability for commercial purposes.[13] But by 1843 Mulholland Street, which ran past the south side of the Temple, was becoming a rival commercial thoroughfare prompted by the residential neighborhood which had developed on the "hill." Meanwhile, Church properties on the "flat" remained unsold. In February, 1843, it was proposed in the city council that two markets be established by the city, one in the upper town and the other on the "flat." Smith opposed the idea, saying that one market was enough to begin with, and that it should be established in the lower town on Main Street, about a quarter mile north of the river. "If we began [*sic*] too large," he said in opposing the idea of two markets, "we should do nothing." But then he betrayed what was perhaps his basic objection: "The upper part of the town had no right to rival those on the river. Here, on the bank of the river, was where we first pitched our tents; here was where the first sickness and deaths occurred; here has been the greatest suffering in this city. We have been the making of the upper part of the town. We have located the Temple on the hill, and they ought to be satisfied. We began here first; and let the market go out from this part of the city; let the upper part of the town be marketed by wagons, until they can build [their own] market."[14] Despite Smith's displeasure the "hill" prospered and grew. The location was drier, with fewer insects, than the "flat," and was therefore more healthful. And the price of building lots was generally lower.[15] By 1844 the

<hr/>

[13] Correspondence of the author with Dr. T. Edgar Lyon, historian of Nauvoo Restoration, Incorporated.

[14] Joseph Smith's History, 5:271. Smith urged the Council to "hold an influence over the prices of markets, so that the poor should not be oppressed, and that the mechanic should not oppress the farmer. . . ."

[15] Lyon correspondence.

Prophet was feuding bitterly with many of the promoters on the "hill," an enmity which led finally to his death.[16] The commercial character of Mulholland Street has survived to the present, while that of Main Street has entirely disappeared.

At the annual conference in April, 1843, Smith complained that "there is no place in this city where men of wealth, character, and influence from abroad can go and repose themselves, and it is necessary we should have such a place. . . . This is the most important matter for the time being. . . . The Church must build it or abide the result of not obeying the commandment." Smith complained privately about the laxity and mismanagement of the Nauvoo House finances, especially in collecting funds. He urged that the business be regularized and pointed to the Twelve as the most likely agency to carry it on. Consequently, Brigham Young ordered laborers to work on the Nauvoo House "even if they have to beg food of their neighbors to commence with. . . ."[17] On April 24, 1843, Smith told the Twelve to "wake up the people to the importance of building the Nauvoo House, as there was a prejudice against it in favor of the Temple." He asked Young, Kimball, Hyde, Taylor, Woodruff, Richards, and George A. Smith to go to Augusta, Iowa, a settlement on the Skunk River ten miles north of Ft. Madison, "to spend the next Sabbath and devise means to secure the property which has been purchased of Moffat by the Nauvoo House trustees." Young recorded in his journal that he received $15,000 in stock certificates to sell; he grumbled at being required to post a $2,000 bond, but the experience with Galland had made the bonding of trusted brethren in the pursuit of business a standard procedure. Lucian Woodworth provided the Twelve with exterior and interior drawings of the building to take along. A congregation of about two hundred were on hand on Sunday, April 30, in Augusta, a flourishing little town that boasted three saw mills and two flour mills. Young said that promises of help were received and Smith reported that they "had a good time," but neither mentioned the sale of any stock.[18]

The prospects of the Nauvoo House were waning, however, despite the considerable energy which Smith exerted in its behalf. Its conception was too grand for the available resources. Finally work

[16] The schismatic party of Mormon leaders which published the *Nauvoo Expositor* included the Laws, the Higbees, and Foster. See Chapter 11.
[17] Joseph Smith's History, 5:328 ff. 366, 368.
[18] Brigham Young's journal in the *Millennial Star*, 26:183, 184, March 19, 1864; and Joseph Smith's History, 5:369–371.

languished and then stopped altogether. In the summer of 1843 even the Prophet lost faith to the extent that he built a wing on his own house, the "Nauvoo Mansion," and opened it as a hotel. In February, 1844, Miller and Wight were asking to leave the project to go to Texas; and on March 7, Brigham Young, never as much interested in the hotel as he was in the Temple, urged the completion of the one and the abandonment of the other. In a sermon he said, "I expect that the Saints are so anxious to work [on the Temple], and so ready to do right, that God has whispered to the Prophet, 'Build the Temple, and let the Nauvoo House alone at the present.'" [19] In 1845, plans were made to resume the work, but they were not carried out. In the confusion over Smith's estate and the liquidation of Mormon properties in Nauvoo in 1846 and 1847, Smith's widow retained title to the Nauvoo House block; Smith's deed of the land to the Association might have been a contingent one. L. C. Bidamon, who married Emma Smith in 1847, dismantled a large portion of the walls of the Nauvoo House down to the stonework of the basement story, and built a modest two-story structure with the bricks on the southwest corner of the original foundation. The resulting structure was used as a residence for the family. The building is now owned by the Reorganized Church and is used as a youth hostel.

The Nauvoo Temple was the greatest of the construction projects in the city. The excavation was commenced in the fall of 1840, the cornerstones were laid in April, 1841, and work continued more or less steadily for the ensuing five years. The building was dedicated in April, 1846, two years after the Prophet's death, though the interior was never finished. [20] It was destroyed by fire in 1848. The commandment to build a temple in Nauvoo was a part of the revelation of January 19, 1841, which also contained the Nauvoo House commandment and authorization to baptize the living as proxies for the unbaptized dead:

Verily I say unto you, let all my Saints come from afar; and send me swift messengers, yea, chosen messengers, and say unto them: Come ye, with all your gold, and your silver, and your precious stones, and with all your antiquities; and with all who have knowledge of antiquities, that

[19] Brigham Young's journal in the *Millennial Star*, 26:328, May 21, 1864.
[20] A controversy with theological implications has persisted between Utah and Reorganized Latter-day Saints as to whether the Temple was completed or not. For a description of its unfinished condition see the *Memoirs of Joseph Smith III*, p. 103, and Smith and Smith, *History of the Reorganized Church*, 3:667.

will come, may come, [*sic*] and bring the box-tree, and the fir-tree, and the pine-tree, together with all the precious trees of the earth;

And with iron, and copper, and with brass, and with zinc, and with all your precious things of the earth, and build a house to my name for the most high to dwell therein;

For there is not a place on earth that he may come and restore again that which was lost unto you, or which He hath taken away, even the fullness of the Priesthood;

For the baptismal font there is not upon the earth, that they, my Saints, may be baptised for those who are dead;

For this ordinance belongeth to my house, and cannot be acceptable to me, only in the days of your poverty, wherein ye are not able to build a house unto me. . . .

Therefore, verily I say unto you, that your anointings, and your washings, and your baptisms for the dead, and your solemn assemblies, and your memorials for your sacrifices, by the sons of Levi [the priesthood], and for your oracles in your most high places, wherein you receive conversations, and your statutes and judgments for the beginning of the revelations and foundations of Zion, and for the glory, honor and endowment of all her municipals, are ordained by the ordinance of my holy house which my people are always commanded to build unto my holy name . . . that I may reveal mine ordinances therein. . . .

For I deign to reveal . . . things which have been kept hid from before the foundation of the world, things that pertain to the dispensation of the fullness of times;

And I will show unto my servant Joseph all things pertaining unto this house, and the priesthood thereof; and the place whereon it shall be built; and ye shall build it on the place where you have contemplated building it [the temple was well begun when the revelation was given], for that is the spot which I have chosen for you to build it;

If ye labor with all your might, I will consecrate that spot and make it holy. . . .[21]

Smith made it clear that the Nauvoo Temple was to be no ordinary meeting house but was to play an integral and indispensable role in new religious modes which were to come: "The temple of the Lord is in process of erection here," he wrote ten days before he proclaimed the above revelation, "where the Saints will come to worship according to the order of His house and the powers of the Holy Priesthood, and will be so constructed as to enable all the functions of the Priesthood to be duly exercised, and where instructions from the Most High will be received and will go forth to dis-

[21] Joseph Smith's History, 4:276–278. The entire document is more than eight thousand words long, the first extensive revelation of Smith in several years. It is in *ibid.*, pp. 274–287, Reorganized Church *Doctrine and Covenants*, Section 107, and Utah Mormon *Doctrine and Covenants*, Section 124.

tant lands." [22] The following year, on May 1, 1842, when discussing "the keys of the kingdom" in a sermon, Smith said, "The keys are certain signs and words by which false spirits and personages may be detected from true, which cannot be revealed to the Elders until the Temple is completed." Freemasonry had been established in Nauvoo only six weeks before this, and Smith and other high churchmen were new Masons. He continued: "The rich can only get [the keys] in the Temple, the poor may get them on the mountain top as did Moses. The rich cannot be saved without charity, giving to feed the poor . . . as well as building. There are signs in heaven, earth, and hell; the Elders must know them all, to be endowed with power, to finish their work and prevent imposition. The devil knows many signs, but does not know the sign of the Son of Man, or Jesus. No one can truly say he knows God until he has handled something, and this can only be in the holiest of holies." [23] Discussing the nature of the Godhead in a sermon in June, 1843, the Prophet explained:

Gods have an ascendancy over angels. . . . In the resurrection, some are raised to be angels: others are raised to become Gods.

These things are revealed in the most holy place in a Temple prepared for that purpose. . . . Why gather the people together in this place? For the same purpose that Jesus wanted to gather the Jews—to receive the ordinances, the blessing, and glories that God has in store for His Saints.

I will now ask this assembly and all the Saints if you will now build this house and receive the ordinances and blessings which God has in store for you; or will you . . . let him pass you by and bestow these blessings on another people? I pause for a reply.[24]

Under the leadership of Brigham Young, the Twelve after their return from England in 1841 added their voices to that of the Prophet to explain to the Saints that the Temple was to play an integral role in the religion of the new dispensation. Promoting the Temple became an important part of their new tasks concerning the temporalities of the Kingdom. In a "General Epistle" of October 12, 1841, they wrote: "Here He has commanded a house to be built unto His name where He may manifest Himself unto His people as in former times, when he caused the ark, the tabernacle, and the temple to be reared, and the cloud, and the fire to rest thereon; and

[22] "A Proclamation of the First Presidency to the Church," January 8, 1841, in Joseph Smith's History, 4:269.
[23] *Ibid.*, 4:608.
[24] *Ibid.*, 5:427.

not that the temple be built only, but that the temple be completed quickly. . . . The time has come when the great Jehovah would have a resting place on earth, a habitation for His chosen where His . . . servants may be endowed from on high." [25]

The finance and construction of the Temple was nominally supervised by a Temple Committee composed of Elias Higbee, Reynolds Cahoon, and Alpheus Cutler. But they were primarily functionaries; the Prophet retained the real authority.[26] The builders were mostly the Saints themselves, sometimes selling and sometimes donating their labor. Costs were met through donations and tithes, both of money and more particularly of goods and labor. There is no indication that borrowing was important to Temple finance. The walls of the structure were of limestone quarried in the city by the Saints, and lumber for the interior came primarily from the Wisconsin "pineries."

In general the plan of the Nauvoo Temple was like that of the temple built at Smith's revelatory command in Kirtland. Each had identical large meeting rooms on the first and second floors served by narthexes and stairs at the front corners. Even the proportions of length to breadth to height were similar, i.e., roughly 4:3:6. The Kirtland Temple was smaller, however, and contained neither a basement nor a story between the main floors, as did the Nauvoo Temple. The Kirtland Temple was a frame structure finished with stucco, whereas the Nauvoo Temple was of masonry. The buildings differed in many other details, and were quite different in appearance. There was no baptismal font in the Kirtland Temple.[27] Smith retained an Elder William Weeks as "architect" for the Nauvoo Temple; but Weeks's actual function may have been more nearly that of draftsman-engineer. The conception of the building was the Prophet's own; at least he gave that impression. The following episode recounted in Smith's journal illuminates the relation between the two men:

[25] *Ibid.*, 4:434, 437.

[26] *Times and Seasons*, 3:909, September 1, 1842. After the death of Higbee in 1843 Hyrum Smith was appointed to the committee. Joseph Smith's History, 6:53.

[27] Temples built in Utah appear to have included the main features of the Nauvoo and Kirtland Temples, such as the characteristic high, boxlike appearance, the general interior layout, and the arched ceilings and pillared side aisles in the main assembly rooms. Presumably they all contain a large baptismal basin in the basement after the manner of the Nauvoo Temple.

In the afternoon, Elder William Weeks (whom I had employed as architect of the Temple) came in to me for instruction. I instructed him in relation to the circular windows designed to light the offices in the dead work of the arches between stories. He said that round windows in the broad side of a building were a violation of all the known rules of architecture, and contended that they should be semicircular—that the building was too low for round windows. I told him I would have the circles, if he had to make the Temple ten feet higher than it was originally calculated; that one light at the center of each circular window would be sufficient to light the whole room, and when the whole building was thus illuminated, the effect would be remarkably grand. "I wish you to carry out my designs. I have seen in vision the splendid appearance of that building illuminated, and will have it built according to the pattern shown me." [28]

That the plan evolved as building progressed is suggested further by a Weeks drawing used to decorate Gustavus Hills's 1842 engraving of the Nauvoo Plat.[29] The design was that of a classic pedimented Greek temple with philasters instead of columns, surmounted by an incongruously tall and massive Georgian tower. The actual temple turned out to be quite different in appearance, especially on the front.

The Temple was 128 feet long, 88 feet wide, and 165 feet from the ground to the top of the tower. The walls were made of solid blocks of cut limestone from four to six feet thick, quarried in the northwest and southwest parts of the city. Temple stones still to be seen in Nauvoo reveal that the finishing was very fine indeed. Charles Lanman, a traveler who saw the building in 1846, described it as "principally after the Roman style of architecture, somewhat intermixed with Grecian and Egyptian." Henry Lewis, a traveling artist who painted the Temple in 1848, said: "It bears a nearer resemblance to the Bysantium of [or?] Roman Grecian style than any other altho' the capitals and bases are entirely unique still the cornices are grecian in part . . . considering . . . that is of no particular style it [does] not in the least offend the eye by its uniqueness like almost all innovations from established standards do." [30]

[28] Under entry of February 5, 1844, in Joseph Smith's History, 6:196, 197.
[29] The Hills engraving was sold for fifty cents in the city perhaps both as a city guide and as a promotional piece. Correspondence of the author with Dr. T. Edgar Lyon, historian of Nauvoo Restoration, Incorporated.
[30] These descriptions of the Temple and those that follow are from an article in the *New York Sun*, n.d., printed in *Apostolic Interregnum*, 7:434, 435, ascribed to W. W. Phelps; from Charles Lanman, *A Summer in the Wilderness* (Philadelphia, 1847), pp. 31, 32; from Henry Lewis, *Making a Motion Picture in 1848* (Minnesota Historical Society, St. Paul, 1936), p. 51; and from

The building was tall and severely boxlike in appearance which, with the massive walls, gave it a character of monumental solidity. Across the front was a high, massive porch, and on top of the building across the front was a low rectangular story called the "attic" that served as a platform for the octagonal tower and dome. The walls were very heavily ornamented with thirty tall pilasters, nine to a side and six front and back; with round, half-round, and Romanesque windows between them; and with heavy, uniquely carved capitals and bases for the pilasters. The bases had inverted crescent moons, and the capitals had what Lanman called "an uncouth head, supported by two hands holding a trumpet," but which was supposed to represent a blazing sunface. All were painstakingly hand-chiseled on the site from great blocks of limestone.[31] A double cornice around the eave was decorated by a wide, heavily molded frieze ornamented with escutcheoned circles and stars and a balustrade around the low-pitched roof. The suns, moons, and stars were a decorative motif symbolic of the three heavenly glories of Mormon eschatology. Under the tower across the front was inscribed in golden letters, "The House of the Lord. Built by the Church of Jesus Christ of Latter Day Saints. Commenced April 6, 1841. Holiness to the Lord."

The Temple was entered from a roofless, pedestal-shaped porch through three arches perhaps nine feet wide and thirty-five feet high. Beyond the narthex was the first floor nave or auditorium with a choir containing three pulpits. Over the Prophet's pulpit was the inscription: "The Lord has beheld our sacrifice: Come after us." The room was lighted by sixteen tall Romanesque windows on the sides. The second floor auditorium was, said Lanman, "in every particular . . . precisely like that of the first." Between the two great rooms was a low story divided into two long rooms running the length of the building, each lighted by eight round windows in the outside wall. The attic story contained a spacious hall in the center, around which were twelve small rooms lighted by round windows. Each of the small rooms had a massive lock on its door. The basement room contained the great baptismal font.[32]

Lewis' paintings of Nauvoo and the Temple in his *Das Illustrirte Mississippitahl* (Leipzig and Florence, 1923).

[31] The cost of the pilasters alone, said Smith, was $90,000. See Mulder and Mortensen, eds., *Among the Mormons*, p. 138.

[32] In the summers of 1961 and 1962 Dr. Melvin Fowler, Curator of North American Archaeology at Southern Illinois University, directed an exploratory

The Nauvoo Temple was an impressive edifice, especially in its remote, pastoral setting. Henry Lewis said of it, "Taking into consideration the circumstances under which it was built it is a wonderful building. . . ." And Lanman was moved to call it "unquestionably one of the finest buildings in this country." Much of the peculiar flavor and character of the Mormon kingdom of Nauvoo inhered in and was symbolized by the Temple—the devotion of material goods to attain spiritual goals and rewards, the sacrifices and Herculean efforts of a humble and almost blindly faithful people to build God's Kingdom on a grand scale and in a hurry from small means, the feverish last-minute dispensing of "endowments" in the Temple before its abandonment. Like the city and kingdom it was left unfinished.

Its dramatic destruction shocked gentile and Saint alike. Fired by the torch of an arsonist in the predawn night of October 9, 1848, the all-wood interior quickly became a gigantic white-hot pyre that lighted the sky over many miles of country. Awed spectators watched zinc from the roof and lead from the shim plates used to set the stone flow in molten rivers down the walls. The walls were left standing, but were struck soon after by a violent wind storm which toppled three of them. The remaining pile was blown up as a precautionary measure.[33]

Joseph Smith took a special proprietary interest in the Temple. It was an extension of his leadership, his prophetic vision of the joining of temporal and spiritual kingdoms, his theology, his power, his ego, and his taste. When it was begun, Smith wrote that it was to be built on a "magnificent scale and will undoubtedly attract the attention of the great men of the earth." [34] He considered it symbolically

study of the Temple site for the Church of Jesus Christ of Latter-day Saints, the owners. A partial excavation of the basement tended to verify contemporary descriptions of the dimensions of the building at the foundation and the arrangement of the basement, while discovering some previously unknown details of design and construction. Completion of the work may add substantially to the slender store of knowledge about the structure. The project field reports and Fowler's report on the recovered artifacts were furnished the author through the courtesy of Nauvoo Restoration, Incorporated.

[33] The firing of the Temple may have resulted from a widespread conspiracy among anti-Mormons in the county who feared the return of the Saints to Nauvoo. See Joseph Earl Arrington, "Destruction of the Mormon Temple at Nauvoo," *Journal of the Illinois State Historical Society*, 40:422 and *passim* (1947).

[34] Letter to the Twelve in England, October 19, 1840, in Joseph Smith's History, 4:229.

as well as actually to be the crown or capstone of the Nauvoo kingdom, the progress of which he came to gauge by the progress of the great building on the hill. He could not let the direction of its affairs slip from him too far; he was suspicious of those who in any way seemed to challenge his exclusive proprietorship. Smith reminded the Temple Committee frequently that their authority was strictly subordinate. On December 11, 1841, Smith wrote, ". . . I directed Brigham Young . . . to go immediately and instruct the building committee in their duty, and forbid them receiving any more property for the building of the temple, until they received it from the Trustee-in-Trust, and if the committee did not give heed to the instruction, and attend to their duty, to put them in the way so to do."[35] In May, 1843, the committee had apparently remonstrated with the Prophet for taking Temple money or supplies for other uses. He replied: "Told the Temple committee that I had a right to take away any property I chose from the Temple office or store, and they had no right to stand in the way. It is the people who are to dictate me, and not the committee. All the property I have belongs to the Temple; and you have no authority only as you receive it from me."[36] Smith's relation to the project is further illustrated by the account of Josiah Quincy upon the occasion when he and Charles Francis Adams were shown the building by the Prophet. Wrote Quincy,

It was a wonderful structure, altogether indescribable by me. Being presumably like something Smith had seen in vision, it certainly cannot be compared to any ecclesiastical building which may be discerned by the natural eye . . . odd and striking as it was, [it] produced no effect that was commensurate with its cost. . . . The city of Nauvoo, with its wide streets sloping gracefully to the farms enclosed on the prairie, seemed to be a better temple to him who prospers the work of industrious hands than the grotesque structure on the hill, with its queer carvings of moons and suns. . . . Near the entrance to the Temple we passed a workman who was laboring upon a huge sun which he had chiseled from the solid rock. The countenance was of the negro type with the conventional rays.

"General Smith," said the man, looking up from his task, "is this like the face you saw in vision?" "Very near it," answered the prophet, "except (this was added with an air of careful connoisseurship that was quite overpowering)—"except that the nose is just a thought too broad."
. . . In a tone half-way between jest and earnest, and which might have been taken for either at the option of the hearer, the prophet put this inquiry: "Is not here one greater than Solomon, who built a Temple with

[35] Joseph Smith's History, 4:470.
[36] Ibid., 5:382.

the treasures of his father David and with the assistance of Huran, King of Tyre? Joseph Smith has built his Temple with no one to aid him in the work." [37]

But when Smith saw the Temple for the last time, in June, 1844, the walls were still only half built. After his death its completion became a sacred obligation to his memory and his commandment; it was the perpetuation of his will beyond his death. Besides, the Saints were convinced that their salvation depended on it. [38]

Baptism for the dead was the first function performed in the Temple, and was perhaps the only special religious ordinance carried on there until 1845. The rite was emphasized constantly in efforts to convince the Saints of the importance of completing the structure. Immersion in the great basement font for healing of the sick was also to be practiced. Characteristic of the information transmitted by the leaders to the Church was the statement of the Twelve in their "General Epistle" of October, 1841. The Temple, they wrote, was to be a place "where the Saints may enter the baptismal font to be baptized for their dead relatives, so that they [the dead] may be judged according to men in the flesh, and live according to God in the spirit, and come forth in the celestial kingdom; a place over which the heavenly messengers may watch and trouble the waters as in days of old, so that when the sick are put therein, they shall be made whole: a place wherein all the ordinances may be made manifest. . . ." [39] The baptismal font was dedicated on November 8, 1841, and was after that used more or less continuously for baptism for the dead. The first such rites were held on November 21, when about forty were baptized for the dead by Apostles Brigham Young, Heber C. Kimball, and John Taylor, with Apostles Willard Richards, G. A. Smith, and Wilford Woodruff "confirming," or laying on hands in a spiritual baptism for the dead. On December 28, Joseph Smith wrote in his journal: "I baptized Sidney Rigdon in the font, for and in behalf of his parents; also baptized Reynolds Cahoon and others." [40]

[37] Mulder and Mortensen, eds., *Among the Mormons*, p. 138.
[38] Ebenezer Robinson, in *The Return*, 2:301, July, 1890.
[39] Joseph Smith's History, 4:434, 437.
[40] *Ibid.*, 4:446, 454, 486. The ordinance was probably practiced earlier; a recorder for baptisms for the dead had been appointed for Zarahemla Stake the previous July. *Ibid.*, 4:382. Nor were all baptisms for the dead in the font after its construction. Charlotte Haven, a gentile resident of Nauvoo, wrote of observing the rite in the river in May, 1843. See Mulder and Mortensen, eds., *Among the Mormons*, p. 123.

The baptismal basin was an extraordinary structure. It was an oval sixteen feet long, twelve feet wide, and four feet deep. The rim stood seven feet above the floor. The molding of the rim and the base were, according to Smith, "formed of beautiful carved work in antique style." The sides were paneled. The most striking feature of the font was that it rested upon the backs of twelve life-size wooden oxen, painstakingly carved out of blocks formed by glueing pine planks together. Smith said they were "copied after the most beautiful five-year-old steer that could be found in the country, and they are an excellent striking likeness of the original. . . ." Eight months were required by the sculptor, Elder Elijah Fordham, for their completion. Water for the font was drawn from a well thirty feet deep, dug in the east end of the Temple basement. "This font was built for the baptisms for the dead," the Prophet concluded, "until the Temple shall be finished, when a more durable one will supply its place." Though stone oxen later replaced the wooden originals, the font probably remained unchanged otherwise. It was entered from stairways at either end, and at each side was a room for recording clerks. The basement room was paved with brick in a pattern converging to the font in the center, and was circled by sixteen "preparation rooms," small cubicles lighted by semicircular windows near ground level.[41]

Work on the Temple was pushed feverishly from the beginning, and the Saints were hounded and badgered to ever greater zeal in its behalf. The revelation commanding the Temple had stipulated a dire condition regarding its building: ". . . I grant unto you a sufficient time to build a house unto me, and during this time your baptisms shall be acceptable unto me. But behold, at the end of this appointment, your baptisms for your dead shall not be acceptable to me [and] you shall be rejected as a church, with your dead, saith the Lord your God." [42] Just what the length of that "sufficient time" was, Smith did not say; but the threat was taken seriously. It was a constant goad and spur to greater effort. The Prophet urged the Temple on the people with rewards of great spiritual blessings to be received when it was done, of mysteries to be revealed, and of powers and gifts to be bestowed. An I. R. Tull, a resident of Pontoosuc, a village a few miles up the river, came to Nauvoo frequently to sell

<hr />

[41] Joseph Smith's History, 4:446, 447; Lanman, *A Summer in the Wilderness*, p. 32.
[42] Joseph Smith's History, 4:277.

produce. He related a conversation with a Massachusetts man who had gathered to Nauvoo in hope that Smith could heal his blind eyes. "I asked him why the Prophet did not open his eyes. He replied that Joseph had informed him that he could not open his eyes until the Temple was finished. . . ." [43]

In October, 1841, the Prophet made another dramatic threat to speed the work on his two public houses. When the semiannual General Conference opened, "The President made some remarks on the inclemency of the weather, and the uncomfortable situation of the Saints with regard to a place of worship, and a place of public entertainment." The following day Smith, "by request of the Twelve Apostles, gave instructions on the doctrine of baptism for the dead, which were listened to with intense interest by the large assembly. He presented baptism for the dead as the only way that men can appear as saviours on Mount Zion." But at the conclusion of his discourse the Prophet announced: "There shall be no more baptisms for the dead, until the ordinance can be attended to in the Lord's House; and the church shall not hold another General Conference until they can meet in said house. *For thus said the Lord!*" [44] The conference adjourned *sine die.* The threat was not carried out; the font was ready for use the following month, and there continued to be conferences, though that of the following April was styled a "special" rather than a "general" conference. But the Prophet's threatened interdict was not without effect; it was repeated in communications to the Saints outside of Nauvoo and stood as an example of his vindictive zeal. [45]

According to the original revelation, God might declare the "sufficient time" ended at any time. "The brethren seemed to vie with each other in their diligence," said Ebenezer Robinson, "as many of them felt . . . if they failed to have the work accomplished by the time appointed, they lost not only their own souls' salvation, but also that of their dead friends, for whom they had been baptized. . . . I confess that was too strong meat for me. . . ." Robinson reasoned that the baptism of the living could not be revoked and that the salvation of the dead could not rightly be made to depend on the performance or nonperformance of the living. "I came to the conclusion that the Lord did not give that revelation." [46]

[43] Gregg, *History of Hancock County,* p. 372.
[44] Joseph Smith's History, 4:424–426.
[45] See for example the Apostolic epistles of November 15 and December 13, 1841, in *ibid.,* 4:449, 472 ff.
[46] *The Return,* 3:12, 13, January, 1891.

None of the Saints who were not contributors to the building might share in the blessings to be given in the Temple. The Twelve made the situation clear in a public letter to the Church on December 13, 1841:

One of those [Temple] privileges which is particularly attracting . . . notice . . . is baptism for the dead . . . and several have already attended to this ordinance by which the sick have been made whole and the prisoner set free; but we have been led to inquire into the propriety of baptising those who have not been obedient and assisted to build the place for baptism; and it seems unreasonable to us that the Great Jehovah will approbate such . . . for if the Church must be brought under condemnation and rejected with her dead, why should not individuals, who thus neglect, come under the same condemnation? For if they are to be rejected, they may as well be rejected without baptism as with it . . . and the time [it would take] to baptize them may be appropriated to building the walls . . . and this is according to the understanding we have received from him who is our spokesman [Smith].[47]

Those Saints who lived thousands of miles away, said the Apostles, came under the same law as those living in Nauvoo. They were all commanded to gather, and when they arrived, they could get into the Temple only if the Book of the Law of the Lord, the master ledger of Temple contributors, showed that they had already tithed for its building.[48] Offerings and consecrations were requested, but tithes were mandatory, said the Twelve:

The tithings required, is one-tenth of all anyone possessed at the commencement of the building, and one-tenth part of all his increase from that time until the completion of the same, whether it be money, or whatever he be blessed with. Many in this place are laboring every tenth day for the house, and this is the tithing of their income, for they have nothing else; others . . . are sick, therefore excusable; when they get well, let them begin; while there are others who appear to think their business of more importance than the Lord's. . . . Our God will not wait always. . . . We hope this gentle hint will suffice, that we may not be compelled to publish the names of those referred to.[49]

The tithing of time had been inaugurated when the building was begun, by a conference resolution of October 3, 1840. Smith wrote the Twelve on October 19 that "every tenth day is devoted by the brethren to quarrying rock, etc. . . ."[50]

In order to build the Nauvoo Temple the Mormon leadership had

[47] "An Epistle of the Twelve Apostles to the Saints of the Last Days," in Joseph Smith's History, 4:473.
[48] Joseph Smith's History, 4:473.
[49] Ibid., 4:473, 474.
[50] Ibid., 4:229.

to refine the management of their human and material resources on a scale they had never before attempted. Brigham Young addressed the elders at the October, 1841, conference "on the propriety of many of the Elders remaining at home, [rather than going away on missions] and working on the Lord's House; and that their labors will be as acceptable to God . . . and more profitable to the Church." They should, said Young, "make consecrations more abundantly than before." [51] All were to labor every tenth day, but some were to labor full-time. Such men were said to be on "Temple missions." Brigham Young saw to it that those assignments were fulfilled. "We would remind some two or three hundred Elders," he said in December, 1841, "who offered to go on missions, some six months, others one year, and some two years, and had their missions assigned them at the general conference to labor on the Temple, that most of their names are still with us, and we wish them to call and take their names away, and give up to the building committee." Many "Temple mission" workers were to be boarded in the homes of Nauvoo Saints; Young reminded such hosts, "you are not forgotten, we have your names also, and we expect soon to send someone to your table, therefore put your houses in order and never be ready to refuse the first offer of a guest." [52] Two months later, in February, 1842, the Trustee-in-Trust published an announcement concerning the management of the Temple labor crews: "a superabundance of hands one week, and none the next, tends to retard the progress of the work; therefore every brother is requested to be particular to labor on the day set apart for the same, in his ward. . . ." They should be on hand "in good season in the morning" with their tools or teams. Ward captains were to keep an accurate account of each man's work, "and be ready to exhibit a list of the same when called for." It was hoped, said Smith, that "neither planting, sowing, or reaping will hereafter be made to interfere with the regulations hinted at above"; the Saints should remember while doing their Temple labor, "that he who sows sparingly, shall also reap sparingly." [53] Though no specific data are available, on an average more than a hundred men at a time must by conservative estimate have been employed, quarrying, hauling, shaping and raising stone, laying bricks, making mortar, and doing carpentry on the great building.

[51] *Ibid.*, 4:427.
[52] *Ibid.*, 4:474.
[53] *Ibid.*, 4:517.

Providing materials for construction and provisions for the laborers was a task of major proportions. "We would invite the brethren for many miles distant around us," wrote the Twelve, "to send in their teams for drawing stone, lumber, and materials for the building; and at the same time load their wagons with all kinds of grain and meat, provisions, and clothing, and hay, and provender in abundance, that the laborer faint not, and the teams be made strong; also that journeyman stonecutters, etc., come, bringing their tools with them, and enlist in the glorious enterprise." If the sisters could do nothing more, they should at least knit mittens and socks.[54] As winter closed in, even more extensive provisioning was ordered, and the Twelve instructed the Saints in a two-hundred-mile radius to supply cattle and hogs in droves "while meat is plenty . . . and the weather is cool . . . for packing." Nor were the "maimed, the lean, the halt and the blind, and such as you cannot use" to be sent as offerings. In addition the sisters were to send bedding, socks, mittens, shoes, and "clothing of every description." All money and goods brought for the Temple were to be presented to the Trustee-in-Trust, and credited at the Temple Recorder's office in the Book of the Law of the Lord.[55] The Temple Recorder advertised in the newspaper from time to time for the kinds of goods that were currently in demand. A series of advertisements beginning June 18, 1842, in the *Neighbor* was headed "Meal, Flour, and Provisions of every kind wanted on tithing," and included a request for bench and molding planes; another series in the fall of 1844 read: "Notice— About 6 or 8 thousand good lath wanted immediately. The amount shall be credited on tithing. William Clayton, Recorder." [56] The Twelve went about the countryside in person to collect for the Temple. At an 1841 stake conference at Lima, Adams County, attended by Taylor and Richards and presided over by Young, a motion was put and carried unanimously that those present "consecrate one tenth of their time and property to the building of the Temple . . . under the superintendence of [stake] President Morley and counsellors. . . ." Three months later Young, Kimball, Richards, and Taylor attended a conference at Ramus Stake and returned with "horses, wagons, provision, clothing, etc., for the Temple [worth] nearly a thousand dollars. . . ." [57] Nor did the Twelve neglect to

[54] Letter of the Twelve to the Church, October 12, 1841, in *ibid.*, 4:434.
[55] Letter of the Twelve, December 13, 1841, in *ibid.*, 4:474, 475.
[56] *Nauvoo Neighbor*, June 18, 1842, November 27, 1844.
[57] It was at this conference that action was taken to transfer lands, bonds, and notes from the stake Bishop to the Trustee-in-Trust. See Chapter 5.

solicit the English Mission despite the impoverished condition of many members there. In March, 1842, a company of 172 English immigrants arrived with "about $3,000 in goods" for the Temple and Nauvoo House. Between May and December, 1842, another $975.04 in Temple funds were credited to English Saints. Brigham Young was serious when he said, "We should be prepared to keep each commandment as it came from the Lord by the mouth of the Prophet, and as the Lord had commanded us to build a Temple, we should do it speedily." [58]

The demands made by the Temple tended to make more explicit the dichotomy between those Saints who had gathered, as the Prophet said, "to share in the tribulation, that they may ultimately share in the glory and triumph," and those who had failed to gather. At a district conference in Boston in 1843 Brigham Young stated the issue plainly. God did not expect all the Saints to gather as soon as they first obeyed the Gospel, but "He *does* require them to hearken unto counsel." If the ungathered Saints believed they could be saved where they were, they were wrong. "Can you get an endowment in Boston or anywhere, except where God appoints? No. . . . Has the Lord spoken in these last days, and required us to build Him a House? Then why query about it? If he has spoken, it is enough." The Saints should not be forced to gather, he said, but should freely choose "whether they will gather and be saved with the righteous, or remain with the wicked and be damned." But Young still wanted money from them, "all you have to spare," and they need not fear that they would have too little left to enable them to gather to Nauvoo. "If I had a wife and ten children, I would give all my money to build the Temple and the Nauvoo House, and would trust to God for their support. Yet I will be richer for it; for God would prosper me in business." Furthermore, said Young, if the Saints did not give their substance it might very likely be stolen, like the ivory cane belonging to a local elder after he had refused to give it to Young. "Now it does neither of us any good." When the Lord shook the earth, as he surely would, ". . . and every valley shall be exalted, and every mountain and hill shall be made low . . . you will have no use for gold, for money and goods as you have now." [59]

Temple finance became an exacting business considering the costs

[58] Joseph Smith's History, 4:438, 440, 467–479, 569.
[59] In the afternoon Parley P. Pratt preached to the conference in a similar vein:

involved and the fact that the economy of Nauvoo rested predominantly on barter rather than monetary exchanges. All manner of goods were received to further the work. When I. R. Tull of Pontoosuc was unable to sell his produce in regular Nauvoo trade channels, he took it to the Temple store, where, he said, he "could always trade it off for something." They had "almost every conceivable thing, from all kinds of implements and men's and women's clothing, down to baby clothes and trinkets, which had been deposited by the owners as tithing, or for the benefit of the Temple." All tithes and offerings were ordinarily received on Saturdays, said Joseph Fielding, "to prevent confusion," and often totaled more than a thousand dollars a week.[60]

Administering such a variety of capital caused problems. The value of goods was a matter of opinion rather than fact, and mismanagement or the suspicion of it was endemic. The fact that "temple timber" was going into private trade was already well known, and suspicions of speculation grew among the Saints. Public accounting was not made, and the integrity of the great project depended finally on Joseph Smith, who assumed and retained the whole responsibility. The Prophet seemed unruffled. "I . . . sent for the Temple Committee to balance their accounts and ascertain how the Temple business was going on," Smith recorded on October 1, 1842:

Some reports had been circulated that the committee was not making a righteous disposition of property consecrated for the building of the Temple, and there appeared to be some dissatisfaction amongst the laborers. After carefully examining the accounts and inquiring into the manner of the proceedings of the committee, I expressed myself perfectly satisfied with them and their works. The books were balanced between the trustee and the committee, and the wages all agreed upon.

"What Elder Young said is good. We want all he spoke of, and a great deal more . . . we have a Prophet who tells us how, when, and where to use it . . . we should [thus] get as much wisdom as the world. If they want a railroad built, all they have to do is open books. The people subscribe stock, a railroad is soon built, and an income is realized. The Saints ought to be as well united as the world, and do the things that God has required, that a great nation may be saved from all nations. . . . Take your means and unite your exertions in this work. . . . We want you to take that course that will save you."

Ibid., 6:12–14, 16. Seven of the Apostles were present at the conference, held September 9, 1843. The proceedings were reported by Wilford Woodruff. See also ibid., 4:590 ff.

[60] Gregg, History of Hancock County, pp. 374, 375; the Millennial Star, 3:78, August, 1842.

I said . . . I was amenable to the state as trustee-in-trust, and that the Temple committee were accountable to me, and to no other authority; and they must not take notice of any complaints from any source, but let the complaints be made to me, if any were needed, and I would make things right.[61]

Two months later, however, in November, 1842, the Temple stone-cutters as a group made formal complaints against the Temple Committee and two of its members, Reynolds Cahoon and Elias Higbee in particular, for "unequal distribution of provisions, giving more iron and steel tools to Reynolds Cahoon's sons than to others, giving short measure of wood to father Huntington, also letting the first course of stone around the Temple to the man who would do it for the least price, etc." Smith decided to bring the disputants together at his house for a formal hearing of the charges. Hyrum Smith and Henry G. Sherwood acted as counsel for the defendants and complainants respectively, with Joseph Smith and William Law presiding. In reporting the affair, which lasted all afternoon and evening, Smith said only that brother Hyrum spoke of "the important responsibility of the committee, also the many difficulties they have to contend with," and advised them to "have charity one with another, and be united." William Law made "a few pointed remarks," though on which side the Prophet did not say. When all had finished, said Smith, "I gave my decision, which was that the committee stand in their place as before. . . . [They] were responsible to me and had given bonds to me [for] $12,000. . . ." [62] While the Prophet's enormous power and prestige enabled him to hold disputing brethren together most of the time as on this occasion, he could not solve all the difficulties inherent in the situation. Brigham Young in later years recalled the problems of tithe goods:

In the days of Joseph, when a horse was brought in for tithing, he was pretty sure to be hipped or ringboned, or have the poleevil, or perhaps had passed the routine or horse-disease until he had become used up. The question would be, "What do you want for him?" "Thirty dollars in tithing, and thirty in cash." What was he really worth? Five dollars, perhaps. They would perhaps bring in a cow after the wolves had eaten off three of her teats, and she had not had a calf for six years past; and if she had a calf, and you ventured to milk her, she would kick a quid of tobacco out of your mouth. These are specimens of the kind of tithing we used to get.[63]

[61] Joseph Smith's History, 5:166.
[62] *Ibid.*, 5:196, 197.
[63] *Journal of Discourses*, 8:346. Young may have exaggerated somewhat for

The Nauvoo Temple could not have been built with any amount of old plows, sacks of potatoes, baby clothes, and ringboned horses, no matter what their undoubted cumulative worth. Of greater significance were tithes and consecrations of land. Between May, 1843, and July, 1844, the county records show 2,558 acres of farm land and an undetermined number of city acres deeded to Joseph Smith as Trustee-in-Trust in consideration of "the love and good will [the grantees] bear the Church of Jesus Christ of Latter Day Saints." Most of the tracts were no larger than 160 acres, though one of 1,760 acres, contributed by James Adams, constituted more than half of the total. There may have been other such tithes and offerings recorded in the Nauvoo register but not in the county records, which would thus not be included in the above total. The management and disposition of such properties kept Smith in the land business after most original Church purchases were sold.[64]

The experience gained in Nauvoo in the use of land, goods, and labor tithes as Temple capital must have been invaluable in Utah where the "law of tithing" was generally interpreted as one-tenth of gross income or more, rather than one-tenth of net increase. In the first twenty years there poverty was more severe and money more scarce than in Nauvoo, and tithing was almost the only available capital for public buildings, roads, canals, bridges, and mills. Tithing in kind rather than money was the general rule throughout the nineteenth century; and its management as well as its collection was a major occupation of the Church, one in which a great deal of proficiency was achieved. For example, Young as Trustee-in-Trust contracted to build a section of the Union Pacific Railroad for $4,000,-000; he then subcontracted portions of the work totaling $2,125,000 to Mormon contractors at a 10 per cent discount, in order to assure the collection of the tithe in advance.[65]

The cost of the Nauvoo Temple is impossible to reckon in terms of money with any accuracy, though various estimates were made. Travelers to Nauvoo in 1847 and 1848 reported the cost at $750,000

---

effect; tithing in kind was then the common practice in Utah, and he was declaiming against its abuses there as well as in Nauvoo.

[64] Hancock County Deed Books L, p. 261; M, pp. 6–12, 85, 274, 275, 398, 401; N, p. 369. Only one such grant was recorded after Smith's death: a third of a section to Newell Whitney and George Miller as Trustees-in-Trust, February, 1845. Deed Book N, p. 233.

[65] See Leonard J. Arrington, Great Basin Kingdom, pp. 54, 109 ff., 119, 134, 137, 262, 270, 290.

and $800,000, figures quoted to them that included estimates of materials and labor consumed.[66] There is no doubt that whatever the cost it was a severe drain on the meager economy of the Mormon kingdom by the Mississippi. "In consequence of the impoverished condition of the Saints," wrote Smith in April, 1841, "the buildings [Temple and Nauvoo House] do not progress as fast as could be desired, but . . . we hope to accomplish much by a combination of effort, and a concentration of action. . . ."[67] But capital had to be taken from productive enterprises that were needed to provide employment, and to manufacture and process consumers' goods. The people were left poorer in things that they might be richer in spirit. Participation in Temple building became a test of faith, since anyone who did not tithe was barred from its ordinances. Although Smith seldom admitted that the great structure was anything but a benefit to the Saints, in January, 1843, he said: "I prophesy, in the name of the Lord God, as soon as we get the Temple built, so that we shall not be obliged to exhaust our means thereon, we will have means to gather the Saints by thousands and tens of thousands."[68]

While the Temple took the capital that might have supplied many jobs in factory and mill, it became itself the city's largest employer. Together with the Nauvoo House, the Masonic Temple, and the Seventies Hall, it constituted a public works project that perhaps prevented the unemployment problem from being disastrous. The tithe-labor system alone removed one-tenth of the laborers from the employed laboring force, though it returned only board in lieu of income. But hired labor on the Temple and other public buildings was of great economic significance. "These buildings have furnished many of the poor with work," wrote Joseph Fielding. John Taylor complained that skilled mill hands were carrying the hod instead of plying their trades as they should; but the fact was that there were few mills to man, and many hods.[69] The indirect effect on the Nauvoo economy was of equal significance. The Temple was a voracious

[66] Lanman, *A Summer in the Wilderness*, p. 32; and Buckingham, "Illinois As Lincoln Knew It; A Boston Reporter's Record of a Trip in 1837," pp. 170–173.
[67] "Report of the First Presidency" to the General Conference, in Joseph Smith's History, 4:338.
[68] *Ibid.*, 5:255.
[69] *Millennial Star*, 3:78, August, 1842; *Nauvoo Neighbor*, May 13, 1843. See Chapter 6.

consumer of bricks, mortar, woodwork, and metalwork of both whitesmith and blacksmith. Crews had to be fed and clothed, teams provided and provisioned, and wagons, sleds, and chains supplied. Many of these necessities were donated, but many were purchased. Nauvoo was a busy marketplace, and the Temple was its best customer.

The cost of the Temple was not a consideration to Smith or to most of the Saints. It was a necessity, not a luxury. In it new religious mysteries were to be revealed and new blessings dispensed. Through its instrumentality the Church would be saved; without it, they would be damned, together with their dead. The building was intrinsically awesome, and was made doubly so to the Saints by its religious significance and the enormous toil and sacrifice they invested in it. It was the symbol of God's Kingdom built upon the earth expressed in a rich and elaborate manner. It was Nauvoo's greatest single achievement, and it told of the real design and purpose of that community. When the Saints abandoned it under duress for an unknown destiny in the West, their sense of alienation from society was heightened by such a loss. The martyred Prophet, the lost city, the great Temple destroyed in a pillar of fire all became interwoven in a fabric of romance, a great lost cause both righteous and glorious. From such a past, myths and legends easily sprang; and Nauvoo is in Mormon culture more a legend than a chapter of history.

The Nauvoo Temple was the focus of religious innovations which revolutionized Mormonism. Ordinances for the dead, as well as novel and secret ordinances for the living, including marriage for eternity, plural marriage, and other extraordinary familial arrangements, were introduced by Smith and Young in Nauvoo for temple observance. It is difficult to know which was conceived first—a temple needing special rites, or special rites needing a temple. At any rate the "temple work" which became central to Mormon life in Utah had its beginnings in the Nauvoo Temple. It had been from the beginning of its construction a particular kind of Mormon shrine. On the other hand the New Mormonism ushered in by the Temple was a stumbling block to some who preferred the Original Mormonism to which they had been converted.[70] Dissenters who broke with the Church over the radical innovations in doctrine

[70] For a discussion of the controversy over new doctrines in Nauvoo, see Chapter 9.

tended to view the Temple as a symbol of apostasy, and its destruction as a righteous judgment.[71]

[71] A private, unpublished manuscript by Joseph Earl Arrington reportedly is an extensive treatment of the Nauvoo Temple. Unfortunately it was unobtainable at the time this book was being written.

8

The Church Corporate as Body Politic

*FREEMEN! A Tremendous Conflict is close at Hand! On its results de-
pends the preservation of our LIBERTIES and sacred RIGHTS—Freemen to the rescue!* . . .

> *March to the battlefield,—*
> *The foe is now before us*
> *Each heart is freedom's shield*
> *And Heaven's banner o'er us.*

Harrison campaign notice in the Springfield, Illinois, *Sangamo Journal,* October 23, 1840.

*The great cause of popular fury was, that the Mormons had at several
preceding elections cast their vote as a unit; thereby making the fact
apparent that no one could aspire to office . . . within their sphere of
influence, without their approbation and votes. It appears to be one of
the principles by which they insist on being governed as a community
to act as a unit in all matters of government and religion. They express
themselves to be fearful that if division should be encouraged in politics,
it would soon extend to their religion, and rend their church with schism,
and into sects. This seems to me to be an unfortunate view of the subject,
and more unfortunate in practice.* . . .

Thomas Ford, "Message of the Governor of Illinois in Relation to the Disturbances in Hancock County, December 21, 1844," *Reports made to the Senate
and House of Representatives of the State of Illinois, 1844* (Springfield,
1844), p. 71.

Mormon life in Illinois expressed itself in such a way as
to suggest to the gentiles that the community of the Saints was
tightly knit and centrally directed, an exclusive corporation, zealous
in purpose and monolithic in action. This gentile apprehension persisted and became more widespread despite the fact that non-Mormons were welcome in Nauvoo, where their religious rights were
protected by law and where an influential gentile minority flourished. Although the Saints were a majority of the population of
Hancock County, the county government remained more or less in
gentile hands—a fact which suggests that the Church had no real desire to control it. Still, Mormon corporatism lay close to the heart of
Mormon-gentile conflict; and in no area of life was it a more sensi-

tive issue than in that of party politics. Mormon political action was bound to arouse resentment.

In the 1840's Illinois politics was in a state of ferment; the whole Midwest was a kind of storm center for national politics. "To all human appearance," wrote Caleb Atwater, "the Census of 1840 will place national government in the hands of the people of the Mississippi Valley. To resist this event would involve the necessity of preventing the revolution of the earth around the sun and upon its axis, and the whole course of nature." [1] In particular Illinois, Indiana, and Ohio became an arena for national political issues and struggles. Cultural crossroads between North and South, East and West, beneficiaries of spectacular population growth and economic development, bellwethers of national political trends—these states had an unusual political significance. Their citizens were a political people, in all senses of the term "political"—in ideals and philosophy, in social attitudes, in party actions and manipulations. Local politics— town, county, and state—offered a turbulent training ground for lawyers, country school teachers, newspaper editors, and others of ambition who worked for political careers. In Illinois, Indiana, and Ohio, American political life was in its heyday. Perhaps never before nor since has it occupied such a position.[2]

From 1840 to the mid-1850's "the Progressive Western Democracy," as the western wing of the Democratic party styled itself, predominated through the southern portion of Illinois and around the Lake. It was the heir of both Jeffersonian and Jacksonian Democracies, and stressed human above property rights, "the right of revolution, of Universal suffrage, of freedom of trade, of overthrow of banks, [and] of the establishment of constitutional currency." [3] It blamed the Whigs for the fiscal troubles caused by the overemphasis of internal improvements and commercial development, and it lauded farmers, laborers, mechanics, and the "simple life." Though it exalted the "Common Man," it had no interest in the Negro, either slave or free. However, it espoused the interests of newly arrived immigrants, especially Irish and German Catholics who labored on canals and railroads. In return it received their solid vote. Despite their view on Negroes and the presence of numbers of pro-southern men in the area just north of the Ohio, the Democrats and the lead-

---

[1] Quoted in Buley, *The Old Northwest*, 2:259.
[2] Hubbart, *The Older Middle West*, pp. 9, 10.
[3] Samuel Medary, the *New Constitution*, September 22, 1849, quoted in *ibid.*, p. 10.

ers to whom they looked—Benton, Cass, Medary, William Allen, Douglas—were western, not southern, in their orientation to national politics. [4]

The Whigs, despite their victory in the 1840 election, were the minority party in the Old Northwest during the forties. For all the charges made against them by the followers of Jackson and Van Buren, they were, like most westerners, quite democratic in spirit. But as followers of Clay, they would not admit that they were like the Jackson and Polk men, whom they considered demagogues. The Whigs befriended bankers, merchants, and men of "moderate wealth." Moreover, the Whigs in the Great Lakes region were antislavery.[5]

The first thirty years of Illinois state politics, said the Illinois historian Theodore Pease, "began with the ruffled gentility of Ninian Edwards and ended with the shirt-sleeve democracy of Stephen Douglas." Though their careers almost touched midway in the period 1818–1848, Edwards was a figure not unlike George Washington, and Douglas was a man more akin to Theodore Roosevelt. Men seemingly of two different worlds, Edwards and Douglas typify the revolution in Prairie State politics that took place in a very few years.[6] During the thirties and forties in Illinois party politics developed slowly. There were followers of Edwards and of his enemies, followers of Jackson and of his enemies, and the same for Van Buren, Harrison, Tyler, Polk, and Douglas. There were pro-National Bank men, including many Democrats, and anti-Bank men. The Democracy was helped by its adoption of the convention-nominating system which prevented small factions from paralyzing the party. The Whigs, however, did not adopt such a discipline and suffered accordingly; they failed to develop as a coherent, consolidated party. Between the mid-thirties and mid-forties, however, a real Democratic party organization gradually developed; and it became the dominant party in Illinois. The Democratic governor Thomas Ford (1842–1846) gave the state a program of fiscal recuperation from the near bankruptcy attending its internal improvement ventures of the thirties and did much to restore political as well as economic integrity to the state.[7]

[4] Hubbart, *The Older Middle West*, pp. 10–13.
[5] *Ibid.*, pp. 14, 15.
[6] Theodore C. Pease, *Illinois Election Returns, 1818–1848*, Vol. XVIII, *Collections of the Illinois State Historical Library* (Springfield, 1923), p. xvii.
[7] *Ibid.*, p. iv; Buley, *The Old Northwest*, 2:230.

At this time Illinois was a conscious seedbed for national politics and the mania for public office was insatiable. Ford said that at the beginning of the 1842–1843 legislative session there were more than a hundred aspirants for the offices of Doorkeeper of the House and Sergeant-at-Arms of the Senate. Legislators controlled most of the patronage—more than the governor or the congressmen. They appointed the United States Senators, "and in a general way provided henchmen for the offices and offices for their henchmen." The fight for office polarized friendships and enmities and provided powerful followings for powerful leaders. It is more than coincidental that Lincoln and Douglas, probably the most important national political figures of the fifties and sixties, were both from Illinois.[8]

Well seasoned with bitterness by the campaign and election of 1836, Illinois politics was occupied from 1838 to 1841 with two important issues, each related to the growing power of the Democratic Party: (1) the right of the victorious party to control the spoils of office and (2) the alien vote. Each heightened political tensions and made the election of 1840, the first in which the Mormons participated, an especially complex canvass.

The first of these issues centered on the problem of tenure in office for Alexander Pope Field, Secretary of State of Illinois. Field was a renegade Jacksonian-turned-Whig who had been Secretary of State since 1828, continuing in office through successive administrations under the interpretation of his ill-defined tenure of office that it extended for life or during good behavior. The Democrats were determined to turn him out and to settle the issue of the rights of the winning party to the patronage "regardless of sentiment or the force of custom." In 1838 when the Democrat Thomas Carlin was elected Governor, he appointed a Democrat, John A. McClernand, to the office of Secretary of State. The Senate, however, would not overturn the precedent under which Field had held office for a decade, and refused to ratify the nomination. Carlin submitted other names for the post with the same result. After the adjournment of the legislature, McClernand was again nominated, and he carried his fight for the office into the courts. The Democratic Justice Sydney Breese of the Fayette County Circuit Court ruled for McClernand in *quo warranto* proceedings; but Field appealed to the State Supreme

---

[8] Stevens, "Life of Stephen A. Douglas," pp. 356, 357. The Stevens study devotes particular attention to Douglas' career in Illinois politics which the biographies of Gerald Capers and George Fort Milton do not do.

Court, a tribunal of three Whigs and one Democrat. The case attracted widespread attention and noted counsel for the plaintiff, including Stephen A. Douglas. The court overturned Breese's decision with an exhaustive opinion based on constitutional grounds. With Douglas leading the attack the Democrats assailed the "Whig court" throughout the state; and the problem of "Life Tenure for Whigs" became a major Democratic issue in the campaign of 1840. In face of the Democratic victory in the state that year, Field resigned and Carlin appointed Douglas to succeed him.[9]

The second great issue in Illinois politics in the late thirties concerned the right of aliens to the vote. The franchise had been granted some ten thousand aliens based on the provision of the Constitution of 1818 that "all male inhabitants, above the age of twenty-one years, having resided in the state six months preceding an election, shall enjoy the right of an elector." Democratic power in Illinois depended on the fact that the Democracy garnered about ninety per cent of the alien votes, and the election of 1838 showed that that vote was crucial. During the campaign the Democratic candidate for Governor, James W. Stephenson, was found to be in default to the United States government for many thousands of dollars and was forced to withdraw. The Democracy, lacking a candidate and burdened with scandal, hastily nominated Carlin, "an honest but ignorant man," and managed to get him elected by a vote of 30,648 to 29,722. The *Quincy Whig* said bitterly, "It is humiliating to reflect, that the political destinies of this large State, are controlled by a transient population . . . of voters. But such is the fact." [10]

On the assumption that the constitutional proviso giving "male inhabitants" the vote implied citizenship, the Whigs brought a test case in a circuit court and won a ruling in August, 1838, that non-naturalized persons were indeed ineligible to vote. The ruling startled the Democrats, and Douglas took steps to have the decision appealed. Since any new ruling on appeal would normally be given at the June, 1840, session of the Illinois Supreme Court, the Democrats expected the "treacherous Whig Court" to deprive them of the alien vote apparently necessary for their success in the August and November elections. But Douglas was able to win a continuance on a technicality and by postponing the decision "save" the alien vote.

[9] Stevens, "Life of Stephen A. Douglas," pp. 330–335.
[10] *Ibid.*, p. 336; Buley, *The Old Northwest*, 2:232.

With this respite, Douglas launched an all-out attack on the Court. "No Supreme Court," said a Douglas biographer, "has ever received the denunciations that Douglas poured out upon the heads of its members."[11] In the 1840–1841 legislative session the Democratic majority enacted a law assuring the franchise to all adult males without reference to citizenship. During the same session, which quite incidentally passed the Nauvoo charters, the Democrats sought to protect their alien vote law by the enactment of a Supreme Court reorganization measure that would add five new justices. The Whigs were especially embittered by that proposal and charged that it was revolutionary. Despite personal rancor, a near-duel, a veto by the Council of Revision, and plausible charges of a "corrupt bargain" in the House, the bill was passed. Carlin appointed the five new justices, all Democrats, including Thomas Ford and Douglas. Although himself a beneficiary, Ford in later years wrote that the measure was "confessedly violent and revolutionary, and [it] could never have succeeded except in times of great party excitement. The contest in the Presidential election of 1840, was of such a turbulent and fiery character, and the dominant party in the state had been so badly defeated in the nation at large . . . that they were more than ever inclined to act from motives of resentment and a feeling of mortification."[12] The close contest for supremacy between the parties in Illinois had honed partisanship to a keen edge and made political emotions raw just at the time that the Mormon element was interjected into the political situation.

The geographical center of Illinois population, and thus of political power, moved steadily north by northwest through the thirties and forties. The shift of the state capital from Vandalia to Springfield symbolized the movement. Before 1832, settlement north of Springfield and Jacksonville was small and scattered and had little significance in state politics. But after the Black Hawk War, settlers flooded into the area. It was a place for ambitious beginners to seek their political fortunes. Stephen A. Douglas of Springfield, twenty-five years old and four years a resident of the state, decided to make it his constituency and in 1838 ran unsuccessfully for Congress in the Third District, which comprised roughly the northern half of the

[11] Stevens, "Life of Stephen A. Douglas," p. 337. In the 1858 debates Lincoln scored his opponent heavily for this episode after Douglas had demanded that Lincoln have respect for the U.S. Supreme Court's decision in the Dred Scott Case.

[12] *Ibid.*, pp. 337–339; Pease, *Illinois Election Returns*, p. lxvii.

state. When he sat on the Supreme Court, he made the northwest central part of the state his curcuit and claimed residence in Quincy, though he was there infrequently. From there he won election to Congress in 1843 and 1844.[13] Hancock County was in this area, where by 1840 a whole new complex of political alignments was being formed and where many new political fortunes were being sought.

Despite the statewide Democratic trend in the thirties, Hancock remained a Whig county; in the congressional, gubernatorial, and state legislative elections of 1838, it went Whig by a three to two margin. Whigs were also in the majority in McDonough, Fulton, Tazewell, and McLean Counties on the east, in Warren County on the north, and to the southeast in Sangamon County (Springfield), which then included modern Logan, Menard, and Christian Counties. So by 1840 the Whigs considered the area bounded roughly by a line drawn through Warsaw-Springfield-Bloomington-Peoria-Monmouth as a party stronghold. The Mormon move into the area seemed unlikely to disturb the pattern, since the Saints went solidly Whig in the elections of 1840 and 1841.[14]

The Mormon vote had not been so Whiggish before the election of 1840, however. In Missouri the Saints had tended in general to be Jacksonian Democrats; Ford said that they had "always supported" the Democratic ticket there. But they had been driven from the state by the Democrat Lillburn Boggs; the Van Buren administration had demurred from acting on their petitions seeking redress for the Missouri grievances; and those petitions had been sponsored in Congress by a Whig Senator and a Whig Representative from Illinois. In addition the Nauvoo charters were guided to enactment by State Senator Sidney Little of McDonough County, a Whig, as well as by Douglas.[15] A reaction in favor of the Whigs, at least temporarily, was a natural result. The first apparent note of Mormon partisanship in Illinois was voiced by Lyman Wight, soon to be one of the Twelve Apostles, in the spring of 1839 in a letter which appeared in the *Quincy Whig*. He attacked not only the Democrats of Missouri but all Democrats generally, and said that Thomas Hart Benton, senator from Missouri and revered leader of the western Democracy, was a demagogue. The Democrats of Quincy who were

[13] Stevens, "Life of Stephen A. Douglas," pp. 314, 315.
[14] Pease, *Illinois Election Returns*, pp. lv ff. and *passim*.
[15] Ford, *History of Illinois*, p. 262.

217

assisting the Mormon refugees were exercised over the attack. "Yesterday I was waited on by Mr. Morris," wrote Robert B. Thompson to the First Presidency of the Church, "who asked me what was intended by such publications . . . when they are doing all in their power to assist us." Thompson had been told that "the feelings of the governor [Democrat Thomas Carlin] are very much hurt. . . . The Whigs are glad of such weapons, and make the most of them." He hoped that the Presidency would not think him too officious, but he believed that the Church should insist that Wight not continue his partisan attacks. "I think we ought to correct the public mind on this subject," said Thompson, "and, as a Church, disavow all connection with politics. . . . The tears of widows, the cries of orphans, and the moans of the distressed, are continually present in my mind . . . if through imprudence . . . three, four, or five years hence, our altars should be thrown down, our houses destroyed, our brethren slain, our wives widowed, and our children made orphans . . . your unworthy servant wishes to . . . appeal to [God] and say . . . I am innocent in this matter." [16] Smith responded with a letter to the *Quincy Whig* expressing a strictly nonpartisan position for the Church. It was Elder Wight's privilege, he said, to express his opinion in either political or religious matters, but "we profess no authority in the case whatever, [and] we have thought, and still think, that it is not doing our cause justice to make a political question of it in any manner whatever." The Missouri barbarities were not the responsibility of any party or religion, said Smith, but were committed by a mob "composed of all parties. . . ." By the same token, members of all parties and religious societies had befriended the cause of the exiled Saints in Illinois, and thanks was due them all. "Favors of this kind ought to be engraven on the rock, to last forever." [17] Smith wrote Lyman Wight privately:

We do not at all approve of the course which you have thought proper to take, in making the subject of our sufferings a political question. At the same time . . . we . . . feel . . . a confidence in your good intentions. And (as I took occasion to state to the Council) knowing your integrity of principle, and steadfastness in the cause of Christ, I feel not to exercise even the privilege of counsel on the subject, save only that you will endeavor to bear in mind the importance of the subject, and how easy it might be to get into a misunderstanding with the brethren concerning it;

[16] Joseph Smith's History, 3:351, 352.
[17] *Ibid.*, 3:354, 355. The letter was sent over the signatures of all three members of the First Presidency.

and . . . whilst you continue to go upon your own credit you will also steer clear of making the Church appear as either supporting you or opposing you in your politics, lest such a course may . . . bring about persecution on the church, where a little wisdom and caution may avoid it.[18]

The Prophet's nonpartisan spirit soon received a severe test. In October, 1839, he went to Washington to attend personally to the business of the Missouri damage claims before the federal government. He met Van Buren, whose response to the affair, according to Smith, was: "What can I do? I can do nothing for you! If I do anything, I shall come in contact [sic] with the whole state of Missouri." Before they parted, however, the President "promised to reconsider what he had said, and observed that he felt to sympathize with us, on account of our sufferings." [19] But the petitions of the Church failed to achieve anything substantial, and Smith returned to Nauvoo in disappointment. His later recollection of the audience with Van Buren caused him, in February, to set down in his journal a somewhat different version from the one just recounted. The President, he said, "treated me very insolently," and listened "with great reluctance" to what he and Higbee had to say. "When he had heard, he said: 'Gentlemen, your cause is just, but I can do nothing for you'; and 'If I take up for you I will lose the vote of Missouri.' His whole course went to show that he was an office-seeker, that self aggrandizement was his ruling passion, and that justice and righteousness were no part of his composition. I found him such a man as I could not conscientiously support at the head of our noble Republic." While in Washington, Smith had also talked with John C. Calhoun, "whose conduct towards me very ill became his station." Officially, however, the Prophet sought to remain neutral regarding politics. At the April, 1840, General Conference he declared that "he did not wish to have any political influence, but wished the Saints to use their political franchise to the best of their knowledge." [20] Unofficially he seems to have expressed partisan feelings freely. "Information has reached this place, through some of the newspapers," Higbee wrote Smith from Washington in March, 1840, "that you have come out for Harrison." [21]

[18] *Ibid.*, 3:366, 367.
[19] Letter of Joseph Smith and Elias Higbee to Hyrum Smith, December 5, 1839, in *ibid.*, 4:40.
[20] *Ibid.*, 4:80, 109.
[21] *Ibid.*, 4:99.

But by fall the Prophet no longer pretended to be politically neutral. "He gave us distinctly to understand that his political views had undergone an entire change," said a gentleman of Montrose, reporting a conversation he had had with Smith to the *Quincy Whig.* Of Van Buren, Smith reportedly said, "*He is not as fit as my dog, for the chair of state.*" He concluded that the Mormons intended to use their political influence in the coming election, when the near hundred thousand Mormon votes in the nation "must be extensively lost to Mr. Van Buren." The gentile who reported these political observations of Smith remarked that "these remarkable sectaries . . . hold in their hands a fearful balance of political power . . . should they ever become disposed to exert their influence for evil, which may Heaven prevent, they would surround our institutions with an element of danger, more to be dreaded than an armed and hundred-eyed police." [22]

The effect of the Mormon settlement on the election rolls of Hancock County is suggested by a comparison of election returns for 1838, 1840, and 1841. The total vote for Congressman increased from 1,087 in 1838 to 1,724 in 1841. Similarly, the vote cast for Governor in 1838 was 1,069, while the vote cast for President two years later was 1,976 (there was no gubernatorial election in 1840). Further analysis suggests that the Mormon vote in 1840 and 1841 strongly favored the Whigs.

HANCOCK COUNTY VOTING SUMMARIES, 1838–1841 [23]

Congress 1838	Whig 629 (58%)	Democrat 458 (42%)
Governor 1838	Whig 633 (59%)	Democrat 436 (41%)
State Senate 1838	Whig 699 (71%)	Democrat 287 (29%)
State Assembly 1838	Whig 578 (57%)	Democrat 437 (43%)
President 1840	Whig 1352 (68%)	Democrat 624 (32%)
State Assembly 1840	Whig 1042 (61%)	Democrat 670 (29%)
Congress 1841	Whig 1201 (70%)	Democrat 523 (30%)

A comparison of votes for Congress, Governor, and legislature in 1838, before the Mormon immigration, and the votes for President and State Assembly in 1840 and Congress in 1841, after the Mormon settlement, shows an increase in the average total vote from 1,035 to 1,804, in the average Whig vote from 635 to 1,198, and in the aver-

[22] *Quincy Whig,* October 17, 1840.
[23] Pease, *Illinois Election Returns.*

age Democratic vote from 404 to only 606. In the 1841 congressional election, the Whig candidate John T. Stuart won in the Third District with fifty-two per cent of the vote; he carried McDonough County with fifty-one per cent, lost Fulton with forty-eight per cent, won Adams with fifty per cent, but carried Hancock with seventy per cent. Of his 1,201 votes in Hancock County, 481 were cast in Nauvoo Precinct alone.[24] The Whigs, frustrated over their inability to carry Illinois even for Harrison, seemed at least to have captured the potentially powerful Mormon vote.

As had been the case in Missouri, the exercise of their franchise brought the Mormons many enemies but few friends. After the election of 1840 jealousy over the Mormon vote began to arise in Hancock County. The "Old Citizens" realized that the Mormon voting strength was potentially greater than their own, whether Whig or Democrat. "On account of this," wrote a historian of Illinois politics, "the old party lines were pretty much broken down," and a new Mormon–anti-Mormon polarity began to develop.[25] Struggling in an already Whig county, Hancock Democrats were especially embittered. William H. Roosevelt, a prominent Democrat, suggested the formation of an anti-Mormon party and pledged that all gentile Democrats "will vote the Anti-Mormon ticket." [26] The beginnings of an organized anti-Mormon political party occurred in the spring of 1841. The *Warsaw Signal* said on May 19: "We believe they have the same rights as other religious bodies possess. . . . But whenever they, as a people, step beyond the proper sphere of a religious denomination, and become a political body, as many of our citizens are beginning to apprehend will be the case, then this press stands pledged to take a stand against them. . . . It is bound to oppose the concentration of political power in a religious body, or in the hands of a few individuals." On June 19 a citizens' meeting was held at Warsaw to elect delegates to a county anti-Mormon convention; the meeting concluded that "there exists serious grounds of apprehension that the leaders of the Mormon body design, so soon as the numbers of their church constitute a majority of the votes, to control

[24] *Ibid.*, p. 123 and *passim;* George W. Gayler, "The Mormons in Illinois Politics: 1839–1844," *Journal of the Illinois State Historical Society*, 49:50, 51 (1956).

[25] E. B. Greene and Charles Thompson, *Governor's Letter Books, 1840–1853*, Vol. VII, *Collections of the Illinois State Historical Library* (Springfield, 1911), p. lxxxii.

[26] Gayler, "The Mormons in Illinois Politics," p. 51.

the offices of this county." The county-wide anti-Mormon convention met on June 28 to nominate for the forthcoming election a slate of candidates who would be "in opposition to Mormon influence and dictation." The gathering called upon the gentile citizens to "lay aside former party feelings and oppose, as independent freemen, political and military Mormonism." [27] But despite the disenchantment of local gentile partisans with the Mormon bloc vote, others continued to court it.

The Census of 1840 had increased the apportionment of Illinois seats in the United States House of Representatives from three to seven, and in anticipation of the election of four new congressmen, ambitious men in both parties were eager to serve the Mormons. In June, 1841, when Smith was arrested as the result of an extradition order from the governor of Missouri, he sought release under a writ of *habeas corpus* in Monmouth and engaged as counsel Orville H. Browning, who was soon to be the first Whig candidate from a newly created Fifth Congressional District. Browning defended Smith with ardor. "Great God! have I not seen it? Yes, my eyes have beheld the bloodstained traces of innocent women and children, in the dreary winter, who had traveled hundreds of miles barefoot . . . to seek refuge from their savage pursuers. . . . And shall this unfortunate man, whom their fury has seen proper to select for sacrifice, be driven into such a savage land, and none dare to enlist in the cause of Justice?" [28] The counselor "has done himself immortal honor," said Robert B. Thompson, who accompanied the Prophet to Monmouth,

in the sight of all patriotic citizens who listened . . . for more than two hours. . . . We have heard Browning on former occasions, when he has frequently delighted the audience with his eloquence; but on this occasion he exceeded our most sanguine expectations. The sentiments he advanced were just, generous, and exalted; he soared above the petty quibbles which the opposite counsel urged, and triumphantly, in a manner peculiar to himself, avowed himself the friend of humanity, and boldly, nobly and independently stood up for the rights of those who had waded through seas of oppression and floods of injustice, and had sought shelter in the State of Illinois.

[27] Gayler, "The Mormons in Western Illinois," pp. 161, 162; and Gayler, "The Mormons in Illinois Politics," p. 50. Greene and Thompson wrote that the "antis" won the county election of 1841, but "thereafter the Mormons succeeded in filling county offices with their own people or so called jack-Mormons." Greene and Thompson, *Governor's Letter Books*, p. lxxxii. However, the abundant trouble the Mormons had with various county officers through the years casts some doubt on this generalization.

[28] *Joseph Smith's History*, 4:370.

Browning had sympathized with the Mormons when they were first driven from Missouri, said Thompson, and the Saints rejoiced "that he yet maintains the same principles of benevolence. His was not an effort of a lawyer anxious to earn his fee, but the pure and patriotic feelings of Christian benevolence. . . ."[29] Looking forward to the congressional election of August, 1841 (the last which would take place in Illinois' old Third District), the Whig nominee, John T. Stuart, sought in various ways to insure that the Mormon vote would continue in the Whig column. "It is [the Whigs'] great object to palter to the Mormons," lamented the Democratic *Illinois State Register* of Springfield:

They need their votes to elect . . . Stuart. Therefore he and they are coquetting with this sect, and have made great efforts, *if not pledges,* to secure their votes, by making them believe that their particular views will be promoted, by the instrumentality of Mr. Stuart.

We have not any prejudice against the Mormons, believing that every man has a right under his own vine and fig tree to worship God as to him shall seem right. But we think it portends some danger, when a candidate for Congress, *bargains in advance* with any particular sect, to foster their especial interests at all hazards—without reference to such christian sects, as have, to say the least of them, equal claims to attention and patronage. Let Mr. Stuart beware that he does not dig a pit for himself to fall into; he may meet the fate of Mr. Little of Hancock, who after having paid his address with great assiduity to the Mormons, while he was toying with others, has been jilted, and now finds himself the discarded of all.[30]

Stuart won the Mormon vote in 1841; but it was the last time that the Whigs were to be so favored. The political sentiment of Nauvoo in 1840 was doubtless anti-Van Buren rather than pro-Whig. Nor did all Mormons stand together to vote for Harrison. On two hundred ballots the name of the Whig elector Abraham Lincoln was marked out and that of the Democrat James Ralston substituted. The *Quincy Whig* editorialized that there was "something connected with the vote at Nauvoo Precinct, which needs explanation. . . . Rumor says that the Hon. Richard M. Young, of the U.S. Senate, and the 'Little Giant' Stephen A. Douglass, who wants to go to Congress, were present at this election and of course their names are mentioned in connection with this little petty trick."[31] Furthermore, the Whig opposition to the vote of aliens could not win favor with the Mormons, whose numbers were being enlarged regularly by new

[29] *Ibid.,* 4:369, 370.
[30] *Illinois State Register,* June 11, 1841.
[31] Gayler, "The Mormons in Illinois Politics," pp. 50, 51n.

immigrants from Britain. Conversely, it was a regular policy of the Democracy to approbate the cause of alien immigrants and to enlist their votes.[32]

The politician who sought most earnestly to win the Mormon vote away from the Whigs was the twenty-eight-year-old State Supreme Court Justice, former Illinois Secretary of State, and aspiring congressman, Stephen A. Douglas. Seated by choice in the Mormon circuit, the young judge successfully curried the favor and friendship of the young Prophet; perhaps the two men recognized kindred spirits in one another. Smith wrote the *Times and Seasons* on May 6, 1841:

I wish, through the medium of your paper, to make known that, on Sunday last, I had the honor of receiving a visit from the Hon. Stephen A. Douglas, Justice of the Supreme Court, and Judge of the Fifth Judicial Circuit . . . and Cyrus Walker, Esq., of Macomb, who expressed great pleasure in visiting our city, and were astonished at the improvements which were made. They were officially introduced to the congregation who had assembled on the meeting ground, by the mayor; and they . . . addressed the assembly.

Judge Douglas expressed his satisfaction of what he had seen and heard respecting our people, and took that opportunity of returning thanks to the citizens of Nauvoo, for conferring upon him the freedom of the city; stating that he was not aware of rendering us any service sufficiently important to deserve such marked honor; and likewise spoke in high terms of our location and the improvements we had made, and that our enterprise and industry were highly creditable to us, indeed. . . .

Judge Douglas has ever proved himself friendly to this people, and interested himself to obtain for us our several charters, holding at that time the office of Secretary of State.

Mr. Walker also ranks high. . . . How different their conduct from that of the official characters . . . of Missouri, whose minds were prejudiced to such an extent that, instead of mingling in our midst and ascertaining for themselves our character, kept entirely aloof, but were ready, at all times, to listen to those who had "the poison of adders under their tongues," and who sought our overthrow. . . .

What makes [their] visit more pleasing is the fact the Messrs. Douglas and Walker have long been held in high estimation as politicians, being champions of the two great parties that exist in the state; but laying aside all party strife, like brothers, citizens, and friends, they mingle with us, mutually disposed to extend to us that courtesy, respect, and friendship, which I hope we shall ever be proud to reciprocate.[33]

Douglas served the Mormons on several occasions. He appointed one Esquire Davis, "who had spoken favorably of the Saints," to the

[32] See Buley, *The Old Northwest*, 2:245, 246.
[33] Joseph Smith's History, 4:356–358.

post of County Clerk, an action, according to Joseph Smith, which "much enraged" the citizens of Warsaw who were members of the anti-Mormon party.[34] Though Orville Browning offered able and eloquent counsel at the Monmouth hearing in June, 1841, Douglas had arranged with Smith to have the proceedings take place before his bench, where the Prophet was swiftly discharged. Governor Carlin had, upon request of the Missouri governor, issued two writs for Smith's arrest; but the first one had been returned for some reason unexecuted. The nonexecution of the first writ of arrest invalidated the second, said Douglas. Thomas Ford observed that in view of such a line of reasoning, "Smith was . . . the more inclined to esteem his discharge as a great favor from the Democratic party." [35] Finally, Douglas, according to his biographer Frank Stevens, "proceeded to clinch the Mormon vote by an act in which no Whig could divide honors." He appointed General John C. Bennett a Master-in-Chancery for Hancock County. Douglas' exercise of the power and patronage of the bench in behalf of the Mormons bore its fruit in time for the campaign of 1842.[36]

In December, 1841, the Illinois Democracy nominated State Senator Adam W. Snyder to be their candidate for Governor in the next election. Snyder appeared to be a strong candidate. He was a colonel of militia, a widely known attorney, and a legislator of tact and ability who inspired confidence in his followers.[37] As chairman of the Senate Judiciary Committee during the 1840–1841 session, he had promoted the passage of the Nauvoo charters, and the Saints felt indebted to him. Joseph Smith immediately announced his support for Snyder in a kind of political manifesto in the *Times and Seasons* addressed "To my Friends in Illinois." John C. Bennett had reported, said Smith, "that no men were more efficient in assisting him to procure our great chartered privileges, than were Colonel Snyder and Colonel Moore [the Democratic candidate for Lieutenant-Governor]. . . . With such men at the head of our State, government will have nothing to fear." The Saints had voted for Harrison, Smith explained, "because we loved him—he was a gallant officer and a tried statesman." But this was not to say that they were bound to be governed by his friends; Harrison was dead, "and all of his friends are not ours."

[34] *Ibid.*, 4:471.
[35] See Stevens, "Life of Stephen A. Douglas," pp. 342, 343; and Joseph Smith's History, 4:365, 374.
[36] Stevens, "Life of Stephen A. Douglas," p. 342.
[37] Greene and Thompson, *Governor's Letter Books*, p. xx.

In the next canvass, we shall be influenced by no party consideration . . . so the partizans of this county, who expect to divide the friends of humanity and equal rights, will find themselves mistaken—we care not a fig for Whig or Democrat; they are both alike to us, but we shall go for our friends, our tried friends, and the cause of human liberty, which is the cause of God. We are aware that "divide and conquer" is the watchword of many, but with us it cannot be done . . . we have suffered too much to be easily duped. . . . Douglas is a master spirit, and his friends are our friends. . . . Snyder and Moore are his friends—they are ours. These men are free from the prejudices and superstitions of the age, and such men we love, and such men will ever receive our support, be their political predilections what they may. . . . We will never be justly charged with the sin of ingratitude—they have served us, and we will serve them.[38]

Smith's candid avowal that the Mormons would vote as a bloc, that they had no party loyalties or interests, that they would vote for those whom they thought would serve them best, and that presently at least their favor rested upon the Democrats, set the Church upon a complex and hazardous political course. Such an avowal was bound to arouse jealousy and resentment; in addition, any candidate who frankly courted the Mormon vote had to weigh the liability of offending the anti-Mormon vote, which likewise knew no party label. Smith's assessment of the motives of politicians, both "friends" and "enemies," and of his own abilities to determine the true self-interests of his people and to guide and deliver their vote *en bloc* suggests that his political understanding was inadequate for the exacting game he had set himself to play.

The Whig press was swift in its reaction to the new Mormon political position. In the issues of January 14 and 21, 1842, the influential Springfield *Sangamo Journal* opened an attack on the Mormons that was to continue until the sect ceased to be a political factor in Illinois. Another Whig paper, the *Peoria Register and Northwestern Gazeteer*, in its edition of January 21 editorialized:

As we at various times expressed ourselves pretty decidedly against political tendencies of this sect, when they were acting with the Whigs, we cannot be charged with sudden hostility now that their leader has gone over, horse, foot, and dragoons, to our opponents. This is probably the first time that a public manifesto of this sort has been issued by a religious leader of this country. The Roman-Catholics in New York last fall, under the call of Bishop Hughes, voted a separate ticket,—in some of the canal counties of this state, the Irish have voted in a body for their candi-

[38] Joseph Smith's History, 4:479, 480. The Prophet signed his manifest "Joseph Smith, Lieutenant-General of the Nauvoo Legion." See also Ford, *History of Illinois*, pp. 263, 266, 267, 269.

date and elected them over both parties. But we have no recollection anywhere of a movement similar to that of the Mormon prophet. We trust that all parties will see its dangerous tendency, and at once rebuke it. The [fiscal] credit of Illinois abroad is bad enough now. What will it be when the fact is proclaimed that Mormonism sways its councils? [39]

The *Quincy Whig* for January 22 described the Prophet's announcement as a "highhanded attempt to usurp power and to tyrannize over the minds of men."

We are sorry to see this movement on the part of President Smith—not so much on account of the influence which his people voting in a body will have in the election—but because, it will have a tendency to widen the breach which already exists between his people and those who are not of their faith, and as a consequence create difficulties and disturbances growing out of an unsettled . . . feeling in the community. . . . Have the Whigs so far departed from the principles of liberality which have always governed them, as to call forth this public demonstration of opposition? We have seen no evidence of it. Many of the Mormons . . . are men of intelligence and patriotism, who will not be swayed to and fro in their support of men or party, by the *dictum* of their leader . . . and to those we look for aid and assistance in carrying the principles of reform into our State Government. The Mormons have a right to vote for SNYDER and MOORE, if they choose, as a matter of course . . . but this clannish principle of voting in a mass, at the dictation of one man, and this man who has acquired an influence over the minds of his people through the peculiar religious creed which he promulgates, is so repugnant to the principles of our Republican form of Government, that its consequences . . . will be disagreeable to think of—bitter hatred and unrelenting hostility will spring up, where before peace and good will had an abiding place.[40]

In the spring of 1842, when the parties were preparing for the elections the following August, the mass of voters in the state were despondent and apathetic about political matters, a situation traceable to the state's fiscal chaos. Indecision and pessimism characterized Carlin's administration in its final months. Since no program had been inaugurated to pay the state's staggering debt, Illinois suffered from a growing reputation for fiscal irresponsibility. It was

[39] Quoted in Snider, "Attitudes in Sectarian Conflict," pp. 22, 23, 37. Snider called the *Sangamo Journal*, the *Alton Telegraph*, and the *Warsaw Signal* "a press triangle that 'went to seed' on Mormon propaganda. The *Journal* was radically prejudiced against the sect. . . . These [were] the source papers opposing Mormonism, with the *Warsaw Signal* leading. . . . Most of the editors of Illinois papers realized that [those three] were ultra-radical . . . yet they allowed that propaganda to filter through their columns." See also Gayler, "The Mormons in Illinois Politics," pp. 51–53.

[40] Snider, "Attitudes in Sectarian Conflict," pp. 34, 35.

frequently called "a ruined state." Specie payments had been suspended at the State Bank since 1840, and the Bank of Cairo, which had furnished much of the state's sound small note currency, in December of 1841 found its notes unsalable in St. Louis and Chicago. The Bank of Cairo declined steadily and lost its charter in 1843. Liquidation of the State Bank, which was liable for much of the internal improvements debt, was to begin in the same year. By July of 1842, business in Illinois cities was near a specie basis; most of the paper that was in circulation was that of the State Bank of Indiana and the Wisconsin Marine and Fire Insurance Company. Political party squabbles had hampered the state's financial officers, who had not even kept proper accounts. Illinois bonds had been hypothecated at thirty-three cents on the dollar. Confusion prevailed in government and in parties, neither of which had a constructive program to offer the voters. The campaign and election promised to be lackluster affairs.[41]

The Whigs were so divided that a convention to nominate a gubernatorial candidate was almost certain to wreck the party. To prevent such a result, Lincoln and other factional candidates agreed privately to withdraw in favor of former Governor Joseph Duncan. Duncan had made a good record as a congressman, legislator, and governor, and was a vigorous campaigner. Furthermore he was "available" as far as the Mormon issue was concerned. He had been in private life when the Nauvoo charters were enacted, and he had previously taken no stand that would compromise him with the anti-Mormon vote. Duncan assessed the political situation astutely. The Mormons had already decided to support the Democrats, and the Whig press was in full anti-Mormon cry. Of greater importance, during the late spring and summer, the state was agog with John C. Bennett's exposé, a lurid attack on the Mormon kingdom from which he had just withdrawn. The Whig papers were happy to carry Bennett's articles in full. It was perhaps the most sensational scandal yet carried by the Illinois press, and it was reaping a strong anti-Mormon sentiment throughout the state. The Nauvoo City Charter, though favored by both parties, had been passed by a Democratic, not a Whig, legislature. The Mormons and gentiles had in practice interpreted its ambiguous provisions so differently that a strong reaction had begun against the charter. Many people might hesitate to vote, it appeared, for any candidate favored by the sect. So Duncan

---

[41] Pease, *Frontier State*, pp. 232, 233, 312 ff.

avoided the obvious, but perhaps unpopular, issues of internal improvements and public finance, and made anti-Mormonism in general and the repeal of the Nauvoo charters in particular the chief issues of his campaign.[42] "Governor Duncan . . . took the stump on this subject in good earnest," wrote Thomas Ford, "and expected to be elected governor almost on this question alone. There is no knowing how far he might have succeeded, if Mr. Snyder had lived to be his competitor." [43]

Remembering their romantic and emotional campaign of 1840, the Whigs concurred in Duncan's strategy, hoping the campaign of 1842 would be another sensation, a crusade against Mormon depravity in morals and conspiracy in politics. Perhaps a popular Whig issue in 1842 might turn the tide in what both parties believed would be a close election.[44]

John C. Bennett and the Whig press cooperated so closely during the summer of 1842 in attacking the Mormons that the Democrats, not without some reason, began to charge "conspiracy." The Whig newspapers gave Bennett abundant publicity and the freedom of their columns, and Bennett profited from his sudden notoriety by stumping the state to make inflammatory speeches against the Mormons. He had, he declared, joined the Saints in the first place merely to find them out, and now his chief purpose was to save the state and nation from their hellish designs. His immediate goal was to get Smith into Missouri, by legal process if possible but by force if necessary. "The whole affair has . . . the appearance of a mere political controversy," wrote historians Greene and Thompson, "the *Sangamo Journal* taking one side and the [Democratic] *State Register* the other. . . . [It] attracted more attention than its importance warranted. Bennett's profligate life and character ought, in great measure, to have detracted from the influence his charges would otherwise have had. As it was, the minds of a great many were unusually receptive, and the scandalous accusations were believed in their entirety in many quarters." [45]

Adam Snyder, the Democratic candidate, died suddenly in May.

[42] For a typical attack on the Nauvoo Charter and expression of the Mormon-Democrat conspiracy charge, see "The Mormon Plot and League, by which THOMAS FORD and JOHN MOORE hope to be elected Governor and Lieut. Governor of Illinois," *Sangamo Journal*, July 7, 1842.
[43] Ford, *History of Illinois*, p. 269.
[44] Greene and Thompson, *Governor's Letter Books*, pp. xx ff.
[45] *Ibid.*, pp. lxxxiii, lxxxiv. For a detailed discussion of the Bennett affair, see below, Chapter 9.

Party managers designed to turn the emergency to advantage if possible; a judicious choice of successor might steal some of the thunder from the Whig anti-Mormon attack, while perhaps still retaining the Mormon vote. Men with such "availability" were scarce; practically every well-known Democrat was on record for the Mormons —state legislators who had favored the Nauvoo charters, lawyers who had vouched for their constitutionality, judges who had had to render decisions where their validity was in question. In the circumstance the choice fell easily upon Supreme Court Justice Thomas Ford. Ford was modest, sincere, widely known, and well liked, especially in the North. He was a man of integrity, with a strongly legalistic turn of mind. Most important, Ford had not been in any way involved with the Mormons or the "Mormon Question," and he had not previously committed himself in the matter.[46]

The Mormons endorsed Ford's candidacy even before he was named officially as Snyder's successor, leading the Whigs again to charge that a "conspiracy" and "corrupt bargain" existed between the Democrats and Mormons. The Whigs also tried to make the voters believe that Ford, like Snyder, was a "Jack-Mormon." [47] But Ford conducted a campaign that confounded both his friends and his enemies. He was not a "locofoco," or "ultra" Democrat, and his stern preachments of the need to face the public debt boldly and begin to retire it were ill-received by party leaders. Particularly startling was his speech at Mt. Carmel on July 9 in which he called Joseph Smith an impostor and a scoundrel, and pledged himself to support the repeal or revision of the Nauvoo charters. Although Duncan was a more colorful campaigner, the people appeared to like Ford's frankness and sincerity. His position on Mormonism was taken apparently from conviction rather than political strategy, and he did not attempt to hedge on this or any other controversial issue. Ford won the election by a margin which rendered the Mormon vote indecisive. But the Whigs were dumfounded that despite Ford's "betrayal" of Mormon interests, he nevertheless carried Hancock County 1,174 to 711, suggesting an almost solid Democratic Mormon vote.[48] The Whig press explained that it was the result of a "corrupt bargain" between Mormons and Democrats, by which Ford had agreed to take an insincere anti-Mormon position publicly

[46] *Ibid.*, pp. xx ff.
[47] *Nauvoo Wasp*, May 28, 1842; *Sangamo Journal*, July 7, 1842.
[48] Pease, *Illinois Election Returns*.

to garner gentile votes.[49] There was nothing in the governor's subsequent actions, nor any other evidence, to support the charge. It is
probable that the Mormons did not take Ford's anti-Mormon campaign pronouncements very seriously.

The role of the Mormons in Illinois politics, exaggerated and distorted by the press of both parties, and grossly overestimated by the
Saints themselves, understandably failed to gain accurate reporting
in the eastern press. The *Niles National Register* of August 6, 1842,
estimated that the Mormons had "about six thousand votes under
their immediate control, sufficient to give them the balance of power
between parties in the state. It is alleged that they have found out
how to make a profitable market of this power. . . . They are now
accused of having contracted to support the [Democratic] party . . .
in consideration of which the City of Nauvoo had a charter granted
to it with very extraordinary powers. . . . Legislative powers [are]
conferred upon its officers equal to those possessed by the legislature itself."[50] Numbering Mormon voters at six thousand was an
absurd exaggeration, though a more accurate figure was probably
unavailable. The Mormons did not at any rate hold a balance of
power between the two parties in Illinois, nor did the passage of the
charters, favored routinely by both parties, figure in any "bargain"
with the Democrats. Such a garbled account added to the budding
national image of a Mormon Power in the sovereign state of Illinois.
That image was to blossom when the Bennett exposé was published
in Boston in the fall of 1842 and "Mormonism" became a national
scandal.

Between the August, 1842, elections and the special congressional
elections a year later nothing occurred to relax the tense political
atmosphere in Illinois. The state sank deeper into depression. Debts
were large and the ability to repay them was small; no adequate
monetary exchange existed and business failures were a daily occur-
rence. Wages were low; farmers could get little for their produce,
and in some localities, nothing at all. The increase of Illinois congressional districts from three to seven portended a "fruit basket
upset" situation. The Whig stronghold north and west of Springfield
was split, the northern part going into the new Sixth District and the
southern part into the Fifth. The border of the two districts was the
Adams-Hancock county line; and since Adams [Quincy] contained

[49] Greene and Thompson, *Governor's Letter Books,* p. xv.
[50] Quoted in Gayler, "The Mormons in Illinois Politics," p. 54.

a considerable Mormon population, the Saints were a political issue
in both districts. In 1842, many Whig candidates from the legislature had campaigned on pledges to repeal the Nauvoo charters; and
since some of them had been elected, the Mormons were bound to
be an issue in the 1842–1843 session of the Assembly. Bills of repeal
were introduced and vigorously advocated; and while the majority
would not yet consider such a politically delicate matter, Nauvoo
was shocked and disturbed by the proceedings. "At first it was supposed that this was merely an electioneering intrigue," wrote Sidney
Rigdon. "But it assumed a formidable appearance, and began to assume the character of a fixed determination to carry the design into
execution. The subsequent acts of the legislature have given but too
much evidence that such was the real intention of a very considerable portion of the members. . . . Not that [we] supposed that
there was any such power vested in the legislature, either in the constitution or in common sense; but [we] did not know how far a reckless spirit might lead men in the violation of both." [51] Joseph Smith,
alarmed by the ferocity of the Whig attack on his kingdom and perhaps disillusioned about the benefits to be gained by corporate political action, announced in January, 1843, that he would have nothing
further to do with politics. "I have of late had repeated solicitations
to have something to do in relation to the political farce about dividing the county," he wrote for publication in the *Nauvoo Wasp:*
". . . but as my feelings revolt at the idea of having anything to do
with politics, I have declined, in every instance, having anything to
do on the subject. I think it would be well for politicians to regulate
their own affairs. I wish to be let alone, that I may attend strictly to
the spiritual welfare of the Church." [52] However, as summer approached and the Prophet encountered his annual ordeal with Missouri extradition, he and the Saints were inadvertently drawn again
into the political maelstrom.

[51] Greene and Thompson, *Governor's Letter Books*, xl, xli; Joseph Smith's
History, 5:437.
[52] Joseph Smith's History, 5:259, 437. Governor Ford believed that the
Mormons had decided to switch their political support to the Whigs early in
1843 when Smith was vindicated in his test of an 1842 writ of arrest before the
Federal Justice Pope, a Whig. "As in the case decided by Judge Douglass,
Smith was too ignorant of the law to know whether he owed his discharge to
the law, or to the favor of the court and the Whig party. . . . The Mormons this
time were made to believe that they were under great obligations to the Whigs
for the discharge of their Prophet from what they believed to be the persecutions of the Democrats; and they resolved to yield their support to the Whig
party in the next election." Ford, *History of Illinois*, pp. 314.

In June, Missouri Governor James Reynolds asked Governor Ford for armed assistance to bring Smith into Missouri. The "Jack-Mormon" Sheriff of Hancock County, William Backenstos, assured the Mormons that he knew, on good authority, that Smith had nothing to fear from Ford as long as the Democrats could count on the Mormon vote. Ford later admitted that such a pledge had been made by a "prominent Democrat of Springfield" in the governor's name but without his knowledge or consent. The evidence does not indicate whether Smith believed Backenstos, though he may well have done so. Ford thought that he did, and that the Sheriff's message "produced a total change" in the minds of the Mormon leaders, a shift from Whig back to Democratic support. The governor described Backenstos as "a managing Democrat" of Hancock County. Ford said that he did not know of the pledge until the "prominent Democrat" himself disclosed it in October, 1846, when the Mormons had become extremely unpopular and most had fled the state. Since they no longer could be a support to anyone, "this man, following the example of hundreds of others of a similar class, has joined the anti-Mormon excitement, and has been a strong advocate of the expulsion of the Mormons and all who sought to do them but simple justice." [53]

But while the Prophet was visiting his wife's relatives in Lee County, some 130 miles northeast of Nauvoo, he was surprised and taken into custody by Missouri officers and a Hancock County constable armed with Ford's order for his arrest. Smith immediately sought legal aid in the form of a writ of habeas corpus, issued him by the Master-in-Chancery of Lee County, and the counsel of Cyrus Walker of Macomb, whom the Prophet said was "considered the greatest criminal lawyer in that part of Illinois." Walker, the Whig candidate for Congress from the Sixth District (which included Hancock County), happened to be campaigning nearby at the time. He came; but, according to Smith, "told me that he could not find time to be my lawyer unless I could promise him my vote. . . . I determined to secure his aid, and promised him my vote. He afterwards went to [Stephen] Markham and joyfully said, 'I am now sure of my election, as Joseph Smith has promised me his vote, and I am going to defend him.'"

After complex legal maneuvers Smith managed to get back to Nauvoo where he expected to be freed on a writ of habeas corpus

[53] Ford, *History of Illinois,* pp. 317, 318.

233

issued by his own Municipal Court. But he was alarmed at the readiness of the Missouri officers to abduct him by force if necessary. He was also frightened by the rumors that John C. Bennett was inciting an "invasion" mob in Missouri, that Ford had honored Reynold's extradition order, and that there was sentiment in Carthage to raise a posse to see that the order was carried out. In a legal sense his safety seemed to him to depend on the power of the Nauvoo Court, and perhaps ultimately on the strength of the Legion. In an emotional address to the citizens of Nauvoo on June 30, 1843, he referred to Nauvoo's sovereign and inviolable chartered rights again and again. Of Walker he said, "I have converted this candidate for congress that the right of habeas corpus is included in our charter. If he continues converted, I will vote for him. . . . If any lawyer shall say there is more power in other places and charters with respect to habeas corpus than in Nauvoo, believe it not." When Smith had finished, Walker "addressed the people to the effect that, from what he had seen in the Nauvoo City Charter, it gave the power to try writs of habeas corpus, etc." [54] In order to vitiate a renewed wave of anti-Mormon feeling aroused by Smith's apparent evasion of Ford's writ, the Prophet directed the Twelve to send elders throughout the state "to preach the gospel and disabuse the public mind with regard to my arrest." At a special Elder's Conference on July 3, eighty-one elders were appointed to go on "special missions" to all sixty-seven counties of Illinois.[55]

As the congressional elections of 1843 approached, the political parties scarcely knew what to expect from the Mormons. The Whigs had not changed their anti-Mormon positions, but Walker, long a friend of Smith, had by a *quid pro quo* secured the promise of the Prophet's vote, and, he assumed, the Mormon bloc vote of Hancock County along with it. The Democrats still counted themselves the beneficiaries of the Mormon vote, however, and assumed that the alignment of 1842 had not changed. "The public is already aware," said the Democratic *Illinois State Register* (Springfield) in mid-July, "that a demand was lately made upon the Governor of this State for the arrest of Joseph Smith, and that a writ was accordingly issued against him. We propose now to state some of the facts, furnishing strong ground of suspicion that the demand which was made

[54] Joseph Smith's History, 5:467, 468, 472. The occasion was reported by Wilford Woodruff.
[55] *Ibid.*, 5:483, 484.

on the Governor here, was a manoeuvre of the Whig party." John C. Bennett, said the *Register*, was the man responsible for renewing the attempt in Missouri to extradite Smith on the old charge of treason, and Bennett, "it is well known, has for a year past been a mere tool of the Whig junto at Springfield. He has been under their absolute subjection and control, and has been a regular correspondent of the *Sangamo Journal*, the principal organ of the Whig party. He has been a great pet of both the *Journal* and the junto, and that paper has regularly announced his removal from place to place, until latterly, and within the last year has published more of his writings than any other person except the editor." According to the *Register*, Walker had despaired of both the Mormon vote and the election, unless he could make a political coup of some kind. So Bennett and the Whig conspirators agreed to arrest Smith near Dixon where Walker "miraculously *happened* to be within six miles, ready and convenient to be employed by Smith to get him delivered from custody. . . . We say these facts . . . produce a strong suspicion, that the whole affair is a Whig conspiracy to compel a Democratic governor to issue a writ against Smith, pending the Congressional election, so as to incense the Mormons, create a necessity for Walker's and perhaps Browning's professional services in favor of Smith, to get him delivered out of a net of their own weaving, and thereby get the everlasting gratitude of the Mormons and their support of the Whig cause." [56] Whether or not the *Register*'s charges were true, they represent a quasi-official Democratic interpretation. Smith thought the editorial worthy of inclusion in his journal; but whether it was because he believed the Whig conspiracy idea to be an explanation for his arrest, or only because it placed the responsibility on Bennett, it is impossible to know.

Both Walker and his Democratic opponent, Joseph P. Hoge, considered the Mormon vote uncertain and worth their particular attention. They came together to Nauvoo on July 29 for four days of campaigning. "There was a political meeting at the Temple," Smith recorded, "when Mr. Joseph P. Hoge . . . addressed the citizens for three hours, and was replied to in short by Mr. Cyrus Walker." Two days later he wrote, "Hyrum [Smith] and Hoge called at the office, when Hoge acknowledged the power of the Nauvoo Charter habeas

[56] *Ibid.*, 5:513–515. Orville H. Browning was the Whig candidate in the Fifth Congressional District (including Adams County). His Democratic opponent was Stephen A. Douglas.

corpus. Esquire Walker gave a stump speech at the stand until dusk, and was immediately replied to by Esquire Hoge for over two hours, having lit candles for the purpose to hear them politically castigate each other."[57] Though Hyrum Smith chose to guide Mr. Hoge about the city, the Prophet gave no hint in his journal that he was anything but aloof and nonpartisan.

The Mormon leader undoubtedly felt himself to be in an equivocal position politically and thought it unfortunate that he had bargained with Walker. Although the Whigs were the avowed "enemies" of the Saints, he had given his support to their candidate. The Democrats, supposed advocates of the Mormons, were perhaps now alien too. Ford had already cooperated with Missouri to bring about Smith's undoing. The Prophet was bewildered. In a Fourth of July speech at Nauvoo he said:

> With regard to elections, some say all the Latter-day Saints vote together, and vote as I say. But I never tell any man how to vote or whom to vote for. But I will show you how we are situated by bringing a comparison. Should there be a Methodist Society here and two candidates running for office, one says, "If you will vote for me and put me in governor, I will exterminate the Methodists, take away their charters," etc. The other candidate says, "If I am governor, I will give all an equal privilege." Which would the Methodists vote for? Of course they would vote *en masse* for the candidate that would give them their rights.
>
> Thus it has been with us. Joseph Duncan said if the people would elect him he would exterminate the Mormons, and take away their charters. As to Mr. Ford, he made no threats, but manifested a spirit in his speeches to give every man his rights; hence the members of the Church universally voted for Mr. Ford and he was elected governor. But he has issued writs against me the first time the Missourians made a demand for me, and this is the second one he has issued against me, which has caused me much trouble and expense.[58]

Either by accident or design Smith found a way to keep his promise to Walker without diverting the Mormon vote from the Demo-

---

[57] Though both Walker and Hoge were "distinguished lawyers," Thomas Ford said that in the matter of advising the Nauvooans of the habeas corpus power of their charters, "the Mormons were deluded and deceived by men who ought to have known better and did know better. . . . If judicious and legal advice were given to [the Saints], they rejected it with scorn, when it came in conflict with their favorite projects; for which reason all persons designing to use them, made it a rule to find out what they were in favor of, and advise them accordingly. In this mode the Mormons relied for advice, for the most part, upon the most corrupt of mankind, who would [advise] them to their destruction, as a means of gaining their favor." Ford, *History of Illinois*, p. 316.

[58] Joseph Smith's History, 5:490.

crats. Publicly he would take a nonpartisan position, cast his own vote for Walker, but let his brother Hyrum direct the vote of the Saints into the Democratic column. That such a course would compromise his own integrity and the political position of the Church seems not to have occurred to him. Willard Richards wrote Brigham Young that on Sunday, July 9, "Joseph gave a sweet conciliatory discourse at the stand, expressive of good feeling for all men." The following Sunday, said Richards, Smith "said he would not prophesy any more; Hyrum should be the prophet; (did not tell them he was going to be a priest now, or a king by and by;) told the elders not to prophesy when they go out preaching." [59] Hyrum Smith had previously been appointed by Joseph to be a "Prophet and Revelator" as well as Patriarch of the Church in January, 1841; but he had always stood in his brother's shadow, and had apparently not much exercised the charismatic offices conferred on him.[60] Now these offices were to have a function. However, Joseph said on Sunday, July 23, that his renunciation should not be taken too seriously. "It has gone abroad," he said,

that I proclaimed myself no longer a prophet. I said it last Sunday ironically: I supposed that you would all understand. . . . Last Monday morning certain brethren came to me and said they could hardly consent to receive Hyram as a prophet, and for me to resign. But I told them, "I only said it to try your faith; and it is strange, brethren, that you have been in the Church so long, and not yet understand the Melchisedek priesthood. . . ." It was not that I would renounce the idea of being a prophet, but that I had no disposition to proclaim myself such. But I do say that I hear the testimony of Jesus, which is the spirit of prophecy.[61]

Charlotte Haven, a young gentile resident of Nauvoo, wrote of the affair: "Our Gentile friends say that this falling of the prophetic mantle on to Hyrum is a political ruse. Last winter [*sic*] when Joseph was in the clutches of the law, he was assisted by some politicians of the Whig party, to whom he pledged himself in the coming elections. Now he wants the Democratic party to win, so Hyrum is of that party, and as it is revealed to him to vote, so go over all the Mormons like sheep following the bell sheep over the wall." [62] On August 2, five days before the election, Apostle John Taylor's *Nauvoo Neighbor* encouraged all the Saints to vote for

[59] *Ibid.*, 5:511, 512.
[60] See *ibid.*, 4:286.
[61] *Ibid.*, 5:516–518.
[62] Quoted in Mulder and Mortensen, eds., *Among the Mormons*, p. 127.

Hoge. "It can serve no good purpose that half the citizens should disfranchise the other half, thus rendering Nauvoo powerless as far as politics is concerned." [63] On Saturday, August 5, two days before the election, Hyrum Smith announced to a large assembly that it was the Will of Heaven that the Saints should vote for Hoge. President William Law created a sensation by challenging the validity of such a revelation, and said that Joseph would not sanction it.[64] The following day Joseph addressed the assembled Sabbath-day gathering as follows:

> I am above the kingdoms of the world, for I have no laws. I am not come to tell you to vote this way, that way, or the other. In relation to national matters, I want it to go abroad unto the whole world that every man should stand on his own merits. The Lord has not given me a revelation concerning politics. I have not asked him for one. I am a third party, and stand independent and alone. . . . As for Mr. Walker he is . . . a high-minded man. He has not hung onto my coattail to gain his election, as some have said. I am going to give a testimony, but not for electioneering purposes. Before Mr. Walker came to Nauvoo, rumor came up that he might become a candidate. Said I—He is an old friend, and I'll vote for him. When he came to my house, I voluntarily told him I should vote for him. . . . He withdrew all claim to your vote and influence if it would be detrimental to your interests as a people.
>
> Brother Hyrum tells me this morning that he has had a testimony to the effect it would be better for the people to vote for Hoge; and I never knew Hyrum to say he ever had a relevation and it failed. Let God speak and all men hold their peace. I never authorized Brother Law to tell my private feelings, and I utterly forbid these political demogogues from using my name henceforth and forever. It is my settled opinion that if Governor Ford erred in granting a writ against me, it is an error of the head, and not of the heart; and I authorize all men to say I am a personal friend of Governor Ford.[65]

The following day, August 7, Joseph recorded in his journal, "Election of Representatives to Congress and state and county officers, the Democratic ticket prevailing in Nauvoo by an overwhelming majority." [66]

[63] *Nauvoo Neighbor,* August 2, 1843.
[64] Ford, *History of Illinois,* pp. 318, 319; Gayler, "The Mormons in Illinois Politics," pp. 56, 57. See also Linn, *The Story of the Mormons,* pp. 248, 249, and Brodie, *No Man Knows My History,* p. 353.
[65] Joseph Smith's History, 5:526. Fawn Brodie states that "Hyrum had promised the Democrats the Mormon vote in return for a seat in the state legislature the following year. In the last week before the election he began openly campaigning for Hoge. . . . William Law was outraged at what he believed was a political sellout to further Hyrum's personal ambitions and fought him at every turn." *No Man Knows My History,* p. 353.
[66] Joseph Smith's History, 5:527.

The Mormon vote was decisive in the election of the Democrat Joseph Hoge in the Sixth Congressional District; and it became apparent that a continuation of Mormon support for the Democracy would mean the permanent eclipse of the Whigs in the County and District. Hoge's margin of victory was only 574 (7,796 to 7,222) while his plurality in Hancock County was 1,355 (2,088 to 733). Without the Mormon vote the Democrats had polled only 624 votes in Hancock in the 1840 presidential election, and 523 in the 1841 congressional election.[67]

In 1844 the Mormon vote again may have been decisive in the re-election of Hoge. He carried the district 8,752 to 7,563; in Hancock County, Hoge won 2,251 to 702. A normal split of the Mormon vote between the major parties would have made the election a very close one.[68]

In neighboring Adams County the considerable Mormon vote in the 1843 election apparently went for the Whig O. H. Browning. Word of Hyrum's "revelation" did not reach them, and they apparently assumed that they were to vote with the Prophet for the Whigs. Perhaps their vote was not considered of importance by the leaders in Nauvoo. But the Mormon vote in Adams was small comfort to Browning and the Whigs, since they lost the election anyway to Douglas. Furthermore, they could look forward to a shift in the Mormon vote to Douglas in the election of 1844.[69] Adams County Whigs had won small majorities in the elections of 1840, 1841, 1842, and 1843 despite the state-wide Democratic trend. They had been in the Whiggish Third Congressional District; but in the first election in the new Fifth District, the Democrats won in the District with 51 per cent of the vote. Douglas had carried Adams County in 1838 with 53 per cent of the vote; in 1843, without the Mormon vote, he won only 41 per cent, with 54 per cent for Browning and 5 per cent for the Liberty Party candidate. In 1844, with Mormon support, Douglas won Adams with 51 per cent, to 44 per cent for the Whig and 5 per cent for the Liberty Party. The result of the poll for presidential electors was identical.[70] The loss in 1844 of what the Whigs

[67] Pease, *Illinois Election Returns,* pp. 117, 125, 140.

[68] *Ibid.,* p. 147. Another important factor in the 1844 election in the Sixth District was the Liberty Party, which polled 506 votes. These undoubtedly included many "Conscience Whigs," and thus cut into the normal strength of the Whig Party.

[69] Letter of the Fifth District Democratic Party to the *Illinois State Register,* quoted in the *Nauvoo Neighbor,* September 27, 1843.

[70] Pease, *Illinois Election Returns,* pp. 109, 117, 122, 124, 126, 139, 146; Stevens, "Life of Stephen A. Douglas," pp. 359–362.

saw as a perfidious Mormon vote was only one factor in the decline
of their party; Douglas' political power, the congressional redistrict-
ing, the Whig weakness as a party in state and nation, and the
strong Democratic trend in 1844 contributed as well. But Adams
County Whigs, along with others of their party in Illinois, were especially bitter against the Saints; and their unrelenting attack on
corporate Mormonism began to suggest that the only "final" solution
to the problem of corporate Mormonism was its destruction or expulsion. Nor did the Democrats espouse the defense of the Saints as
anti-Mormon feeling in Illinois increased. The Church had tried to
use its political power, actual and potential, as both a promise and a
threat; the Saints got little in return but a fear and hatred that was
soon to prove fatal to them. "From this time forth," wrote Thomas
Ford, "the Whigs generally, and a part of the Democrats, determined upon driving the Mormons out of the state; and everything
connected with the Mormons became political. To this circumstance
in part, is to be attributed the extreme difficulty ever afterwards of
doing anything effectually in relation to the Mormon and anti-Mormon parties, by the executive government." [71]

The majority of Mormons were not chastened in political matters
by their expulsion from Illinois, and continued to espouse the bloc-
vote principle. As the election of 1848 approached they sought to
turn their presence in Iowa to political advantage. "The Whig and
Democratic parties were nearly equally balanced in the state" wrote
Brigham Young, "and both appeared solicitous of the welfare of our
people; they wanted us to vote in the . . . election." The solicitude
of which Young spoke enabled the Mormons to create their own
county out of the Pottawottamie Indian lands. Orson Hyde edited a
newspaper favoring the Whigs, and the Saints voted Whig in 1848,
1849, and 1850. The Democrats, who carried the state of Iowa in
1848, were angered and sought the disorganization of Pottawattamie
County. An explosive political situation might have been one reason
why Young urged the abandonment of Kanesville [Council Bluffs]
in 1851.[72]

The notion that the Mormon Kingdom should present a solid
front politically matured in Utah; it was one of the chief levers by
which Utah sought statehood, and one of the main political reasons

[71] Ford, *History of Illinois*, p. 319.
[72] James K. Melville, "The Political Ideas of Brigham Young" (unpublished
Ph.D. dissertation, University of Utah, 1956), pp. 51, 52.

why statehood was denied for so long. In 1881 a Bishop Lunt of the Mormon Church is reported to have said, "Our vote is solid, and will remain so. It will be thrown where the most good will be accomplished for the church. Then, in some great political crisis, the two present political parties will bid for our support. Utah will then be admitted as a polygamous state, and the other territories we have peacefully subjugated will be admitted also. We will then hold the balance of power, and will dictate to the country. . . . We possess the ability to turn the political scale in any particular community we desire. Our people are obedient. When they are called by the church, they promptly obey." [73] While perhaps not the official position of the Church, Bishop Lunt suggested the climate of opinion that existed among the hierarchy. The Mormons had developed in Illinois a view of politics that was to be a characteristic of the Great Basin Kingdom—a view that the vote was the instrument not of individual action but of group power. The individual might be saved in the kingdom, but the kingdom itself must be saved by the group action of individuals. "Every religion is to be found in juxtaposition to a political opinion," observed de Tocqueville, "which is connected with it by affinity. If the human mind be left to follow its own bent, it will regulate the temporal and spiritual institutions of society upon one (and the same) uniform principle; and man will endeavor . . . *to harmonize the state in which he lives on earth with the state he believes to await him in heaven.*" [74]

[73] Anson P. Stokes, *Church and State in the United States* (New York, 1950), 2:281.
[74] Alexis de Tocqueville, *Democracy in America*, Third American Edition (New York, 1839), p. 299.

9

Conflict Within the Kingdom

*There is nothing to which the minds of good men, when once passed the
bounds of sound discretion, and launched on the ocean of feeling and
experiment, may not come . . . nothing so terrible and unmanageable
as the fire and whirlwind of human passion, when once kindled by mis-
guided zeal. . . . For, in every church, there is wood, hay, and stubble
which will be sure to take fire on the wrong side. . . . New England of
the West shall be burnt over . . . as in some parts of New England it
was done eighty years ago.*

Lyman Beecher to Nathaniel Beeman, 1828, quoted in Cross, *The Burned-
Over District*, p. 110 facing.

Internal strife, disunion, and schism were always as great
a danger to Mormonism as attacks from the outside; and although
persecution finally destroyed the Nauvoo community, disagreement among brethren divided the Church. There had been de-
fections by individuals almost from the founding of the movement, and serious revolts had occurred in Kirtland and Far West in
1837 and 1838. But the untimely death of Joseph Smith and the
difficult problem of succession occasioned the breakup of the
Church into hostile, disputatious groups. The succession crisis was,
however, only one of a long series of troubles. From the beginning
Mormonism was prone to excesses, resulting in inner tensions and
conflicts which brotherly love and common conviction could not always overcome. As a result, alienation worked two ways; sometimes
the individual member displeased the group and was cast out, and
sometimes the group or the leadership displeased the individual so
much that he withdrew.[1] Often, of course, the disaffection was

---

[1] Contention between brethren prompted a reproof from the Nauvoo High
Council early in 1842. "We are grieved at the conduct of some," they wrote
in *Times and Seasons*, "who . . . instead of promoting union, appear to be
engaged in sowing strifes and animosities . . . spreading evil reports; brother
going to law with brother, for trivial causes, which we consider a great evil,
and altogether unjustifiable, except in extreme cases, and then not before the
world. Saints are to judge both the world and the angels, therefore such lawing
before the world is shameful. Why do ye not rather take wrong? Why do ye
not rather suffer yourselves to be defrauded? The law of the Lord as well as

mutual. While members were disfellowshipped for failure to observe the "Word of Wisdom," usually either by using alcohol, tobacco, or "hot drinks," the Church subjected itself to similar criticism when the Nauvoo city government legalized liquor. The Church had condemned secret societies, but then encouraged a Masonic lodge in Nauvoo. The Church denounced "priestcraft," but employed a priestly hierarchy of control that grew stronger and more absolute with the passing of time and the purge of dissenters. Theocracy in government and mandatory cooperation in social and economic matters conflicted with the individualism of many devout believers. The Church had insisted on strict morality among its members; but the scandalous amours of John C. Bennett, the charges of immorality made against the Mormon hierarchy by both "enemies" and "apostates," and finally the teaching and practice of the spiritual wife doctrine (which implied plural marriage) was unsettling to many Saints. In short, Mormons had the same ardor for morality and social uplift which characterized other Christian sects and the various reform movements of the period; but at the same time the Church exhibited aspects of what Cross calls "ultraism"—novel modes of belief and practice at variance with established mores. Though Mormonism demanded orthodoxy of its adherents, it was an unorthodox sect that sometimes shocked its own members as well as its "enemies." [2]

Since Joseph Smith assumed the ultimate authority and responsibility for everything in the Church and since whatever he espoused or opposed became more or less the official position, he was naturally the crux of most of the really serious controversies, and final dissent was usually against his authority, regardless of the initial causes of disagreement. After Smith's death, the same was true of Brigham Young. Descriptions of the numerous schisms or "apostasies" have tended to present an incongruous dichotomy of those utterly faithful to Smith and those utterly opposed to him, with no apparent middle ground and no obvious issue other than the Prophet and his works. Such a picture is much oversimplified and fails to include the difficulty that the Mormons had in achieving a

---

the law of the land should guide." *Times and Seasons*, 3:699, 700, February 15, 1842.

[2] Cross, *The Burned-Over District*, contains a thoughtful treatment of the social and religious climate of western New York, the cradle of Mormonism, in the twenties. See also D. B. Davis, "The New England Origins of Mormonism," *New England Quarterly*, 26:147–168 (1953).

consensus about other things. But Smith did assume too much of the burden, both of responsibility and of acrimony. Being courageous as well as vain, he played all the roles of absolute leader, including martyrdom. He was bound to be loved, hated, and feared by Mormons as well as gentiles. The language of Smith's revelations was always cast in the first person, "Thus saith the Lord" fashion of the Biblical prophets. But by the Nauvoo period he was using the mode with less restraint than at first, and using it to give force not only to formal *ex cathedra* communications but to assorted miscellaneous pronouncements as well. When Smith failed to separate the prophetic role from that of administrator, entrepreneur, political aspirant, and plain disputant, the sacredness of his spiritual leadership became jeopardized in the eyes of many Mormons. When "thus saith God" mixed in temporal affairs, as it did in the Nauvoo House enterprise, trouble resulted. "It seems to me, General," said Josiah Quincy to Smith in April, 1844, "That you have too much power to be safely trusted to one man." "In your hands or that of any other person," Smith replied, "so much power would, no doubt, be dangerous. I am the only man in the world whom it would be safe to trust with it. Remember, I am a prophet!" Smith's concluding remark, Quincy related, was a "rich, comical aside," as though it must have sounded ridiculous to a gentile.[3]

In February, 1833, the Church had been admonished by the word of revelation against the use of alcohol. The document is unique among all Smith's revelations in that it was not a "commandment" but merely inspired counsel. It was "A word of wisdom," says the preface, "for the benefit of the . . . church. . . ."[4] The "Word of Wisdom" was particularly esteemed by Latter-day Saints. Its observance was sometimes made a test of fellowship. The second General Conference held in Nauvoo "voted that Ephraim Owen's confession for disobeying the Word of Wisdom be accepted."[5] In June,

---

[3] Mulder and Mortensen, eds., *Among the Mormons*, p. 140.

[4] The document continues:

"Behold, thus saith the Lord unto you, in consequence of the evils and designs which do and will exist in the hearts of conspiring men in the last days, I have warned you, and forewarn you . . . that inasmuch as any man drinketh wine or strong drink among you, behold, it is not good, neither meet in the sight of your Father. . . . And again, strong drinks are not for the belly, but for the washing of your bodies. And again, tobacco is not for the body, neither for the belly, and is not good for man, but is an herb for bruises, and all sick cattle, to be used with judgment and skill. And again, hot drinks are not for the body or belly." Book of *Doctrine and Covenants*, Section 86.

[5] "Minutes of Conference at Commerce, Illinois, October 6th, 7th, and 8th, 1839," in Joseph Smith's History, 4:12.

1841, the High Council of Zarahemla Stake resolved unanimously to revoke the elder's license of Calvin Beebe "for breaking the covenent and keeping a tippling shop." Brother Beebe was then disfellowshipped, and the Council issued a warning that other offenders would meet a similar fate. The following August the Zarahemla Stake Conference decided to disfellowship any brethren "who are in the habit of drinking ardent spirits." [6]

With such emphasis it appeared at the outset that Nauvoo was to be a dry town. The charter of the Nauvoo House forbade the sale or use of liquor on the premises.[7] "As chairman of the committee [on the vending of spiritous liquors]," said Smith in February, 1841, "I reported a bill to the City Council, which, after a long discussion, passed into 'An ordinance in relation to temperance!' " The ordinance forbade the sale of "whisky in a less quantity than a gallon, or other spiritous liquors in less quantity than a quart . . . excepting on the recommendation of a physician, duly accredited in writing by the Chancellor and Regents of the University of the City of Nauvoo [Bennett]." So liquor by the drink was outlawed. "In the discussion of the foregoing bill," wrote Smith, "I spoke at great length on the use of liquors, and showed that they were unnecessary, and operate as a poison to the stomach, and that roots and herbs can be found to effect all necessary purposes." [8] Reporting the proceedings at the laying of the Temple cornerstones the following April, the Prophet wrote: "What added greatly to the happiness we experienced on this interesting occasion, is the fact that we heard no obscene or profane language; neither saw we anyone intoxicated. Can the same be said of a similar assemblage in any other city in the Union? Thank God that the intoxicating beverage, the bane of humanity in these last days, is becoming a stranger in Nauvoo." [9] In November, 1841, the city council ordered the Legion to raze a "grocery" near the Temple

[6] *Times and Seasons*, 2:498–499, June 7, 1841, and 2:548, August 2, 1841. See also Joseph Smith's History, 4:106. The Prophet himself used neither alcohol nor tobacco. See William Clayton's testimonial in the *Millennial Star*, 3:76, August, 1842.
[7] Joseph Smith's History, 4:302.
[8] *Ibid.*, 4:298, 299. It is false to assume, however, that Smith held strictly abstemious views. In 1836, for example, he blessed and partook of the wine served at the wedding dinner of Apostle John Boynton, a feast which was, said Smith, "conducted after the order of heaven." Two years later President Hyrum Smith advised the Kirtland Camp Company "not to be too particular in regard to the Word of Wisdom." Joseph Smith's History, 2:378; 3:95. See also *ibid.*, 2:369, 447.
[9] *Ibid.*, 4:330, 331.

where spirits were being dispensed unlawfully. Despite criticism by gentile citizens of such an order, it was summarily executed.[10]

Although Nauvoo was a city of temperate or abstinent Saints, it was also a burgeoning western river town. Doubtless most of its gentiles and many Mormons did not hold prohibitionist views, and the demand for alcohol in its various forms must have been more or less constant. Such pressure is evident in the gradual relaxation of the official attitude toward liquor. As early as July, 1841, Smith recorded, "I was in the City Council, and moved that any person in the City of Nauvoo be at liberty to sell vinous liquors in any quantity, subject to the city ordinances." He offered no further explanation, nor did he say whether his motion carried the council.[11] There was apparently never any prohibition on the sale of beer and ale, and on April 9, 1842, the council acted to license taverns and ordinaries in the town to sell beer but not spirits.[12] But on May 14, Smith recorded, "I attended city council in the morning, and . . . spoke at length for the repeal of the ordinance . . . licensing merchants, hawkers, taverns, and ordinaries, desiring that this might be a free people, and enjoy equal rights and privileges, and the ordinances were repealed."[13] Furthermore, there was illicit whisky to be had in Nauvoo. Fines levied against violators were small, and scarcely a deterrent to those engaged in so attractive a business.[14]

By 1843 Smith's attitude toward intoxicants had grown more liberal and urbane. In March of that year he noted in his journal, "I told Theodore Turley that I had no objection to his building a brewery." When the Prophet opened his own hostelry in September he allowed O. P. Rockwell to establish a bar there. Emma Smith was in St. Louis at the time; when she returned she was furious, and told Joseph he had to choose between the bar and his wife, since he could not have both under the same roof. Smith protested that the arrangement was only temporary, and that Rockwell would soon open a barber shop–bar across the street. But Emma was adamant, and the bar was removed.[15] However, in December, the city council

---

[10] *Times and Seasons*, 3:599, 600, November 15, 1841.

[11] Joseph Smith's History, 4:383.

[12] *Times and Seasons*, 3:765, April 15, 1842.

[13] Joseph Smith's History, 5:8. The same council session acted to prohibit "brothels and disorderly characters." Smith had told them that there were "certain characters in the place, who were disposed to corrupt the morals and chastity of our citizens, and that houses of infamy did exist. . . ."

[14] *Ibid.*, 5:57, 198, 541.

[15] Memoirs of Joseph Smith III, pp. 74, 75. The Prophet's son added that the building begun across the street for Rockwell was never finished.

passed "An Ordinance for the health and convenience of travelers and other persons" that authorized the Mayor (Smith) to sell or otherwise dispense spirits at his house "in any quantity as he shall judge . . . wisdom. . . ."[16] In October, 1844, the sale of liquor by the drink in Nauvoo was fully authorized. Liquor licenses were granted by the Mayor's Court at a fee of from two hundred to four hundred dollars, with heavy fines authorized for violators.[17] The same ordinance contained a prohibition on drunkenness.

One can only surmise how extensive was the use of alcohol in Nauvoo, based upon the fragmentary kinds of information given above, or a comment such as that of Hosea Stout on the occasion when he took his first plural wife. The celebrants drank "what wine we wanted" before listening to some "edifying remarks by President Amasa Lyman." Stout noted in his journal another social event where the Twelve and other Church authorities "were provided with as much beer, wine, cakes, etc., as we could eat and drink."[18] Nor is it possible to do more than guess at the degree of the Saints' disapproval of conviviality in Nauvoo. Undoubtedly Emma Smith was not the only one who reacted strongly against this additional secular trend within the Kingdom. By the time the Mormons established themselves in Utah, the prohibition of tea, coffee, tobacco, and alcohol that had existed in the thirties in the Church apparently had eroded away almost completely, and those products were in common use among them. But in the middle sixties, a move to revive the Word of Wisdom was undertaken not for moral but for economic purposes. The stimulants were luxuries that had to be mostly imported, with a consequent drain of hard money to the outside. Brigham Young admonished the Saints to produce such goods themselves or do without; and in less than two decades abstinence from tea, coffee, tobacco, and alcohol was almost as strong a test of faith and fellowship as willingness to take a mission.[19]

Another indication that the Kingdom was not intended to lack urbanity or the accouterments of American middle class culture was evidenced in the enthusiasm with which Joseph and Hyrum Smith and other leading Mormons established Freemasonry in Nauvoo, apparently through the urging of John C. Bennett. On March 15,

[16] Joseph Smith's History, 6:111.
[17] *Nauvoo Neighbor*, October 23, 1844.
[18] Brooks, *John Doyle Lee*, pp. 68, 69.
[19] Leonard Arrington, "An Economic Interpretation of the Word of Wisdom," *Brigham Young University Studies*, 1:37–49 (1959); and Arrington, *Great Basin Kingdom*, pp. 223 ff., 250.

1842, before a large crowd assembled in the Grove, the Prophet himself presided with obvious delight as "grand chaplain" at the installation of the Nauvoo Lodge. "The day was exceedingly fine," he wrote in his journal, "all things were done in order, and universal satisfaction was manifested." In the evening the neophyte Masons met in the Prophet's office, where Smith was awarded the first Masonic degree. The next day he "rose to the sublime degree." President Hyrum Smith was chosen the first master of the Nauvoo Lodge.[20] The Prophet enjoyed being a Mason, as his unfailing interest in the affairs of the fraternity and the pleasure he took in its social life attested. But Masonry apparently made additions to the theology as well as the society of the Kingdom. Six weeks after his introduction to the mysteries of the Order he preached a sermon on "the keys of the kingdom." "The keys are certain signs, and words," he said, "by which false spirits and personages may be detected from true, which cannot be revealed to the Elders till the Temple is completed. . . . There are signs in heaven, earth, and hell; the Elders must know them all, to be endowed with power, to finish their work and prevent imposition. The devil knows many signs, but does not know the sign of the Son of Man, or Jesus. No one can truly say he knows God until he has handled something, and this can only be in the holiest of holies."[21] The Biblical term "keys," meaning religious authority or power, had been used frequently by Smith from the beginning of his ministry both in revelations and in sermons. But here was a new connotation suggestive of the influence of Masonry; it also was a clue to the relation existing in the Prophet's mind between special, perhaps secret, new priesthood rites and the Temple. The Nauvoo Lodge of Masonry, however, was to have its own temple. The cornerstone was laid by Hyrum Smith in June, 1843, and the building was completed in April, 1844. Details of its size and cost are lacking, but the Prophet described it as "the most substantial and best finished of all Masonic Temples in the western states." More than five hundred Masons attended its dedication.[22] The fraternity did not, however, prevent the persistence of antagonism between Mormon and gentile Masons. A Master Mason named Nye whom Smith described as an adulterer and a "hypocritical

---

[20] Joseph Smith's History, 4:550–552; *The Return*, 2:287, June, 1890.
[21] Joseph Smith's History, 4:608.
[22] See Joseph Smith's History, 5:422, 430, 446; 6:287, 349, 350. Ebenezer Robinson recalled that the lower room of the Masonic temple was fitted as a theater. *The Return*, 2:287, June, 1890.

Presbyterian preacher" who tried to "pull me by the nose and trample on me" established a rival lodge up on the "hill" in April, 1843. The Prophet did not elaborate, but it probably appealed for members to the gentiles of the Order.[23] As in the matter of Nauvoo temperance, there is little direct evidence of the public reaction or opposition to Masonry in Nauvoo and its patronage by the hierarchy. It is difficult to imagine, however, that opposition did not exist. The widespread influence of the anti-Masonic movement, like the temperance movement, must have left its impress on numerous Latter-day Saint converts. The *Book of Mormon* stressed the dangers and abominations of secret societies; and a revelation from Smith in 1831 voiced the warning that "a thing . . . is had in secret chambers, to bring to pass even your destruction in process of time, and ye know it not. . . ."[24] Ebenezer Robinson viewed the introduction of Freemasonry into the Kingdom with disgust. "Heretofore," he wrote, "the church had strenuously opposed secret societies such as Freemasons, [and] Knights of Pythias . . . not considering the 'Order of Enoch' and 'Danites' of that class; but after Dr. Bennett came into the Church a great change of sentiment seemed to take place. . . ."[25]

Joseph Smith and other Mormon officials were frequently charged by their critics with extorting converts' money. The charge was stoutly denied, apparently with justification. Extortion as such was not a problem, but there was an unsettled area of relations between private and public enterprise in the Kingdom. Successful gentile businesses were sometimes subjected to pressure if they did not meet with official approval for whatever reason—as when the Prophet attacked the housebuilders who hired the Nauvoo House workmen away from their jobs on the hotel. But faithful brethren could be victims of such interference, too, as was illustrated when the Twelve took the *Times and Seasons* away from Ebenezer Robinson. Robinson was a Nauvoo pioneer of 1839. He and Don Carlos Smith began the *Times and Seasons* in a dank basement using a press and type that had been buried in Missouri to save it from the mob. In addition to publishing the paper, they added to their busi-

[23] Joseph Smith's History, 5:370, 371. Smith received news of Nye's death with satisfaction just before the rival chapter opened. ". . . any man or Mason who attempts to ride me down or oppress me," he said, "will run against the boss of Jehovah's buckler and will be quickly moved out of the way."
[24] *Doctrine and Covenants*, Section 38:4; Joseph Smith's History, 1:141.
[25] *The Return*, 2:287, June, 1890.

ness job printing, a type foundry, a book bindery, and a stationery shop. To house the operation they built a "commodious" brick building at the corner of Bain and Water Streets, two blocks west of the Prophet's house. "I felt that the blessing of the Lord rested upon my labors," wrote Robinson, "as I was endeavoring with all my heart, to try and help establish righteousness and truth in the earth, and at the same time build up a permanent business for myself and family, little dreaming of what was in store for me." [26]

In the summer and fall of 1841 the Twelve were assuming the enlarged duties as administrators in the Kingdom conferred on them by Joseph Smith. One of their decisions was that the official paper should be owned and operated by the Church, "they being not satisfied with the manner in which Gustavus Hills [then Robinson's associate] had conducted the editorial department since the death of Robert B. Thompson." Robinson was adjured to sell the paper to them, or else they would start a competing paper of their own.[27] According to Robinson, the Prophet had warned him previously that the Twelve wanted to control the paper. "I thought it would be well to tell you," Robinson quoted Smith as saying, "for I am sorry to see any difference arise between you brethren who have borne the burden in the heat of the day." [28] Robinson balked, however, and additional pressure was applied. On January 17, 1842, the Nauvoo Stake High Council, according to Smith, who was in attendance, "were unanimously opposed to Robinson's publishing the *Book of Mormon* and other books." [29] Eleven days later, the Prophet recorded the following revelation to the Twelve: "Verily thus saith the Lord unto you, my servant Joseph, go and say unto the Twelve, that it is my will to have them take in hand the editorial department of the *Times and Seasons* according to that manifestation which shall be given unto them by the power of my Holy Spirit in the midst of their counsel [*sic*] saith the Lord, Amen." [30] At that Robinson gave in but insisted that the Church buy his entire business. On February 4, a week after the revelation, the Prophet wrote, "closed a contract with Ebenezer Robinson for the printing office . . . also the paper

[26] *The Return*, 2:324, 325, September, 1890.
[27] Meetings of the Council of Twelve, November 20 and 30, 1841. Joseph was present at the latter meetings. Joseph Smith's History, 4:454, 463: Brigham Young's journal in the *Millennial Star*, 26:104, February 13, 1864.
[28] *The Return*, 2:324, September, 1890.
[29] Joseph Smith's History, 4:494, 495.
[30] *Ibid.*, 4:503.

fixtures, bookbindery, and stereotype foundry, by proxy, namely, Willard Richards, cost between 7,000 and 8,000 dollars." Robinson, writing many years later of the event, reported a price of $6,600 recorded in his account book, of which he said he consecrated $4,-561.91 to the Temple, credited to his name in the Book of the Law of the Lord. Whoever received what was apparently a handsome commission on the transaction, the real agent may have been Brigham Young. He called the price paid Robinson "exorbitant." "The reason I paid such a price," he wrote in his journal, "was [because] the Prophet directed the Twelve to pay him whatever he asked." [31] Whatever may have been the merits of the Twelve's case against continued private management of the *Times and Seasons*, such a takeover by the Church of a flourishing private business, and the manner in which it was accomplished, pointed up the growing centralization of power in the hierarchy and the difficulty even the most faithful members could experience as a result.

Of consequence to a larger number of Saints was the animosity of Church leaders in Nauvoo to the Kirtland congregation. Kirtland had been the scene of unpleasantness and failure in 1837 and 1838. There the first large-scale schism in the Church had occurred, and there many of the dissidents had remained. Smith had fled Kirtland in 1838, leaving behind hatred, debt, and lawsuits, both within and without the Church. He never returned.[32] In 1840, however, he began to fear that Kirtland was a potential competitor to Nauvoo as a gathering place for new converts, especially the anticipated surge of immigrant English Saints who in the beginning came via the New York–Erie Canal route, and found Kirtland on Lake Erie a more convenient destination than Nauvoo.[33] In the spring of 1839, before Nauvoo was well founded, it appeared that Smith intended to salvage Kirtland as an alternate gathering point for Saints whose intentions to migrate to Missouri had been frustrated.[34] Even a year

[31] *Ibid.*, 4:513, 514; *The Return*, 2:346, 347, October, 1890; *Millennial Star*, 26:119, February 13, 1864; *Times and Seasons*, 3:695, 696.

[32] See Fielding, "The Growth of the Mormon Church in Kirtland, Ohio," chap. 9.

[33] *Millennial Star*, 1:262, February, 1841.

[34] See Joseph Smith's History, 3:345, 350. Smith hoped that the Kirtland Saints would aid his trusted agent Oliver Granger with "money, lands, chattels, and goods," and, with reference to the rebellion there against his authority in 1837, he hoped, that Granger would "contend earnestly for the redemption of the First Presidency of the Church."

later, in a letter to his agent, Oliver Granger, Smith hoped "that you will be enabled to free the Lord's house [Kirtland Temple] from all encumbrance. . . ." But the Prophet was concerned with the conduct of one of the Kirtland elders, Almon W. Babbitt, whose actions were "calculated to destroy the confidence of the brethren in the Presidency" and who had "led [recent converts] to Kirtland instead of to this place [Nauvoo]. . . ." Fellowship was withdrawn from Babbitt until he should repent. "It is in consequence of aspiring men," wrote Smith, "that Kirtland has been forsaken."[35] An airing and amicable settlement of the real or imagined grievances against Babbitt momentarily benefited relations between Nauvoo and the old Ohio stake. The Prophet told the October, 1840, conference that "something should be done with regard to Kirtland, so that she might be built up . . . that the brethren from the east might gather there. . . ."[36] But Babbitt's term of office as Kirtland Stake President proved inauspicious. Among the numerous items of Church business considered in Smith's revelation of January 19, 1841 (including the Temple, Nauvoo House, and baptism for the dead) was Kirtland, with which the Lord apparently was not well pleased. "I the Lord will build up Kirtland, but I the Lord have a scourge prepared for the inhabitants thereof." Babbitt was singled out for reproof. "And with my servant Almon Babbitt, there are many things with which I am not pleased; behold, he aspireth to establish his council instead of the council which I have ordained, even the Presidency of my Church, and he setteth up a golden calf for the worship of my people."[37] But in October, 1841, the festering affair came to a head and broke. The conference minutes reported that Hyrum Smith, the new Patriarch for the Church, reproved "the course pursued by some Elders in counteracting the efforts of the presidency to gather the Saints, and enticing them to stop in places not appointed for the gathering, particularly referring to the conduct of Elder Almon W. Babbitt of Kirtland." Lyman Wight and Henry Miller charged that Babbitt had also "taught doctrine contrary to the revelations of God and detrimental to the interests of the Church" since he had returned to Kirtland. The conference dis-

[35] Joseph Smith's History, 4:164–167.
[36] *Ibid.*, 4:187, 188, 205. See also Smith's letter to the Kirtland Saints the following month in *ibid.*, pp. 225, 226.
[37] Joseph Smith's History, 4:281; *Doctrine and Covenants*, Section 107:27. William Law, soon to become a member of the First Presidency, was counseled, "If he will do my will, let him not take his family unto the eastern lands, even unto Kirtland."

fellowshipped him "until he shall make satisfaction." [38] Whatever
the exact nature of the course being taken by Babbitt and the Kirtland brethren that was so displeasing to the Church at Nauvoo, certainly a part of it was their independent action, a quality not in
keeping with the "spirit of unity" which was becoming a dominant
Mormon characteristic. Smith had recently dissolved the Kirtland
Stake in a move to make the Nauvoo region the center of the gathering; so whereas in the mid-thirties Kirtland had been the center of
the Church and the seat of the Prophet, by 1840 it was downgraded,
neglected, and virtually abandoned. The Kirtland Saints in all likeli-
hood resented such treatment, and their actions under the circumstances may have been deserving of censure. But the fault that most
displeased the hierarchy was that the Ohio Saints were employing
their substance to "build up" Kirtland, instead of forwarding it to
Nauvoo.

On the very same day when the Nauvoo brethren were suspend-
ing his membership, President Babbitt was presiding over his own
semiannual stake conference, the actions of which were to bring
down a full measure of ecclesiastical wrath upon all their heads.
They acted to solicit money to establish their own stake newspaper
to be titled *The Olive Leaf*.[39] When the news of this seemingly inoffensive project reached Nauvoo the response was swift and
peremptory. "All the Saints that dwell in that land are commanded
to come away, for this is 'Thus saith the Lord,'" wrote Hyrum Smith
to the Kirtland Saints on October 31. They were to make no more
investments or expenditures of any kind in Ohio. Their property
they would be unable to possess in peace any more, for they would
be "scourged with a sore scourge." The plans to establish a press,
"and the ordaining of Elders, and sending out Elders to beg for the
poor, are not according to the will of God." The primary charge that
Hyrum Smith made against Kirtland, however, was that "they have
neglected the House of the Lord [and] the baptismal font, in this
place. . . ." Smith promised in the name of God that Kirtland
should one day be built up and "polished and refined according to
my word"; but only after the Nauvoo Temple was completed, and
Nauvoo was "filled up, and polished, and sanctified according to my
word, saith the Lord." [40] On November 16 the Kirtland Saints wrote

---

[38] Joseph Smith's History, 4:424.
[39] *Ibid.*, 4:443.
[40] *Ibid.*, 4:445. The Kirtland Saints were assured that their children might
one day be able to repossess the lands and properties that they were ordered
to leave, "but not until many years shall pass away."

the Prophet a formal epistle entreating him to reconsider the harsh order, and he granted their petition at least in part. He reminded them that all stakes except those in Hancock and Lee Counties were discontinued, and Kirtland was no exception. But "as it appears that there are many in Kirtland who desire to remain there, and build up that place," they might have their press and do what they could "in righteousness" to build up Kirtland. "But do not suffer yourselves to harbor the idea that Kirtland will rise on the ruins of Nauvoo," he warned them. "It is the privilege of brethren emigrating from any quarter to come to this place, and it is not right to attempt to persuade those who desire it, to stop short." [41] On this basis the matter rested, with Babbitt able gradually to restore himself in the confidence of the hierarchy. He and his brethren had learned that they and "Saints abroad" like them were subordinate to Nauvoo.

Adding to such difficulties as those discussed above was a series of little apostasies and rebellions, heresies, and transgressions in the Church that seemed impossible to end. Typical was the case in 1840 of an Elder Sydney Roberts of New York who commanded a brother by the word of revelation to give him a fine suit and a gold watch. He was also given to "saluting the sisters with what he calls a holy kiss." "Much good counsel" was given Elder Roberts to convince him of his error, but to no avail. So he was excommunicated and asked to give up his elder's license, which he refused to do. [42] Later the same year an Elder John A. Hicks was cut off from the Church for "false and schismatical conversation" and for unspecified breeches of the city ordinances. [43] Early in 1842 two brethren were tried before the Nauvoo High Council, one for "teaching that the Church ought to unsheath the sword" and the other for "preaching that the authorities of the Church were done away with, etc." [44] Two other elders were excommunicated, one for "setting himself up as a false prophet," the other for publishing and teaching "certain 'revelations' and doctrines not consistent with the Doctrine and Covenants of the

---

[41] *Ibid.*, 4:476. The Kirtland letter was signed by "acting Presidents" Lester Brooks and Zebedee Coltrin, Bishop Thomas Burdick, and the old stake high council. The April, 1843, Conference at Kirtland resolved by unanimous vote that all should gather to Nauvoo as a group. Evidence is lacking to indicate how many of them did so. *Ibid.*, 5:352; *Times and Seasons*, 4:284, August 1, 1843.

[42] Joseph Smith's History, 4:237.

[43] *Ibid.*, 4:428.

[44] *Ibid.*, 4:501, 514. One of these proved himself innocent to the satisfaction of the Council. He had, said Smith, "been complained of by those who had prejudice and hardness against him."

Church . . . the whole mass of which appeared to be the extreme of folly, nonsense, absurdity, falsehood, and bombastic egotism—so much so as to keep the Saints laughing, when not overcome with sorrow and shame."[45] A more serious problem was the false prophets who attracted a following among the Saints. One such was James Collin Brewster, a sixteen-year-old youth of Springfield, who created a sensation among the considerable group of Mormons in Sangamon County by introducing a book of scripture which he said was one of the "lost books of the Bible." He claimed to have received it by revelation as Smith had received the *Book of Mormon*. Brewster announced that the proper location for Zion was in California, and some of the Saints made plans to go. Joseph Smith's attention was sufficiently arrested so that he saw Brewster and read his manuscript. "I inquired of the Lord," said Smith, "and the Lord told me the book was not true—it was not of Him. If God ever called me, or spoke by my mouth, or gave me a revelation, he never gave revelations to that Brewster boy or any of the Brewster race." Nonetheless, Brewster prophesied the death of Joseph and Hyrum Smith and the downfall of Nauvoo, which, after the events, added to his prestige and following. He never went to California, but after a brief association with Strang, went to Kirtland with his followers and organized a church.[46]

The Mormon leaders tried to retard heretical and divisive tendencies by exhorting the Church to remember Christian love and wisdom. In April, 1842, the Prophet published a lengthy treatise on the subject of discerning true from false prophets. He prefaced his essay by saying that "Recent occurrences that have transpired among us render it an imperative duty devolving upon me to say something in relation to the spirits by which men are actuated."[47] Smith warned the priesthood to beware of pride, vanity, and flattery, and urged

[45] *Ibid.*, 4:550, 552. The two were Oliver Olney and Francis Gladden Bishop. Smith "gave Mr. Bishop over to the buffetings of Satan until he shall learn wisdom." Apparently Bishop failed to do so, for in 1851 after a period of adherence to the movement of J. J. Strang he went to Kirtland, proclaimed himself the true Mormon prophet, gathered a group of followers, and went west to Iowa to build Zion. See Flanders, "The Mormons Who Did Not Go West," p. 29; and Dale L. Morgan, "A Bibliography of the Churches of the Dispersion," *Western Humanities Review*, 7:116 (1953).

[46] Interstate Publishing Company, *History of Sangamon County, Illinois* (Chicago, 1881), p. 535; Joseph Smith's History, 5:214; Flanders, "The Mormons Who Did Not Go West," p. 30; Smith and Smith, *History of the Reorganized Church*, 3:53, 62.

[47] Joseph Smith's History, 4:571–581; *Times and Seasons*, 3:743–748, April 1, 1842.

them to be forgiving of one another. In one conference he "exhorted the brethren who had charges to make against individuals; and made some very appropriate remarks respecting the pulling of the beam out cf their own eye, that they may see more clearly the mote that is in their brother's eye." [48] The practice of making complaints against one another at conference became so onerous that finally it was forbidden. Smith also urged disputants to settle their differences privately, without resort to the courts of the Church or, more especially, the civil courts. In addressing the High Council in 1840 about one such dispute he said, "there was in reality no cause of difference, [and the contending parties] had better be reconciled without [a] vote of the council, and henceforth live as brethren, and never more mention their former difficulties." [49] Brigham Young counseled the brethren in an 1844 sermon to avoid contention at all costs: "To cure lawing, let us pay attention to our own business. When we hear a story, never tell it again, and it will be a perfect cure. If your brother mistreats you, let him go; cease to deal with men who abuse you; [then] we should not have such disorderly men in our midst. . . . Our difficulties and persecutions have always arisen from men right in our own midst. . . . I would not sue a man if he owed me five hundred, or a thousand dollars, and he came to me and said he would not pay me." [50] Despite the emphasis on reconciliation and sound doctrine many differences persisted. Two of the rifts in the Church that went unhealed were most spectacular and damaging. They were the quarrels between Smith and Sidney Rigdon, and of greater significance, between Smith and John C. Bennett, mayor and major general of the Legion.

Rigdon played a part in the Mormon movement second only to that of the Prophet in the thirties; but in Nauvoo his role was minor. The change was probably due both to Rigdon's poor health and to increasing friction between the two leaders. Rigdon seems to have been emotionally and intellectually intemperate, and Smith may well have felt that, considered in retrospect, his counsels in Kirtland and Far West had been less than wise. Rigdon planned in 1840 to leave Nauvoo, a move tantamount to resigning his position. But he was dissuaded by a revelation which advised him that "it is not my will that he shall seek to find safety and refuge out of the city which

[48] Joseph Smith's History, 3:295; 4:105, 358–359.
[49] *Ibid.*, 4:105.
[50] Brigham Young's journal in the *Millennial Star*, 26:328, May 21, 1864.

I have appointed . . . even the city of Nauvoo." If he would "remain with my people" and "make an acceptable offering" he could continue to stand in his office and was even promised a healing of his infirmities.[51] He remained, but was never in the inner circle of leadership which Smith shared with Bennett, brother Hyrum, the Twelve, and the High Council.

In January, 1843, Smith began to suspect that Rigdon was secretly in league with Bennett, who by then had become the Prophet's mortal enemy.[52] Rigdon was the postmaster of Nauvoo, and Smith convinced himself that his private correspondence was being opened and read, and that his safety, for which he already feared, was thus further jeopardized. "Few if any letters for me can get through the post office in this place," he wrote Horace Hotchkiss, "and more particularly letters containing money, and matters of much importance. I am satisfied that Sidney Rigdon and others connected with him have been the means of doing incalculable injury, not only to myself, but to the citizens in general. . . ."[53] Smith had apparently wanted the postmastership himself, and was piqued when the appointment went to Rigdon, as he thought, with the assistance of Bennett.[54] Consequently Smith sought to have Rigdon removed. In a letter to U.S. Senator R. M. Young requesting the change, the Prophet included "some affidavits, proving that letters had frequently been broken open, money detained, and letters charged twice over, etc., etc. . . ." He added that "It will be seen by the petition, that I was nominated for the office. I can only say that, if I receive the appointment, I will do my utmost to give satisfaction." Whoever the replacement, Smith urged that he be appointed "as soon as circumstances will possibly admit."[55]

On March 27 Smith wrote a long letter to Rigdon "with sensations of deep regret and poignant grief." "I can no longer forbear throwing off the mask and letting you know the secret wranglings of my heart . . ." he said. "I believe and am laboring under the fullest convictions that you are actually practicing deception and wickedness against me and the Church of Jesus Christ of Latter-day Saints; and that you are in connection with John C. Bennett and George W.

[51] Joseph Smith's History, 4:283.
[52] See Bennett's letter to Rigdon and Orson Pratt and Smith's reaction in *ibid.*, 5:250–252.
[53] *Ibid.*, 5:196.
[54] See the Smith-Rigdon correspondence of March, 1843, in *ibid.*, 5:312–316.
[55] *Ibid.*, 5:266, 267.

Robinson [Rigdon's son-in-law] in the whole of their abominable practices, in seeking to destroy me and this people . . . and that you are in the exercise of a traitorous spirit against our lives and interests, by combining with our enemies and the murderous Missourians." [56] Since Bennett first came to Nauvoo, Smith said, he had been aware of "something dark and mysterious hovering over our business concerns . . . in relation to the post office," and that he had kept Rigdon's "secret plottings and connivings" with Bennett locked in his bosom. Despite such charges, the letter was conciliatory in tone, inviting an explanation and denial. But unless he could be satisfied that he was wrong, ". . . I must . . . publish my withdrawal of my fellowship from you to the Church . . . and demand of the conference a hearing concerning your case [on conviction of which] they will demand your license." [57] Rigdon replied on the same day with a long, careful, conciliatory letter denying all Smith's charges and attempting to explain various incidents that might have aroused Smith's suspicions. Rigdon also alluded to some old feud between them that was obviously of major significance. "I had hoped that all former difficulties had ceased forever. On my part they were never mentioned to any person, nor a subject of discourse at any time or any place. I was tired of hearing of them, and was in hopes they slumbered for ever." [58] Smith let the matter rest for a while, but when in the summer he narrowly escaped being returned to Missouri for trial, he charged Rigdon publicly. "There is a certain man in this city who has made a covenant to betray and give me up to the Missourians . . . [He] is no other than Sidney Rigdon. This . . . I have from gentlemen from abroad, whose names I do not wish to give." Smith then announced that he was withdrawing the

[56] Rigdon's son-in-law, George W. Robinson, withdrew from the Church in 1842 amidst charges and counter-charges of swindling which even reached the pages of the *Quincy Whig*. Carlos Granger, a reputable Nauvoo gentile and presumably a disinterested third party, said that he had had unsatisfactory land deals with Robinson, and believed him to be a "dishonest man." *Nauvoo Wasp*, August 4, 1842; George Q. Cannon, *Life of Joseph the Prophet* (Salt Lake City, 1888), p. 427. See also Joseph Smith's History, 5:122.

[57] *Ibid.*, 5:312–314.

[58] *Ibid.*, 5:314, 315. The reference was perhaps to the embarrassment created when John C. Bennett described the quarrel between Smith and Rigdon as resulting from Smith's improper advances to one of Rigdon's daughters. It was commonly anticipated, at least outside Nauvoo, that Rigdon would follow Bennett in "exposing" Mormonism and its founder; but instead he publicly reaffirmed his faith and quoted his daughter Eliza as saying under the spirit of inspiration that Bennett "was a wicked man and . . . the Lord would tread him under his feet." See *ibid.*, 5:6, 8, 46, 121–123.

hand of fellowship from Rigdon "on condition that the foregoing be true," and asked the Saints to endorse his action by the uplifted hand. Willard Richards reporting the event said that the Sunday afternoon crowd voted unanimously to disfellowship Rigdon and demand his license.[59] Rigdon tried to clear himself by forwarding a garbled letter which he claimed to have received from Thomas Carlin showing that the governor knew Rigdon to be loyal to Smith. The Prophet read the letter publicly to another Sabbath day crowd, and concluded, "The letter is one of the most evasive things, and carries with it a design to hide the truth." Rigdon mounted the stand in the afternoon of the same day and declared, "I never . . . exchanged a word with any man living on the subject [of betraying Smith]. I ask pardon for having done anything which should give occasion to make you think so." [60] But Smith was unconvinced, and when the semiannual conference met October 9, 1843, the first item of business was the President's request to have Rigdon removed as his counselor by conference action. He detailed the various reasons why he believed the man in league with "enemies," and in addition expressed his dissatisfaction with Rigdon's contribution in his high office, "not having received any material benefit from his labors or counsels" since the Saints came to Illinois. Nevertheless, said Smith, he desired Rigdon's salvation, "and expressed his willingness that he should retain a place among the Saints." Rigdon replied to the charges one by one, and concluded with "a moving appeal to President Joseph Smith, concerning their former friendship, associations, and sufferings; and expressed his willingness to resign his place, though with sorrowful and indescribable feelings." The conference minutes note that "During [Rigdon's] address, the sympathies of the congregation were highly excited." Whether moved by Rigdon's defense or unimpressed by Smith's charges, the conference rallied behind the accused. Almon W. Babbitt and President William Law spoke in his behalf, and Presiding Patriarch Hyrum Smith spoke of the mercy of God "and the propriety and importance of the Saints exercising the same attribute toward their fellows, and especially toward their aged companion and fellow servant in the cause of truth and righteousness." Then on motion of William Marks and Hyrum Smith the conference voted to sustain Sidney Rigdon as Counselor in the First Presidency. Joseph Smith had a final word,

[59] *Ibid.*, 5:532.
[60] *Ibid.*, 5:553, 554, 556.

however. "I have thrown him off my shoulders," he said, "and you have again put him on me. You may carry him but I will not."[61] After that Rigdon's influence was small. He tried to assert his authority ten months later, at the August, 1844, conference considering the leadership problem of the Church following the death of Smith. Not surprisingly, his claims to the succession received little response.[62]

The Rigdon-Smith rift might have attracted more attention than it did both within and without the Church had it not been overshadowed by the sensational Bennett estrangement. Bennett's attachment to Mormonism in the first place was, like that of Isaac Galland, not motivated primarily by religious considerations. His desire was to have place in a dynamic corporation and to share the rewards accruing from its growth. Smith apparently received both men on this basis. To build a kingdom in the world required men in the management who knew the affairs of the world. They were to be the Mormon equivalent of a paid professional staff. But both men proved to be personally unfit, and when they were "fired" they added their voices to the rising anti-Mormon chorus. Bennett, having failed in his career with the Mormons, decided to make another, perhaps more successful career, by attacking them.

Bennett was in Nauvoo from September, 1840, to May, 1842. During that time he had part in drafting and promoting the city charter, was mayor from the first election in February, 1841, until his departure, and was instrumental in starting the Masonic lodge. He was chancellor of the city university, a job of small significance inasmuch as there was no university yet; and Bennett made only preliminary moves to begin one. His *chef d'oeuvre* was the Nauvoo Legion, of which he was architect, organizer, and functional commander. Smith's generalship was largely ceremonial, and what he knew of martial affairs he learned from Bennett. Smith's growing sophistication in other areas stemmed in part from Bennett's influence. He taught the Prophet the manners and conventions of "society," how to move and feel comfortable in the world of affairs, of politics, of lawyers, legislators, and editors. Smith adopted many of Bennett's demagogic traits into his own energetic oratory—the affectation of superiority, the exaggerated manner, the strident phrase, the extremity of self-righteous denunciation, the techniques of bathos and ha-

[61] *Ibid.*, 6:47–49.
[62] Paradoxically Smith included Rigdon in the Council of Fifty, formed early in 1841. See below, Chapter 10.

rangue. Smith was also impressed by Bennett's use of Latin phrases, an affectation of learning habitual to the latter's speaking and writing. The Prophet incorporated the technique into his own communication, where it sometimes got out of hand.[63] Up to a point Bennett's "worldliness" was his most valuable characteristic. In the realm of morals it was his undoing. He was an attractive man, and entered Nauvoo society as a very eligible bachelor. Soon his philandering became the spice of Nauvoo gossip. Smith became uneasy. Soon after Bennett's arrival, the Prophet received a letter from "a person of respectable character" who claimed that Bennett had a wife and three children in McConnelsville, Ohio, and that he was "a very mean man." But, said Smith, "knowing that it is no uncommon thing for good men to be evil spoken against, the . . . letter was kept quiet, and held in reserve." Nevertheless, when Bennett's attentions to one young woman were such that she anticipated marriage, the Prophet ordered him to stop, finally threatening "to expose him" if he did not desist. Bennett broke off the relationship. But, said Smith, he sank "deeper and deeper into wickedness and hypocrisy," and privately began to implicate the Prophet:

He went to some of the females of the city who knew nothing of him but as an honorable man, and began to teach them that promiscuous intercourse between the sexes was a doctrine believed in by the Latter-day Saints, and that there was no harm in it . . . and that I myself and others of the authorities of the Church, not only sanctioned but practiced the same wicked acts, and when asked why I publicly preached so much against it said that it was because of the prejudice of the public, and that it would cause trouble in my own house. He . . . endeavored to keep it a matter of secrecy, persuading them there would be no harm if they did not make it known . . . he seduced an innocent female by his lying, and subjected her character to public disgrace, should it ever be known.[64]

[63] See for example Smith's "Views of the Powers and Policy of the Government of the United States," his letter of November 13, 1843, to James Arlington Bennett, and his "Appeal to the Green Mountain Boys," in which there are phrases from four, seven, and sixteen foreign languages respectively. *Millennial Star,* 22:276, 326, 743, 744, May 5, 1860–December 1, 1860. In Joseph Smith's History these passages were omitted with an apology from the editor, B. H. Roberts, who attributed them not to Smith but to W. W. Phelps, a scribe, "who had some smattering knowledge of languages, which he was very fond of displaying. . . . Because these displays of pedantry mar these documents . . . and are not really the work of President Smith, they are omitted. . . ." Joseph Smith's History, 4:75n.

[64] Joseph Smith's History, 5:35, 36. This is Smith's account embodied in "An Address to the Church . . . and to All the Honorable Part of the Community," June 23, 1842. Ebenezer Robinson confirmed Smith's story in general in *The Return,* 2:262, 263, November, 1890.

On June 15, 1841, Hyrum Smith and William Law wrote the Prophet from Pittsburgh that Bennett indeed had a wife in Ohio who had left him because of his adultery there. When confronted with the letter, Bennett candidly admitted its truth.[65] The profundity of the official embarrassment may be gauged by the fact that until the spring of 1842 nothing was done about Bennett, except to urge him to stop his amours. No public recognition was made of the trouble, except that Bennett's influence in official matters steadily diminished. Ebenezer Robinson thought the business was kept covered for fear of the reaction of the gentile neighbors to such a sordid scandal. Considering its subsequent acrimony, it seems likely that Smith had good reason to be apprehensive.[66]

In the spring of 1842, however, the affair was gradually brought into the open. In an epistle to the English Saints March 20, the Twelve included an elaborate and extraordinary testimonial to Smith's character and sacred calling. "We . . . know," they concluded, "that his words are true, his teachings sacred, his character unsullied among men of truth. . . ." At the General Conference in April, Smith "spoke in contradiction of a report in circulation about Elders Heber C. Kimball, Brigham Young, [myself] and others of the Twelve, alleging that . . . they endeavored to induce [a certain sister] to believe in having two wives." No one "that is acquainted with our principles would believe such lies," he said, "except [Thomas] Sharp, editor of the *Warsaw Signal*." "I preached in the Grove," he wrote under entry of April 10, 1842, "and pronounced a curse upon all adulterers, fornicators, and unvirtuous persons, and those who have made use of my name to carry on their iniquitous designs. . . . We have thieves among us, adulterers, liars, hypocrites. . . . The Church must be cleansed, and I proclaim against all iniquity." On April 29 he confided to his journal, "A conspiracy against the peace of my household was made manifest, and it gave me some trouble to counteract the design of certain base individuals, and restore peace. The Lord makes manifest to me many

---

[65] Joseph Smith's History, 5:36, 37; *The Return*, 2:263, November, 1890. "Soon after," according to both Smith and Robinson, Bennett attempted suicide by poison, and strenuously resisted efforts made to save his life. It is possible that this was the occasion in January, 1842, when Smith was elected mayor *pro tem*, though it was six months after the Law–Hyrum Smith letter. In such a case, the suicide attempt must have been prompted by another incident.

[66] The Twelve returned from England in the fall of 1841 to assume important duties, some perhaps previously belonging to Bennett. It may be that the Bennett difficulty was one reason why the Prophet recalled his Apostles.

things, which it is not wisdom for me to make public, until others can witness the proof of them." [67]

If Smith was looking for "proof" to expose Bennett, he found it a week later when he became convinced that Bennett had plotted to have him assassinated. On May 7 during parade ground maneuvers of the Legion arranged by Bennett, Smith said that his major general had arranged to have him killed and make it appear an accident. The suspected strategy was countermanded by Captain A. P. Rockwood, commander of Smith's bodyguards, "who kept close by my side." [68] After that, an open rupture was imminent. On May 17 Bennett resigned as mayor. Smith continued to fear a plot against his life, and on May 19 spoke to the city council, which had just elected him the new mayor, "concerning the evil reports which were abroad in the city concerning myself, and the necessity of counteracting the designs of our enemies, establishing a night watch, etc., whereupon the council resolved that the mayor be authorized to establish a night watch, and control the same."

Whatever had occurred in the previous fortnight apparently had thoroughly frightened Bennett too, if he were not so already. He was present at the May 19 council session; when Smith asked him to declare whether he had any charges to make, "on account of the reports in circulation this day, and to quiet the public mind," he replied with near hysterical vehemence that he did not. "I have no difficulty with the heads of the Church," he said, "I publicly avow that anyone who has said that I have stated that General Joseph Smith has given me authority to hold illicit intercourse with women is a liar in the face of God. Those who have said it are damned liars; they are infernal liars. He never in public or private gave me any such license, and any person who states it is a scoundrel and a liar." Some had said, he continued, that he would become "a second Avard," referring to the chief of the Danite band of Mormon terrorists at Far West who was expelled from the Church and who then publicly turned on the Mormons. Nothing could be further from the truth, "and should the time ever come . . . to test my faith, it will then be known whether I am a traitor or a true man." His wish was to be restored "to full confidence, fellowship, and my former standing in the Church," and his conduct would show that he deserved such restoration. Smith then said to him, "Will you please state defi-

[67] Joseph Smith's History, 4:562, 563, 585–588, 607.
[68] *Ibid.*, 5:4; Brooks, *John Doyle Lee*, p. 51.

nitely whether you know anything against my character, either in public or private?" Bennett replied, "I do not. In all my intercourse with General Smith, in public and in private, he has been strictly virtuous." Smith concluded the drama, enacted before "a house filled with spectators," with a statement concerning "those who had been guilty of circulating false reports. . . . Let one twelve months [twelvemonth] see if Brother Joseph is not called for . . . to keep them out of their graves; and I turn the key on them from this very hour if they will not stop their lyings and surmisings; let God curse them, and let their tongues cleave to the roofs of their mouths." [69] Bennett's recital before the council on May 19 was so palpably false there can be little doubt that he believed himself to be under duress, which was to be the first of the sensational charges he would soon make against the Church. Although many Mormon leaders solemnly denied the accusation, the event appears to have been a "confession" staged for public consumption.

Just what occurred in the succeeding month is unclear, but no accommodation was reached, and, if anything, the apprehension of both Smith and Bennett about what the other might do increased. Bennett was notified of his expulsion from the Church on June 25, and of Smith's intention to "publish him in the paper"; but he pleaded "for his mother's sake" to be spared from that, and public notice was not made. The next day before "nearly a hundred brethren" in a private meeting, Bennett "acknowledged his wicked and licentious conduct toward certain females . . . and that he was worthy of the severest chastisements, and cried like a child, and begged that he might be spared, in any possible way; so deep was his apparent sense of guilt . . . so deeply did he feign, or really feel contrition," said Smith, "that he was forgiven still. I plead for mercy for him." [70] Bennett left Nauvoo, "very abruptly" according to Smith, probably soon after the episode of the twenty-fifth. On the twenty-seventh he wrote the *Burlington* [Iowa] *Hawkeye* that Smith had promised to kill him. "The holy Joe fears the consequences of my disclosures, and has threatened to take my life, and has ordered some of his Danite band to effect the murder clan-

[69] *Ibid.*, 5:13, 14. See also Bennett's affidavit of June 17, 1842, sworn before Alderman Daniel H. Wells, a gentile, in which he makes substantially the same denials. *Ibid.*, 5:38.

[70] *Ibid.*, 5:18, 19. Hyrum Smith and William Law said the date of Bennett's excommunication was May 11. *Ibid.*, 5:74, 76.

destinely—but *he shall* be exposed. If he murders me, others will avenge my blood, and expose him. . . ." [71] On July 30, he wrote the *Logansport Telegraph*, ". . . I am threatened with death by the holy Joe and his Danite band of murderers, in case I dare make any disclosures in relation to the conduct of that polluted mass of corruption, iniquity, and fraud—that king of Impostors—the holy and immaculate Joe Smith." [72] The Bennett disclosures included descriptions of maidens seduced by Mormon leaders, fantastic polygamous pseudo-religious sexual rites, a reign of terror by Smith's murderous band of "Danite" bullies, enormous swindles in which the hierarchy victimized Saint and gentile alike, and a grandiose plot to conquer the Northwest States and convert them into a Mormon empire. They were printed serial-fashion in the *Sangamo Journal* during the summer of 1842, and were wisely copied by other western newspapers, particularly the Whig press in Illinois. They were reported though not often reprinted in the eastern press. In the fall of 1842, Bennett collected his accounts and published them, with additions, as *The History of the Saints; or an Exposé of Joe Smith and the Mormons.*

The Prophet offered no public explanation for Bennett's unusual confession before the city council on May 19. On July 20, in answer to Bennett's charges, thirteen members of the city council swore an affidavit that Bennett was under no duress on May 19. "There was no excitement at the time, nor was he in anywise threatened, menaced, or intimidated. His appearance . . . was voluntary . . . and [he] went . . . as free as any member of the Council. We further testify that there is no such thing as a Danite Society in the city, nor any combination, other than the Masonic Lodge of which we have any knowledge." [73]

The spring and summer of 1842 was altogether a very difficult time for Smith. In addition to the Bennett affair Galland's fraudulence was discovered, finances became desperate, and the Prophet applied for bankruptcy; he was involved in the takeover of the *Times and Seasons* and became its editor, Duncan was running for Governor on an anti-Mormon platform, and the shooting of Boggs led to Smith's arrest as a conspirator. The Bennett accusations supplied much grist for the Nauvoo rumor mill, and the Prophet was occu-

[71] Quoted in *Niles National Register*, 62:323, July 23, 1842.
[72] Quoted in Gayler, "The Mormons in Western Illinois," p. 156.
[73] Joseph Smith's History, 5:68.

pied extensively in suppressing the scandal. Cryptic entries in his journal attest the fact.[74] Speaking before the Relief Society, a sort of "ladies' aid" of Nauvoo, he cautioned the women to "put a double watch over the tongue." If there were unvirtuous persons, they needed to be guided back to the path of virtue, but "keep it all in silence." "The truth on the guilty should not be told openly, strange as this seems," said Smith, "yet this is policy. We must use precaution . . . lest in exposing these heinous acts we draw the indignation of a Gentile world upon us (and, to their imagination, justly too). It is necessary to hold an influence in the world, and thus spare ourselves an extermination . . . beware, be still, be prudent, repent, reform, but do it in a way not to destroy all around you. . . ."[75]

On June 18 Smith denounced Bennett publicly for the first time. He called the citizens to a special public meeting, and "spoke his mind in great plainness concerning the iniquity, hypocrisy, wickedness and corruption of General John Cook Bennett." On June 23 he published "an Address to the Church of Latter-day Saints and to All the Honorable part of the Community" in which he recited in general terms the whole history of the affair, and included Bennett's affidavit of May 17 and his statements before the city council on the nineteenth. The tone of Smith's account was moderate, and had none of the character of a diatribe against Bennett.[76]

[74] Entries in Smith's Journal from May 12 to June 29 are illustrative: "Dictated a letter to Elder Rigdon concerning certain difficulties, or surmises which existed. . . ." ". . . had an interview with Elder Rigdon, concerning certain evil reports put in circulation by Francis M. Higbee, about some of Elder Rigdon's family. . . ." "Hiram Kimball has been insinuating evil and forming evil opinions against [me] with others. . . ." "Charges have been filed against Robert D. Foster . . . for abusive language against Samuel H. Smith [the Prophet's brother]. . . ." "Chauncey L. Higbee was cut off from the Church . . . for unchaste and unvirtuous conduct toward certain females, and for teaching it is right, if kept secret, etc. He was put under $200 bonds to keep the peace, on my complaint against him for slander, before Ebenezer Robinson, Justice of the Peace." "In company with Bishop Miller, I visited Elder Rigdon and his family, and had much conversation about John C. Bennett, and others, much unpleasant feeling was manifested by Elder Rigdon's family, who were confounded and put to silence by truth." "I held a long conversation with Francis M. Higbee [who] found fault with being exposed [but] appeared humble and promised to reform." *Ibid.*, 5:6, 8.

[75] *Ibid.*, 5:19. Smith's address to the Relief Society on May 26 was reported by Eliza Roxy Snow. The women were apparently in high moral dudgeon. See also Smith's second address to them on June 9. "Sisters of the society, shall there be strife among you? I will not have it. . . . Away with self-righteousness." He concluded by promising to give them a lot and an unfurnished house to aid in their work. *Ibid.*, 5:24, 25.

[76] *Ibid.*, 5:35–40.

Despite Smith's best efforts to soften the impact of the Bennett affair on the Saints, there were many apostasies in 1842. The *Sangamo Journal* for September 14 carried the following notice: "We, the undersigned, feeling ourselves aggrieved by the conduct of Joseph Smith, and others of the leaders of the Church of Latter Day Saints—and feeling that we have been most scandalously imposed upon in matters and things of a Divine character, wish publicly to withdraw from said Church, and no longer claim allegiance thereto." The signers were Joseph D. Conoly, Mary Ann Conoly, Mary A. Converce, Robert Angould, Martha Angould, Charles Chase, Jr., Richard Chase, Sarah McMullen, E. H. McMullen, and H. H. Ogle, Sr. The *Sangamo Journal* had the previous week carried notice of the withdrawal of Oliver H. Olney, who was to write his own exposé of Mormonism.

During the summer of 1842 the attention of Nauvooans gradually shifted from the internal rumblings produced by Bennett to the possibility or probability that his exposé, coupled with the anti-Mormon feeling in the Illinois election campaign and the storm rising in Missouri over the Boggs shooting, would bring a wave of persecution against them. They tended to draw together in the face of these new threats from the outside and to dismiss Bennett's accusations of immorality in high places as the acts of a cornered scoundrel. The historian would tend likewise to discount Bennett's charges, were it not that polygamy was soon to become a central feature of the Mormon religion.

The celestial marriage, or "spiritual wife," doctrine held that marriage, as well as other family relationships, were eternal in duration when properly solemnized or "sealed" in special Mormon rites. These everlasting families were to play a great part in the "exaltation" of the Saints in the life to come. Since a man whose wife had died often remarried, in the life to come both women would be his wives. It was but a simple and logical step to forsake monogamy in this life in favor of "plurality," as the Mormons later referred to it. Just who took the first step, or when, is impossible to determine from reliable sources. Bennett's charges and the extraordinary stir they caused, together with other incidents described below, suggest that the process had begun by 1841, but privily and in a very limited circle. Bennett, a promiscuous and lascivious man, stumbled onto a developing religious principle which he apparently distorted to aid and justify himself in his amours. The shocked indignation aroused among the leaders by Bennett's actions was similar to that aroused among the Saints after "plurality" was established and the gentile world accused them of immorality. Plural marriage was to orthodox Mormons a solemn, sacred duty, not the servant of lust and license. The principle of celestial marriage was in process of formation at least as early as 1841. In the spring of that year Ebenezer Robinson had a conversation with Don Carlos Smith, the Prophet's young brother. Although writing a half-century later, Robinson described it in detail. "Any man," said young Smith, "who will teach and practice the doctrine of spiritual wifery will go to hell; I don't care if it is my brother Joseph." Robinson reflected that "[Don Carlos Smith] was one of the most perfect men I ever knew. He was a bitter opposer of the 'spiritual wife' doctrine which was being talked quite freely, in private circles, in his lifetime." [77] He died in August, 1841.

On November 7, 1841, an Elder William Clark preached in Nauvoo "reproving the Saints for lack of sanctity, and a want of holy living, enjoining sanctity, solemnity, and temperance in the extreme, in the sectarian style." Then Joseph Smith mounted the stand and, perhaps to the surprise of the congregation, rebuked Clark as "Pharisaical and hypocritical," and proceeded to show the Saints "what temperance, faith, virtue, charity, and truth were. . . . If you will not accuse me, I will not accuse you. If you will throw a cloak of charity over my sins, I will over yours—for charity covereth a multitude of sins. What many people call sin is not sin: I do many things to break down superstition, and I will break it down." [78] Ebenezer Robinson took strong exception to this sermon, and saw it as part of a process of preparing the people for new and different moral standards. "The foregoing, and kindred doctrine," he said, "coming from such a source [the Prophet], could not fail to bear evil fruit, as is evidenced by the subsequent course pursued by the Church. It began to be frequently talked by the people, that what was formerly considered sin was not sin. This had a direct tendency to lower the standard of vital piety, which the masses of the people were endeavoring to maintain." [79]

Until February, 1842, Robinson had lived with his family in the *Times and Seasons* building, but was summarily evicted by Apostle Willard Richards the day that he sold it to the Twelve. His family, having no place to go, was taken in by the neighbor next door.

[77] *The Return*, 2:287, June, 1890.
[78] Joseph Smith's History, 4:445.
[79] *The Return*, 2:323, 327, September, 1890.

"That evening," said Robinson, "Willard Richards commenced living with Nancy Marinda [Mrs. Orson] Hyde, in the rooms we had vacated . . . where they lived through the winter." [80] Richards' wife was living in Massachusetts at the time, and Apostle Orson Hyde was on a mission to Jerusalem. Disquieting rumors may have reached Jenetta Richards, for the Prophet wrote her a cryptic letter of reassurance on June 23, 1842, "agreeable to your request." He assured her that his heart's desire and prayer was especially in behalf of the brethren with heavy and important responsibilities, "among [whom] is your husband. . . . You say I have got him; so I have, in the which I rejoice for he has done me great good. . . . Never did I have a greater intimacy with any man than with him. May the blessings of Elijah crown his head forever and ever." Richards would soon be on his way to see her, said Smith, "and I want you, beloved sister, to be a general in this matter, and help him along, which I know you will. He will be able to teach you many things which you have never heard; you may have implicit confidence in the same. . . . I hope that you may be steadfast in the faith, even unto the end." [81]

When Orson Hyde returned from his mission the following December, his mind "temporarily gave way," said Robinson, when he "learned of the secret teachings of the spiritual wife doctrine." He suddenly disappeared, and, because of his demented state, it was feared that he might have come to harm or even have committed suicide. An extensive search discovered him sitting alone on the riverbank five miles below the city, "without a hat." At the April, 1843, General Conference, on a vote to sustain Joseph Smith as Prophet and President, Hyde alone, according to Robinson, voted "no." [82]

Apostle Orson Pratt also suffered a loss of faith in 1842 for reasons which were not explained; and, though the difficulty was not made public, it became so serious that Pratt (and presumably his wife as well) was quietly expelled from the Church on August 20. "I spent several days laboring with Elder Orson Pratt," said Brigham Young of the affair; "[his] mind became so darkened by the influence and statements of his wife, that he came out in rebellion against Joseph,

[80] *Ibid.*, 2:346, October, 1890.
[81] Joseph Smith's History, 5:40, 41.
[82] The conference minutes indicate that after Smith rather testily asked for a vote of confidence, Brigham Young led the group in a "unanimous" show of hands. *Ibid.*, 5:328.

refusing to believe his testimony or obey his counsel. . . . Joseph told him if he did believe his wife and follow her suggestions, he would go to hell." The day Pratt was excommunicated, Amasa Lyman, whom, ironically, Pratt had converted to Mormonism, was ordained to take his place as the twelfth Apostle.[83]

John C. Bennett knew Pratt's feelings, and seemed to be certain that Rigdon and Pratt were two high churchmen who would substantiate his charges of Smith's immoral teachings and practices. According to Bennett, Pratt had written that he and his wife were preparing to leave Nauvoo and join in exposing Mormonism. But, whatever his other difficulties, Pratt had no desire to be associated with Bennett, and wrote a letter on September 26, 1842, to the *Wasp* disclaiming any correspondence or other connection with the deposed general. Pratt said he and his wife "intend to make Nauvoo our residence, and Mormonism our motto." Bennett continued to believe, however, that Pratt and Rigdon were his "contacts" in Nauvoo, for he wrote them in January, 1843, of his plans to bring Smith forcibly to trial in Missouri. Pratt brought the letter to the Prophet immediately and reaffirmed that he had no connection with Bennett. Pratt was just then repenting of whatever heresy caused his expulsion in August, and on January 20, 1843, Joseph Smith rebaptized Pratt and his wife and reordained Pratt to the Twelve. The resulting anomalous situation of Amasa Lyman was settled by making him a fourth member of the First Presidency.[84]

The month before Pratt was cut off, Hyrum Smith swore out an affidavit which vehemently denied the accusations of Bennett and rejected all his works; but in so doing Smith was explicit about Bennett's use of a spiritual wife doctrine (though he implied that Bennett was its author). "Several females . . . testified that John C. Bennett attempted to seduce them, and accomplished his designs by saying it was right; that it was one of the mysteries of God, which was to be revealed when the people were strong enough in faith to bear such mysteries . . . bringing witnesses of his own clan to testify that there were such revelations and commandments, and that they were of God. . . ." Hyrum described the private confrontation

---

[83] Brigham Young's journal in the *Millennial Star*, 26:151, March 5, 1864. Smith was in hiding outside the city, fearing extradition for the Boggs crime; but he was in contact with affairs in Nauvoo, and Pratt's excommunication was probably done at least with his knowledge and consent, though it may have been initiated by Brigham Young.

[84] *Ibid.*, 5:250–252, 255, 256.

between Bennett and his brother Joseph, whom he reported as saying: "Doctor! Why are you using my name to carry on your hellish wickedness? Have I ever taught you that fornication and adultery were right, or polygamy or any such practice? He [Bennett] said, You never did. Did I ever teach you anything that was not virtuous—that was iniquitous, either in public or private? He said, You never did." [85]

Despite continuing public disclaimers of secret teachings in the Church as described by Bennett, there were indeed secret rites initiated by Joseph Smith into the inner circle of leadership in the spring of 1842. On May 4 the Prophet recorded in his journal:

I spent the day in [the council room above the store] in council with General James Adams of Springfield, Patriarch Hyrum Smith, Bishops Newel K. Whitney and George Miller, and President Brigham Young, and Elders Heber C. Kimball and Willard Richards, instructing them in the principles and order of the Priesthood, and so on to the highest order of the Melchisidek Priesthood, setting forth the order pertaining to the Ancient of Days, and all those plans and principles by which anyone is enabled to secure the fullness of those blessings which have been prepared for the Church of the First Born, and come up and abide in the presence of Eloheim in the eternal worlds. In this council was instituted the ancient order of things for the first time in these last days. And the communications I made to this council were of things spiritual, and to be received only by the spiritual minded; and there is nothing made known to these men but what will be made known to all the Saints of the last days, as soon as they are prepared to receive, and a proper place is prepared to communicate them, even to the weakest of Saints; therefore let the Saints be diligent in building the Temple . . . knowing assuredly that all these things . . . are always governed by the principle of revelation.[86]

By 1843 Ebenezer Robinson knew of the existence of a secret group of Saints, including women, called the "Holy Order," whose private rites included symbolic re-enactment of the Garden of Eden. The initiates wore a peculiar undergarment called a "robe," all in one piece, with a hole in the center of the breast and in one knee, and a square on the left breast and a compass on the right. It was claimed that no harm could befall the wearer. This robe was believed to be the reason for Willard Richards' miraculous escape from

[85] *Ibid.*, 5:71, 72. President William Law, who less than two years later was openly to charge the doctrine of polygamy against the Smiths, made a similar affidavit. Both Hyrum Smith and Law affirmed that Bennett was highly emotional and willing to make full confession, but that he was not coerced to do so. *Ibid.*, 5:75–77.

[86] *Ibid.*, 5:1, 2; *Millennial Star*, 19:390–393, June 20, 1857.

injury when he was with the Smiths at their assassination. John Taylor, describing the event, said Richards "through the promises of God, escaped without even a hole in his robe."[87] The rites included special signs, grips, tokens, key words, and a girdle worn in addition to the robe. The members of the "Holy Order" were bound with ironclad oaths of secrecy. "I could tell you many things," Robinson remembered being told by one of the order, "but if I should, my life would pay the forfeiture." Robinson never attended any of the meetings, but said he saw the Prophet go to them. Once he accidentally saw John Taylor standing outside the door of the council room above the store, turbanned and clothed in a white robe, with a sword in his hand, "evidently," said Robinson, "representing the 'cherubins and flaming sword which was placed at the east of the Garden of Eden, to guard the tree of life.' "[88]

During the spring and summer of 1843 the doctrine and practice of celestial marriage was formally woven into the fabric of secret observances. The Prophet publicly alluded to the new rite several times in the period. On May 16 in a sermon at Ramus he said:

Except a man and his wife enter into an everlasting covenant and be married for eternity, while in this probation [life], by the power and authority of the Holy Priesthood, they will cease to increase when they die; that is, they will have no children after the resurrection. But those who are [so] married and continue without committing the sin against the Holy Ghost, will continue to increase and have children in the celestial glory. . . .

In the celestial glory there are three heavens or degrees; and in order to obtain the highest, he must enter into this order of priesthood. . . . He may enter into the other, but that is the end of his kingdom: he cannot have an increase.[89]

[87] *The Return*, 2:252, April, 1890; Utah Church *Doctrine and Covenants*, 135:2; Reorganized Church *Doctrine and Covenants*, 113:2; Hyrum M. Smith and Janne M. Sjodahl, *Doctrine and Covenants Commentary* (Salt Lake City, 1951), p. 855. In Joseph Smith's History, 6:619, the account by an unnamed author, perhaps Taylor, said: "Dr. Richards' escape was miraculous; he being a very large man, and in the midst of a shower of balls. . . . His escape literally fulfilled a prophecy [of Joseph] that the balls would fly around him like hail . . . but that there should not be a hole in his garment."

[88] *The Return*, 2:253, 254, April, 1890. "We believe they were as conscientious in this matter as Saul of Tarsus was when he held the garments of those who stoned Stephen to death. But we never believed those measures were God's work, or we should have gone with them instead of opposing them, as we did, notwithstanding the threatened curse, of which we have records to show. As this is the time of Utah's sore trial [1890] we felt it our duty to publish the foregoing . . . that the responsibility may rest where it belongs," i.e., on Joseph Smith.

[89] Joseph Smith's History, 5:391, 392; Utah Church *Doctrine and Covenants*, 131:1–4.

On June 11 in a Sabbath day address in Nauvoo, Smith urged the necessity to finish the Temple in order that the fullness of the Gospel could be revealed, "for there are certain ordinances and principles that, when they are taught and practiced, must be done in a place or house built for that purpose." With reference to those who opposed new revelations Smith said: "Many men will say, 'I will never forsake you, but will stand by you at all times.' But the moment you teach them some of the mysteries of the kingdom of God that are retained in the heavens and are to be revealed to . . . men when they are prepared . . . they will be the first to stone you and put you to death. . . . Where there is no change [progression?] of priesthood, there is no change of the ordinances, says Paul. . . . Have ye turned revelators? Then why deny revelation?"[90] In another sermon, July 16, Smith said he "slightly touched upon the subject of the everlasting covenant, showing that a man and his wife must enter into that covenant in [this] world, or he will have no claim on her in the next world. But on account of the unbelief of the people, I cannot reveal the fullness of these things at present." Preaching a funeral sermon on August 13, Smith discussed the end of the world and the future life of the Saints.

Elijah the prophet shall reveal the covenants of the father in relation to the children, and the covenants of the children in relation to the fathers. Four destroying angels holding power over the four quarters of the earth, until the servants of God are sealed in their foreheads, which signifies sealing the blessing upon their heads, meaning the everlasting covenant, thereby making their calling and election sure [*sic*]. When a seal is put upon the father and mother, it secures their posterity, so that they cannot be lost, but will be saved by virtue of the covenant of their father and mother.[91]

On May 26, Smith took his brother Hyrum, Apostles Kimball, Young, and Richards, James Adams, Bishop Whitney, and President William Law into his upper chamber "and gave them their endowments and also instructions in the priesthood on the new and everlasting covenant, etc."[92]

[90] *Ibid.*, 5:423, 424. The report of this sermon is from the journals of Wilford Woodruff and Willard Richards.

[91] *Ibid.*, 5:530. The sermon was reported by Willard Richards.

[92] *Ibid.*, 5:409. According to Juanita Brooks in her biography of John D. Lee, the various unpublished elders' journals with which she worked indicated that in April, 1843, Smith explained the principle of celestial marriage to Benjamin F. Johnson, Erastus and Lorenzo Snow, and John Benbow; and William Clayton married his first plural wife during the same spring. Brooks, *John Doyle Lee*, pp. 56–57.

Ebenezer Robinson said that early in the summer of 1843 the spiritual wife doctrine was "so closely pressed that I felt that the time was at hand when I must determine whether to accept or reject it." He decided on the latter course "after much turmoil and prayer." Soon after July 12, he was told that on that day the Prophet had received a revelation on celestial marriage; it was not made public, and he never saw a copy of it, but he heard it discussed many times. Near the end of July, William Marks, like Robinson an opponent of the doctrine, confirmed the fact. "They have got a revelation on the subject," he said. Robinson, Marks, and President William Law, together with their wives, "freely discussed" the matter. They were all at a loss to know what to do. When the document was read in the High Council, Marks, Austin Cowles, who was an associate in the Stake Presidency, and Leonard Soby refused to accept it. Cowles was "far more outspoken and energetic in his opposition to that doctrine than almost any other man in Nauvoo," said Robinson. Cowles straightway resigned his presidency, and "after that . . . was looked upon as a seceder, and no longer held a prominent place in the Church, although morally and religiously speaking he was one of the best men in the place." [93] He left Nauvoo the following June with other seceders. William Marks's account, though not detailed, tends to confirm that of Robinson.[94]

The document of July, 1843, on celestial marriage has had an unusual history. It was not made public during the lifetime of the Prophet, and its contents remained known only in a limited circle. In 1852 Brigham Young published in Utah what William Clayton, scribe and close friend of Smith, declared to be an exact copy of the original, made by his own hand in July, 1843. The original was al-

[93] *The Return*, 3:29, 30, February, 1891.
[94] "During my administration [as stake president]," said Marks, "I saw and heard many things that were practiced and taught that I did not believe to be of God; But I continued to do and teach such principles as were plainly revealed as the law of the Church. . . . Therefore, when the doctrine of polygamy was introduced into the Church I took a decided stand against it; which stand rendered me quite unpopular with many of the leading ones of the Church." *Zion's Harbinger and Baneemy's Organ*, 3:52, 53, July, 1853, quoted in *The Saints' Herald*, 51:73, January 27, 1904. Marks's statement appeared with slightly altered wording the *True Latter Day Saints' Herald*, 1:22, 23, 1860; and Smith and Smith, *History of the Reorganized Church*, 3:733. *Zion's Harbinger* was the paper of Charles Blanchard Thompson, leader of a Mormon splinter sect in western Iowa. Marks was associated with the Thompsonites for a time, and then became counselor to President Joseph Smith III in the Reorganized Church.

legedly burned by Emma Smith, though she denied ever having seen such a document.[95] The reason given by Brigham Young in 1852 for its long secrecy was fear of the reaction from the gentile world. But polygamy had been practiced openly in Utah from the beginning, and when knowledge of the custom passed from United States territorial officials to the nation, there was no longer any reason to keep it secret. Besides, by 1852 there were many scattered bodies of antipolygamous Mormons who claimed that Brigham Young and not Joseph Smith was its author. Since then there has been a controversy between Utah Mormons and the antipolygamy Saints, notably the Reorganized Church, over the veracity of the document. Until recently the popular and quasi-official view of the latter group has been that the document was authored in Utah and was a forgery, and that the abundant testimony to the contrary was part of a conspiracy to conceal the truth.[96] Whether the manuscript was altered or not before its publication can probably never be known from documentary sources, if possibly biased testimony be excluded. Though Smith said in 1844 that those who accused him of authoring polygamy "had taken the truth of God and made it a lie," there was something in the original document to which Marks and Cowles, both antipolygamists then and later, strongly objected.[97] At the very least it must have implied "plurality" or its possibility.

In a letter of September 8, 1843, Charlotte Haven spoke of the

[95] Smith and Smith, *History of the Reorganized Church*, 3:351–352. For the most extensive treatment of the subject in the literature of the Reorganized Church, see *ibid.*, pp. 348–366.

[96] More recently the view has been changing to an admission that Smith entertained the spiritual wife doctrine, and even authored in 1843 a revelation on marriage; but, it is held, the document was no more than a basis for later distortions placed upon it in Utah. This view assumes that Smith's repeated denials of personal complicity in the practice of polygamy and his public denunciations of the doctrine are sufficient proof to exonerate him from any connection with the tenet. See for example articles by the official historian, C. A. Davies, "Spiritual Marriage," and "Section 132, Utah D. & C.; A New Look at that Document on Polygamy," *Saints' Herald*, 109:322 ff., May 1, 1962, and 109:433 ff., June 15, 1962. The fact that before 1843 Smith denied even the existence of the spiritual wife doctrine, as official policy, though he could not have failed to know the untruth of such a denial, has apparently not been considered. The assumption that Smith would allow others than himself to promulgate doctrine and practice for the Church which were contrary to his own beliefs likewise tortures reason.

Denial of the doctrine and practice of plurality continued to be the official position of the Mormon Church until 1852.

[97] Smith's statement is from the city council proceedings of June 8, 1844, in *The Nauvoo Neighbor*, June 19, 1844.

new order of marriage in a letter to her family. She noted Joseph Smith's declaration a few weeks before that his prophetic mantle had fallen on his brother Hyrum. "We hear that [Hyrum] has already had some wonderful revelations not yet made public, but that a few of the elders put their heads together and whisper what they dare not speak aloud." A month or so before, she said, an Elder George J. Adams had returned from a two-year mission in England with a new wife and child, though he already had a wife and family in Nauvoo. "I am told that his first wife is reconciled to this at first unwelcome guest in her home," said Charlotte Haven, "for her husband and some others have reasoned with her that plurality of wives is taught in the Bible, that Abraham, Jacob, Solomon, David and indeed all the old prophets and good men, had several wives, and if right for them, it is right for the Latter Day Saints. Furthermore, the first wife will always be first in her husband's affection and the head of the household, where she will have a larger influence. Poor, weak woman!" Charlotte Haven ascribed the doctrine to Hyrum Smith, of whom she held a low opinion. "I cannot believe that Joseph will ever sanction such a doctrine. . . ." [98]

Brigham Young and Willard Richards had written Adams in February to come to Nauvoo "according to the decision of the council, and answer to the charges of adultery which had been preferred against him, before the First Presidency." [99] But on September 2, Stake President William Marks gave notice that Adams had been "honorably acquitted by the High Council in Nauvoo, from all charges heretofore preferred against him from any and all sources. . . ." [100] Marks's opposition to polygamy was not as strong at that time as it was to become later. After the Prophet's death, he may have felt relieved of personal fealty to the extent that his criticism became more vocal. "When I found that there was no chance to rid the Church of that damnable doctrine," he said, "I made my arrangements to leave Nauvoo, and I did so firmly believing that the plans and designs of the Great Jehovah, in inspiring Joseph to bring forth the Book of Mormon, would be carried out in his own time, and in his own way." By action of the October, 1844, conference, Marks was not continued as stake president.

[98] Quoted in Mulder and Mortensen, eds., *Among the Mormons*, pp. 126, 127. Charlotte Haven called Adams "Apostle," which was incorrect.
[99] Joseph Smith's History, 5:271.
[100] *Times and Seasons*, 4:303. The edition is dated August 15, 1843, but was not published until September, "owing to sickness in the office."

In December, 1843, according to Ebenezer Robinson, Hyrum Smith came to his home and expounded the doctrine of "plurality" to his wife and him personally. But they continued adamant in refusing to embrace it. "Hyrum opposed it at first," said Robinson, "but afterwards became its warm advocate, to my certain knowledge." The same month, Brigham Young instructed a group of Saints gathered for prayer and testimony of "the necessity of following our file leader, and Saviour, in all his laws and commandments, without asking any questions why they are so." [101]

Young's enjoinder pointed up the dilemma that shook the whole community. There were so many questions; yet doubt led to apostasy, and unquestioning faith supposedly led to salvation. The unity of Nauvoo was shattered because not all solved the dilemma in the same way. The questions, the doubts, the scandals, and the zeal to deal with questioners and doubters, created grave pressures within the Kingdom. There were many aspects of Mormonism as expressed in Nauvoo which were "strong meat," to use Robinson's phrase, and not to the taste of some of the Saints. Divisions within the Church over controversial matters of policy and doctrine led finally to the death of the Prophet, and abetted the ultimate destruction of the Nauvoo community.

[101] *The Return,* 3:29, February, 1891; Brigham Young's journal in the *Millennial Star,* 26:311, May 14, 1864.

10

The Kingdom as Empire

Be it ordained by the Senate and House of Representatives of the United States . . . *that Joseph Smith, of the city of Nauvoo, in the State of Illinois, is hereby authorized and empowered to raise a company of one hundred thousand armed volunteers in the United States and territories, at such times, and places, and in such numbers, as he shall find necessary and convenient for the purposes specified in the foregoing preamble, and to execute the same.*

> From Joseph Smith's proposed "Ordinance for the Protection of the Citizens of the United States Emigrating to the Territories, and for the Extension of the principles of Universal Liberty," March 26, 1844, in Joseph Smith's History, 6:275–277.

Should the inherent corruption of Mormonism fail to develop . . . sufficiently to convince its followers of their error, where will the thing end? A great military despotism is growing up in the fertile West, increasing faster, in proportion, than the surrounding population, spreading its influence around, and marshalling multitudes under its banner, causing serious alarm to every patriot.

> The *New York Sun*, September 4, 1843.

May Nauvoo become the empire seat of government!

> Toast drunk in the Nauvoo Mansion, January 29, 1844; in Joseph Smith's History, 6:188, 189.

Perhaps John C. Bennett's most sensational and alarming charge against the Mormons was that they had "a vast and deeplaid scheme . . . for conquering the states of Ohio, Indiana, Illinois, Iowa, and Missouri, and erecting upon the ruin of their present governments a despotic military and religious empire, the head of which, as emperor and pope [would be] Joseph Smith . . . and his ministers and viceroys, the apostles, high priests, elders, and bishops of the Mormon Church." [1] As stated by Bennett the idea was absurd, as was his earlier suggestion that the Nauvoo Legion should make a holy war of revenge on Missouri. But there was a kernel of truth in the imputation of an imperious, expansionist Mormonism, and events kept the idea alive and nurtured gentile apprehension.

[1] Quoted in Joseph Smith's History, 5:80n.

The rapid growth of Nauvoo and of the Church, the burgeoning Nauvoo Legion, the unusual independence of the Nauvoo government, Mormon participation in Illinois politics, and Smith's candidacy for President of the United States, considered together with the aggressive, energetic, strident qualities which seemed to pervade Mormonism, all tended to leave an unquiet wake among the gentiles. When finally the unrealized and only half-suspected Mormon ambitions of the forties blossomed in Utah into a full-scale attempt to create a vast Mormon empire in the West, a whole generation of Americans became convinced that Mormonism threatened to subvert not only their morals, but their republic as well.

Dreams of empire were in fact born in Nauvoo, and plans were laid to make them come true; but the empire was to be a peculiarly Mormon one—chaste, inoffensive, properly constitutional, and within the American expansionist tradition, a means to help God's Kingdom "roll forth." The developing Mormon view of government in the Kingdom of God and its proper relation to the existing governments of the land was a compound of Mormon thought about the Kingdom itself, the habitual failure of state and federal government to protect the Saints from persecution or to redress wrongs done them, and their expectations of rapid and infinite Mormon population expansion. Influenced by specific developments in Nauvoo and conditioned in a time and a region much concerned with western expansion and the Texas and Oregon questions, Smith and others began to think in terms of a quasi-sovereign church-state whose influence would spread into Texas, Oregon, Mexico, and Central America. Such a development they viewed not as rivaling the normal course of American expansion into those areas but rather as a vital part of it.

The concept of a Mormon state originated in the doctrine that the restored Church of Christ was to "build up" the Kingdom of God upon the earth. The early references to the Kingdom in Mormon scriptural and evangelistic writing are mostly general and sometimes ambiguous. Often it was identified with the Church, often with a righteous society, sometimes with one righteous individual, the priesthood, or the "pure in heart." Sometimes the implication was of an actual government embracing the whole world, "wearing the vestments of a sovereign state." [2] Popularly the Kingdom was identified

[2] Melville, "The Political Ideas of Brigham Young," p. 8. See also Hyrum Andrus, "Joseph Smith, Social Philosopher, Theorist, and Prophet," chap. XIV, "The Establishment of the Kingdom of God," and *passim.*

with Mormon communitarianism, that is, Zion at Independence and her stakes at Kirtland, Far West, and Nauvoo. Apostle Parley Parker Pratt, in a widely circulated missionary tract written in 1837, was more specific. "Now, when we speak of the kingdom of God, we wish it to be understood that we mean His organized government on the earth." Pratt proceeded to explain that organization: "Four things are required in order to constitute any kingdom in heaven or on the earth; namely, first, a king; secondly, commissioned officers duly qualified to execute his ordinances and laws; thirdly, a code of laws by which the subjects are governed; and fourthly subjects who are governed where these exist in their proper and regular authority, there is a kingdom. . . . In this respect the kingdom of God is like other kingdoms. . . ."[3] Apostles John Taylor and Brigham Young further explicated Pratt's definition: "The Lord is that king," said Taylor, "his people are his subjects; his revealed will is the law of his kingdom; the priesthood is the administrator of those laws." The Mormon priesthood, said Young, is "the perfect system of government."[4] The prophet Daniel's interpretation of the dream of Nebuchadnezzar was popularly believed by Mormons to be prophecy concerning the Kingdom in the Latter Days. It should be as a "stone cut out of the mountain without hands" which would roll forth to fill the whole earth, "a kingdom which shall never be destroyed . . . but it shall break in pieces and consume all these kingdoms, and it shall stand forever."[5] In 1841, Pratt used the second and seventh chapters of Daniel, the twenty-fourth and fortieth chapters of Isaiah, and the *Book of Mormon*, first Nephi, as texts in writing a long letter to Queen Victoria in which he warned that soon all the kingdoms of the world, including that of Her Majesty, would fall. Upon the ruins, the Kingdom of God would rise. "I have given the above," wrote Pratt, "in order that your majesty, and the people of your dominion, may be aware of future events which are nigh, even at the door. I must close this letter by forewarning the Sovereign and people of England, in the most affectionate manner, to repent and turn to the Lord. . . . I mean my message for the lords and nobles, clergy and gentry as well. . . ." Repentance would be achieved by aiding the poor rather than oppressing them, said Pratt. "Now if the rulers, clergy, and people of England hearken to this message, they

---

[3] Pratt, A *Voice of Warning and Instruction to All People*, p. 85.
[4] *Times and Seasons*, 4:24, December 1, 1842; Joseph Smith's History, 5:550
[5] Book of Daniel, Authorized Version, 2:44.

shall have part in this glorious kingdom [of God]; but if they will not hearken to the words of the prophets and apostles, they will be overthrown with the wicked, and perish from the earth." [6]

Although the Mormon vision of the Kingdom was apocalyptic, as it was in other millennialist sects of the period, and the language used to express it sometimes implied violence, Joseph Smith insisted that the work of God was the cause of peace. The great states of the past were all "raised to dignity amidst the clash of arms and the din of war," whereas "the designs of God . . . have been to promote the universal good of the universal world; to establish peace and good will among men . . . to make the nations of the earth dwell in peace, and to bring about the millennial glory." [7] In another discussion of Daniel's prophecies, the peaceful processes of God were affirmed: "it is not our intention to be understood that this destruction is to be accomplished by physical force by the people of God, but by the preaching of the gospel, and the judgments and power of God." [8] Nevertheless, the details of the process by which the Kingdom of God would supersede the kingdoms of this world remained unspecified and subject to differing speculations.

The Mormon view of the Constitution of the United States seemed in the beginning not untypical of Jacksonian Democracy.[9] The Constitution set the framework and limits of government and forbade government encroachment upon civil rights. Of particular importance were its guarantees of the right to free conscience and worship, individual liberty, and protection of property. The Mormons, however, tended to see constitutional guarantees as specific demands for government action to redress violated rights, a view not prevalent until after the Civil War. But constitution and government failed to redress their grievances in Missouri, and the Saints discov-

[6] Pratt wrote as head of the British mission on May 28, 1841; *Times and Seasons*, 3:591–596, November 15, 1841. His letter fulfilled the commandment in Smith's revelation of January, 1841, to proclaim the Kingdom of God to the kings and rulers of the earth. Reorganized Church *Doctrine and Covenants*, 107:1–4; Utah Church *Doctrine and Covenants*, 124:3–12. See also Joseph Smith's History, 4:483; 6:80.

[7] From "The Government of God," an article in *Times and Seasons*, 3:855, July 15, 1842.

[8] Erastus Snow and Benjamin Winchester in *The Gospel Reflector*, quoted in *Times and Seasons*, 3:612, December 1, 1841.

[9] Jackson was a heroic figure to both Joseph Smith and Brigham Young. "General Jackson's administration may be denominated the *acme* of American glory, liberty, and prosperity," wrote Smith, "for the national debt . . . was paid up in his golden day. . . ." Joseph Smith's History, 6:203.

ered to their distress that a government of laws is also a government of men. During the Nauvoo period a perceptible change of attitude took place, and the Church began to seek political as well as legal solutions to the problems of conflict with gentile society. In the process the concept of the Kingdom became less legalistic and more political.[10] Political action was a practical necessity for kingdom building, said Smith in 1843. "It is our duty to concentrate all our influence to make popular that which is sound and good, and unpopular that which is unsound. 'Tis right, politically, for a man who has influence to use it. . . . From henceforth I will maintain all the influence I can get." [11]

The first time the Mormons gave serious thought to their need for assistance from the federal government was in 1839, at the time of the founding of Nauvoo. After their failure in the state courts to recover lands in Jackson County, Missouri, of which they were dispossessed in 1833, and feeling themselves lucky to be left with their lives after being expelled from their Far West homes in 1839 by Boggs's executive order, they naturally turned to higher authority. Sidney Rigdon conceived a grand scheme to present the Mormon case before the United States Congress through petitions and deputations, and to "impeach" the state of Missouri for not having a republican form of government. Inasmuch as Illinois officials were sympathetic to the plight of the Saints and anxious to win their friendship, official support was inferred and much importance was attached to it. The "leading men" of Illinois were favorable, said Smith; even Governor Carlin's assistance was expected. "The Bishops of the Church are required to ride and visit all scattered abroad, and to collect money to carry on this great work. Be assured . . . that operations of an all-important character are under motion. . . ." [12]

[10] See Joseph Smith's letter from the Liberty jail, March, 1839, in Joseph Smith's *History*, 3:304, 305, and *Times and Seasons*, 1:133, 134, July, 1840; the discussion of the government of the Kingdom of God and Mormon constitutional thought follows that of Melville, "The Political Ideas of Brigham Young," pp. 8–17.

[11] Joseph Smith's *History*, 5:286. A passive and nonpolitical philosophy was early expressed in a revelation of 1831. "Let no man break the laws of the land, for he that keepeth the laws of God hath no need to break the laws of the land; wherefore, be subject to the powers that be, until He reigns whose right it is to reign, and subdues all enemies under his feet." Utah Church *Doctrine and Covenants*, 58:21, 22; Reorganized Church *Doctrine and Covenants*, 58:5.

[12] Governor Lucas of Iowa Territory gave Rigdon noncommittal letters of introduction to the governor of Ohio and to President Van Buren, which the Saints interpreted as influential letters of endorsement. E. H. West, ed., *Calendar of the Papers of Martin Van Buren* (manuscript, Library of Congress); Joseph Smith's *History*, 3:310, 311, 333 ff.

In April, 1839, the project was undertaken, and preparations were pushed throughout the summer. The Saints were in great need of money, and the notion grew upon them that a cash settlement would be made, either by Missouri, acting under orders from Washington, or by the federal treasury itself, to recompense them for their losses. Four hundred ninety-one individual petitions of grievances and bills of damages were obtained from the Saints amounting to $1,381,044; but there were still "a multitude more of similar bills hereafter to be presented," said Smith, "which, if not settled immediately, will ere long amount to a handsome sum, increasing by compound interest." [13] It appears that the Mormons never contemplated bringing any action in the courts of the United States; the petitions were to go before Congress and the President. To carry out the mission of state, on September 29 the Prophet, accompanied by the venerable Rigdon and "Judge" Elias Higbee as companions and Orrin Porter Rockwell as general factotum, set out for the Capital in a proper two-horse carriage. They were armed with letters and petitions and possessed of the most sanguine expectations. Their hopes were quickly dispelled by the reception they got eight weeks later on their arrival in Washington. Smith's various accounts of his brief audience with the President differ somewhat depending on how angry he was at the recollection, but Van Buren was obviously candid in admitting that if he responded to the Mormon pleas in any way he would lose the vote of Missouri in the election the following autumn.[14] Although the President would undoubtedly have refused to take any action in such a matter regardless of the effect on his political future, the Prophet considered the rejection to be based on personal political considerations alone. Smith seems in large measure to have developed his view of the ideal chief executive— fearless, righteous, unselfish, above political consideration, willing and able to override vacillating or wicked courts and legislatures— from his reaction to the encounter with Van Buren. The reception given the Mormon leaders at the Capitol was as unsatisfactory as that in the President's Mansion. Both Clay and Calhoun reacted "coldly." The latter reportedly said, "It involves a nice question . . . of States' rights; it will not do to agitate it"; and though Clay moved the Mormon petition in the Senate, he said, "I am indifferent as to the motion; but . . . the subject ought to be referred, and that in-

[13] Joseph Smith's *History,* 4:75.
[14] See *ibid.*, 6:203, for one of Smith's subsequent heated attacks upon Van Buren.

quiry should be made by the [Judiciary] Committee whether Congress has any power to redress." [15] The Senate Judiciary Committee made a lengthy report on the matter in March, 1840. Although the memorial of the Mormons had been "drawn up in great length . . . with feeling and eloquence," it failed to allege any offense committed by the officers or courts of the United States. Therefore, "The committee . . . after full examination . . . unanimously concur in the opinion that the case presented for their investigation is not such a one as will justify or authorize any interposition by this Government . . . the petitioners must seek relief in the courts of judicature of the State of Missouri. . . ." Such an appeal "will never be made in vain by the injured or oppressed. It can never be presumed that a state either wants the power, or lacks the disposition, to redress the wrongs of its own citizens committed within her own territory, whether they proceed from the lawless acts of her officers, or any other persons." The committee resolved that they "be discharged from the further consideration of . . . this case." [16] Even assuming the sincerity of the Judiciary Committee, such a report was based on the presumptions of law and justice rather than the circumstances of politics and power. It was received in Nauvoo with disappointment, cynicism, and bitterness. The Mormons continued to press the petitions through their congressman, John T. Stuart, but without the enthusiasm of 1839, and without success. [17]

The experiences of the Missouri persecutions and the fate of the petition to the national government taught the Mormons the prime fact of ante-bellum federalism: the states were sovereign and supreme. The lesson caused them grave concern. They felt that their former reliance on the promises of the Constitution and the American tradition of liberty had been naive, and that they needed new means to guarantee the safety and integrity of the Kingdom. The Nauvoo Charter was the result. Machinery for the protection of individual and group liberty for the Saints was assumed to inhere in the city council and municipal court; and the Legion likewise was assumed to make the Kingdom sovereign. "I concocted it [the

[15] *Niles National Register,* 57:364, February 1, 1840; Joseph Smith's History, 5:393; Gayler, "The Mormons in Western Illinois," p. 6. The official petition is in Joseph Smith's History, 4:24–38.

[16] "Senate Judiciary Committee report on the memorial of the delegation of the Latter Day Saints, March 4, 1840," *Senate Documents,* 1st Session, 26th Congress, Vol. V, 1839–1840.

[17] See Joseph Smith's History, 4:427. A petition was again sent in November, 1843. *Ibid.,* 6:84–88.

Charter]," said Smith, "for the salvation of the Church, and on principles so broad, that every honest man might dwell secure under its
protective influence. . . ." [18] But as soon as its unique objectives
became known, opposition to the charter began to develop in Illinois, and a resolve to amend or repeal it paralleled a rising tide of
anti-Mormon feeling. By the autumn of 1843 some in Nauvoo believed that the approaching session of the legislature might indeed
change the chartered status of the city, though such a possibility was
not admitted publicly. During this season crimes of violence committed against individual Mormons increased alarmingly. Robberies,
kidnappings, burnings, shootings, and stabbings, mostly of Mormon
farmers in the outlying settlements, spread terror to the whole Mormon community. Most of the perpetrators were believed to be Missourians living within a few miles of Hancock County, among whom
a belief had grown that Mormons were beyond the law, fugitives
from justice, and fair game. Smith wanted to activate the Nauvoo
Legion as a police force and even pursue the offenders into Missouri
if need be; but Governor Ford would not permit it.[19] The stage was
set for a new turn in the development of a Mormon state.

"I suggested to the Council the idea of petitioning Congress to receive the City of Nauvoo under the protection of the United States
Government," wrote Smith in his journal on December 8, 1843, "to
acknowledge the Nauvoo Legion as U.S. troops, and to assist in for-
tifications and other purposes, and that a messenger be sent to Congress for this purpose at the expense of the city." John Taylor, Orson
Spencer, and Orson Pratt were appointed a committee to draft a
memorial to this effect.[20] Two weeks later the petition, together
with a draft of a federal ordinance to enact the proposal, was finished. Basing a constitutional argument on the reserved powers,
privileges and immunities, and territorial clauses, the petition requested Congress to bestow upon Nauvoo "all the rights, powers,
privileges, and immunities belonging to Territories, and not repug-

---

[18] *Ibid.*, 4:249. See also G. Homer Durham, "A Political Interpretation of
Mormon History," *Pacific Historical Review*, 13:136–150 (1944).

[19] See Ford's letter to Smith and Smith's reaction in *Joseph Smith's History*,
6:113–115. The governor notwithstanding, Smith ordered a hundred men of
the Legion to take an accused kidnapper of Warsaw into custody when it was
believed that his arrest would "be resisted by an armed force," perhaps the
county militia. *Ibid.*, 6:119. For an understanding of the general situation from
the Mormon viewpoint, see the November and December issues of the *Nauvoo
Neighbor*, and *Joseph Smith's History*, Vol. VI, chap. 5 *passim*.

[20] *Joseph Smith's History*, 6:107.

nant to the Constitution of the United States," and to confirm and
secure "the spirit, letter, meaning, and provisions of the [Nauvoo]
charter" for the new territory. The mayor of the city should be empowered "by . . . consent of the President of the United States,
whenever the actual necessity of the case and the public safety shall
require it, to call to his aid a sufficient number of United States
troops, in connection with the Nauvoo Legion, to repel the invasion
of mobs, keep the public peace, and protect the innocent from the
unhallowed ravages of lawless banditti that escape justice on the
western frontier." Officers of the United States were to be required
to obey "the requisitions of this ordinance"; and the Nauvoo Legion,
". . . for all services rendered in quelling mobs and preserving the
public peace . . . shall be under the same regulations, rules, and
laws of pay as the troops of the United States." [21] Amid a growing
sense of frustration and fear, the Mormons were now seeking a truly
novel solution to their problem. The proposal to create a self-
governing, well-garrisoned, largely independent Mormon enclave
under the guise of a federal territory within the sovereign State of
Illinois approached the extreme limits of possibility, if the Kingdom
on the Mississippi were to remain within the general framework of
the American federal union. The time was approaching when individual Mormons would in effect have to choose between their American citizenship and literal citizenship in the Kingdom of God. The
choice when made tended to divide those who went to Utah from
those who did not.

Except for the passage of the Nauvoo charters the Prophet's relations with gentile governments since the founding of the Church
had ranged from unsatisfactory to disastrous. That he should feel
himself and his movement increasingly alienated from the nation's
legal and political fabric is not unnatural. At various times he made
dire predictions of the fate that was in store for those who oppressed
or failed to aid the Saints of God. On his way home from Washington early in 1840 he "did not fail to proclaim the iniquity and inso-
lence of Martin Van Buren, toward myself and an injured people,
which will have its effect upon the public mind; and may he never
be elected again to any office of trust or power, by which he may
abuse the innocent and let the guilty go free." [22] "My heart faints
within me," Smith wrote in his journal, "when I see, by the visions of

[21] *Ibid.*, 6:125–132.
[22] Joseph Smith's History, 4:89. The editor noted Van Buren's subsequent
political failure.

the Almighty, the end of this nation, if she continues to disregard the cries and petitions of her virtuous citizens, as she has done, and is now doing."[23] The following July he wrote: "Since Congress had decided against us, the Lord has begun to vex this nation. . . . A hailstorm has visited South Carolina . . . which swept crops, killing some cattle. Insects are devouring crops on the high lands, where the floods of the country have not reached, and great commercial distress prevails everywhere. . . . [God] will continue except they repent; for they now stand guilty of murder, robbery, and plunder, as a nation, because they have refused to protect their citizens, and execute justice according to their own constitution."[24] In May, 1843, he told Stephen A. Douglas, who was a guest at his table, "I prophesy in the name of the Lord God of Israel, unless the United States redress the wrongs committed upon the Saints . . . in a few years the government will be utterly overthrown and wasted, and there shall not be so much as one potsherd left. . . ." Failure to help the Mormons against Missouri was a "foul and corroding blot upon the fair fame of this great republic," the knowledge of which would have caused the Founding Fathers "to hide their faces with shame." Smith further prophesied that Douglas would one day aspire to the presidency; "and if ever you turn your hand against me or the Latter-day Saints, you will feel the hand of the Almighty upon you. . . ."[25]

In 1843, despite the innumerable concerns of the moment in Nauvoo, plans were being conceived for the future development of the Kingdom on a scale imagined by few. "I prophesy [that] as soon as we get the Temple built, so that we shall not be obliged to exhaust our means thereon," said Smith in January, 1843, "we will have means to gather the Saints by thousands and tens of thousands." In the same vein he told an inner circle of leaders, "from the sixth day of April next, I go in for preparing with all present for a mission through the United States, and when we arrive at Maine we will take ship for England and so on to all countries where we shall have a mind to go. . . . If I live, I will yet take these brethren through the United States and through the world, and we will make just as big a wake as God Almighty will let me. We must send kings and governors to Nauvoo, and we will do it."[26] The need to settle those

[23] *Ibid.*
[24] *Ibid.*, 4:145.
[25] *Ibid.*, 5:394. See also Smith's address of June 30, 1843, in *ibid.*, 5:467.
[26] *Ibid.*, 5:255, 256. Smith was addressing what he called simply "the council." Probably it was a nascent group of top leaders which became the secret Council of Fifty, described below.

tens of thousands, and perhaps the kings and governors too, eventuated in plans for a vast Mormon empire in the West. Though never developed as envisioned, the concept formed the basis of Brigham Young's Mormon domain in the Great Basin and gave to Latter-day Saint culture and history a great part of its unique character. The idea of establishing Mormon colonies beyond the western boundaries of the United States was probably coincident with the rising national interest in Texas, Oregon, and California during the thirties and forties. Henry Clay advised the Mormons in 1839 that the best way for them to solve their problems was to move to Oregon.[27] It occurred to others that such a move would solve "the Mormon question" and perhaps help to secure Oregon as an American territory. The *Quincy Whig* on September 24, 1842, advanced the argument explicitly:

If [Smith] will listen to word from us, we would advise him to locate his new Jerusalem, away to the far West, in the Oregon country and there . . . govern the Saints in his own way . . . he would procure peace and quietness [without] molestation in the enjoyment of their peculiar notions in that distant country;—to the Government, the location of [the Mormons] would be an advantage, because it greatly needs settlers in that region; and doubtless, Government would do something right handsome for Joseph, in the grant of a gift of lands, etc., if he would guarantee the emigration of any number of settlers. . . .[28]

James Arlington Bennett of New York, sometime friend and honorary convert of Mormonism, wrote a letter to James Gordon Bennett of the *New York Herald* which in part also advised westering for the Saints. Missouri and Illinois had better leave them alone, for if they were to be driven farther west, they might set up an independent government of their own. "Indeed," said Bennett, "I would recommend to the Prophet to pull up stakes and take possession of the Oregon territory in his own right, and establish an independent empire. In one hundred years from this time, no nation on earth could conquer such a people." The Prophet could then "make his own laws by the voice of revelation, and have them executed like the act of one man." If Smith would do this, Bennett was sure that "millions would flock to his standard and join his cause."[29] Such heady no-

---

[27] Joseph Smith's History, 5:393.
[28] *Times and Seasons*, 3:953, October 15, 1842. Joseph Smith professed horror at the suggestion of such an idea, but nevertheless considered it worthy of republication in full in his own paper.
[29] Smith included the entire document in his journal under entry of October 16, 1842; Joseph Smith's History, 5:170.

tions began to fit into the more advanced Mormon thinking about the future of the Kingdom.[30]

Smith himself was an ardent expansionist and Texas annexationist. It was better to take Texas despite slavery, he said, than have the British get it. "Don't let Texas go, lest our mothers and the daughters of the land should laugh us in the teeth. . . ." The objection had been advanced that the South already held the balance of power in the nation; but the Prophet would solve that problem by liberating the slaves in "two or three states, indemnifying their owners, and send the Negroes to Texas, and from Texas to Mexico, where all colors are alike. And if that was not sufficient, I would call upon Canada, and annex it. . . . We should grasp all the territory we can." [31] Apparently little was done before the winter of 1843–1844 to implement any scheme for colonizing Mormons in the West except to send a small expedition into Iowa in July and August of 1843 to make some preliminary explorations, possibly of routes across that territory from Nauvoo to the Missouri River.[32] But after the memorial to Congress of December, 1843, the leaders began earnestly to consider the possibilities of movements to the West. Historians of Mormonism have assumed that plans were undertaken at this time for the abandonment of Nauvoo in favor of a western Kingdom for all Mormons, an event which was actually to transpire in two years. Such an assumption seems to be an argument after the fact and ignores the large plans continually being made up until the autumn of 1845 for the future development of Nauvoo. More accurate is the explanation that plans were considered for the establishment of Mormon colonies in the West; and in case of emergency, such plans could serve as an avenue of escape for all Nauvoo Mormons. In the event, the emergency did occur and has obscured what was actually intended by Smith.[33] Early in February, 1844, the Twelve discussed

[30] Smith is purported to have prophesied in the summer of 1842 that the Saints would be driven into the Rocky Mountains and there become a mighty people. The account is so confused, however, that this author considers it suspect. See editor Brigham H. Roberts' discussion in *Joseph Smith's History*, 5:86n.

[31] From a public address of Smith in Nauvoo, March 7, 1844, in *Joseph Smith's History*, 6:243, 244. The Prophet was then beginning his "campaign" for the presidency.

[32] See the report of Jonathan Dunham, the expedition leader, in *ibid.*, 5:541 ff.

[33] Brigham Young, writing perhaps in justification of his attempted establishment of the State of Deseret, said that the Prophet created the Council of Fifty in part to determine "the best manner to settle our people in some distant and unoccupied territory, [free from] constant oppression and mobocracy,

the propriety of establishing a "mock congress for the purpose of investigating and informing ourselves on the rules of national intercourse, domestic policy, and political economy." The Prophet advised against it, however, "lest we might excite the jealousy of our enemies." [34] Smith did instruct the Apostles to select an exploring company to go to California "to select a location for the settlement of the Saints." [35] Meanwhile, Lyman Wight and George Miller had been investigating the advisability of establishing Mormon colonies in the Wisconsin country where they had located their sawmills. Miller arrived in Nauvoo March 8 with a formal report.[36] The colony at the "pinery" had had a very difficult season, and the Wisconsin brethren advised against further colonizing for a variety of reasons. But they had a specific proposal to make as an alternative. They wished to take the "pineries" colony to the "table lands" of Texas, and there establish a Mormon mission. They would sell the mills, urge the friendly Indians to sell their lands to the government, and all go west together. Many things would thus be accomplished: the opening of the Church "in all the South and Southwestern States, as also Texas, Mexico, Brazil, etc., together with the West Indian Islands"; it would provide "a place of gathering for all the South (they being encumbered with that unfortunate race of beings the Negroes)"; and in general enable the colonists "to employ our time and talents in gathering together means to build according to the commandments of our God, and spread the gospel to all nations." Both Wight and Miller wrote separate letters; but both were endorsed by a committee of brethren at the mills, and the authors' signatures were therefore not attached. One of the letters stated the general proposition as outlined above. In the other, the implications of the proposal were further explored. The Wisconsin Indian friends, "if counselled by us so to go," had a strong desire to move to the Southwest, "where game is more plenty," and would there aid in large-scale conversions of Indians. "This committee is therefore led to take a brief view of the south and western part of North America, together with the Floridas, Texas, West Indian Islands, and the ad-

under the protection of our own laws, subject to the constitution." *Millennial Star*, 26:328, May 21, 1864.
[34] *Ibid.*, 26:327.
[35] *Ibid.*
[36] The report dealt with the nature and disposition of the Indians, their receptivity to the Gospel, relations with the Indian agent, the climate, agricultural and mineral resources, availability of game, etc.

jacent islands of the Gulf of Mexico, together with the Lamanites [Indians] bordering on the United Territories from Green Bay to the Mexican Gulf, all crying with one voice, through the medium of their Chiefs, Give us [your Gospel], for . . . your ways are equal, and your righteousness far exceeds the righteousness of all the missionaries that we have yet become acquainted with. . . ." Indian missions were a cherished objective of the Mormons, but they had never been extensive or successful. Here was a stirring prospect for a much neglected responsibility. There would be in addition the advantage of evangelizing among southern slave-owners. "Are there not thousands of rich planters who would embrace the gospel, and, if they had a place to plant their slaves, give all the proceeds of their yearly labor, if rightly taught, for building up the kingdom . . . ? We answer, Yes. . . ." They were "well informed" that the Cherokee and Choctaw nations lying between Arkansas and the Red River owned "large plantations and thousands of slaves," and that they were "very desirous to have an interview with the Elders, upon the principles of the Book of Mormon." It would be far better to establish a kind of "Southern gathering" where slaveowners could go with their blacks "and keep them in lively exercise according to their former customs and habits." The alternative, if such converts had to gather to Zion in the North, would be the necessity to abolish slavery and settle the southerner "in a climate uncongenial to his nature and entirely derogatory to his former occupations in life." [37] Here were proposals for kingdom building on a grand scale indeed. Convert gatherers could be sent out to such colonies which would become subcenters of Mormon population. It would be a way of establishing "concert and reciprocity" through the agency of the Kingdom between North and South. Furthermore, what could be done for planters, slaves, and Indians might be done for other kinds of converts too. The Miller-Wight letters struck fire in the Prophet's heart. "Brother Miller, I perceive the Spirit of God is in the Pineries as well as here, and we will call together some of our wise men and proceed to set up the Kingdom of God by organizing some of its officers." [38]

[37] The letters were signed by Wight, Miller, Phinias Bird, Pierce Hawley, and John Young, "Select Committee to write expressing the views of the branch of the Church at Black River Falls"; Wight and Miller were "to write the views of the Committee," but when each wrote separate letters, it was "resolved that both productions be sent without alterations." Joseph Smith's History, 6:255–260.

[38] Miller, *Correspondence*, p. 20.

According to Smith's journal, "The brethren went into council on the subject matter of the letters during the evening [March 10, 1844]." The following day the Prophet began the formal organization of the secret leadership group which became known as "the Council of Fifty." The move was apparently precipitated by a resolve to implement some such program as that suggested by the Miller-Wight letters; but Smith had for some time been developing a private, informal core of leadership as a latent power structure for the Kingdom.[39] The Council of Fifty was to be no mere committee, but rather an elaborate organization endowed with awesome trappings and ritual. Miller, who belonged to the group, said the Prophet organized the members "as princes in the Kingdom of God." William Marks, referring apparently to the same event, said, "I was witness . . . of the introduction (secretly) of a kingly form of government, in which Joseph suffered himself to be ordained a king, to reign over the House of Israel forever." [40] So secret was the Council of Fifty that few people even knew of its existence before Smith's death. Its records remain hidden, and it is therefore possible to construct only a general picture of its purpose and function from scattered references in the journals and reminiscences of some of the members. Smith intended apparently that it be a shadow government for the Church and for the city of Nauvoo, ready to assume direct control in case of any emergency. In addition, it prepared memorials to Congress, planned political strategy, decided various economic questions, established businesses, secured building materials, provided bodyguards for the leaders, and dealt with apostates and "enemies." It further served to gain obedience to Church directives that might not be legally binding. But beyond this it was to plan for the growth of the Kingdom, and specifically to direct the expected vast influx of converts and to establish Mormon colonies in the West and Southwest, and in Central and South America.[41]

[39] Juanita Brooks, writing from the unpublished journals of such members of the Council of Fifty as John D. Lee and Hosea Stout, said that Smith began its formation in April, 1842, but that organization was "completed" on March 11, 1844. *John Doyle Lee*, p. 56.

[40] Miller, *Correspondence*, p. 20. *Zion's Harbinger and Baneemy's Organ*, 3:53, July, 1853, reprinted in *Saints' Herald*, 51:73, January 27, 1904. Marks was a member of the group at first; but he apostatized from the leadership of the Twelve after the death of Smith. "I could not conceive [the kingly government] to be in accordance with the laws of the Church," he said, "but I did not oppose this move, thinking it to be none of my business."

[41] Brooks, *John Doyle Lee*, p. 81; Leonard Arrington, *Great Basin Kingdom*, pp. 31, 32. See also Lyman Wight's statement about the functions of the Council of Fifty in Smith and Smith, *History of the Reorganized Church*, 2:790, 791.

The Council of Fifty included Young, Kimball, Woodruff, Hyde, Orson and Parley Pratt, George A. Smith, Richards, Wight, and Taylor of the Twelve, Hyrum Smith, Bishops George Miller, Newel Whitney, and Edward Hunter, and such men as Erastus Snow, Joseph Fielding, Joseph Coolidge, C. C. Rich, John D. Lee, George J. Adams, Amasa Lyman, W. W. Phelps, John M. Bernhisel, Lucian Woodworth, Alexander Badlam, Reynolds Cahoon, Amos Fielding, Lorenzo D. Wasson, James Emmett, O. P. Rockwell, Sidney Rigdon, Uriah Brown, William Marks, Theodore Turley, Charles Shumway, Alpheus Cutler, Samuel Bent, Peter Haws, A. P. Rockwood, Orson Spencer, Joseph L. Heywood, William Clayton, and Jedediah M. Grant, many of whom were officers in the Nauvoo Legion. The membership grew slowly, reaching a total of fifty-three by the time of Smith's death. Others were added to the membership in succeeding years until it became a numerous group. It contained an inner circle of leaders whom Smith sometimes called "the living constitution of the Kingdom." [42] "Its settings were always strictly private," wrote Benjamin F. Johnson in his journal, "and its rules [directives] were carefully and promptly observed. . . . I was present at every session, and being about the youngest member of that Council I was deeply impressed with all that transpired, or was taught by the President." [43] The Council of Fifty was apparently bound to the Prophet personally by strong ties of fealty.

After Smith's death the Council of Fifty was a power behind Brigham Young, and while he purged some members who opposed him, he was careful to consult it when formulating policy. The martyrdom of the Prophet gave a special sanctity to the tasks Smith had directed its members to undertake. The handling of Church property in Nauvoo became a function of the Fifty. Joseph Coolidge, Joseph Heywood, Almon Babbitt, and John Fullmer, the trustees-in-trust for the Church from 1844 to 1846, were all Council members. The organization and conduct of the trek west into the Great Basin was largely the work of the Fifty. Two members, Alpheus Cutler and Lyman Wight, believed that their westering missions differed from that directed by Brigham Young, and they launched independent Mormon colonies in Texas, Iowa, Kansas, and Minnesota. From 1844 to 1849, according to Leonard Arrington, the Fifty more or less

[42] Joseph Smith's History, 6:260, 263, 341; Smith's journal in the *Millennial Star*, 23:150, March 9, 1861; Brooks, *John Doyle Lee*, pp. 81 ff.; Brigham Young's journal in the *Millennial Star*, 26:328, May 21, 1864.

[43] Quoted in James D. Clark, "The Kingdom of God, the Council of Fifty, and the State of Deseret," *Utah Historical Quarterly*, 26:141 (1958).

directed the civil and temporal affairs of Mormonism; and in the Great Basin the Council was the government of the new Mormon state of Deseret. Despite their failure to gain annexation to the Union for Utah the Council of Fifty continued as a kind of shadow government into the 1870's.[44]

The first tasks of the Council concerned the proposals of Wight and Miller about the Texas colony and the associated notion of an empire of Mormon settlements in the West. Smith said the Council formed on March 11, 1844, was "to take into consideration the subject matter . . . in the [Miller-Wight] letters, and also the best policy for this people to adopt to obtain their rights from the nation and insure protection for themselves and children: and to secure a resting place in the mountains, or some uninhabited region. . . ."[45] The Council met almost daily in lengthy sessions for two weeks after March 11, drawing in additional members frequently. An early item of business was Texas. Not only would a colony be planted there, but territory would be sought for a Mormon state. The Republic of Texas was in need of aid to defend itself against Mexico; the Mormons would render such aid by settling west Texas, thus creating a neutral buffer zone between the Texans on the one side and the Mexicans and perhaps the Indians on the other. All that was wanted in return from the government in Austin was a grant of the western two-thirds of Texas for the new Mormon state.[46] On March 14, Lucian Woodworth, a gentile and erstwhile Nauvoo House architect, was dispatched to Austin to begin negotiations with the Texas government; and George Miller left for Wisconsin to notify the colony there of its move to Texas "to take possession of the newly acquired territory." Miller and Wight then hurried back to Nauvoo, hoping to arrive by the time Woodworth returned. They arrived on April 30, and Woodworth on May 2. Woodworth's report to the Council of Fifty was, said Miller, "altogether as we could wish it"; a treaty had been "partly entered into" with the Texas cabinet.[47]

[44] See Leonard J. Arrington, *Great Basin Kingdom*, pp. 431, 432, chap. 1, notes 105–108. For Brigham Young's thinking in 1855 about the Kingdom of God and the Council of Fifty, see *Apostolic Interregnum*, pp. 381, 382.

[45] Joseph Smith's History, 6:261.

[46] Miller, *Correspondence*, p. 20. According to Miller the territory which the Mormons wanted was all of Texas lying north and west of the falls of the Colorado River upstream from Austin, in addition to the corridor lying between the Nueces and the Rio Grande, to connect the whole with the Gulf of Mexico.

[47] *Ibid.*, Joseph Smith's History, 6:349, 350. The author has searched the published documents of the Republic of Texas and its chief officers for references to

Woodworth, Miller, and A. W. Brown were appointed commissioners to complete negotiations in Austin, Lyman Wight was to move the Wisconsin colony to the "newly acquired territory" during the summer, and then all were to "report to the Council of the kingdom." If these projects were successful, said Miller, "we should have dominion in spite of the United States." On May 3, Brigham Young wrote Reuben Hedlock in England, "If any of the brethren wish to go to Texas [instead of Nauvoo], we have no particular objection. . . . In eighteen months . . . you may send a hundred thousand there. . . ."[48]

But the project was interrupted by the troubles which led to the death of Smith seven weeks later. That summer Miller tried to get the official papers from Brigham Young that the commissioners to Texas would need for their mission; but, said Miller, "to my utter astonishment, [he] refused anything to do with the matter; that he had no faith in it, and would do nothing to raise means for our outfit or expenses. Thus all hopes cut off to establish dominion of the kingdom. . . ." This was the cause of the break between Wight and Young. Wight left Nauvoo, never to return. He took the Wisconsin colony, which was personally loyal to him, on an epic trek to Texas and established them near the falls of the Colorado, the point which was to have been a corner of the envisioned Mormon domain. He was convinced that in so doing he fulfilled the martyred Prophet's commission. Wight remained in Texas until his death in 1858 and became locally famous as a pioneer colonist. Miller broke finally with Young in 1846, followed J. J. Strang to Beaver Island, then joined Wight's colony in Texas. But he was unhappy in all these situations and finally emigrated to California, where he too became a noted pioneer.[49] Brigham Young never recognized Wight's Texas venture as legitimate after the death of Smith, since it was undertaken against Young's orders; and finally he commanded Lyman Wight, his brother Apostle, to be cut off from the Church because .
Wight refused to recognize Young's authority and move to Utah.

Woodworth's mission, but without success. It is not difficult to imagine, however, that such an extraordinary negotiation would be kept in confidence.

[48] Joseph Smith's *History*, 6:354.
[49] The considerable detail with which Miller was able to describe the events of earlier years in his letters to the *Northern Islander* was due to his journal, which he kept faithfully as a Mormon elder should. See Mills, "De Tal Palo Tal Astilla" ["A Chip off the Old Block"], 10:3:86–174. This is an account of Miller and his son and namesake as important California founders, and contains parts of the journal and most of text of Miller's letters to the *Northern Islander*.

Records of the Texas scheme as envisioned by the Prophet and the Council of Fifty were apparently suppressed, and general histories of Mormonism are silent on the subject.

After the Texas matter, the Council of Fifty considered further steps toward making an empire of the Kingdom. On March 21 Smith recorded, "In council . . . discussing the propriety of petitioning Congress for the privilege of raising troops to protect the making of settlements in the uncivilized portions of our continent." Willard Richards was appointed to embody the thinking of the group in suitable form. Five days later the draft of a memorial was read and approved by the Council. Its proposals are surely among the most extraordinary in the history of American filibustering. It reveals perhaps more clearly than any other document extant the dimensions of Mormon expansionist thinking just at the point when the Joseph Smith period of Mormon history gave way to that of Brigham Young. The memorial began with an introduction expressive of Smith's patriotism and anxiety to serve his country, phrased in florid, spread-eagle language strongly reminiscent of John C. Bennett. The body of the document was formulated as a proposed congressional ordinance, of which the following is a partial quotation:

Whereas, many of the citizens of these United States have been and are migrating to Texas, Oregon, and other lands contiguous to this nation; *and whereas* Texas had declared herself a free and independent nation, without the necessary power to protect her rights and liberties, *and whereas* Oregon is without any organized government [or] protection . . . *and whereas* the United States desire to see the principles of her free institutions extended to all men, especially where it can be done without loss of blood and treasure to the nation, *and whereas* there is an almost boundless extent of territory on the west and south of these United States, where exists little or no organization of protective government, *and whereas* the lands thus unknown, unowned, or unoccupied, are among some of the richest and most fertile on the continent, *and whereas* many . . . would gladly embrace the opportunity of extending their researches and acquirements so soon as they can receive protection [from] the red man, the robber, and the desperado . . . *and whereas* Joseph Smith . . . does hereby offer to prevent . . . bloodshed on our frontiers, to [deliver] Texas, to protect . . . Oregon from foreign aggression and domestic broils, to prevent the crowned nations from encircling us . . . on our western and southern borders . . . to open the vast regions . . . to our enterprising yeomanry . . . and thus strengthen the government and enlarge her borders. . . .

Section 1. *Be it ordained* . . . that Joseph Smith, of the city of Nauvoo . . . is authorized . . . to raise a company of one hundred thousand armed volunteers in the United States and Territories . . . as he shall find necessary and convenient for the purposes specified in the foregoing preamble, and to execute the same.

Succeeding sections prescribed heavy fine and imprisonment for any "person or persons who shall hinder . . . Joseph Smith . . . in raising said volunteers, and marching and transporting them to the borders of the United States and Territories. . . ." They further prescribed membership in the regular army of the United States for Smith, and ordained that neither he nor the forces under his command would "disturb the peace of any nation or government acknowledged as such, break the faith of treaties between the United States and any other nation, or violate any known law of nations, thereby endangering the peace of the United States." Smith would "confine his operations to those principles of . . . the preamble, the perpetuity of which shall be commensurate with the circumstances and specifications which have originated it." All of this would "save the national revenue" by superseding the necessity of maintaining a standing army at public expense in the West, serve to explore the unknown regions of the continent, "search out antiquities," and "break down tyranny and oppression." [50]

Orson Pratt was delegated to carry the memorial to Washington, together with a similar one "to the President, in case the other should fail." Hyde wrote on April 25 that the Mormon proposition found great favor with several leading senators, some members of the cabinet, and especially Congressman Stephen A. Douglas. But they feared a misunderstanding with Great Britain, with whom the United States had a treaty for the joint occupation of Oregon. This fear, said Pratt, had made the Government decline.[51] The memorial was introduced into the House of Representatives by John Wentworth of Chicago; but the reading was objected to. One member observed "that if memorials of this kind were to be read, he was entrusted with one of a peculiar character, from certain citizens of Frederick county, Maryland." Wentworth moved to suspend the rules to read the Mormon petition in connection with a general consideration of the Oregon Territory bill, but the motion was defeated. So apparently the document was not even heard on the floor of the Congress.[52]

[50] Joseph Smith's History, 6:275–277.
[51] See Hyde's letters to Smith in Joseph Smith's History, 6:369–376.
[52] *Congressional Globe*, May 25, 1844, quoted in Joseph Smith's History, 6:282.

While in Washington, Hyde received a map of the Oregon country from Stephen A. Douglas, together with John C. Frémont's description of the Far West and the Platte River–South Pass route to the Umpqua and Klamath valleys of Oregon. Douglas promised to mail a copy of Frémont's report to Smith. "There is no government established there," wrote Pratt, "and it is so near California that when a government shall be established there, it may readily embrace that country likewise. . . . Judge Douglas says he can direct Mr. Smith to several gentlemen in California who will be able to give him . . . information on the state of affairs [there]."[53]

On April 8, 1844, during the General Conference, Smith began to reveal the new imperial concept of the Kingdom to the Saints. The congregation was dismissed, but the elders were asked to stay to hear "a great, grand, and glorious revelation . . . in relation to the economy of the Church." There had been much discussion, said the Prophet, "in relation to Zion—where it is, and where the gathering of this dispensation is. . . ." The dilemma of a Zion located in Jackson County, Missouri, and a temple for the salvation of all Mormons in Nauvoo continued to bother many of the faithful. Such constructs, however, were too narrow—"I will make a proclamation that will cover a broader ground. *The whole of America is Zion itself from north to south, and is described by the Prophets, who declare that it is the Zion where the mountains of the Lord should be, and that it should be in the center of the land.*" A temple in a central place was absolutely essential, he said, but "wherever the Elders . . . shall build up churches and branches . . . throughout the States, there shall be a stake of Zion." Nauvoo would be the center of vast Zionic operations, and "the particular spot for the salvation of our dead." Smith was careful that the new expanded view should not detract from the completion of the Temple.[54] Brigham Young added an enthusiastic note to Smith's proclamation. The following day he told the elders, "It was a perfect sweepstakes when the Prophet called North and South America Zion. . . . It is a perfect knock-down to the devil's kingdom."[55] Writing to Reuben Hedlock the following month Young revealed the new principle to the head of the British Mission. "Joseph said . . . after the Temple was done, and the Elders endowed, they would spread and build up cities all over the

[53] Joseph Smith's History, 6:374, 375.
[54] *Ibid.*, 6:318, 319.
[55] *Ibid.*, 6:321.

United States; but at present we are not to teach this doctrine. . . .
But you can see why it is wisdom for the [British] Saints to get into
the United States. . . ." [56]
The second strategic move to "establish dominion of the Kingdom" as Miller put it was to run Joseph Smith for President in 1844.
Though the decision was made before the formal establishment of
the Council of Fifty, it was the work of that nascent inner circle.
The reasons for such an extraordinary proposal were basically the
same that prompted the drift toward Mormon political separatism
—a sense of alienation from parties and politicians, the insecure
situation of Nauvoo, and the conviction that novel means must be
employed to insure the safety and future growth of the Kingdom.
The *Times and Seasons* for October 1, 1843, carried an editorial entitled "Who Shall Be Our Next President?" The answer was that it
must be a man who would secure the Mormon rights. Early in November Smith sent letters to John C. Calhoun, Henry Clay, Lewis
Cass, Richard M. Johnson, and Van Buren, all considered likely
presidential candidates. Since the Mormons, "who now constitute a
numerous class in the school politic of this vast republic," had been
sorely oppressed by Missouri and no succor had been forthcoming
from the federal government, each was asked: "*What will be your
rule of action relative to us as a* people, should fortune favor your
ascension to the chief magistracy?" To Van Buren's letter was
added, "also whether your views or feelings have changed since the
subject . . . was presented you . . . in 1841, and by you treated
with a coldness, indifference, and neglect, bordering on contempt?" [57]
Calhoun replied in December that in case of his election he would
administer the Constitution and laws impartially; and "as they
make no distinction between citizens of different religious creeds
I should make none." As far as Missouri was concerned, "can-
dor compels me to repeat what I said to you at Washington,
that . . . the case does not come within the jurisdiction of the Federal Government, which is one of limited and specific powers." [58]
Clay also replied within the month. He did not consider himself a
candidate; but should he become so, ". . . I can enter into no engagements, make no promises, give no pledge to any particular portion
of the people of the United States. If I ever enter into that high

[56] *Ibid.*, 6:353.
[57] *Ibid.*, 6:64, 65.
[58] *Ibid.*, 6:115, 156.

office I must go into it free and unfettered. . . ." Nevertheless, he did not consider it "inconsistent with this declaration" to say that he sympathized with the "sufferings under injustice" of the Mormons; and he believed that "in common with other religious communities, they ought to enjoy the security and protection of the Constitution and laws." [59] Smith responded angrily to both letters. In a long, indignant letter to Calhoun he revealed his own view of the sovereign power of the national government, a view conditioned by the needs of the Mormons as he conceived them and by his belief in power and authority as they were exercised within the Church. He admonished Calhoun to read the Constitution of the United States to understand "what can be done to protect the lives, property, and rights of a virtuous people, when [President and Congress] are unbought by bribes, uncorrupted by patronage . . . unawed by fear, and uncontaminated [by] tangling alliances. And God . . . will raise your mind above the narrow notion that the General Government has no power, to the sublime idea that Congress, with the President as Executor, is as almighty in its sphere as Jehovah is in his." The reply to Clay was apparently so intemperate that the editor of Smith's journal did not see fit to include it in the published version. It was, Roberts admitted, "written in a caustic and, at times vehement vein." [60]

"Who shall be our next President?" asked the *Nauvoo Neighbor* of February 7, 1844. "Do you want to know? . . . We have our eyes upon the man, when the proper time comes . . . as American citizens, we will go it with a rush." The matter was "of the most paramount importance" to Latter-day Saints, wrote editor John Taylor in the February 14 *Neighbor*. "Our situation in regard to the two great political parties is a most novel one." He rehearsed again the Missouri persecutions and the refusal of the government to give redress, as well as the refusal of leaders of the major parties to espouse the Mormon cause. "We have paid hundreds of thousands of dollars into the coffers of Congress for their lands [i.e., public lands in Missouri] and they stand virtually pledged to defend us in our rights, but they have not done it. . . . Hear it therefore ye mobbers! proclaim it to all the scoundrels in the Union! . . . rob at pleasure; murder until ye are satiated with blood; drive men, women, and chil-

[59] *Ibid.*, 6:376. If replies were received from any of the others, they were not included in Smith's journal.

[60] *Ibid.*, 6:376, 377n; Smith's letter to Calhoun, *ibid.*, 6:156–160.

dren from their homes, there is no law to protect them, and Congress has no power to redress their grievances, and [the President] has no ear to hear their complaints." Possibly there was worse yet to come for the Saints. Senator Benton of Missouri had an understanding with Van Buren, said Taylor, to support the former President in a bid for re-election. If successful, Van Buren would use the executive power "to wipe away the stain from Missouri by a further persecution of the Mormons, and wreaking out vengeance on their heads, either by extermination, or by some other summary process." Taylor admitted that he did not know for a fact that such a bargain existed, "but we have . . . good reason to believe we are correctly informed." Under these circumstances whom could the Saints support for President? There could be only one answer: "*General Joseph Smith.* A man of sterling worth and integrity, and of enlarged views; a man who has raised himself from the humblest walks of life. . . ." Both parties had sought Mormon votes; but each had betrayed the Mormons to seek gentile votes by demagogic attacks on the Saints. No more would they suffer themselves to be the targets "for the filthy demagogues of the country to shoot their loathsome arrows at. . . . We refuse any longer to thus be daubed for either party . . . we withdraw." If it was necessary for the Saints to "throw away our votes," said Taylor, it was better to do so "upon a worthy, than upon some unworthy individual, who might make use of the weapon we have put in his hand to destroy us with."[61]

Despite Taylor's reference to a "throw away" protest vote, the Mormons were serious about Smith's candidacy. While realizing that the odds against success seemed enormous, anything was possible in the Kingdom of God. Whether Smith was author of the project, or merely a willing participant, it is impossible to know. He completed on February 7 a long document entitled "Views of the Powers and Policy of the Government of the United States" which served as a basis for subsequent statements about the Prophet's political philosophy, and which showed him to be a willing candidate.[62] George Miller said that the campaign was planned by the Council of Fifty.

[61] *Nauvoo Neighbor,* February 7, 14, 1844. The February 15 issue of *Times and Seasons* likewise declared the candidacy of Smith. Both papers carried "For President—General Joseph Smith" banners until the Prophet's death.
[62] See Joseph Smith's History, 6:197–209. The document was first published in the *Times and Seasons* for May 15, 1844. Brigham Young believed Smith had a chance to win. See *Apostolic Interregnum,* p. 210.

Elders were to go on campaigning missions to every state in the Union, get up electoral tickets, "and do everything in our power to have Joseph elected President; and if we succeeded in making a majority of the voters converts to our faith . . . the dominion of the kingdom would be forever established in the United States." If the project were unsuccessful, said Miller, "we could fall back on Texas, and be a kingdom notwithstanding." A hundred elders were called to campaign missions, and many more volunteered. "All things are going on gloriously," wrote Brigham Young in May. "We shall make a great wake in the nation. . . . We have already received several hundred volunteers to go out electioneering and preaching, and more offering. We go for storming the nation. . . . The kingdom is organized; and, although as yet no bigger than a grain of mustard seed, the little plant is in a flourishing condition, and our prospects are brighter than ever." [63] The campaign was to be "the entire united effort of all the official members of the Church," said Miller. "At no period had there been half so many elders in the vineyard in proportion to the number of members in the Church." [64] The Council of Fifty adjourned *sine die* on April 25 to go campaigning. Though Miller on his mission in Kentucky "preached and electioneered alternately," John D. Lee, another member of the Council of Fifty, on his mission labored only at evangelical preaching. While Lee was unmolested, Miller was told, "If you do not leave this country and put a stop to preaching your religious views and political Mormonism, the negroes are employed to hang you to an apple tree." [65] When the news of Smith's assassination on June 27 reached the campaigning elders, they quickly returned to Nauvoo.

After the death of the Prophet, the mission-colony plan already set in motion was but one of many forces tending to pull people away from Nauvoo and disrupt Mormon catholicity. James J. Strang and Sidney Rigdon soon began to gather members under their leadership, and fear of renewed persecutions prompted many to flee Nauvoo. Brigham Young fought against all such centrifugal tendencies, including those which resulted from western ventures specifically ordered by the Prophet and the Council of Fifty. Young hesi-

[63] Brigham Young to Reuben Hedlock, May 3, 1844, in Joseph Smith's History, 6:351, 354.
[64] Miller, *Correspondence*, pp. 20, 21.
[65] *Ibid.*; Joseph Smith's History, 6:343; Brooks, *John Doyle Lee*, p. 58. For the minutes of a political "convention" held May 17 in Nauvoo see Joseph Smith's History, 6:386 ff.

tated to forbid the Wight-Miller expedition to Texas since the principals were men of importance and the scheme had carried a great deal of prestige in the Fifty. But Young's hostility was apparent nevertheless, and increased to wrath when Wight left against his wishes (Miller decided to remain). At the October, 1844, conference Young went so far as to say that Wight had gone to Texas "because he was a coward," and predicted that he and his company would return (they did not). Although James Emmett was one of the Council of Fifty who was to have been a member of the Oregon-California exploring party commissioned by the Prophet in February, 1844, when summer came Young forbade Emmett to go.[66] But he went anyway, apparently convinced, like Wight, that he was doing the Prophet's will. Young denounced Emmett and threatened to cut him off. He and his company were gone a year, and suffered severe hardship. Finally, broken and submissive to Young's authority, Emmett returned to Nauvoo in 1845.[67]

At the April, 1845, conference Brigham Young felt himself secure enough to broach the subject of the expanding Kingdom again. In a "proclamation of the Twelve Apostles of the Church of Jesus Christ of Latter Day Saints to all the Kings of the World, To the President of the United States of America, To the Governors of the Several States, And to the Rulers and Peoples of All Nations," he stated that God's Kingdom was soon to enjoy a spectacular growth and expansion. No nation, ruler, community, or individual could remain neutral toward the Kingdom; all would be either for it or against it. Zion would supersede all national differences, bounds, and rivalries.[68] Six months later, in the face of rising persecution, Young decreed the abandonment of Nauvoo and the westward hegira of the entire Church. His subsequent thinking about the geopolitics of a western Mormon state were based on the concepts first outlined in Nauvoo.

Young did not at first conceive his empire as being confined to the Great Basin alone, as is indicated by an 1846 proposal to the Crown for the settlement of Vancouver Island by British Saints. Young suggested the idea, and a petition addressed to Queen Victoria was

[66] See Joseph Smith's History, 6:222. The Twelve had organized personnel for the company pursuant to Smith's request.
[67] See *Apostolic Interregnum*, pp. 269, 302, 377, 383–385, 435.
[68] G. Homer Durham, "A Political Interpretation of Mormon History," 13:141, 1944. The document is unpublished, and is in the Church Historian's Office in Salt Lake City.

signed by nearly thirteen thousand Saints, many of them presumably British. It suggested that a Mormon colony on Vancouver Island
would remove many of the British unemployed and the industrious
poor, and would be advantageous to the Empire in opening the
China trade. In addition, the petition suggested blandly, such a colony would forestall American seizure of the island. Moneys advanced by the Crown to aid emigrants would be repaid by labor
performed at Vancouver on harbors and other public works. The
colony would prove self-supporting, and would soon have export-
able products of agriculture, as the soil was rich. The British government was interested, but negotiations broke down when it became
clear that no public money could be advanced to support the project. Orson Spencer, then president of the British Mission, continued
to urge an Oregon or Vancouver migration, but to no avail. In December, 1847, Young sent word that the British Saints were to
gather to the new Zion in the Great Basin.[69]

Young's ordering of settlements in the valleys of the Great Basin
demonstrated his strategic planning for the growth of the Kingdom
on an imperial scale. There were two colonizing phases: the first
comprised a "heartland" of Salt Lake, Weber, Utah, Toole,
Parowan, Box Elder, Pahvant, and Juab valleys, where settlement
was initiated between 1847 and 1851. To this group was added the
colony in the Cache Valley in 1856. The second was an outer ring of
communities apparently designed in part for defense, in part for
support and aid for those gathering to the inner settlements, and for
the convenience of traders and missionaries going to the outside.
These settlements included Carson Valley, Nevada, 1849–1851, San
Bernardino, 1851, Las Vegas, 1855, and Lemhi on the Salmon River
in 1855. Another part of Young's concept was to plant a string of
twenty-seven settlements between the Utah "heartland" and the
California coast at Los Angeles to facilitate communication over the
route. It became known as the "Mormon Corridor." Between 1847
and 1857, ninety-six separate communities were founded by Mormon colonists, a number which was to grow to more than five hundred by the end of the century.[70]

Mormon faith in the apocalyptic triumph of God's Kingdom, and
the persecution which followed all their corporate endeavors in the
more settled parts of the country fostered concepts of Mormon sepa-

[69] Cannon, "Migration of English Mormons," 52:444.
[70] Leonard J. Arrington, *Great Basin Kingdom*, pp. 84 ff.

ratism, nationalism, and manifest destiny. Yet Mormon expansionism was at the same time an expression of political pluralism: Mormons were American nationalists trying to blend the idea of the Kingdom of God with the prevailing expansionist spirit of their generation. The Saints were descended from a long line of New England expansionists, and westering was their heritage. The American federal system made possible the notion that a sovereign Mormon state or states could be created in the West and yet be a part of the American Union. During the near half-century struggle of Utah to achieve statehood, her opponents charged the Mormons with separatist, subversive motives.[71] The Saints protested their loyalty as Americans who wanted nothing more than to have a government and laws of their own choosing in their own state. They professed to see no inconsistency in being loyal Mormons and loyal Americans at the same time.

[71] For an example of such a view, see Daniel Dorchester, *Christianity in the United States* (New York, 1881), p. 648.

11

The Fall of the Kingdom

[A] *cause of mobs is, that men engaged in unpopular projects expect more protection from the laws than the laws are able to furnish in the face of popular excitement. They read in the Constitution the guaranty of their rights, and they insist upon the enjoyment of these rights to the fullest extent, no matter what may be the extent of popular opposition. . . . In such a case, it may be that the whole people may be on one side, and merely the public officers on the other. [They] are appealed to for protection, when it is apparent that, being separated from the strength of the people, they form the mere dead skeleton of government. . . . If the government cannot suppress an unpopular band of horse thieves . . . how is it to suppress a popular combination which has the people on its side? I am willing enough to acknowledge that all this is wrong, but how is it to be avoided? . . . This brings us to treat of the Mormons.*

Ford, *History of Illinois*, pp. 250–251.

now fixing to leave Our Home and all we have except what too wagons can Draw and our Place of Destenation We know not.

Journal entry of Lorenzo Dow Young, Nauvoo, February 1, 1846, from "Diary of Lorenzo Dow Young," *Utah Historical Quarterly*, 14:133 (1946).

On June 27, 1844, Joseph Smith and his brother Hyrum were murdered in Carthage, the seat of Hancock County, by a mob while the Mormon leaders were under a guarantee of safety given personally by Governor Thomas Ford. It was the beginning of the end for Nauvoo. To the burden caused in the Church by the issue of polygamy was added the tragedy of the Prophet's death, the contest for succession to Church leadership, and, the following winter, the repeal of the Nauvoo City Charter by the state legislature. By 1845 the civil authorities in county and state were either unwilling or unable to protect the city from a rising tide of depredations, and in September, 1845, Brigham Young, leader of the Mormons in Nauvoo since August of 1844, announced that the city would be abandoned the following spring. Preparations were undertaken during the winter of 1845–1846 to move not only the Illinois Saints but the whole Church to the West. Nauvoo was evacuated during the spring and summer of 1846 under intermittent goading from mobs. By autumn what had been the most populous city in Illinois was virtually deserted. Its founder was left buried in a secret, unmarked grave to prevent desecration of the body.

The murder of the Prophet resulted from a rift between Saints and gentiles in Hancock County which had been growing since 1841. Politics was the main divisive issue. But there were other less tangible factors, such as the competition between Nauvoo and Carthage and Warsaw for pre-eminence in the county, a competition easily won by Nauvoo on the basis of population; but it was a victory never conceded by the gentiles. The fact that Nauvoo operated its own government including law enforcement and judiciary separate from the county made for constant conflicts. Furthermore, any Mormon in the county accused of crime could get a Mormon jury which would acquit him, and an anti-Mormon could do the same. Each was entitled to a jury of the county, and the state had no power to change the venue. "No leading man of either party," said Governor Ford, "could be arrested without the aid of an army, as individuals of both parties were justly afraid of surrendering for fear of being murdered; and when arrested, each trial was likely to lead to a civil war, and . . . as a conviction was impossible . . . the administration of criminal justice was completely at an end, whilst the Mormons remained in the county."[1] Such a situation encouraged the lawless on both sides, as well as the lawless who took whichever side best suited their purposes. The rural areas of the county were by the end of 1843 virtually without law enforcement except that provided by posses of one side or the other, or by vigilante action. Hatred of the Mormons and particularly of Smith increased as the Mormons grew more numerous and apparently more powerful and aggressive. Particularly galling to the anti-Mormons was the notion that Smith was a fugitive from Missouri justice and that he repeatedly escaped his just punishment by flight or by legal maneuvers, the most prominent of which was his automatic release from any arrest by writ of habeas corpus from his own Nauvoo Court. Many gentiles seemed obsessed with the need to see Smith punished. Since the Prophet seemed able to frustrate all legal moves to accomplish that end, even prominent men among his enemies in Hancock County began to

[1] Thomas Ford, "Report of the Governor in Relation to the Difficulties in Hancock County," December 10, 1846, in *Reports made to the Senate and House of Representatives of the State of Illinois, 1846* (Springfield, 1847), p. 1. See also Ford, *History of Illinois*, pp. 366–369.

think in extralegal terms. It was a situation not dissimilar to that which had led to the murder of the abolitionist editor Elijah Lovejoy by a mob at Alton in 1837. The desire to see Smith eliminated was in addition abetted by the widespread belief that the Mormons were held together in a kind of captivity by the Prophet's diabolical powers, and that if he were gone Nauvoo and the whole Mormon Power would disintegrate.

When an opportunity to murder Smith finally came, it grew paradoxically out of events within the Mormon Church. Conflict over the issues of plurality of wives and other "ultraist" doctrines, including plurality of gods, had grown within the circle of Mormon leaders until an open break occurred in the spring of 1844. A number of prominent men withdrew and formed their own reform church. They were led by William Law, a member of the First Presidency since 1841, Wilson Law, a brigadier general in the Legion, Austin Cowles, a member of the Nauvoo High Council, James Blakeslee, a prominent Seventy, and Robert D. Foster, Chauncey Higbee, and Charles Ivins, prominent businessmen. They resolved to publish their views and to "expose" the secret and abominable teachings of the Mormon hierarchy in an opposition newspaper, to be named *The Nauvoo Expositor*. On June 7 they issued the first and only edition of their paper. Smith moved swiftly to put down the seceders. At his instigation the city council declared the *Expositor* a public nuisance and ordered the press destroyed. Within three days the city marshall had executed the order and had confiscated all available copies of the paper. The editors feared for their safety and fled to Carthage, determined to bring retribution on Smith and the hierarchy. They swore out a warrant for the arrest of the Prophet on a charge of riot. News of the affair spread quickly through the county, and feeling ran high on both sides. The *Warsaw Signal*, a perennial anti-Mormon paper, declared: "We have only to state that this is sufficient!" Said editor Thomas Sharp in the *Signal* on June 12: "War and extermination is evitable! CITIZENS ARISE, ONE AND ALL!!! Can you *stand* by, and suffer such INFERNAL DEVILS! to ROB men of their property rights, without avenging them. We have no time for comment! everyman will make his own. LET IT BE WITH POWDER AND BALL!" Citizens' committees were formed in Warsaw and Carthage resolved to bring Smith to justice, but they feared that there was no force of sufficient strength that could be put together in the county to bring Smith into custody, defended as he presumably would be by the Nauvoo Legion. So on June 17 the Carthage committee requested Governor Ford to mobilize a sufficient force of state militia to execute legal process in Nauvoo. Ford decided to go to Hancock County himself since it was, as he said, "an occasion . . . of considerable perplexity," and since "great excitement existed in the minds of the people." Ford arrived in Carthage on June 21, anxious both to see the laws obeyed and to prevent civil war. He found a large armed force of Hancock men constituted as a *posse comitatus*. To bring in a third and presumably neutral force he mobilized the whole militias of neighboring Schuyler and McDonough Counties. In Nauvoo, Smith had mobilized the Legion and placed the city under martial law but seems not to have considered bringing about an armed conflict unless he was attacked in force. His first disposition with regard to his own safety was to flee, but others prevailed upon him to give himself up to the governor. On June 24, the Prophet and seventeen others named in the writ, including Hyrum Smith, went voluntarily to Carthage, where the Smiths were comfortably lodged in the county jail for their own protection. The Legion's arms were also surrendered at the governor's demand, an action taken by Ford because of the illegal use of the Legion in destroying the *Expositor* press and in resisting the county officers seeking to arrest Smith. Ford had achieved one of his two aims by bringing Smith into custody, and he hoped to achieve the other by disbanding the forces at Carthage and by going to Nauvoo personally to urge the Mormons to keep the peace. He retained a force of three independent companies of Carthage militia to guard the jail, and departed for Nauvoo on June 27.[2] He was aware of collusion among the gentiles to precipitate a general conflict with the Mormons, but was ignorant of a plot to kill the Prophet in Carthage, and foresaw no such possibility. The guards at the jail had by prearrangement charged their guns without balls. Late in the afternoon they were set upon by a large group of disguised men, apparently members of the Warsaw posse, and, after a show of resistance, they allowed themselves to be overpowered. The assailants then entered the jail and shot the Prophet and his brother to death; they left Apostle John Taylor, who was also in the room at the time, seriously wounded. Ford confessed that the news of the slaying was

[2] Ford argued later in defense of his actions that he assigned Carthage men to guard the jail rather than militia from Schuyler or McDonough Counties for the sake of convenience to the troops themselves. He had no reason, he said, to doubt the loyalty of the Carthage companies.

"perfectly astounding" to him. Fearful of a Mormon uprising, betrayed by militiamen supposedly under his command, and feeling himself in the confidence of none, Ford despaired of preventing bloodshed on a massive scale. But the leaderless Mormons were paralyzed with shock and fear, and in the absence of Brigham Young or Heber Kimball, away campaigning for Smith, they listened to the moderate counsel of the wounded Taylor and did nothing.[3] The gentiles for their part were incapable of further action. Many families fled Carthage and Warsaw from fear of Mormon vengeance, and leaders of the anti-Mormon movement, fearful of both the Mormons and the law, were silent. Hancock County lapsed into a terrified quiet.[4]

Notwithstanding widespread antagonism toward the Mormons in the state, reaction to the murder of the Prophet was one of shock and outrage. The *Quincy Herald* (date uncertain) carried a statement of the governor calling the murders a "disgrace"; the Mormons had done, said Ford, "all that was required or which ought to have been required of them." The *Herald* added: "It will probably never be known who shot Joseph and Hirum [*sic*] Smith—but their murder was a cold-blooded and cowardly act, which will consign the perpetrators if discovered to merited infamy and disgrace—They have broken their pledges to the Governor—disgraced themselves and the state to which they belong. They have crimsoned their perfidy with blood." The *Illinois State Register* (Springfield) of July 5 called the assassination one of "the most disgraceful and cold-blooded murders ever committed in a Christian land."[5] Even the rabid *Warsaw Signal*, although more concerned about the possibilities of Mormon vengeance and guilt devolving upon Warsaw citi-

[3] All of the Twelve except Taylor and Willard Richards were away on missions at the time. Richards was in the room with Taylor at the time of the fatal shooting, but was unhurt.

[4] Ford, *History of Illinois*, pp. 322–354; Ford, "Message of the Governor of Illinois in Relation to the Disturbance in Hancock County," December 21, 1844, in *Reports Made to the Senate and House of Representatives of the State of Illinois, 1844* (Springfield, 1845), pp. 67–70; Hancock County Circuit Court Docket "D," pp. 114, 115, 122; Greene and Thompson, *Governor's Letter Books*, pp. lxxxviii, xcvi; *The Nauvoo Neighbor*, January 24, 1844; *The Nauvoo Expositor*, June 7, 1844; George W. Gayler, "Governor Ford and the Death of Joseph and Hyrum Smith," *Journal of the Illinois State Historical Society*, 50: 391–411 (1957); Snider, "Attitudes in Sectarian Conflict," pp. 176, 177, 179–182, 235; Mulder and Mortensen, eds., *Among the Mormons*, pp. 143–145. Many documents and details relating to the events described above are in Joseph Smith's History, 6:416–627.

[5] Quoted in Gayler, "Governor Ford and the Death of Joseph and Hyrum Smith," p. 408.

zens, called the event a "calamity," a "catastrophe," and a "dreadful outrage." [6] Ford qualified the apparent sympathy for the Mormons in a letter to Nauvoo, July 22, 1844. "The naked truth," he said,

is that most well informed persons condemn in the most unqualified manner the mode in which the Smiths were put to death, but nine out of every ten [express also] their pleasure that they are dead. The disapproval is most unusually cold and without feeling . . . called for . . . by decency, by a respect for the laws and a horror of mobs, but does not flow warm from the heart. The unfortunate victims . . . were generally and thoroughly hated throughout the country, and it is not reasonable to suppose that their death has produced any reaction in the public mind resulting in active sympathy; if you think so, you are mistaken.[7]

Nevertheless, the Mormons were spared any further serious threat during the summer and the hierarchy was able to devote itself to pressing internal concerns.[8]

Most critical was the problem of leadership. The whole structure of authority was geared to Smith's pre-eminence as charismatic leader, and the vacuum created by his death was intolerable. Furthermore, the assassination was almost totally unexpected by a people who saw the activity of their church as the working out step by step of the Divine Will, and who expected therefore that divine aid would protect the Prophet. Smith was only thirty-eight, in the vigorous prime of life. He had survived sickness, accident, and constant persecution; and few, including Smith himself, seem to have seriously considered the possibility of his death. When it came, perplexity was added to shock and grief. There had been three in the quorum of First Presidency; William Law had apostatized, so Sidney Rigdon was the sole remaining member.[9] Rigdon's standing with the people as well as his capacity were questionable, however, following his virtual repudiation by the Prophet. A man of both unquestioned prestige and ability was Brigham Young; but the Twelve stood next below the Presidency in the hierarchy of Mormon authority. The situation of the Council of Fifty was anomalous since the group was as yet unknown to the people and had been organized around the person of the Prophet. Finally it was remembered by

[6] Quoted in Snider, "Attitudes in Sectarian Conflict," pp. 240, 241. The date of issue is uncertain, but was immediately after the assassination.

[7] Roberts, *Comprehensive History*, 2:303.

[8] Hancock County elections in August were dominated by a division between those who wanted an end to violence against the Mormons and those who did not. The former party prevailed, aided of course by a large Mormon vote. See *Apostolic Interregnum*, pp. 223, 226, 227.

[9] Amasa Lyman's ordination to the quorum of First Presidency was apparently an *ad hoc* arrangement. See *Joseph Smith's History*, 5:255.

some that Smith had at least twice publicly designated his eldest son, Joseph III, to be his successor in the prophetic office; but in 1844 young Smith was still only twelve years old.[10]

Almost all Mormon leaders were away campaigning when the Smiths were killed, but hastened back to Nauvoo when they received the news. Most of them arrived late in July or early in August, and they began to confer immediately about the problem of leadership. There seemed to be some consensus, expressed outwardly at least, that the new head should be no more than a *pro tempore* authority. But there was serious disagreement about who it should be. George Miller and Alexander Badlam believed that the Council of Fifty should be convened to "organize the church" anew, a contention with which Apostle Lyman Wight apparently agreed. Other members of the Twelve disagreed on the grounds that the Fifty was not an official Church organization and contained gentiles who ought not to figure in such a decision.[11] Sidney Rigdon arrived on Saturday, August 3. He addressed a large Sabbath day gathering the following morning to the effect that he should be a "guardian" for the Church, and that there could be no successor to the dead Prophet. His actions, he said, were pursuant to a revelation he had received in Pittsburgh on the day of Smith's death. Rigdon commanded the tentative support of some leading elders, including Stake President William Marks, and the ratification of his leadership by a vote of the Nauvoo Saints appeared certain. He appointed a conference for that purpose to convene on Tuesday, August 6, but then rescheduled it for two days later. The delay was momentous in its consequences, for Brigham Young arrived in Nauvoo Tuesday evening.[12]

[10] The occasions were when Smith was in Liberty jail early in 1839, and in Nauvoo sometime in 1843. Among the witnesses were Lyman Wight and James Whitehead, one of the Prophet's scribes, Bishop Newel K. Whitney, Alpheus Cutler, Reynolds Cahoon, George J. Adams, Ebenezer Robinson, and Apostles John Taylor and Willard Richards. See *Memoirs of Joseph Smith III*, pp. 13, 14; and Davis, *Story of the Church*, pp. 288, 385, 386, 444, 445.

[11] *Apostolic Interregnum*, p. 213. Wight said many years later: "the first thing to have been done would have been to call the fifties together . . . which contained all the highest authorities of the Church. As you will readily see . . . had not the fifty constituted the highest authorities, it would have been a species of weakness to have ordained all the highest authorities into that [body]. The fifties assembled should have . . . called on young Joseph, and held him up before the congregation of Israel to take his father's place in the flesh!" Letter of Lyman Wight to the *Northern Islander*, July, 1855, quoted in Smith and Smith, *History of the Reorganized Church*, 2:789.

[12] Roberts, *Comprehensive History*, 2:414; *Apostolic Interregnum*, pp. 224–228.

The events of the next few days were to pass the reins of leadership irrevocably into the hands of Brigham Young and the Quorum of Twelve, although the fact was unknown at the time. When the senior Apostle returned, he was prepared to assume control of the Church, and he acted both with care and dispatch to accomplish that end. He met first with the members of his own quorum who were present—Kimball, Taylor, Woodruff, Richards, Wight, George A. Smith, and the brothers Pratt—in order to seek agreement and present a common front.[13] Then at four o'clock on Wednesday he met with a general council including the Twelve, Stake High Council, and the assembled high priests, where for the first time he confronted Rigdon. Rigdon stated his position concerning a "guardianship," explaining further that "Joseph sustains the same relationship to this church as he has always done. No man can be a successor to Joseph. . . . The martyred prophet is still head of this church. . . . I have been consecrated a spokesman to Joseph, and I was commanded to speak for him. . . . I propose to be a guardian to the people; in this I have discharged my duty and done what God has commanded me, and the people can please themselves whether they accept me or not." Brigham Young replied in a manner that both refuted Rigdon's proposal and made clear the vigor of his own intentions:

I do not care who leads the church, even though it were Ann Lee; but one thing I must know, and that is what God says about it. I have the keys and the means of obtaining the mind of God on the subject.

I know there are those in our midst who will seek the lives of the Twelve as they did the lives of Joseph and Hyrum. We shall ordain others and give the fullness of the priesthood, so that if we are killed the fullness of the priesthood may remain.

Joseph conferred upon our heads all the keys and powers belonging to the Apostleship which he himself held before he was taken away, and no man or set of men can get between Joseph and the Twelve in this world or in the world to come.

How often has Joseph said to the Twelve, "I have laid the foundation and you must build thereon, for upon your shoulders the kingdom rests!"

The Twelve, as a quorum, will not be permitted to tarry here long; they will go abroad and bear off the kingdom to the nations of the earth, and baptize the people faster than mobs can kill them off. I would like, were it my privilege, to take my valise and travel and preach till we had a people gathered who would be true.

My private feelings would be to let the affairs of men and women alone,

---

[13] A week earlier Willard Richards had signed the licenses of two newly ordained elders "TWELVE APOSTLES, President." *Ibid.*, p. 213.

only go and preach and baptize them into the kingdom of God; but, whatever duty God places upon me, in his strength I intend to fulfill it. Then by way of showing that he had as much authority as Rigdon to call a special conference, he concluded by saying, "I want to see this people, with the various quorums of the priesthood, assembled together in special conference on Tuesday next at 10 a.m." [14]

But that conference was unnecessary, for Young was able on the following day to obtain the ratification of a dominant position for himself and his quorum and a secondary role for Rigdon. At the hour which Rigdon had appointed, the old Mormon leader spoke for an hour and a half to the assembly to advance his claims, but no action was taken. Then Young appointed a reassembly of the throng for 2 p.m. At that time, he arose and began to address the conference as follows:

> *Attention all!* . . . For the first time in my life, for the first time in your lives, for the first time in the Kingdom of God in the nineteenth century, without a Prophet at our head, do I step forth to act in my calling in connection with the Quorum of Twelve. . . . Apostles whom God has called by revelation through the Prophet Joseph, who are ordained and annointed to bear off the keys of the Kingdom of God in all the world. . . . The Twelve are appointed by the finger of God. Here is Brigham, have his knees ever faltered? Have his lips ever quivered? Here is Heber and the rest of the Twelve, an independent body who have the keys of the priesthood. . . . They stand next to Joseph, and are as the First Presidency of the Church.

Young was emphatic in his repeated refutations of Rigdon's claim to a "guardianship":

> You cannot fill the office of a prophet, seer, and revelator: God must do that. You are like children without a father and sheep without a shepherd. You must not appoint a man at your head; if you should, the Twelve must ordain him. . . . You cannot take Elder Rigdon and place him above the Twelve. . . . I tell you there is an over anxiety to hurry matters here. . . . Do you want the Church properly organized, or do you want a spokesman [Rigdon's term to describe his new relation to the martyred Prophet] to be a chief cook and bottle-washer? . . . If [Rigdon] wants now to be a spokesman to the Prophet, he must go to the other side of the veil, for the Prophet is there, but Elder Rigdon is here. Why will Elder Rigdon be a fool? Who knows anything of the priesthood, or of the organization of the Kingdom of God. I am plain. . . . Now if you want Sidney

[14] *Apostolic Interregnum*, pp. 229, 230. Young described the occasion in his journal as follows: "I followed [Rigdon] and showed the brethren the errors and fallacies which [he] manifested on the occasion." *Millennial Star*, 26:359, June 4, 1864.

Rigdon or William Law to lead you or anybody else, you are welcome to them; but I tell you in the name of the Lord that no man can put another between the Twelve and the Prophet Joseph. . . . *All that want to draw away a party from the Church after them, let them do it if they can, but they will not prosper.*

After Young finished speaking, Amasa Lyman arose and hastened to explain that he did not arrogate any special position to himself as a counselor to Joseph, and was happy to subordinate himself to the Twelve. "President Young has stood next to the Prophet Joseph. . . . There is no need of a President, we have a head here. . . . We now see the necessity of the Apostleship." [15] Sidney Rigdon did not speak to the assembly, but asked W. W. Phelps to do so for him. Phelps, however, proceeded implicitly to support the Twelve rather than Rigdon. At some point in the meeting, according to Jacob Hamblin who was seated nearby, Rigdon attempted to call upon the body for a vote to sustain him as President and "guardian" but Young interrupted him, saying, "I will manage the vote for Elder Rigdon. He does not preside here. This child will manage this flock for a season." [16] The manner in which Young managed all the voting that afternoon was informal to say the least; it was not his intention that the gathering should be treated as a deliberative body. "There is more business than can be done this afternoon, but we can accomplish all we want to have done without calling this convention of the whole church. I am going to present to you the leading items." The crucial matter was the elimination of Rigdon's claims and the endorsement of the Twelve to direct the Church. Young wanted there to be no misunderstanding about the authority he intended for his quorum to exercise. "Don't make a covenant to support [the Twelve] unless you intend to abide their counsel; and if they do not counsel you as you please, don't turn round and oppose them. I want every man, before he enters into a covenant, to know what he is going to do. . . . The Twelve have the power now—the seventies, the elders, and all of you can have the power to go and build up the kingdom. . . ." Without the formality of a motion from the body, Young then put the question:

[15] Lyman had been ordained an Apostle by the Prophet in 1842, replacing the disaffected Orson Hyde. Upon Hyde's reinstatement the following year, Lyman was made an *ad hoc* counselor to Smith. On September 12, 1844, the Twelve resolved that he "stand as a member of the Quorum of Twelve," bringing the membership of that body to thirteen.

[16] P. H. Corbett, *Jacob Hamblin, the Peacemaker* (Salt Lake City, 1952), pp. 21, 22.

Do you want Brother Rigdon to stand forward as your leader, your guide, your spokesman. [*sic*] President Rigdon wants me to bring up the other question first. . . . Does the church want, and is it their only desire to sustain the Twelve as the First Presidency of this people? . . . If the church want the Twelve to stand as the head, the First Presidency of the church, and at the head of this kingdom in all the world, stand next to Joseph, walk up into their calling, and hold the keys of this kingdom. . . . Manifest it by holding up the right hand. ["There was a universal vote."] If there are any of a contrary mind . . . lift up your hands in a like manner. ["No hands up."] This supercedes all other questions, and trying it by quorums.

In a like manner, Young asked for a show of hands to support the proposition that the Church "be tithed until the Temple is finished, as they hitherto have been," and that the Twelve be supported "in all the world in their missions." Finally Young asked, "Will you leave it to the Twelve to dictate about the finances of the Church? and will it be the mind of this people that the Twelve teach what will be the duties of the bishops in handling the affairs of the Church? I want this, because twelve men can do it just as well as calling this immense congregation together at any other times." The show of hands appeared unanimous. Concerning the future role of Rigdon, Young said, "He has been sent away by brother Joseph to build up a kingdom; let him keep the instructions and calling; let him raise up a mighty kingdom in Pittsburgh, and we will lift up his hands to Almighty God. I think we may have a printing office and a gathering there." In closing the meeting, Young said, "The Twelve will dictate and see to other matters . . . and now let men stand to their posts and be faithful." [17]

Less than universal satisfaction was manifest over the establishment of the Twelve as an *ad hoc* presidency for the Church and the manner in which it was accomplished. George Miller, already vexed by the curtailment of the planned Texas mission, described Young's public performance on August 8 as a "long and loud harangue." "I had always took him to be a blunderbuss in speaking, and on this occasion apparently more so, for the life of me I could not see any point to his remarks, than to turn over Sidney Rigdon's pretensions. . . . I must confess that all the proceedings at this time was anarchy and boisterous confusion. . . . Let me be excused from

[17] *Apostolic Interregnum*, pp. 232–242; Cowley, *Wilford Woodruff*, pp. 216 ff. Portions of the proceedings of August 8 are also in Roberts, *Comprehensive History*, 2:415–420; and Smith and Smith, *History of the Reorganized Church*, 3:6–8n.

saying more on this painful subject." [18] Rigdon did not concede victory to the Twelve, but continued privately to promote his own case, and to arouse opposition to the Twelve. He was able to command little support in Nauvoo, however, due in part to the fact that the majority supported the Twelve for one reason or another. Furthermore, Young controlled most of the ecclesiastical machinery. Rigdon was thus cast into the role of dissenter, which tended to make his cause more unpopular. He returned to Pittsburgh shortly and established himself among the Saints in the region as President of the Church. He immediately began publication of a periodical, *The Latter Day Saints' Messenger and Advocate*, in which he attacked the Twelve. The practice of polygamy was central to his charge that they were apostates. "The so-called Twelve Apostles at Nauvoo," he wrote, "are now teaching the doctrine of what is called Spiritual Wives . . . and they are practicing it, and this doctrine is spreading alarmingly through that apostate branch [of the Church]. . . . This doctrine is what has induced these men to put at defiance the ecclesiastical arrangement of the church. . . ." [19] The Twelve acted quickly to declare Rigdon an apostate. On September 8 at a public meeting called for the purpose in Nauvoo he was cut off from the Church by vote of the body. Ten who voted for Rigdon were suspended from fellowship pending trial before the High Council, an action to be extended to all "who shall hereafter be found advocating his principles." Again, not all were satisfied with the proceedings. "As regards the trial of Elder Rigdon at Nauvoo," wrote Benjamin Winchester, a prominent elder, "it was a forced affair, got up by the Twelve to get him out of their way, that they might the better arrogate to themselves higher authority than they ever had, or anybody ever dreamed they would have; and also (as they perhaps hope) to prevent a complete exposé of the spiritual wife system, which they knew would deeply implicate themselves." [20] On September 19, Orson Hyde wrote a letter to Ebenezer Robinson, in Pennsylvania on a mission, which detailed the right of the Twelve to the position they were assuming. He requested that Robinson publish the letter among the Pittsburgh Saints in order to undermine their support of Rigdon. The argument set forth by Hyde was one used by the Twelve to buttress the contention that their primacy re-

[18] Miller, *Correspondence*, p. 23.
[19] *Latter Day Saints' Messenger and Advocate*, October, 1844.
[20] Letter of Benjamin Winchester to John Hardy, quoted in Linn, *Story of the Mormons*, p. 281.

sulted from the established law of the Church. Essentially it was that Joseph had conferred upon them certain secret blessings, or "keys" to authority, which had not been given to Rigdon or their other competitors for power. Hyde wrote that the twelve had received "the Keys of the Kingdom, and every gift, key, and power that Joseph ever had, confirmed upon our heads by an anointing, which Brother Rigdon never did receive. We know the charge which the prophet gave us . . . and we know that Elder Rigdon does not know what it was." The Twelve had agreed to carry out that commission "with signs and with tokens, with garment and girdle." Smith had admonished them the previous March to "let no man take your Crown," and Hyde concluded by testifying, "I know that the curse of God will fall upon everyone that tries to give us trouble . . . for this promise we have received from the Lord in solemn convocation." [21]

The fact that there was still no successor to Joseph Smith in the specific office of Prophet, Seer, and Revelator to the Church (and Young did not intimate that he might be the man) created an anomalous situation for the new leadership, preventing a final settlement of the transfer of power; yet it also conferred benefits by causing potential objectors, who believed the Twelve to be in control only temporarily, to remain silent. The Twelve themselves abetted the impression that all was not finally settled. "Great excitement prevails throughout the world to know, 'who will be the successor of Joseph Smith?'" wrote Apostle John Taylor in the *Times and Seasons* for September 2, 1844. "In reply, we say, be patient, *be patient* a little, till the proper time comes, and we will tell you all. 'Great wheels move slow.'" The Twelve, said Taylor, had been sustained "to preside over the whole church . . . *without a dissenting voice*" at the August 8 conference, and ". . . when any alteration in the presidency shall be required, seasonable notice shall be given; and the elders abroad, will best exhibit their wisdom to all men, by remaining silent on those things they are ignorant of." [22] George Miller said that during the summer and fall of 1844 he made frequent attempts at conversation with Young and Heber Kimball "with regards to Joseph leaving one to succeed him." These, he said, were "invariably met with the inuendo, '*stop*' or '*hush*' brother Miller, let

[21] *The Return*, 2:253, April, 1890.
[22] *Times and Seasons*, 5:632, September 2, 1844.

there be nothing said in regard to this matter, or we will have little Joseph [twelve-year-old Joseph III] killed as his father was, inferring indirectly that Joseph Smith had appointed his son Joseph to succeed him in the prophetic office, and I believe this impression was not alone left on my mind, but on the brethren in general. . . ." In 1845 and 1846, said Miller, his concern over the proper role of the Twelve in the Church grew, but "I bore all this, and more too, as I was yet laboring under the delusion that Joseph Smith, the younger, was really prophet, and Brigham by sufferance, was acting as temporary leader." [23] Young himself spoke in ambiguities that were open to various interpretations. "Let no man presume for a moment that his [Joseph's] place will be filled by another"; he said in mid-August in a general epistle to the Saints, "for, remember *he stands in his own place*, and always will; and the Twelve Apostles of this dispensation stand in their own place and always will, both in time and in eternity, to minister, preside, and regulate the affairs of the whole church." [24] But he was not without apprehension about the Saints' interest in "Young Joseph" as a possible successor, and finally he became suspicious of the Prophet's widow, who was a known opponent of the spiritual wife doctrine and who did not conceal her dislike of the senior Apostle. Emma Smith had been a public figure, in a modest way, both as the "First Lady" of the Church and as founder and president of the Nauvoo Female Relief Society. Apprehensive perhaps that her home might become the center for an opposition party, especially one built around the idea that her eldest son was heir-apparent to the prophetic mantle, Young in 1845 set a watch upon her house, which noted all visitors and observed their subsequent movements. On one occasion she and her family were threatened anonymously with physical harm if they did not leave Nauvoo.[25] She remained, however, and in 1846 refused to go west with the Saints. Other opponents of the Twelve were harassed in other ways. When in 1845 Austin Cowles, former member of the Nauvoo Stake Presidency who had left the Church with William Law, re-

[23] Miller, *Correspondence*, pp. 23, 30. Miller finally broke with Young, in 1848, at Winter Quarters. Miller controverted Young's assumption of the office of First President, Young was suspicious of Miller's loyalty, and the bishop was angered at what he considered Young's mismanagement of Church affairs at Winter Quarters and Young's misuse of Mormon Battalion payroll money.

[24] *Apostolic Interregnum*, p. 250.

[25] Autobiography of Joseph Smith III, in Edward Tullidge, *Life of Joseph the Prophet* (Lamoni, Iowa, 1880), pp. 746, 748.

turned to the city, he was soon set upon by the "Whistling and Whittling Brigade" and hounded out of town.[26] On August 9, 1844, the day after Young had exacted a vote of confidence from the Nauvoo Saints, he and his quorum began to take firm control of the affairs of the Church by issuing a series of executive orders. On that and ensuing days they 1) appointed Bishops Newel Whitney and George Miller to assume the duties of the Trustee-in-Trust "and settle the affairs of the late Trustee"; 2) ordered the Nauvoo House Association to "wind up their business and report"; 3) strengthened the city police force; 4) took Amasa Lyman back into the Twelve; 5) put the *Nauvoo Neighbor* and the *Times and Seasons* under the personal management of John Taylor; 6) ordered that "the general superintendancies' [*sic*] direction and control of emigration from England be in the name of Brigham Young, President of the Quorum of Twelve"; 7) divided the North American Continent into administrative districts presided over by high priests under the direction of Apostles Young, Kimball, and Richards; 8) ordained that "Willard Richards continue the history of the Church and be supported"; 9) said that Lyman Wight and George Miller be allowed to take their company to Texas "if they desire to go"; 10) ordered an increased wage for some Temple workers; 11) decreed that Nauvoo was still the place of gathering and would continue to be so; 12) urged all Saints to "proceed immediately to tithe [themselves of] a tenth of all their property and money . . . and then let them continue to pay in a tenth of their income . . ."; and 13) ordered them to have nothing to do with "politics, voting, or president making at present." [27]

An urgent problem which faced Young was the crisis of confidence in the whole Nauvoo venture precipitated by the murder of

[26] The event was described by young Joseph Smith III. "Upon being asked his opinion of certain things which had been taught, he expressed himself freely in disapproval." His words were noted, said young Smith, and soon he was beset by the "Whistling and Whittling Brigade," the guard of youths whose duty it was to drive undesirables out of town. They followed him all day, "urging him from place to place, annoying him by whistling, and whittling toward him with wicked looking knives, saying nothing to him, except to tell him to move on when he stopped to speak to anyone. . . . Despairing of honorable treatment from his before time brethren, broken down with infirmity, and stricken with grief . . . he was going to the ferry to cross the river. I spoke to him, when his escort struck up their din of whistling and whittling, hustling the poor old man with the ends of broken boards and the sticks they were whittling." *Ibid.*, p. 749.

[27] *Apostolic Interregnum,* pp. 247–252.

the Prophet. Many felt that the city was doomed; the Temple was far from finished, and, it appeared, was likely to remain so. The Emmett exploration and Wight's proposed venture aroused widespread interest. Young responded by forbidding anyone to leave without the permission of the Twelve. In a sermon of August 18, Young suggested his considerable apprehension about the lure of Wight's colony:

I discover a disposition of the sheep to scatter, now the shepherd is taken away. I do not say that it will never be right for this people to go from here . . . but I do say wait . . . until you are counseled to do so. The report has gone forth . . . that the Twelve have a secret understanding with those men who are going away and taking companies with them, that they shall take away all they can. . . . I swear by the Holy Trinity that such a report is utterly false. . . . There is no man who has any right to lead one soul out of this city by the consent of the Twelve, except Lyman Wight and George Miller [who] have had the privilege of taking the "Pine Company" where they pleased, but not another soul has the consent of the Twelve to go with them. . . . I tell you in the name of Jesus Christ that if [Wight and Miller] take a course contrary to our counsel . . . they will be damned and go to destruction—and if men will not stop striving to be great and exalted, and lead away parties from us, thereby weakening our hands . . . I will destroy their influence in this church. . . .[28]

Young affirmed that the Temple would indeed be finished and the Saints endowed therein according to previous intent, and that Nauvoo, "our infant city may grow and flourish, and be strengthened an hundred fold." More missionaries were to be sent out, and more converts gathered in. Careful attention was to be given the economic needs of the city, although Young's program for industrial development was similar to—and no more successful than—that of Smith. Young further urged the people to build permanent homes in Nauvoo. "Stay here," he said. "Plow, sow, and build. . . . One plowshare will do more to drive off the mob than two guns."[29] Young succeeded apparently in restoring confidence. No large scale emigration took place; in fact, the population continued to grow. The state census of 1845 showed Hancock to be the most popu-

---

[28] *Apostolic Interregnum*, pp. 254, 255.
[29] Corbett, *Jacob Hamblin*, p. 23; *Apostolic Interregnum*, pp. 250, 251; Cowley, *Wilford Woodruff*, p. 225. The Quorums of Seventy, the missionary corps of the Church, were soon increased in number by Young from twelve to thirty-two, with a general secretary who collected $5 in dues from each member annually, a potential income from that source of $11,200. Brooks, *John Doyle Lee*, pp. 63, 64; *Apostolic Interregnum*, p. 455.

lous county in the state with 22,559 inhabitants, and Nauvoo the largest city with a population of 11,036.[30] A letter to Lyman Wight in Texas from the Council of Fifty in April, 1845, urged him and his colony to return to share in the joys of a flourishing city. "We are prospering both temporally and spiritually," he was told. "Immigration continues. . . . Several hundred have arrived this spring. . . . There were many thousands present at our conference this month. All of our business was performed with utmost peace and union and not a dissenting voice. . . . Tithings come in for the Temple more liberally than ever before. . . . There is no prospect of any mob at present, and all things bid fair for peace and prosperity."[31]

Young wrote Wilford Woodruff in England on the anniversary of the Prophet's martyrdom that the capstone had been placed on the Temple and that work was proceeding on roof and tower. The Nauvoo House committee had been reorganized, with Apostles G. A. Smith and Amasa Lyman replacing Lyman Wight and John Snyder. "A large quantity of brick is already made for the Nauvoo House, and considerable means are at hand to prosecute the work. We calculate to have it covered in before winter." Young's whole description of the progress of the city suggested prosperity—many new buildings being erected, large outlays of cash for the Temple, etc. "There never was a more prosperous time in general," he said, "amongst the saints, since the work commenced. Nauvoo, or more properly, the 'City of Joseph,' looks like a paradise."[32]

The apparent *détente* in Mormon-gentile affairs which followed the death of Smith proved temporary, and a renewal of persecution began in the autumn of 1844. It grew in intensity until a year later, when Brigham Young agreed to remove his community from the state. The murder of the Prophet had not solved the "Mormon Question," as many had hoped it would. Thanks in part to the efficiency of the new Mormon oligarchy, corporate Mormonism survived and flourished. Even moderate-minded citizens of the state were at a loss to know how to prevent violence against the Mormons, or protect the gentiles in Hancock County from what was presumed to be the constant threat of reprisal by the powerful and numerically superior sect. Governor Ford, plagued by many state-wide problems, heading a machinery of state government that was in his generation inade-

[30] *Reports made to the Senate and House . . . 1846*, p. 70; Charles J. Schofield, *History of Hancock County* (Chicago, 1921), p. 1103.
[31] *Apostolic Interregnum*, p. 400.
[32] *Ibid.*, pp. 400, 430, 431.

quate to cope with major or sustained crises, and tending personally to a legalistic view of public problems, was apparently unable to conceive of a solution that would both pacify the gentiles and leave Nauvoo intact. Thomas Geddes, a Hancock County Colonel of militia, recalled a private conversation he had with Ford just after the governor had left the Smiths in Carthage jail. "It's all nonsense," said Ford, "you will have to drive these Mormons out yet!" Geddes replied, "If we undertake that Governor, when the proper time comes, will you interfere?" "No, I will not," said Ford; then after a pause he added, "until you are through." [33]

The anti-Mormon extremists had hoped after the *Expositor* affair to precipitate a general conflict with the Nauvoo Legion, thus forcing the governor to bring in an overwhelming force of militia to destroy the hated enemy. When this did not occur, a delegation of citizens from Warsaw waited upon Ford in July, 1844, with a petition that he expel the Mormons for the public safety. "It seemed that it had never occurred to these gentlemen," Ford observed drily, "that I had no power to exile a citizen." Finding that they could expect no help from the state, but being emboldened as it became apparent that the murderers of Smith would escape conviction, the militant gentiles resolved to take further direct action as soon as the crops were gathered in the fall.[34] In September, preparations went forward to raise the citizenry against the Mormons, and notices appeared in the papers of Hancock and surrounding counties of a coming "wolf hunt," the well-known code term for night-riding against Mormons. Anticipating a general uprising, Ford again journeyed to Carthage, this time bringing with him a militia force of some five hundred commanded by General John J. Hardin, a Whig, and an officer of unquestioned integrity. The Mormons for their part organized companies of "minute men" for defense. The state force arrived in Carthage on October 25, and, according to Ford, put an end for the time being to the danger of an anti-Mormon pogrom. The ringleaders fled to Missouri, as did the entire "Carthage Greys" militia company. Ford had come armed with writs for the arrest of several implicated in the Smith murders, determined that the perpetrators be brought to justice; but Hardin's officers and men became infected so quickly with local hatreds that the governor was unable to obtain

[33] Gregg, *History of Hancock County*, p. 372.
[34] "Message of the Governor in Relation to the Disturbances in Hancock County," December 21, 1844, p. 83.

aid in executing his writs. Ford complained that he was helpless, since the powers of the chief executive were severely limited by law. Hardin remained in Hancock County through the winter with a small force, and succeeded in maintaining the peace despite complaints from each side that he was partial to the other.[35]

When the State Legislature assembled in December, 1844, there was a general clamor among the members to repeal the Nauvoo Charter. Ford admitted that its privileges had been much abused, but urged the legislators to correct the charter by amendment rather than to repeal it, and to leave the citizens of that city equal, not superior or inferior, to those of other cities in the state. "This is republican and cannot be denied without injustice," he said. "I do not see how ten or twelve thousand people can well do in a city without some chartered privileges."[36] However, after considerable debate, the assembly revoked the city charter in its entirety on January 29, 1845, by a bipartisan vote of twenty-five to fourteen in the Senate and seventy-five to thirty-one in the House.[37]

Thus Nauvoo was deprived of its legal government, with no provision made by the hostile legislature for an alternative to prevent lawlessness and anarchy within the city. Ford wrote Brigham Young to advise that in the emergency the city be reorganized under the existing law governing the incorporation of towns. Towns had the power to make ordinances, prevent nuisances, gaming, disorderly conduct, etc., provide protection from fire, and levy real-estate taxes. The limitations were severe however. Such corporations could be no

[35] Miller, *Correspondence*, pp. 24–25; Ford, *History of Illinois*, pp. 364–366; Corbett, *Jacob Hamblin*, p. 23. Bishop Miller, now a Mormon Trustee-in-Trust, was almost killed by the state troops in an accidental shooting when he was in Carthage on business. He believed it was an attempt on his life. He returned to Nauvoo "after uttering a few formal blessings on the unmanly, cowardly dogs. . . ."
[36] "Message of the Governor . . . ," December 26, 1844, p. 85. Ford advised a repeal of the sections protecting Mormons from arrest, providing excessive punishment for civil officers attempting such arrests, and the militia clause which provided for the Nauvoo Legion. The Legion should then be constituted a brigade of the state militia. He admitted, however, that it would be impossible for this and neighboring militia units "to act together for some time."
[37] *Laws of the State of Illinois, the Fourteenth General Assembly, 1844–1845* (Springfield, 1845), p. 187; Charles M. Thompson, *The Illinois Whigs Before 1846* (Urbana, 1915), pp. 105–106. The vote showed a striking parallel to that on a bill to grant state aid to the Illinois-Michigan canal, suggesting a *quid pro quo* between Mormons and "Jack-Mormons" on the one side, and members from the urban and canal counties of Cook, DuPage, Fulton, Peoria, Kane, and LaSalle on the other, all of whom voted both for the canal bill and to retain the Nauvoo Charter.

more than one mile square, must be governed by a board of trustees, and could have no court higher than that of justice of the peace. Young grumbled that if such a procedure in Nauvoo "were complied with to the letter," twelve corporations would be required to cover the area within the old city limits. He decided to create one such town corporation, but no more.[38]

The Mormons were prepared to meet the emergency in their own way with an ecclesiastical government converted to civil use. In January, 1845, when the repeal of the charter was imminent, Parley Pratt described the governing function of the priesthood as follows:

> The government of the Church . . . is purely a Theocracy . . . under the direct control and superintendance of the Almighty. The legislative, judicial, and executive power is vested in Him. He reveals the laws, and he elects, chooses, or appoints the officers; and holds the right to reprove, correct, or even remove them at pleasure. Hence the necessity for a constant intercourse by direct revelation between Him and His Church. . . . It is true the people have a voice, but it is secondary . . . rather a sanction, strength, and support to what God chooses.[39]

Young began soon after the repeal of the charter to use the governmental machinery of the Church to govern the city. Each ward already had a bishop heading a corps of lesser priesthood. Ward bishops were now empowered to "set apart deacons in their wards to attend to all things needful, and especially to watch . . . that the peace and good order hitherto sustained by the city might still be preserved." The arrangement was efficient, if not universally popular. On April 14 Young wrote in his journal with evident satisfaction, "The deacons have become very efficient looking after the welfare of the saints; every part of the city is watched with the strictest care, and whatever time of night the streets are traveled, at the corner of every block a deacon is found attending to his duty."[40] For apostates, gentiles, or recalcitrant Saints who were not amenable to priestly directives, there were other means of control, such as the "whistling and whittling brigade." Although the new regime was less than democratic, it maintained the peace.

The Nauvoo Legion was not disbanded despite the fact that it was, after January, 1845, outside the law. It continued important both as an instrument of internal social control and as a potential means of defense. Young was now in command of the Legion; but

[38] *Apostolic Interregnum*, pp. 396–400.
[39] *Millennial Star*, 5:150–153, March, 1845.
[40] *Apostolic Interregnum*, pp. 388, 399.

unlike Smith, he was uninterested in the details of its operation. These he turned over to his second in command, Charles C. Rich, thus elevating that officer to a position of power and importance in Nauvoo. Rich tightened discipline and disposed troops in and around the city in such a way as to suggest that the place was virtually under martial law. Guards were posted to prevent anyone from going into or out of the city without permission of the authorities. The close relation between the Legion and the increasingly paramilitary priesthood organization is suggested by an order sent by Young to Rich in September, 1845:

> *To Charles C. Rich:*
> *President of All Organized Quorums of the Church*
> *. . . in Hancock County.*
> Greeting: You are hereby instructed to hold the same in readiness for all duties that shall be necessary in all emergencies.
> > [signed] BRIGHAM YOUNG,
> > President [41]

There was even a "Junior Legion" of some 250 boys who trained every week during the summer of 1845; they marched in the July 4 parade, set off with white caps and pants trimmed in red.[42]

The repeal of the city charter signaled the beginning of the final and decisive campaign of the gentile extremists, by then grown to a numerous party, to drive the Mormons from the state. Ford continued in the spring to be worried about the safety of Nauvoo, assuming as he did that the Legion was no more. He urged the speedy reorganization of the Mormon militia into regular units of state militia. "I have been advised," he wrote Brigham Young on April 8, ". . . of the proceedings of the Carthagenians in removing the cannon from Macomb. As yet I am ignorant of their design. . . . Whether they intend it as mere bravado, to keep up agitation and excitement . . . or . . . a general move and renewal of the designs of last summer and fall I am not aware. . . . These events may for aught I know point to a new war against you."[43] Quiet prevailed, however, until late June, when Dr. Samuel Marshall, clerk of the County Commissioners Court and a bitter Mormon-hater, attacked the acting Sheriff Minor Deming, a Mormon sympathizer. During the fight Deming shot Marshall, and the wound was mortal. Though

---

[41] *Apostolic Interregnum*, p. 444; Evans, *Charles C. Rich*, pp. 76, 82, 84; Gayler, *The Mormons in Western Illinois*, pp. 47, 48.
[42] Brooks, *John Doyle Lee*, pp. 69, 70.
[43] *Apostolic Interregnum*, p. 397.

Deming clearly acted in self-defense he was arrested for manslaughter, and held in jail to protect him from Marshall's friends, who
swore revenge. The passions of the "Antis" were aroused. At the
same time it was discovered that some Mormons had pooled their
property in private trusteeship arrangements, so that when legal
judgments were levied against them for any reason, they could
prove that others owned the property. This further inflamed gentile
feeling. Irritation grew on both sides over a rash of larcenies and
robberies in the county during the summer. The gentiles professed to fear that Mormon incendiaries would burn their farms
and towns.[44] Early in September, a group of gentiles in the Lima–
Green Plains neighborhood, astride the Adams-Hancock county line,
resolved to drive the Mormons from among them. An incident was
staged to make it appear that Mormons had shot at gentiles, and the
country was roused to repel Mormon depredations. A mob of some
three hundred gathered near Green Plains, and started systematic
burnings of Mormon farms. "For such lawless and outrageous acts,"
said a non-Mormon eyewitness, "they were done in such a quiet and
orderly manner as to be astonishing." [45] Brigham Young reported
on September 15 that forty-four buildings had been destroyed,
with the arson continuing. Terrified Mormons were fleeing to Nauvoo, and 134 teams and wagons were sent from the city to aid
in the evacuation. Young declared, "I [am] willing they should do
so [burn the farms] until the surrounding counties should be convinced that we are not the aggressors, peradventure they may conclude to maintain the supremacy of the law by putting down mob
violence and bringing offenders to justice." He advised the brethren to remain calm, to bring in the threatened Saints in outlying neighborhoods, and to prepare for a siege. "There is grain
enough growing within ten miles of the city, raised by the Saints,"
he said, "to feed the whole population for two years if they were to
sit down and do nothing but gather it in and feast upon it, and worship God."

The mob was not unopposed, however. Jacob B. Backenstos, the
acting sheriff elected by Mormon votes to succeed Deming, raised a
small mounted posse, presumably of Mormons, and attacked the
mobbers wherever he could find them, killing two and wounding
many more. Civil war had begun in earnest. The burnings contin-

[44] Ford, *History of Illinois*, pp. 404–406; *Apostolic Interregnum*, pp. 428, 439.
[45] Gregg, *History of Hancock County*, p. 374.

327

ued; more than two hundred buildings were destroyed, and a Mormon was murdered. Backenstos was resolved to take control of the county and put a stop to the rioting and arson. Inasmuch as a large number of citizens had expressed revulsion when the burnings commenced, the sheriff hoped to be able to marshal a substantial force of his fellow gentiles; but so great was the hatred aroused by his forceful actions that not a man responded to his call. So he went to Nauvoo, and called upon the Mormons to follow him. He succeeded in raising a force several hundred strong, according to Ford. The sheriff and his little army swept away all resistance and took and occupied Carthage. Leaders of the opposition fled, mostly to a sure sanctuary in Missouri. By this time many had been killed on both sides, some in open conflict, and some from ambush.[46]

During the same summer, anti-Mormon feeling across the river in Lee County, Iowa, always strong, reached fever pitch. In May a Mennonite minister and his son were murdered there in cold blood. The two perpetrators, juring Mormons, fled to Nauvoo. The authorities there readily surrendered them after ascertaining the charges against them, adding incidentally that they were not regular members of the Church. The Lee County citizens convicted and hanged them, but the belief persisted that the crime was a typical Mormon outrage. Then on July 4, an old and revered Lee County resident was murdered in Rock Island. The culprit was never apprehended; in less excited times, the crime might have been linked to a gang of cutthroats who operated in the Rock River Valley. But at the time it was laid directly to the Mormons, apparently without any evidence. The crime, said a chronicler of the event, "was the boldest and most daring yet committed by the old Mormon banditti." A nonpartisan slate of anti-Mormons was nominated and elected to Lee County offices, and mass meetings passed resolutions of expulsion against the Saints.[47] The days of the small Mormon community in Lee County were clearly numbered.

When Governor Ford learned that Backenstos held Hancock County under a martial law enforced by Mormons, he hurried to a

[46] Ford, pp. 408–410; Miller, *Correspondence,* pp. 25, 26–28; Pease, *Frontier State,* p. 357; *Apostolic Interregnum,* pp. 443, 445. Backenstos was a Democratic politician of the county who had won terms in the legislature and, indirectly, a federal appointment through the support of Mormon votes. He was fiercely hated by the anti-Mormons both as a "corrupt bargain" politician and a gentile traitor.

[47] Western Historical Company, *History of Lee County, Iowa* (Chicago, 1879), pp. 470, 476 ff.

conference in Jacksonville with General Hardin, Attorney-General McDougall, and Congressman Stephen A. Douglas, an old Mormon hand home for the August elections, to determine what course should be pursued by the state. They decided that Hardin should raise a large force and hasten to Hancock "and put an end to these disorders." In addition, said Ford, "It was also agreed that these gentlemen should unite their influence with mine to induce the Mormons to leave the state." Ford appointed Douglas, Hardin, McDougall, and W. B. Warren, Clerk of the Supreme Court and a major of militia, to be a commission empowered to deal with the situation in Hancock County. Their actions were to be based on the assumption that the Mormons must leave, and that the most the state could or should accomplish was to work for the safety of the sect until they could complete preparations for removal. Ford wrote Backenstos from Jacksonville on September 26 a letter expressing privately his approbation of the sheriff's course which he would not do publicly. "I hereby congratulate you on the prospect of peace," wrote the governor, who proceeded to counsel Backenstos to place his trust in Hardin, McDougall, and Douglas. "You have been placed by this in a critical position. . . . You cannot always keep *your posse* about you, and your enemies will never cease to endeavor to arrest you, and if they ever get hold of you they will murder you." [48]

Hardin and the commissioners took three to four hundred volunteers to Hancock County, arriving in Carthage late in September. They found the town in the possession of a Mormon force, which Hardin ordered to disperse within fifteen minutes. They also found that irregular parties of Mormons were plundering and ravaging the county. Hardin brought this to an end, and decreed that any group of more than four persons from either side was proscribed from assembling and marching in the county. [49]

After Sheriff Backenstos's force took control of Hancock County, the citizens of neighboring counties, ordinarily not greatly aroused at the Mormon Menace, became alarmed lest the gentile minority should entirely desert Hancock County, thus leaving it in Mormon hands—an eventuality they regarded as intolerable. Meetings were held to discuss the problem, and on October 1, a congress represent-

[48] Ford to Backenstos, September 26, 1845; Thomas Ford Papers, Illinois State Historical Library.
[49] Ford, pp. 410, 411; Robert W. Johannsen, ed., *The Letters of Stephen A. Douglas* (Urbana, 1961), pp. 124–126.

ing nine counties assembled in Carthage and resolved that the Mormons must either leave voluntarily or be expelled from Illinois.

The Mormon leaders responded surprisingly with an unhesitating agreement to do as they were bid, if they were granted the freedom during the ensuing winter to make preparations to go. The decision had not been hastily made. Western emigration as a last alternative had been in the minds of the hierarchy for at least two years, and when Young cemented his control over the Church at Nauvoo sufficiently to have some hope of success in a corporate emigration, it became a real possibility that was undoubtedly discussed in secret councils. Though the public posture of the authorities previous to September, 1845, had been one of optimism concerning the future of Nauvoo, after the repeal of the charter in January there had been a significant increase in the publication of information and news about the West in the *Neighbor*—reports particularly about California, Oregon, and Frémont's explorations. In February, 1845, a gentleman of Macomb sent a proposal for solving the "Mormon Problem" to George Miller. He suggested the formation of a "Mormon Reserve" in the Public Domain in Wisconsin. The Mormons should purchase an area twenty-four miles square at the federal price of $1.25 an acre at long credit, settle the Saints upon it, and erect a "model republic." None but Mormons should be allowed upon the lands, and the whole reserve should be surrounded by an unsettled *cordon sanitaire* five miles wide. Editor John Taylor considered the idea worthy of a full report on the front page of the *Neighbor*. "The foregoing correspondence," he concluded, "has inspired us with lively interest. . . ." However, the size of the proposed reserve was in his estimation far too small for the anticipated population of three hundred thousand Saints and two hundred thousand additional persons who would "cleave to us from friendship, affection, or interest." An area two hundred miles square would be more appropriate, to be located either in Wisconsin or in Kansas, Oregon, or West Texas.[50] In March John Taylor drafted a letter to be sent by the Twelve to the governors of all the states except Illinois and Missouri, detailing the extremes of oppression suffered by the Mormons and the dangerous situation then existing for them. "Will you favor us by your personal influence," wrote Taylor, ". . . Or will you express your views concerning what is called the *Great Western Measure* of colonizing the Latter Day Saints in Oregon, the Northwestern Terri-

[50] *Nauvoo Neighbor*, February 26, 1845.

tory, or some location, remote from the states, where the hand of oppression shall not crush every noble principle, and extinguish every patriotic feeling?" A slightly altered letter was sent to President Polk asking that he "convene a special session of Congress and furnish us an asylum. . . ." [51] Governor Ford had begun to make his feelings clear in a letter of April 8 to Brigham Young. "Your religion is new," he wrote, "and it surprises the people as any great novelty in religion generally does. They cannot rise above the prejudices excited by such novelty. . . . If you can get off by yourself you may enjoy peace; but surrounded by such neighbors I confess I do not foresee the time when you will be permitted to enjoy quiet. I was informed by General Joseph Smith last summer that he contemplated a removal west; and . . . I think if he had lived he would have begun to move in the matter before this time." Ford continued by suggesting as "a matter of confidence" that the Saints consider emigration to California. Sparsely populated by Indians and the "imbecile Mexican Spaniard," it offered "a field for the prettiest enterprise undertaken in modern time." If the country were conquered, Mexico was "so physically weak and morally distracted" that she would be unable to do anything about it. "Why would it not be a pretty operation for your people to go out there, take possession of and conquer a portion of the vacant country, and establish an independent government of your own subject only to the laws of the nations?" asked the governor. Once there, isolation would be assured for a long time. "If you conclude to do this," he said, "your design ought not to be known or otherwise it would become the duty of the United States to prevent your emigration. But if you once cross the line of the United States Territories you would be in no danger of being interfered with." [52]

When in September, 1845, the implacable mood of the militant gentiles became apparent, Young set in motion numerous activities looking toward a general move west. On September 9 he convened the Council of Fifty to consider the problem, and it decided to send a preliminary company of fifteen hundred men to the Great Salt Lake Valley. A committee was ordered "to gather information relative to emigration, and report the same to the council." Two days later the Twelve met and selected "members of the council to start

[51] Journal of John Taylor, quoted in Roberts, *Comprehensive History*, 2:522–525. The only response was from the governor of Arkansas, who expressed his inability to render any aid.

[52] *Apostolic Interregnum*, pp. 397, 398.

westward next spring." They also prayed "that the Lord would give us wisdom to manage affairs with the mob so as to keep them off till we can accomplish what he requires at our hands in completing the Temple and Nauvoo House, also for wisdom to manage affairs in regard to the western migration." On September 15, Young wrote Elder Samuel Brannan, publisher of a little Latter-day Saint paper in New York: "I wish you together with your press, paper, and ten thousand of the brethren, were now in California at the Bay of San Francisco, and if you can clear yourself and go there, do so." At the end of the month Parley Pratt reported the calculation that an outfit to take a family of five to the Coast would require "one good wagon, three yoke of cattle, two cows, two beef cattle, three sheep, one thousand pounds of flour, twenty pounds of sugar, one rifle and ammunition and a tent and tent poles." Such an outfit would cost $250 if purchased, and would make a wagon load approximating 2,900 pounds, or "calculating them to walk considerably would reduce it to about nineteen hundred pounds." Young wrote in his journal for September 30, "It was decided that all the council [Fifty?] were to go west with their families, friends, and neighbors." [53]

On the same day Hardin and Douglas came to Nauvoo with their force of troops to search for the bodies of some gentiles who had disappeared and were presumed to have been murdered in the city. The annoyance which Hardin and Young felt for each other is readily apparent in the latter's description of the encounter; but when the commissioners learned of the Mormon decision to leave, the necessary conversations were carried on in businesslike fashion. Hardin and Douglas were informed that the Oregon country was a likely objective for Mormon settlement, and the commissioners expressed hearty endorsement. Hardin said he would "do all in his power to help," and Douglas said that since "Vancouver's Island was claimed by the United States . . . he felt sure there would be no objection to its settlement, or to the settlement of Oregon." The question of the firmness of the Mormon intentions was discussed, and Young pointed out that "we were not sowing any winter wheat, and a greater testimony of our intentions to remove should not be asked." Hardin declared his satisfaction with Mormon sincerity, "but had not the assurance we could go," said Young, "if our property could not be sold"; consequently the General urged the appointment of trustees to sell Mormon property. [54]

[53] *Ibid.*, pp. 439, 445. For an account of the saga of Samuel Brannan, see Paul Bailey, *Sam Brannan and the California Mormons* (Los Angeles, 1943).
[54] *Apostolic Interregnum*, pp. 446–448.

The next duty of the commissioners was to persuade the militant citizens that the Mormons would indeed leave. They went from Nauvoo to Quincy, where representatives of nine counties met on October 1 (citizens of Hancock County were excluded) to determine how to take action against the Mormons. Douglas and Hardin convinced them to allow the Mormons peace to prepare for their exodus; but the conference was so hostile that the truce thus arranged was fragile at best. Hardin left a force of one hundred men under Major Warren in Hancock County to enforce his orders, with the understanding that it could quickly be reinforced if necessary.[55] The truce arrangements were entailed in an exchange of letters between the commissioners and the Twelve which were published in the newspapers of the region. Young declared that the Saints had need to sell their property, but that "one thousand families, including the Twelve, the High council, the Trustees and general authorities of the church are fully determined to remove in the spring, independent of the contingency of selling our property, and . . . this company will comprise from five to six thousand souls." Young added that the "church as a body desire to remove with us, and will if sales can be effected, so as to raise the necessary means." In an open letter Young pled with the citizens to "let us alone with . . . vexatious lawsuits . . . and help us to cash, dry goods, groceries, good oxen, milch cows, beef cattle, sheep, wagons, mules, harnesses, horses, etc., in exchange for our property, at a fair price. . . ." Young concluded by saying, "It is a mistaken idea that we 'have *proposed* to remove in six months;' for that would be so early in the spring, that grass might not grow nor water run, both of which would be necessary for our removal; but we propose to use our influence, to have no more seed time nor harvest among our people in this county, after gathering our present crops."[56]

Even if the Mormon communities were unmolested during the ensuing months, the tasks facing the leadership were difficult. Not only had preparations to be made for an epic journey, the destination of which was as yet undecided, but many of the people had yet to be convinced to follow the orders of the Twelve and Fifty in abandon-

[55] For the resolutions of the Quincy Committee regarding the truce, see *Apostolic Interregnum*, pp. 451–453. The activities of the commissioners and their reports are in Johannsen, ed., *The Letters of Stephen A. Douglas*, pp. 121–127, 137, 210.

[56] *Warsaw Signal*, October 15, 1845, and *Lee County Democrat* (Fort Madison), October 18, 1845, quoted in Snider, "Attitudes in Sectarian Conflict," pp. 281, 287, 288.

ing the city. The decision to leave came as a shock to many who had
everything invested in Nauvoo. What of the Temple, now nearly
completed by sacrifice and herculean effort? What of the whole
cause of Zion, if Nauvoo were to fall? Young hinted at the problem
when he said that some would definitely leave, and the rest "desire
to remove with us, if sales can be effected. . . ." He added that "the
organization of the church . . . is such, that there never can exist
but one head or presidency at any time, and all good members wish
to be with the organization," suggesting perhaps that as yet the
whole body did not agree upon the necessity or the desirability of
complying with his policy on removal.[57] But Young proceeded ener-
getically to promote a concert of action. The semiannual conference
of October 6 convened in the Temple, the first time the building had
been used for a general convocation, and the proceedings gave considerable attention to the exodus and the desirability for the Saints
to unite in faith and obedience to accomplish the new objective.
Heber Kimball again likened the Saints to potter's clay. "Let us become passive as clay, in the hands of the potter: If we don't we'll be
cut from the wheel and thrown back in the mill again." [58] The next
day after conference, Young addressed a lengthy formal announcement to the members of the Church "abroad" of the intent to move
the entire body west. He spoke of the "unparalleled union of the
great body of the Saints convened" at the late conference, and said
that "a crisis of extraordinary and thrilling interests has arrived"
which would usher in "a new epoch, not only in the history of the
church, but of this nation." The exodus, he suggested, was not a calamity, but a part of the working out of God's plan for the Saints.
"We discover a merciful design in our heavenly Father towards all
such as patiently endure these afflictions until he advises them that
the day of their deliverance has come." Heavy expenses were ahead
to provide outfits for the emigrants, heavy losses could be expected
from forced sales of property, and local resources had been used for
"an extensive improvement of farms, and the erection of costly public and private edifices"; therefore he urged the brethren abroad to
come to Nauvoo in order to help. "Dispose of your properties and
inheritance, and interests for available means, such as money,
wagons, oxen, cows, mules, and a few good horses adapted to jour-

[57] *Ibid.*, p. 281.
[58] See *Apostolic Interregnum*, pp. 456–477.

neying and scanty feed. Also for durable fabrics suitable for apparel and tents. . . ." In conclusion, Young admonished them:

Wake up, wake up, dear brethren, from the Mississippi to the Atlantic, and from Canada to Florida, to the present glorious emergency in which the God of heaven has placed you to prove your faith by your works, preparatory to a rich endowment in the Temple of the Lord, and the obtaining of promises and deliverances, and glories for yourselves and your children and your dead. . . . And we . . . assure you . . . of our . . . confidence [in your] obedience to the counsel of the Great God through the Presidency of the Saints. . . .

[signed] Brigham Young, President [59]

The completion of the Temple shared first priority with preparations to emigrate in the autumn of 1845. The commandment was to be fulfilled, and the people were to receive their "endowments" before they had to leave the city. When Smith was killed a year-and-a-half earlier, the walls had been no more than half built, so finishing the structure had been no small task. Doubtless Young's tithing procedures plus an enlarged membership and improved economic conditions had been helpful in speeding the work. "When the Temple is done," Young had said, "I expect we shall be baptized, washed, annointed, ordained, and receive the keys and signs of the priesthood for our dead, that we may have full salvation, and thus . . . be saviours on Mt. Zion. . . ." [60] Late in November, 1845, special rooms in the attic story were completed and furnished for the ceremonies, and early in December the ordinances were begun under the supervision of the Twelve. Only those who could produce vouchers that their tithe had been paid in full were to be admitted. Consequently, said George Miller, when the endowment rooms were being outfitted, "tithe gatherers were sent out in every direction [and] there was an immense sum of money and property paid in. . . ." The secret "temple work" was prosecuted day and night, and comprised not only the blessings of endowment, including, said Ebenezer Robinson, signs, grips, tokens, and garments "such as were given in the Holy Order in Joseph's lifetime," but also the sealing of plural wives and a new ceremony of "adoption" whereby Church leaders sealed to themselves men of the priesthood, together with their families, as their own children. The rites continued until February, 1846, when the Twelve left Nauvoo for the West; during that time

[59] *Ibid.*, pp. 479, 480.
[60] Brigham Young's journal for December 28, 1844, in the *Millennial Star*, 26: 316, May 7, 1864.

ordinances were administered to more than five thousand persons. This minority of the Mormons in the Nauvoo region was in years to come to constitute an élite group of the faithful.[61] Meanwhile, the Mormon leaders continued their study of possible destinations in the West. Maps, travelers' accounts, and pamphlets about California and Oregon were perused; particular attention was given to the journal of John C. Frémont, compiled during his 1842 exploration. It contained his extensive description of the isolated valley of the Great Salt Lake, which continued to attract Young's attention. Preparations for the trip went forward slowly. A check made on January 13 disclosed a total of no more than seventy wagons ready to go.[62]

Despite the incompleteness of preparations and the unsettled condition in the Church owing to the activities of the Pretender Prophet James J. Strang, the "apostasy" of Lyman Wight, William Smith, and John E. Page from the Twelve, and the faithlessness of many who were unwilling that Nauvoo be abandoned, a situation arose that suggested to Young the propriety of an early departure for himself and the other leading brethren, long before grass grew and water ran. The activities of counterfeiters who based their operations in Nauvoo had caused a return of indictments at the December term of the United States District Court at Springfield charging Young and eight of his fellow Apostles with the crime. The federal marshal believed that he would be unable to effect the arrests, and appealed to Governor Ford for a force of state militia to give him aid. Ford refused on the grounds that the "Truce of Nauvoo" had granted amnesty from indictment for old crimes; he was certain that convictions could not be obtained even if the Mormons were guilty, which apparently he doubted. Furthermore he feared that the arrest of the leaders would jeopardize the Mormon exodus. However, he wrote Young that the federals would press the charges, and implied that when the ice broke in the river a force of troops would come up from St. Louis to effect the arrests. The implication was without

[61] See Brooks, *John Doyle Lee*, pp. 43, 44, 65, 72–74; *The Return*, 2:301, July, 1890; Miller, *Correspondence*, p. 29; Evans, *Charles C. Rich*, pp. 95, 96. The great enthusiasm of the Saints for the special Mormon rites evident in the final winter in Nauvoo continued for at least two more years, and was paralleled by renewed enthusiasms in Utah during subsequent periods of stress and crisis, such as 1855–1857 and during the Federal "Raid" of the eighties.

[62] Brooks, *John Doyle Lee*, p. 74; Ray Allen Billington, *Far Western Frontier, 1830–1860* (New York, 1956), p. 96n.

basis in fact, but was intended as a spur to the Mormon removal. In this it succeeded.[63]

By the end of January about two thousand persons were relatively well prepared to go, and were organized into companies of fifty and one hundred. On February 2, the Twelve, the trustees, and some other leaders made the decision to go immediately. "We agreed that it was imperatively necessary to start as soon as possible," wrote Young. "If we are here many days, our way will be hedged up. Our enemies have resolved to intercept us whenever we start. I should like to push on as far as possible before they are aware of our movements." He instructed the captains of companies to have each family ready to leave on four hours' notice. That night, Young and Kimball went to visit Willard Richards. "We walked out into his garden," said Young, "and examined his grove of chestnut trees, and his wife Jenetta's grave, and after returning . . . made inquiries of the Lord as to our circumstances and the circumstances of the Saints and received satisfactory answers." [64] Plans for leaving immediately were thwarted, however, by a press of business, including the clamor of the brethren to receive their endowments before that activity was ended in the Nauvoo Temple. Young was vexed that "the brethren would have us stay here and continue the endowments until our way would be hedged up. . . ." He promised them more temples where they would go. "In this Temple we have been abundantly rewarded, if we receive no more." "I also informed them," he continued, "that I was going to get my wagons started and be off." However, he finally relented, since he knew "the multitude . . . were thirsting and hungering for the word. . . ." On that day (February 3) 295 more received temple ordinances. It was February 15 before Young was able to get away from Nauvoo. He joined an already sizable camp in the interior of Lee County, including the plural wives of many of the leaders and what were perhaps the first infant children born to plural marriages.[65]

From the relative safety of the Iowa wilderness, Young continued through February and March to direct affairs in Nauvoo as much as

[63] Ford, *History of Illinois*, p. 413. The zealous marshal went to Nauvoo without a militia escort and very nearly apprehended Young. See *Apostolic Interregnum*, pp. 549 ff.

[64] *Apostolic Interregnum*, pp. 578, 579.

[65] *Ibid.*, pp. 578, 579, 585; Brooks, *John Doyle Lee*, pp. 72, 76, 82, 88. Lee apparently considered the first contingent of emigrants, which left in February and March, to include the most zealous and faithful portion of the Mormon community, of which plural wives were an unmistakable sign.

possible. The brethren were urged to speed up their preparations and to leave as swiftly as possible, now that spring approached. "All the houses in Nauvoo," wrote Ford, "and even the temple, were converted into work-shops; and before spring, more than twelve thousand wagons [doubtless an exaggerated estimate] were in readiness." Almon Babbitt, Joseph Heywood, and John Fullmer were appointed trustees to sell Church property as well as that of individuals. They took the deed to John D. Lee's house and gave him $800 in credit, an exceptionally high price, toward the purchase of teams and store goods. Lee himself ventured into Missouri on a trading mission for the Iowa Camp, offering deeds to Nauvoo property for which he received stock, lead, powder, rifles, blankets, tools, tobacco, bee stands, wagons, and "calicoes." Governor Ford declared that "people from all parts of the country flocked to Nauvoo to purchase houses and farms which were sold extremely low, lower than the prices at a sheriff's sale, for money, wagons, horses, oxen, cattle, and other articles of personal property. . . ." One woman was offered ten dollars for her house, lot, and twenty acres, all fenced. She protested, but was reminded that she had to leave, and that "that amount will ferry you across the river." The purchaser decided at last that he wanted her furniture included as well. Old debts or unfinished business now became critical, and a series of suits were filed in the county court for the attachment of Mormon property to satisfy creditors. The trustees offered the Temple for rent in May, but apparently there was no response.[66]

Brigham Young grew anxious lest the zeal for emigration of those left in the city might decline, now that the leaders were gone. Many of the men in the "Camp of Israel," as Young styled the emigrants, had left their families in the city, and wanted to return for them. He feared perhaps that if they returned to Nauvoo they would stay. "Let your families be!" he told them on April 19. "What can you do at Nauvoo now? Nothing but eat. . . . Go and do what I command you—that you open a farm and raise something to feed them when they arrive." He finally permitted some to return, but without their wagons, "an order which caused much protest." His fears were not groundless. Opposition to the Twelve and dissension about the exodus existed in Nauvoo, although the active opponents may have

[66] Brooks, *John Doyle Lee*, pp. 78, 84; Ford, p. 412; Myron Abbott, "Diary of Myron Abbott" (typescript, University of Utah Library), p. 7; Deed Book L—Index; Hancock County Circuit Court Record Book D, p. 576; *Hancock Eagle* (Nauvoo), May 8, 1846.

been a small minority.[67] Thomas Gregg, a leading anti-Mormon of Warsaw, said that although large numbers left in the spring, "the Strangites, Rigdonites, Smithites and Twelveites, still behind, kept up their dissensions, the former all agreeing in their denunciations of the latter, and all except the latter, censuring the westward movement. . . . It began to be feared [by the gentiles] that many of the Mormons were not intending to leave the city, but to quietly remain, in the hope and expectation that in time the danger would be over." [68]

By mid-May, according to the *Hancock Eagle*, the "new citizen" (gentile) paper of Nauvoo, fourteen hundred teams and twelve thousand persons had crossed the river. But hundreds and perhaps thousands remained. Work continued on the Temple, and it was in constant use, although endowments had been concluded in February. A three-day dedication was planned for May 1–3; one of those days the proceedings were to be open to the non-Mormon public upon the payment of one dollar.[69] Major Warren's militia, reduced to a token force, was due to be disbanded May 1. The Mormons protested their withdrawal, but Ford replied that they were an expense to the state and that they were numerically insufficient anyway to prevent violence if either side were to use it. Under these circumstances anti-Mormon passions arose again in the county and led to violence. In May isolated Mormons were driven off their property, and early in June the anti-Mormons proposed to march a force to Nauvoo for a "demonstration," and applied to the citizens of the counties represented at the Quincy congress the previous October for aid. This action caused an increase in the number of Mormons evacuating the city, including many who had not planned to leave and who consequently suffered great hardship. It also caused alarm among the "new citizens," gentiles who had moved into Nauvoo after having purchased Mormon property. Although they had held a meeting on May 29 to consider forming a town government of their own, the

[67] Brooks, *John Doyle Lee*, p. 83; *Apostolic Interregnum*, p. 610. In September, 1846, William Smith, himself one of the Twelve under the regime of his brother the Prophet, wrote the *Sangamo Journal* a most vitriolic letter of accusation against Young and his coterie, who were "spiritual wife believers, law of Moses believers, consecration believers, and believers in the doctrine of secret murder to save men's souls—as for instance the death of Irvin and Amos Hodge, a Mr. Daniels, and a Mr. Wilcox." *Sangamo Journal*, November 5, 1846.
[68] Gregg, *History of Hancock County*, p. 345.
[69] See Brooks, *John Doyle Lee*, p. 86; Pease, *Frontier State*, p. 359.

anti-Mormons declared that the Mormon leaders still controlled the city, and that there were three thousand Saints there and an equal number nearby in Iowa. The New Citizens feared that the objectives of the mob included not only a pogrom against Mormons, but a sack of the city as well. By June 13 a hostile force of about four hundred was encamped before the city, and about three hundred New Citizens and Mormons were mustered to defend it. The Antis demanded access to the city in order forceably to expel the Mormons; when refused, they attacked, but were repulsed and compelled to withdraw. Civil war again ensued in Hancock County. In September another force attacked the city, this time with a cannon, but the onslaught failed. Nevertheless, the defenders felt the need to come to terms, which they found to be intolerant, particularly with regard to Mormons and those who had aided them. Both Mormons and some gentiles then fled the city, and the *State Register* reported that a reign of terror marked by plunder and violence prevailed in Nauvoo. Ford again marched into the county with a force of militia, but found the citizenry so hostile that he was unable to accomplish anything.[70]

During the ensuing months, a few score Mormons returned, many professing denial of the faith or opposition to the ruling oligarchy, and all professing undoubtedly their desire to live in peace with their neighbors. They prompted the *Madison Express* for February 12, 1846, to observe that "Every Saint, mongrel, or wholeblood, and everything that talked, looked, or acted like a Saint, should be compelled to leave."[71] But by then the "Mormon Problem" was ended; corporate Mormonism in Illinois was destroyed, and Illinoisans found that thereafter the Saints who remained or returned were quite innocuous. The memory remained, however, fresh and virile. Said an official state historian, writing seventy years later: "After full allowance is made for the violence and perhaps the greed of the opponents of the Mormons in Illinois, it must be admitted that they saw clearly how terrible an excrescence on the political life of the state the Mormon community would be, once it had attained full growth . . . and to enforce the will of public opinion, the resort to private war, though to be deplored, was inevitable."[72]

A traveler upon the river visited Nauvoo soon after the exodus

[70] Pease, *Frontier State*, pp. 358–361. Hardin was absent serving in the Mexican War. He was killed at the Battle of Buena Vista.
[71] Quoted in Pooley, *Settlement of Illinois*, p. 523.
[72] Pease, *Frontier State*, p. 362.

and described the scene which he encountered. The empty city appeared sufficiently extensive to contain "a hundred thousand souls. But its gloomy streets bring a most melancholy disappointment. Where lately resided no less than twenty-five thousand people [*sic*], there are not to be seen above five hundred, and these in mind, body, and purse, seem to be perfectly wretched." Fences were in ruins, gardens were grown to weeds, and vegetation was rank in the streets. Not more than one house in ten was occupied; windows were broken, doors were open and sagging. No domestic animals were to be seen. Even the children were silent, and showed the marks of suffering and care.[73] The blight left on Nauvoo by the course of events marked its former residents as well. Writing in Utah in later years, T. B. H. Stenhouse, an astute ex-Mormon high priest and editor, said:

No faith could be more liberal than *written* Mormonism. In the beginning of its mission it was a beautiful ideal. . . . In . . . creed writing they are . . . broadly cosmopolitan in sentiment, warmly inviting to "fair freedom's feast," away up in the Rocky Mountains. . . . But when once the Plains have been traversed, there the reception of . . . the religious stranger have been like the chilling breezes of the frigid zone. . . . In intercourse with mankind [Mormonism] is the trampled worm still in agony, the remembrance of "persecutions" that chills every forward, generous impulse and withers the soul with the baneful teaching that "he who is not for us is against us." . . . No professors of religion . . . could be more bitterly bigoted than the rigidly orthodox among the Mormons today.[74]

[73] Charles Lanman, *A Summer in the Wilderness*, pp. 30–33.
[74] T. B. H. Stenhouse, *The Rocky Mountain Saints* (New York, 1873), p. xxii.

Bibliography

CONTEMPORARY NEWSPAPERS AND PERIODICALS

The Hancock Eagle (Nauvoo).
The Latter-Day Saints' Millennial Star (Liverpool).
The Latter Day Saints' Messenger and Advocate (Pittsburgh).
The Nauvoo Expositor.
The Nauvoo Neighbor.
The Nauvoo Wasp.
The Niles National Register.
The Return (Davis City, Iowa).
The True Latter Day Saints' Herald (Plano, Illinois, and Lamoni, Iowa).
The Times and Seasons (Nauvoo).
Snider, Cecil A. "Development of Attitudes in Sectarian Conflict: A Study of Mormonism in Illinois in Contemporary Newspaper Sources." Unpublished Master's thesis, University of Iowa, 1933.
    This document contains extensive verbatim excerpts of press items concerning the Mormons taken from contemporary newspapers in Illinois and Iowa.

CONTEMPORARY WORKS ON MORMONISM

Bennett, John Cook. *The History of the Saints, or an Exposé of Joe Smith and the Mormons.* Boston, 1842.
Caswall, Henry. *The Prophet of the Nineteenth Century, or, the Rise, Progress, and Present State of the Mormons.* . . . London, 1843.
Jackson, Joseph H. *A Narrative of the Experiences of Joseph H. Jackson in Nauvoo, Exposing the Depths of Mormon Villainy.* Warsaw, Illinois, 1844.
Lee, John D. *Mormonism Unveiled.* . . . St. Louis, 1885.
Stenhouse, Fanny (Mrs. T. B. H.). *Tell It All; the Story of a Life's Experience in Mormonism.* Hartford, Connecticut, 1874.
Stenhouse, T. B. H. *The Rocky Mountain Saints.* . . . New York, 1873.

COUNTY HISTORIES

Clarke, S. J. *History of McDonough County, Illinois.* Springfield, 1878.
Fulwider, A. L. *History of Stephenson County, Illinois.* Chicago, 1910.
Gregg, Thomas A. *History of Hancock County, Illinois.* Chicago, 1880.
Historical Encyclopedia of Illinois and History of McDonough County. Chicago, 1907.
History of Lee County, Iowa. Chicago, 1881.
History of Sangamon County, Illinois. Chicago, 1881.

Hobart Publishing Company. *Biographical Review of Hancock County, Illinois.* Chicago, 1907.
Roberts, Nelson C., and Moorehead, Samuel W. *History of Lee County, Iowa.* Chicago, 1914.
Scofield, Charles J. *History of Hancock County, Illinois.* Chicago, 1921.
Stevens, Frank E. *History of Lee County, Illinois.* Chicago, 1914.
Western Historical Company. *History of Lee County, Iowa.* Chicago, 1879.

JOURNALS AND WORKS BASED PRIMARILY ON JOURNALS AND AUTOBIOGRAPHICAL WRITINGS

Anderson, Mary A. Smith, and Hulmes, Bertha A. Anderson, eds. *Joseph Smith III and the Restoration,* Independence, Missouri, 1952.
Brooks, Juanita. *John Doyle Lee, Zealot—Pioneer Builder—Scapegoat.* Glendale, California, 1962.
Corbett, Pearson H. *Jacob Hamblin, the Peacemaker.* Salt Lake City, 1952.
Cowley, Matthias F. *Wilford Woodruff.* Salt Lake City, 1909.
Evans, John H. *Charles Coulson Rich, Pioneer Builder of the West.* New York, 1936.
Juvenile Instructor's Office. *Heber C. Kimball's Journal.* Salt Lake City, 1882.
Roberts, Brigham H., ed. *History of the Church of Jesus Christ of Latter-Day Saints, Period II: Apostolic Interregnum, from the Manuscript History of Brigham Young and Other Original Documents.* Salt Lake City, 1932.
Smith, Joseph Jr. *History of the Church of Jesus Christ of Latter-Day Saints, Period I: History of Joseph Smith the Prophet, by Himself.* Brigham H. Roberts, ed. 6 Vols. Salt Lake City, 1948–1951.
Snow, Eliza R. *Biography and Family Records of Lorenzo Snow.* Salt Lake City, 1884.
Tullidge, Edward W. *Life of Joseph the Prophet.* Plano, Illinois, 1880.

MANUSCRIPTS

Abbott, Myron. "Diary of Myron Abbott." Bunkersville, Nevada, 1880. Typescript, University of Utah Library.
Abstract of the Probation of the Estate of Joseph Smith Jr. Carthage, Illinois, 1844. (Photostat.)
Abstract of Title to Lot 106, City of Nauvoo. In possession of the Honorable John Gorby, Carthage, Illinois.
"A short sketch of the triels of Mrs. R. F. Smith at the killing of the Smiths. The Mormans Profphet." Illinois State Historical Library.
Correspondence of John Gillet, John Dean Gillett, Smith Tuttle, and Horace Hotchkiss. Gillett Family Papers, Illinois State Historical Library.
Field report of the 1962 archeological excavation of the Nauvoo Temple site, and Dr. Melvin Fowler's report on recovered artifacts. (See Chapter 7, note 32.)

Ford, Thomas. Papers. Illinois State Historical Library.
Letter of Dr. Thomas L. Barnes, n.d. Manuscript Collection of the Illinois State Historical Library.
Peck and Messinger. "Map of the State of Illinois," in *Travellers Directory of Illinois*. . . . 1840. Manuscript Collection of the Wisconsin State Historical Society.
Plat of the City of Nauvoo. 1878. (Photostat.)
Sloan, James. Papers. Illinois State Historical Library.
Smith, Hyrum. Estate Papers. Vault of the Hancock County Clerk, Carthage, Illinois.
Smith, Joseph. Papers. Illinois State Historical Library.
Smith, Joseph Jr. Estate Papers. Vault of the Hancock County Clerk, Carthage, Illinois.
Young, James H. *The Tourist's Pocket Map of the State of Illinois, Exhibiting Its Internal Improvements, Roads, Distance, etc.* 1838. Manuscript Collection of the Wisconsin State Historical Society.

PUBLIC DOCUMENTS

Ford, Thomas A. "Message of the Governor of Illinois in Relation to the Disturbances in Hancock County." December 21, 1844. *Reports made to the Senate and House of Representatives of the State of Illinois, 1844.*
————. "Report of the Governor in Relation to the Difficulties in Hancock County." *Reports made to the Senate and House of Representatives of the State of Illinois, 1846.*
Hancock County, Illinois, Records. Bond and Mortgage Book 1; Deed Books B, E, F, G, 12G, H, I, K, L, M, N; Plat Book 1; Circuit Court Docket D. Vault of the Circuit Clerk and Recorder. Carthage, Illinois.
Journals of the House of Representatives and the Senate, of the Twelfth, Thirteenth, and Fourteenth General Assemblies of the State of Illinois, 1840–1841, 1842–1843, 1844–1845. 6 Vols.
Laws of the State of Illinois, the First, Ninth, Eleventh (Special Session), Twelfth, Thirteenth, and Fourteenth General Assemblies, 1819, 1835–1836, 1839, 1840–1841, 1842–1843, 1844–1845.
The Public Statutes at Large of the United States of America, 1789–1845. 5 Vols. Boston, 1846.
"Senate Judiciary Committee report on the memorial of a delegation of the Latter Day Saints, March 4, 1840." Document No. 247, *Senate Documents*, 1st Session, 26th Congress. Vol. V, 1839–1840.

OTHER PRIMARY SOURCES

Berrett, William E., and Burton, Alma D., eds. *Readings in L. D. S. Church History*, from original manuscripts. 3 Vols. Salt Lake City, 1953–1958.
Ford, Thomas A. *A History of Illinois from Its Commencement as a State in 1818 to 1847.* . . . Chicago and New York, 1854.

Jenson, Andrew, and Stevenson, Edward. "Infancy of the Church." Vol. LXI, No. 20: *Utah Pamphlets*. University of Utah Library.
This pamphlet contains interviews of Jenson and Stevenson with elderly Mormons, and accounts of visits to historical sites, including Nauvoo.

Johannsen, Robert, ed. *The Letters of Stephen A. Douglas*. Urbana, Illinois, 1961.

Journal of Discourses, by Brigham Young, President of the Church of Jesus Christ of Latter-Day Saints, His Two Counsellors, the Twelve Apostles, and others. 26 Vols. London and Liverpool, 1853–1886.

Kilbourne, David W. *Strictures on Dr. I. Galland's Pamphlet, entitled "Villainy Exposed," with some account of his transactions in lands in the Sac and Fox Reservations, etc., in Lee County, Iowa.* Ft. Madison, Iowa, 1850. (Pamphlet.)

Lanman, Charles. *A Summer in the Wilderness*. New York, 1847.

Latrobe, Charles Joseph. *The Rambler in North America*. 2 Vols. London, 1836.

Leopard, Buel, and Shoemaker, F. C., eds. *The Messages and Proclamations of the Governors of the State of Missouri*. 28 Vols. Columbia, 1922–1957.

Lewis, Henry. *Das Illustrirte Mississippithal*. Leipzig and Florence, 1923.
This work contains Lewis' paintings made along the Mississippi, including those of Nauvoo.

Lewis, G. *Impressions of America and the American Churches*. Edinburgh, 1845.

Martineau, Harriett. *Society in America*. 3 Vols. London, 1837.

Miller, George. *Correspondence of Bishop George Miller with the Northern Islander from his first acquaintance with Mormonism up to near the close of his life, 1855.* Compiled and published privately in pamphlet form by Wingfield Watson of Burlington, Wisconsin, 1916.
In the library of the Wisconsin State Historical Society.

Mills, H. W. "De Tal Palo Tal Astilla" ["A Chip off the Old Block"], *Publications [of] the Historical Society of Southern California,* 10: 3:86–174 (1915–1917).
This article contains an account taken from George Miller's journals that parallels that of the *Northern Islander* correspondence.

Minnesota Historical Society. *Making a Motion Picture in 1848; Henry Lewis' Journal of A Canoe Voyage from the Falls of St. Anthony to St. Louis*. St. Paul, 1936.

Mulder, William, and Mortensen, A. R., eds. *Among the Mormons; Historic Accounts by Contemporary Observers*. New York, 1958.

Pease, Theodore C. *Illinois Election Returns, 1818–1848*. Vol. XVIII, *Collections of the Illinois State Historical Library*. Springfield, 1923.

Pratt, Parley P. *A Voice of Warning and Instruction to All People, containing a Declaration of the Faith and Doctrine of the Church of the Latter Day Saints, commonly called Mormons*. New York, 1837.

Quaife, Milo M., ed. *An English Settler in Pioneer Wisconsin; the Letters of Edwin Bottomly, 1844–1850*. Vol. XXV, *Publications of the*

State Historical Society of Wisconsin: Collections. Madison, 1918.

Selby, Mrs. Paul. "Recollections of a Little Girl in the Forties . . ." *Journal of the Illinois State Historical Society* (Springfield, Illinois), 16: 157–186 (1923–1924).

Smith, Joseph. Letter to Oliver Granger, May 4, 1841. Printed in *Journal of the Illinois State Historical Society,* 40:85–86 (1947).

Spencer, Orson. *Letters Exhibiting the Most Prominent Doctrines of the Church of Jesus Christ of Latter-day Saints, by Elder Orson Spencer, A.B.* Liverpool, 1879.

Young, Lorenzo Dow. "Diary of Lorenzo Dow Young," *Utah Historical Quarterly.* 14:133–170 (1946).

GENERAL WORKS

Ackernecht, E. H. *Malaria in the Upper Mississippi Valley, 1760–1900.* Baltimore, 1945.

Allen, E. J. *The Second United Order Among the Mormons.* Columbia University, 1936.

Arrington, Leonard J. *From Wilderness to Empire; The Role of Utah in Western Economic History.* Salt Lake City, 1961.

———. *Great Basin Kingdom; An Economic History of the Latter-Day Saints, 1830–1900.* Cambridge, Massachusetts, 1958.

———. *Orderville, Utah: A Pioneer Mormon Experiment in Economic Organization.* Logan, Utah, 1954.

Beardsley, Harry M. *Joseph Smith and His Mormon Empire.* New York, 1931.

Bestor, Arthur. *Backwoods Utopias; The Sectarian and Owenite Phases of Communitarian Socialism in America: 1663–1829.* Philadelphia, 1950.

Billington, Ray Allen. *The Far Western Frontier, 1830–1860.* New York, 1956.

Briggs, Milton, and Jordan, Percy. *An Economic History of England.* London, 1954.

Brodie, Fawn. *No Man Knows My History: The Life of Joseph Smith, The Mormon Prophet.* New York, 1945.

Buley, Raymond C. *The Old Northwest; Pioneer Period: 1815–1840.* 2 Vols. Indianapolis, 1950.

Cannon, George Q. *The Life of Brigham Young.* Salt Lake City, 1893.

———. *The Life of Joseph the Prophet.* Salt Lake City, 1888.

Carlson, Theodore L. *The Illinois Military Tract; A Study of Land Occupation, Utilization, and Tenure.* Vol. XXXII, No. 2, *Illinois Studies in the Social Sciences.* Urbana, 1951.

Chambers, William U. *Old Bullion Benton: Senator from the New West.* Boston and Toronto, 1956.

Cross, Whitney. *The Burned-Over District; The Social and Intellectual History of Enthusiastic Religion in Western New York, 1800–1850.* Ithaca, 1950.

Davis, Inez Smith. *Story of the Church.* Independence, Missouri, 1934.

Edwards, Maldyn. *After Wesley; A Study of the Social and Political Influence of Methodism in the Middle Period (1791–1849)*. London, 1935.

Ekirch, Arthur A. *The Idea of Progress in America, 1815–1860*. New York, 1944.

Engels, Friedrich. *Condition of the Working Class in England*. London, 1844.

Faulkner, Harold Underwood. *Chartism and the Churches*. Vol. LXXIII, *Columbia University Studies in History, Economics, and Public Law*. New York, 1916.

Geddes, Joseph A. *The United Order Among the Mormons (Missouri Phase)*. Columbia University, 1922.

Greene, E. B., and Thompson, C. M., eds. *Governor's Letter Books, 1840–1853*. Vol. VII, *Collections of the Illinois State Historical Library*. Springfield, 1911.

Gue, Benjamin F. *History of Iowa*. 4 Vols. New York, 1903.

Hammond, J. L. and Barbara. *The Rise of Modern Industry*. New York, 1926.

Hartz, Louis. *The Liberal Tradition in America; An Interpretation of American Political Thought Since the Revolution*. New York, 1955.

Hayes, Carlton J. H. *A Political and Cultural History of Modern Europe*. 2 Vols. New York, 1936.

Hinsdale, B. A. *The Old Northwest*. New York, 1888.

Hubbart, H. C. *The Older Middle West, 1840–1880*. New York and London, 1936.

Jensen, Therald. *Mormon Theory of Church and State*. University of Chicago Libraries, 1938.

Jenson, Andrew, ed. *Latter-Day Saint Biographical Encyclopedia*. 4 Vols. Salt Lake City, 1901, 1914, 1920, 1936.

Larson, Gustive O. *Prelude to the Kingdom; Mormon Desert Conquest; A Chapter in American Cooperative Experience*. Francistown, New Hampshire, 1947.

Linn, William A. *The Story of the Mormons*. New York and London, 1902.

Mathews, Lois K. (Rosenberry). *The Expansion of New England*. Boston and New York, 1909.

McNiff, William J. *Heaven on Earth; a Planned Mormon Society*. Oxford, Ohio, 1940.

Meyers, Marvin. *The Jacksonian Persuasion; Politics and Belief*. Stanford, California, 1957.

Nelson, Lowry. *The Mormon Village*. Salt Lake City, 1952.

The New Cambridge Modern History. Vol. X. London and New York, 1960.

O'Dea, Thomas F. *The Mormons*. Chicago, 1957.

Parrish, William E. *David Rice Atchison of Missouri; Border Politician*. Vol. 34, No. 1, *University of Missouri Studies*. Columbia, 1961.

Pease, Theodore C. *Frontier State: 1818–1848*. Vol. II, *The Centennial History of Illinois*. Springfield, 1918.

Petersen, William. *Steamboating on the Upper Mississippi.* Iowa City, 1937.

Polleys, Abner Dexter. *Stories of Pioneer Days in the Black River Valley.* Black River Falls, Wisconsin, 1948.

Riley, I. Woodbridge. *The Founder of Mormonism: A Psychological Study of Joseph Smith, Jr.* New York, 1902.

Roberts, Brigham H. *A Comprehensive History of the Church of Jesus Christ of Latter-Day Saints Century I.* 6 Vols. Salt Lake City, 1930.

Smith, Joseph III, and Smith, Heman C. *The History of the Reorganized Church of Jesus Christ of Latter Day Saints.* 4 Vols. Lamoni, Iowa, 1896–1903.

Stokes, Anson Phelps. *Church and State in the United States.* New York, 1950.

Taylor, George R. *The Transportation Revolution, 1815–1860.* Vol. IV, *The Economic History of the United States.* New York and Toronto, 1951.

Thompson, Charles M. *The Illinois Whigs Before 1846.* Urbana, 1915.

de Tocqueville, Alexis. *Democracy in America.* Third American Edition. New York, 1839.

Van Deusen, Glyndon G. *The Jacksonian Era, 1828–1848.* New York, 1959.

Wearmouth, Robert F. *Methodism and the Working-Class Movements of England, 1800–1850.* London, 1937.

Weinberg, Albert R. *Manifest Destiny; A Study of National Expansionism in American History.* Gloucester, Massachusetts, 1958.

Werner, M. R. *Brigham Young.* New York, 1925.

West, Ray B., Jr. *Kingdom of the Saints; The Story of Brigham Young and the Mormons.* New York, 1957.

PERIODICAL ARTICLES

Arrington, Joseph Earl. "Destruction of the Mormon Temple at Nauvoo," *Journal of the Illinois State Historical Society,* 40:414–425 (1947).

Arrington, Leonard J. "Early Mormon Communitarianism: The Law of Consecration and Stewardship," *Western Humanities Review,* 7: 341–369 (1953).

———. "An Economic Interpretation of the Word of Wisdom," *Brigham Young University Studies,* 1:37–49 (1959).

———. "The Settlement of the Brigham Young Estate," *Pacific Historical Review,* 21:1–20 (1952).

Billington, Ray Allen. "The Frontier in Illinois History," *Journal of the Illinois State Historical Society,* 43:28–45 (1950).

Buckingham, J. H. and Pratt, Harry E., eds. "Illinois as Lincoln Knew it; a Boston Reporter's Record of a Trip in 1847," *Papers in Illinois History and Transactions for the Year 1937* (Illinois State Historical Society).

Bushman, Richard L. "Mormon Persecutions in Missouri, 1833." *Brigham Young University Studies,* 3:11–20 (1960).

Cannon, M. Hamlin. "Migration of English Mormons to America," *American Historical Review*, 52:436–455 (1946–1947).
Clark, James R. "The Kingdom of God, the Council of Fifty, and the State of Deseret," *Utah Historical Quarterly*, 26:131–150 (1958).
Durham, G. Homer. "A Political Interpretation of Mormon History," *Pacific Historical Review*, 13:136–150 (1944).
Fielding, Robert Kent. "The Mormon Economy in Kirtland, Ohio," *Utah Historical Quarterly*, 27:331–358 (1959).
Gayler, George W. "Governor Ford and the Death of Joseph and Hiram [*sic*] Smith," *Journal of the Illinois State Historical Society*, 50:391–411 (1957).
————. "The Mormons in Illinois Politics 1839–1844," *Journal of the Illinois State Historical Society*, 49:48–66 (1956).
Greene, E. B. "Sectional Forces in the History of Illinois," *Transactions of the Illinois State Historical Society for the Year 1903*, pp. 75–83.
Harstad, Peter. "Disease and Sickness on the Wisconsin Frontier: Malaria [and] Cholera," *Wisconsin Magazine of History*, 43:83–96, 203–237 (1959–1960).
Jackson, Donald. "William Ewing, Agricultural Agent to the Indians," *Agricultural History*, 31:3–7 (1957).
Larson, Gustive O. "Land Contest in Early Utah," *Utah Historical Quarterly*, 29:309–325 (1961).
Stevens, Frank E. "Life of Stephen A. Douglas," *Journal of the Illinois State Historical Society*, 16:247–673 (1923–1924).
    This is a book-length biography that places emphasis on Douglas in Illinois politics.
Van Der Zee, Jacob. "The Half-Breed Tract," *Iowa Journal of History and Politics*, 13:151–164 (1915).

UNPUBLISHED THESES AND DISSERTATIONS

Andrus, Hyrum L. "Joseph Smith, Social Philosopher, Theorist, and Prophet." Doctor of Social Science dissertation, Syracuse University, 1955.
Ellsworth, S. George. "A History of Mormon Missions in the United States and Canada, 1830–1860." Ph.D. dissertation, University of California, 1951.
Fielding, Robert Kent. "The Growth of the Mormon Church in Kirtland, Ohio." Ph.D. dissertation, University of Indiana, 1957.
Flanders, Robert B. "The Mormons Who Did Not Go West: A Study of the Emergence of the Reorganized Church of Jesus Christ of Latter Day Saints." Master's thesis, University of Wisconsin, 1954.
Gayler, George R. "A Social, Economic, and Political Study of the Mormons in Western Illinois, 1839–1846: A Re-Evaluation." Ph.D. dissertation, University of Indiana, 1955.
Jensen, Therald N. "Mormon Theory of Church and State." Ph.D. dissertation, University of Chicago, 1938.
McBrien, Dean Depew. "The Influence of the Frontier on Joseph Smith." Ph.D. dissertation, George Washington University, 1929.

Melville, James Keith. "The Political Ideas of Brigham Young." Ph.D. Dissertation, University of Utah, 1956.

Snider, Cecil A. "Development of Attitudes in Sectarian Conflict: A Study of Mormonism in Illinois in Contemporary Newspaper Sources." Master's thesis, University of Iowa, 1933.

Snider, Helen F. "Mormonism in Illinois: An Analysis of Non-Mormon Press Materials, 1838–1848." Master's thesis, University of Iowa, 1933.

PRIVATE INTERVIEWS AND CORRESPONDENCE

The author had conversations with a number of attorneys of Hancock County, Illinois, which were helpful as an introduction to the county records and to the oral traditions of county history. Of particular significance were interviews with Mr. Preston Kimball, an attorney and life-long resident of Nauvoo and a descendent of pioneer settlers of the locality.

Answers to many questions were kindly supplied by Dr. T. Edgar Lyon, Historian of Nauvoo Restoration, Incorporated, and by Mr. Kenneth Stobaugh and Mr. Floyd Fears of the Joseph Smith Historic Properties, Nauvoo.

Index

Adams, Charles Francis, 6, 7
Adams, George J.: tried for polygamy, 276; in Council of Fifty, 293; mentioned, 72n
Adams, James: lauded by Prophet, 93; instructed in secret rites, 271; receives endowment, 273
Adams County, Ill.: in Military Bounty Tract, 16; Mormon vote, 239. *See also* Quincy
Agricultural and Manufacturing Association. *See* Nauvoo Agricultural and Manufacturing Association
Allred, James: Agricultural and Manufacturing Association trustee, 149n; agent for Nauvoo House, 182
Apostles, Council of. *See* Twelve Apostles
Augusta, Iowa, 189
Avard, Sampson, 27

Babbitt, Almon W.: chastised by Presidency, 252; defends Rigdon, 259; trustee-in-trust, 293
Backenstos, Jacob B., 327–329
Backenstos, William, 233
Badlam, Alexander: in Council of Fifty, 293; supports Council of Fifty in succession struggle, 312
Bankruptcy: general in Illinois, 167; of Mormon leaders, 168–169; legality, 169
Baptism for the dead: in Temple revelation, 191; in Nauvoo Temple, 198; instructions, 200; Ebenezer Robinson on, 200; mentioned, 70
Barlow, Israel: contacts Galland, 30; Agricultural and Manufacturing Association associate, 149n

Barrett, John, 149n
Bear, John, 140
Beebe, Calvin, 245
Bennett, James Arlington, 288
Bennett, John Cooke: on sickness in Nauvoo, 54; joins Church, 93–96; letters to Prophet, 94; lobbyist for charters, 96; mayor, 101; on Nauvoo Legion, 110; on war against Missouri, 113–114; Agricultural and Manufacturing Association trustee, 149n; proposes canal, 151; Master-in-Chancery, 225; supports Democrats, 225; Mormon exposé, 228, 264; cooperates with Whigs, 229; extradition of Prophet, 234; incites mob, 234; approval of liquor, 245; urges Freemasonry, 247; and Smith-Rigdon dispute, 257–258; founds Nauvoo Legion, 260; influence on Prophet, 260–261; break with Mormons, 260–265; and celestial marriage, 266; corresponds with Rigdon and Orson Pratt, 270; charges plan of conquest, 278; mentioned, 243, 249
Bent, Samuel: financial mission, 128; in Council of Fifty, 293
Bernhisel, John M., 293
Bidamon, L. C., 190
Bishop, Francis Gladden, 255n
Blakeslee, James, 308
Boggs, Lilburn: mobilizes militia, 11; assassination attempt on, 104; mentioned, 217
Book of Abraham, 123
Book of the Law of the Lord, 203; consecrations recorded, 251
Brannan, Samuel, 332
Brewster, James Collin, 255

British Mission: 57–59; converts and emigrants, 58n; Mormon evangel, 62–63; opening, 63n; growth, 64–66; first emigrants leave, 67; interest in Nauvoo gatherings, 67; *Millennial Star* as organ, 69; letters of emigrants, 69, 75, 87–89; work of Twelve, 71; emigration, 71–72; instructions to emigrants, 72–74; emigrant route, 77; general shipping office, 79–81; decline of emigration, 81; Conference, April, 1845, 82; emigrants described, 86–87
Brotherton, Thomas, 75
Brown, A. W., 295
Brown, Uriah, 293
Browning, Orville H.: counsel for Prophet, 222, 225; Mormon vote for, 239

Cahoon, Reynolds: signs Kirtland notes, 166; bankruptcy, 169; on Temple Committee, 193; baptized for dead, 198; Temple mismanagement, 206; in Council of Fifty, 293
Caldwell County, Mo.: Mormons in, 10, 92; Mormon militia, 109. *See also* Far West
California, 288, 290, 330
Canal (Nauvoo), 43
Carlin, Thomas: on Nauvoo Charter, 104; Illinois governor, 214; offended by Mormons, 218; writes Rigdon, 259
Carter, Jared: signs Kirtland note, 166; bankruptcy, 169
Carthage, Ill., 234
Celestial marriage: doctrine, 267–269; Prophet on, 272–274; advocated privately, 274, 277; revelation, 274
Charter (Nauvoo). *See* Nauvoo Charter
Chartism, 61, 62
Church of Jesus Christ of Latter-day Saints: described, 1; New

England origins, 2; headquarters in Nauvoo, 45; patronage, 159; repudiation of debt, 165, 167, 168; partisan politics, 217–218; bloc voting, 226, 241; in Illinois politics, 231–232; gentile sentiment against, 240, 279, 290, 307–309; temperance, 244–245; opposition to Freemasonry, 249; western expansion, 279, 287–292, 296, 330; Constitutional views, 281, 282, 284; petitions to federal government, 282, 296; leadership succession, 311–316; priesthood governs Nauvoo, 325; abandonment of Nauvoo, 330, 333, 334; opposition to Twelve, 338–339
Clark, Hyrum, 79
Clark, William, 268
Clayton, William: letter of, 90; Deputy Registrar of Deeds, 102; land agent, 124; Temple Recorder, 203; in Council of Fifty, 293
Commerce, Ill.: 30, 39–41; Prophet settles near, 38; Mormon location near, 38; plat ordered vacated, 43
Commerce City: platted, 41; plat vacated, 43
Committee on Removal (Far West), 12
Coolidge, Joseph: in Council of Fifty, 293; trustee-in-trust, 293
Council of Fifty: 292–294; memorial to Congress, 296–297; plans presidential campaign of Prophet, 301–302; and leadership succession, 311; sends explorers to Great Salt Lake Valley, 331
Council of Twelve. *See* Twelve Apostles
Cowan, (?): promotes Shokoquon, 139–140; mentioned, 166
Cowdery, Oliver, 166n
Cowles, Austin: opposes celestial

marriage, 274; leader of faction, 308; driven from Nauvoo, 319–320

Cutler, Alpheas: Agricultural and Manufacturing Association associate, 149n; heads "pinery," 183; on Temple Committee, 193; western mission, 293; in Council of Fifty, 293

Danites, 10, 249

Davis, Amos W.: officer in Legion, 111; bankruptcy of, 169; in Nauvoo House revelation, 181

Democratic Party: in Illinois, 212, 214; in Hancock County elections, 220–221; in election of 1842, 225; on political views of Mormons, 234–235; influence of Mormon vote, 239–240; and Mormons in Iowa, 240

Deseret, State of: 106; Council of Fifty in government of, 294

Des Moines Rapids: 40; as water power source, 151

Des Moines Rapids Railroad, 150

Douglas, Stephen A.: supports Nauvoo charters, 96; at Legion maneuvers, 112; and alien vote case, 215; congressional candidate, 216; Illinois Supreme Court justice, 216; courts Mormon vote, 224–225; presides at hearing of Prophet, 225; election, 239; prophecy to, 287; on Mormon expansion, 297; commissioner on Mormon problem, 329; on western removal, 332–333; mentioned, 213, 214, 224

Duncan, Joseph, 228

Dunham, Jonathan, 289n

Emmett, James: in Council of Fifty, 293; explorations of, 303

Endowments, 273, 335, 337

Far West, Mo.: Mormons in, 10; surrendered by Mormons, 11; Committee on Removal, 12; exodus, 12, 74; schism, 242; mentioned, 26. *See also* Caldwell County, Mo.

Fielding, Amos: heads emigration of British Mormons, 72; action against, 79; in Council of Fifty, 293

Fielding, Joseph: on Nauvoo industry, 147; in Council of Fifty, 293; mentioned, 208

Fifty, Council of. *See* Council of Fifty

First Presidency: agents in land purchase, 35; urges Nauvoo gathering, 45, 49; sell stock, 148–149

Ford, Thomas: on Hancock County, 21–22; on Nauvoo growth, 56; Illinois governor, 213; Illinois Supreme Court justice, 216; on political views of Mormons, 225, 232n; candidate, 230; and extradition of Prophet, 233; on Mormon rights, 236n; on Mormon-gentile conflict, 240, 307; and Smith assassination, 309–311; anxiety for Mormon removal, 322–323, 336; denies anti-Mormon petition, 323; amending of Nauvoo Charter, 324; on Nauvoo emergency government, 324–325; warns Brigham Young, 326; confers on Mormon problem, 328–329; urges western movement of Mormons, 331; disbands peace force, 339

Fordham, Elijah, 199

Foster, Robert D.: ordained Elder, 44; Agricultural and Manufacturing Association associate, 149n; real-estate promoter, 188; accused by Prophet, 266n; leader of faction, 308

Freemasonry: and Temple rites, 192; established in Nauvoo, 247; and Mormon theology, 248;

Freemasonry (*continued*) ,
Mormon opposition to, 249; mentioned, 243
Frémont, John C., 298
Fullmer, John: bankruptcy of, 169; trustee-in-trust, 293, 338

Galland, Isaac: offers lands to Mormons, 25; in Massac Gang, 27; land speculator, 27–30; at Commerce, Illinois, 30; land sale to Mormons, 35; Half-Breed Land Company, 36; defrauds Mormons, 37; lauded by Prophet, 37; exposed, 55; receives Missouri land deeds, 126; agent for Mormons, 132–134; breaks with Mormons, 134; to be agent at Kirtland, 164; in Nauvoo House revelation, 181
Gallatin, Mo., 11
Gathering: early places of, 10; planned for Nauvoo, 43, 48, 51; to Missouri discontinued, 47; related to Temple, 48; to Nauvoo urged, 49; threatened by sickness, 54; from British Mission, 67, 68, 71–74, 86, 87; and Mutual Benefit Association, 82–83; Prophet on, 89; urged by Twelve, 136–137
General Conferences: April, 1840, 45, 219; October, 1840, 46, 252; April, 1841, 48, 111; October, 1841, 134, 165, 170; October, 1839, 244; October, 1843, 259; April, 1842, 262; April, 1844, 298; October, 1845, 334
Geneva Stake, 49
Gillet, John: speculator in Hancock County lands, 41; and Hotchkiss Purchase, 41, 135; and Mormon debtors, 173
Granger, Gilbert, 167
Granger, Oliver: agent in land purchase, 36; agent in Kirtland, 164, 251; death, 165; signs Kirtland

note, 166n; Prophet's debt to estate, 167
Grant, Jedediah M., 293
Green, E. P., 36
Green, John P.: Agricultural and Manufacturing Association associate, 149n; bankruptcy of, 169

Half-Breed Land Company, 36
Half-Breed Tract: 28–29; Mormon purchases, 36–37
Hall, James, 20
Hancock County, Ill.: site of Nauvoo, 1; in Military Bounty District, 16, 117; bad reputation, 21; Mormon decision to settle, 35; politics, 217; Mormons as political factor, 220–222; Mormon vote, 239; anti-Mormon sentiment, 288, 307, 308, 323; Smith assassination, 310; anti-Mormon depredations, 326–328, 339–340
Hardin, John J.: commands militia, 323; commissioner on Mormon problem, 329; on western removal, 332–333
Harris, George W., 128
Haven, Charlotte: on Mormons in politics, 237; on celestial marriage, 275–276
Haws, John, 149n
Haws, Peter: Agricultural and Manufacturing Association trustee, 149n; in Nauvoo House revelation, 181; heads "pinery," 183; promotes Nauvoo House, 186; in Council of Fifty, 293
Hedlock, Reuben: heads British Mission, 79–80; financial difficulties of, 81; and Mutual Benefit Association, 81–82; action against, 84; signs Kirtland note, 166n
Hendrix, James, 126
Herringshaw and Thompson's addition to Nauvoo, 43
Heywood, Joseph L.: in Council of

Fifty, 293; trustee-in-trust, 293, 338

Hibbard, Davison, 39

Hicks, John A., 254

Higbee, Chauncey: officer of Legion, 111; excommunicated, 266n; leader of faction, 308

Higbee, Francis: officer in Legion, 111; at opening of Nauvoo Mansion, 177; real-estate promoter, 188; accused by Prophet, 266n

Higbee, Isaac, 149n

Higbee, "Judge" Elias: meets Galland, 31; Agricultural and Manufacturing Association associate, 149n; bankruptcy of, 169; on Temple Committee, 193; Temple mismanagement, 206; to Washington, 283; mentioned, 219

High Council. *See* Nauvoo High Council

High Council (Far West), 12. *See also* Nauvoo High Council

Hills, Gustavus: engraving of Nauvoo, 43; Temple engraving, 194; works on *Times and Seasons*, 250

Hoge, Joseph P.: campaigns in Nauvoo, 235; Mormon votes for, 239

"Homestead," 175

Hotchkiss, Horace: speculator in Hancock County lands, 41; business relations with Mormons, 128–132; on Mormon bankruptcies, 172; problem with Mormon debtors, 173

Hotchkiss Purchase: described, 41n; terms, 42, 135n; discussed at General Conference, 45; correspondence, 128–132; and bankruptcy of Prophet, 171–172

Hunter, Edward: buys Nauvoo lands, 120; on Nauvoo water power development, 153; business with Prophet, 161–163; in Council of Fifty, 293

Huntington, William, 149n

Hyde, Nancy Marinda (Mrs. Orson), 269

Hyde, Orson: opening of British Mission, 57, 63n; to England in 1846, 84; sells Nauvoo House stock, 189; opposes celestial marriage, 269; in Council of Fifty, 293

Illinois: as site of Mormon settlement, 13–22; settlement, 14–16; politics, 15, 214–216, 222, 226, 227; sectional conflict, 15; population growth, 15–16; plans for internal improvements, 18; public indebtedness, 18; need for growing population, 19; prejudice against group immigration, 19–20; antireligious feeling in, 20–21; depression, 227–228; Mormons in politics, 231–232; reaction to Smith assassination, 310–311

Illinois and Michigan Canal: in state plan of works, 18; in repeal of Nauvoo charters, 322; mentioned, 15

Illinois State Register (Springfield): on political views of Mormons, 223; on extradition of Prophet, 234

Independence, Mo., 10, 23

Ivins, Charles, 118, 308

Jackson County, Mo., 10

James, Samuel, 118, 149n

Johnson, Benjamin F., 293

Jones, Dan, 86

Kelly, James, 149n

Keokuk, Iowa: bad reputation of, 21; promoted by Galland, 28

Kilbourne, David: on Galland, 30; on Lee County Mormons, 55

Kimball, Ethan, 31, 188

Kimball, Heber C.: cousin of Commerce Kimballs, 31; urges obedience, 50, 334; missionary in

Kimball, Heber Co. (*continued*) Britain, 63–64; sells Nauvoo House stock, 189; baptizes for dead, 198; Temple fund raising, 203; instructed in secret rites, 271; receives endowment, 273; in Council of Fifty, 293; mentioned, 337

Kimball, Hiram: land broker at Commerce, 31; accused by Prophet, 266n; mentioned, 103

Kimball, Phineas, 31, 188

Kingdom of God: in Last Days, 9; concept of in British Mission, 63; and gathering of British Saints, 69, 70, 76; and Mutual Benefit Association, 81–83; relation to Nauvoo government, 106; and Mormon priesthood, 108; economy, 116; Twelve on, 136–137; and North-South sectionalism, 291; and Council of Fifty, 292; political theory, 240, 279–281; and Prophet's presidential campaign, 302. See also Zion

Kirtland, Ohio: gathering to advised, 26, 36; bank, 41–42n; dissension at, 45n; gathering to forbidden, 49; Zionic efforts in, 49; debts in, 164–166; temple, 193; Saints at chastised, 251

Knight, Joseph, 126

Knight, Vinson: agent in land purchase, 36; ward bishop, 44; on city council, 101; solicits aid for poor, 146; Agricultural and Manufacturing Association trustee, 149n; signs Kirtland note, 166n; bankruptcy, 169; in Nauvoo House revelation, 181

Knowlton, Sidney, 149n

La Harpe, Ill., 140

Land speculation. *See* Speculation

Latter-Day Saints' Millennial Star. *See Millennial Star*

Law, William: officer in Legion, 111; Agricultural and Manufac-

turing Association trustee, 149n; in Nauvoo House revelation, 181; real-estate promoter, 188; in Temple dispute, 206; and election of 1843, 238; defends Rigdon, 259; Bennett affair, 271n; receives endowment, 273; opposes celestial marriage, 274; leader of faction, 308; mentioned, 311

Law, Wilson: on city council, 101; officer in Legion, 111; Agricultural and Manufacturing Association trustee, 149n; real-estate promoter, 188; leader of faction, 308

Lee, John D.: on Prophet, 7–8; receives patronage, 158–159; in Council of Fifty, 293; mission, 302

Lee County, Iowa: bad reputation, 21; speculation, 28–29; site of Mormon settlement, 32, 33, 35, 36, 54–56; attempted annexation by Missouri, 40; Zarahemla Stake, 44; anti-Mormon sentiment, 328

Liberty (Mo.) Jail, 24

Lima, Ill.: stake, 49; as satellite town, 140

Lincoln, Abraham, 214, 223, 228

Little, Sidney, 96

Lucas, Robert, 32, 33

Lyman, Amasa: ordained Apostle, 270; in Council of Fifty, 293; supports Twelve, 315; heads Nauvoo House Association, 322; mentioned, 247

Lyon, William P., 169

Maid of Iowa, 86, 161

Malaria, 40, 53

Markham, Stephen, 119n, 233

Marks, William: presides at conference, 25; opposes regathering, 25; presides at Nauvoo, 36; Nauvoo Stake president, 44; on city council, 101; Agricultural and Manufacturing Association trustee, 149n; paid debt by Prophet, 167; in Nauvoo House revelation, 181; supports Rigdon, 259, 312; opposes celestial marriage, 274, 276; in polygamy trial, 276; in Council of Fifty, 293

Marsh, Thomas B., 11

Masonic Order. *See* Freemasonry

Masonic Temple, 208

Methodism (Britain), 62–63

Military Bounty Tract (Ill.), 16, 17, 117–119

Millennial Star: defends emigration, 67; organ of British Mission, 69

Miller, George: on early growth of Nauvoo, 51; on Nauvoo poverty, 145; Agricultural and Manufacturing Association trustee, 149n; on Nauvoo speculation, 158; in Nauvoo House revelation, 180; and Nauvoo House Association, 182; heads "pinery," 184; instructed in secret rites, 271; and Texas colony, 290, 294, 295; in Council of Fifty, 293; breaks with Young, 295; mission, 302; supports leadership of Fifty, 312; supports Joseph Smith III, 318–319

Miller, Henry W.: agent for Nauvoo House, 182; accuses Babbitt, 252

Mississippi River, 52

Montrose, Iowa, 21

Moon, Francis, 147

Moon, John, 67

Morey, George, 169

Morley Settlement, 140. *See also* Lima, Ill.

Mormons. *See* Church of Jesus Christ of Latter-day Saints

"Mormon War" (Mo.), 11

Morrison, Arthur, 169

Mt. Ephraim Stake, 49

Mutual Benefit Association, 81–83, 85

Nashville, Iowa: 5; promoted by Galland, 28; Mormon purchase, 36; as gathering place, 55n; as satellite town, 138

Nauvoo: descriptions, 38–43, 52, 87–88; naming, 41; malaria, 51, 53; school system, 52–53; landscaping urged, 53; growth of population, 56; British immigrants, 86; registry of deeds, 102; real-estate additions to, 125; sale of liquor, 245–247; Freemasonry established, 247; Bennett scandal, 265–266; gentile sentiment against, 279, 307–309; decision to abandon, 330; opposition in to removal, 333–334; opposition to Twelve, 338–339; attacks upon, 339–340

— Economy: 52, 74, 115–117, 144–148, 177–178; as townsite, 40; expected immigration, 46; early growth, 50; plan for industry, 68, 81; land sales, 125–126; banking functions, 126–127; need for industry, 147; railroad projected, 151; industries, 154; producers' cooperative, 154–155; building industry, 156–157; public buildings erected, 158–159; debt forgiveness, 167–168; lumber for, 184; commercial districts, 188; markets, 188; rivalry between upper and lower town, 188; speculative building, 188; effect of Temple on economy, 208–210; sale of property, 337–338

— Mormon religious center: as expression of Mormon communitarianism, 23; founding and settlement, 34–35, 38, 44, 46; gathering to urged, 43–45, 48, 49, 51; first conference, 44; first words appointed, 44; stake appointed, 44; official headquarters, 45

— Politics and government: government established, 101; elections, 221, 223, 235, 238, 239;

Nauvoo: Politics and gov't (*cont.*) proposal to make a federal territory, 285; *ad hoc* government, 325–326
Nauvoo Agricultural and Manufacturing Association: 148–150; plans pottery, 149–150; charter threatened, 150; bill for repeal of charter, 232
Nauvoo Charter: 52, 92–93, 98–100, 104; passage, 96–97; and habeas corpus controversy, 104; speech of Prophet on, 105; and Legion, 109; repeal, 153, 324; bills for repeal, 232; Mormon thought concerning, 284–285; gentile sentiment against, 285
Nauvoo City Council, 99, 151
Nauvoo Expositor, The, 308
Nauvoo Female Relief Society, 266
Nauvoo High Council: urges gathering, 45; appoints Prophet treasurer, 119; and land business, 121–122; opposes Robinson, 250; trials before for apostasy, 254; hears revelation on celestial marriage, 274; polygamy trial before, 276
Nauvoo House: 179, 182; solicitation for, 78; jeopardized by speculative building, 158; revelation, 180; sale of stock, 181; promoted by Prophet, 185, 189; problems, 186; work abandoned, 190; as works project, 208; bill for repeal of Association charter, 232; liquor forbidden in, 245; plans to resume work on, 322
Nauvoo House Association: employs poor, 145; charter, 180; operations, 182–184; reorganized, 322
Nauvoo Legion: 109–113; authorized in charter, 100; gentile apprehension, 113; razes liquor store, 245–246; founded by John C. Bennett, 260; mobilized, 309;

in *ad hoc* government, 325–326
Nauvoo Mansion, 175–177, 190
Nauvoo Municipal Court, 99
Nauvoo Registry of Deeds, 102–103, 170
Nauvoo Temple: 52, 179; related to gathering, 45, 47, 48; purpose, 47; solicitation for, 78; in British Mission policy, 80; described, 88, 194, 195, 199; cornerstones laid, 111; site purchased, 125; jeopardized by speculative building, 158; revelation, 190; Prophet on rites for, 191–192; Committee, 193; design, 193–194; destruction, 196; Prophet supervises construction, 196–197; baptism for dead, 198; baptismal font, 199; promoted by Prophet, 199–201; finance and construction, 201–205; mismanagement of charged, 206; cost, 207–208; as works project, 208; effect on Nauvoo economy, 208–209; significance in Mormonism, 209–210; secret rites for, 271; work to complete, 322, 335; rites in, 335–336; offered for rent, 338; dedication, 339
Nauvoo University, 52
Nauvoo Water Power Company, 153
Needham, John, 88, 148
Niswanger, William, 167, 169

Olive Leaf, The, 253
Olney, John F., 149n
Olney, Oliver: signs Kirtland note, 166n; apostasy, 255n, 267
Order of Enoch, 249
Oregon, 332
Owen, Abel, 165–166

Page, John E.: president of Nauvoo Water Power Company, 153; defection, 336
Partridge, Edward: opposes regathering, 25; meets Galland, 31;

on indigents, 38–39; ward bishop, 44
Patten, David, 11
Payson Stake, 49
People's Charter movement. *See* Chartism
Perpetual Emigrating Company, 78–79, 85
Phelps, William Wine: in Council of Fifty, 293; supports Twelve, 315
Pierce, Robert, 130
Pineries. *See* Wisconsin pineries
Polygamy. *See* Celestial marriage
Pratt, Orson: Agricultural and Manufacturing Association associate, 149n; defection, 269; drafts petition, 285; to Washington, 297
Pratt, Parley Parker: heads British Mission, 68; counsels emigrants, 76; to England, 1846, 84; promotes Temple, 204n; political theory of Kingdom, 280, 325; in Council of Fifty, 293; on outfit for western trek, 332
Priesthood, Mormon, 106–109

Quincy, Ill.: Mormons in, 1, 12, 13, 217; stake discontinued, 219; anti-Mormon congress in, 332. *See also* Adams County, Ill.
Quincy, Josiah: on Prophet, 6–7; on Temple, 197

Ramus, Ill.: as satellite town, 138–139; Temple fund raising in, 203
Remick, James: sues Galland, 30; swindles Prophet, 142
Reorganized Church of Jesus Christ of Latter Day Saints: owns Nauvoo House, 190; rejects revelation on celestial marriage, 275
Rich, Charles Coulson: early settler, 50; on city council, 101; officer in Legion, 111; in Council of Fifty, 293; commands Legion, 326

Richards, Jenetta (Mrs. Willard): letter of Prophet to, 269; grave of visited, 337
Richards, Willard: on opening of British Mission, 63; sells Nauvoo House stock, 189; baptizes for dead, 198; fund raising for Temple, 203; lives with Nancy Hyde, 269; instructed in secret rites, 271; receives endowment, 273; and polygamy trial, 276; in Council of Fifty, 293; Church historian, 320; mentioned, 337, 359
Rigdon, Sidney: meets Galland, 31; favors Galland purchase, 32; preaches mass funeral, 54; on city council, 101; president and trustee of Agricultural and Manufacturing Association, 149; defends Agricultural and Manufacturing Association, 149, 150; signs Kirtland note, 166n; bankruptcy, 169; baptized for dead, 198; dispute with Prophet, 256; Nauvoo postmaster, 257; to Washington, 283; in Council of Fifty, 293; and leadership succession, 311–316; mentioned, 36, 91
Ripley, Alanson: agent in land purchase, 35; on water power development, 152; mentioned, 55
Roberts, Sydney, 254
Robinson, Ebenezer: on landscaping, 53; on registry of deeds, 103; opposes Legion, 114; borrows for *Book of Mormon* printing, 128; Agricultural and Manufacturing Association trustee, 149n; builds tenement, 157; leases Nauvoo Mansion, 177; on baptism for dead, 200; on Freemasonry, 249; sells *Times and Seasons*, 249–251; criticizes Prophet, 268; describes secret rites, 271; opposes celestial marriage, 274, 277
Robinson, George W.: agent in land purchase, 35; takes Galland option, 35; Agricultural and Man-

Robinson, George W. (*continued*)
ufacturing Association trustee,
149n; in Smith-Rigdon dispute,
257–258; mentioned, 118
Rockwell, Orrin Porter: suspected
of Boggs assault, 104; barkeep,
246; to Washington, 283; in
Council of Fifty, 293
Rockwood, A. P.: officer in Legion,
111; in Council of Fifty, 293
Rogers, Daniel, 31
Roosevelt, William H., 221

Sangamo Journal (Springfield): on
Mormon political views, 226;
Bennett a correspondent, 235;
carries Bennett disclosures, 265
Sharp, Thomas, 308
Sherwood, Henry G.: bankruptcy,
169; in Nauvoo House revelation,
181; defends Temple Committee,
206
Shumway, Charles, 293
Smith, Don Carlos: death, 54; in
city council, 101; officer in Legion, 111; Agricultural and Man-
facturing Association trustee,
149n; cofounder of *Times and
Seasons*, 249; opposes celestial
marriage, 268
Smith, Emma (Mrs. Joseph): correspondence with Carlin, 104;
buys lands, 120; retains Nauvoo
House title, 190; attitude toward
liquor, 246; opposes Twelve, 319
Smith, George Albert: missionary to
Britain, 66; sells Nauvoo House
stock, 189; baptizes for dead,
198; in Council of Fifty, 293;
heads Nauvoo House Association,
322
Smith, Hyrum: on gatherers' quali-
fications, 47; on city council, 101;
land broker, 124; business mission east, 130; Agricultural and
Manufacturing Association trustee, 149n; at 1841 conference,
165; signs Kirtland note, 166;

bankruptcy, 169–171; in Nauvoo
House revelation, 181; defends
Temple Committee, 206; and
election of 1843, 237–239; becomes Mason, 248; chastises Kirtland Saints, 252; defends Rig-
dom, 259; and celestial marriage,
270, 276, 277; instructed in secret rites, 271; receives endowment, 273; hosts politician, 286;
in Council of Fifty, 293; death,
306–309
Smith, Joseph Jr.: biographies of,
4n; described by observers, 5–8;
self-evaluation, 8–10; in Liberty
Jail, 11; solicits aid of Galland,
33; arrives in Quincy, 34; lauds
Galland, 37; describes Nauvoo
site, 38; settles near Commerce,
38; on sickness in Nauvoo, 54;
implicated in Boggs assault, 104;
extradition of attempted, 104,
233–235; on Legion, 109; commander of Legion, 111; emoluments, 122, 159, 160; threatened
Iowa arrest, 141; advises abandonment of Iowa settlements,
142; first residence in Nauvoo,
156; as entrepreneur, 160–161;
general store, 161–163; business
dealings with Hunter, 161–163;
financial difficulties, 163, 177;
public officers, 163; signs Kirtland note, 166n; and Oliver
Granger estate, 167; bankruptcy
proceedings of, 168–171; writes
Hotchkiss on bankruptcy, 171;
opens Nauvoo Mansion, 176; supervises Temple building, 196–
197; arrest, 233; dissent against,
243; becomes Mason, 248; dispute with Rigdon, 257–260; influence of Bennett on, 260–261;
charges of polygamy against,
262; fights Bennett scandal, 265–
266; letter to Jenetta Richards,
269; death, 306–309
— Economic leader: counsels Gal-

land purchase, 32; on Nauvoo economy, 52; instructions to British emigrants, 68, 89, 90; economic thought, 116; land broker, treasurer, and Trustee-in-Trust, 119; on speculation, 121, 158; Hotchkiss correspondence, 128–132; on unemployment, 140; on need for industry, 148; Agricultural and Manufacturing Association associate, 149n; on water power development, 151–152; urges domestic manufacturer, 153–154; revelation of on Nauvoo House, 180; on Nauvoo House finance, 183; promotes Nauvoo House, 185, 189; decides Temple dispute, 206; and *Times and Seasons* sale, 249–251

— Political leader: in city council, 101; Registrar of Deeds, 102; elected mayor, 103; speech on charter, 105; promotes satellite towns, 138–140; political views, 218, 219, 225, 226, 232, 236, 238, 281, 283, 286; meets John C. Calhoun, 219; meets Van Buren, 219; on Stephen A. Douglas, 224; on Mormon rights, 234; and election of 1843, 236–237; on sale of liquor, 245–247; political theory of Kingdom, 281; to Washington, 283; proposal to make Nauvoo federal territory, 285; prophecy on government, 287; expansionist plans of, 287–292; orders California exploration, 292; organizes Council of Fifty, 292; memorial on westward expansion, 296; runs for U.S. presidency, 299–302; Constitutional views of, 300; views on westward movement of Mormons, 331

— Religious leader: founder of Mormonism, 4; anticipates end of world, 8–9; counsel on regathering, 25; promotes Nauvoo gathering, 34–35, 43–48, 51; promotes Temple, 47, 48, 190–191, 199–200; commands gathering to Nauvoo, 48; on Zionic policy, 49; in Zarahemla Stake, 55; opens British Mission, 63n; and priesthood, 108; on Temple design, 193–194; baptizes for dead, 198; admonishes forgiveness, 255; views on morality, 268; on polygamy, 271; initiates secret rites, 271; on celestial marriage, 272–274; gives endowments, 273; expanded concept of Kingdom, 298

Smith, Joseph Sr., 54

Smith, Joseph III: on father's household, 175; and leadership succession, 312, 319

Smith, Samuel H.: on city council, 101; bankruptcy, 169

Smith, William: business mission east, 130; defection, 336

Snow, Erastus, 293

Snyder, Adam W.: gubernatorial candidate, 225; death, 229

Snyder, John: mission to England, 78; Agricultural and Manufacturing Association associate, 149n; in Nauvoo House revelation, 180; removed from Nauvoo House Association, 322

Soby, Leonard: Agricultural and Manufacturing Association associate, 149n; opposes celestial marriage, 274

Speculation: in Illinois lands, 17; in Half-Breed Tract lands, 28–29; in Lee County, 28–29; in Half-Breed Land Company stock, 36–37; in Illinois Military Bounty Tract lands, 117–118; and Nauvoo economy, 121; in farm lands about Nauvoo, 140–141; in Nauvoo buildings, 188

Spencer, Augustine, 188

Spencer, Orson: British Mission President, 85; on Nauvoo settlement, 144; at opening of Nauvoo

Spencer, Orson (*continued*)
Mansion, 177; drafts memorial to
Congress, 285; in Council of
Fifty, 293
Springfield, Ill., 49
Stenhouse, T. B. H., 341
Stout, Hosea, 111, 247
Strang, James Jesse, 302, 336

Taylor, John: ordained Apostle: 12;
missionary to Isle of Man, 65; to
England, 1846, 84; criticizes
Agricultural and Manufacturing
Association, 149; advocates cooperatives, 155; criticizes building
industry, 157; at opening of Nauvoo Mansion, 177; business dealings with Prophet, 177; sells
Nauvoo House stock, 189; baptizes for dead, 198; Temple fund
raising, 203; practices secret rites,
272; political theory of Kingdom,
280; drafts territorial petition,
285; in Council of Fifty, 293; political views, 300; wounded, 309;
on leadership succession, 318;
letter to governors, 330
Temple (Nauvoo). *See* Nauvoo
Temple
Texas: Mormon colonies planned,
290; negotiations with, 294
Thompson, Robert B.: death, 54;
sells lands to Prophet, 120; Agricultural and Manufacturing Association trustee, 149n; political
views, 218; lauds O. H. Browning, 222; mentioned, 250
Times and Seasons: business described, 249–250; sale of, 157,
177, 249–251
Tithe: for Temple, 206–207; in
Utah, 207
Trustee-in-Trust: Prophet elected,
119; Young in Utah, 120n;
deeded Ramus lots, 139; conflict of interests, 159; and Prophet's bankrupt proceedings, 170;

transfer of properties to, 170; and
Temple construction, 202; receives Temple funds, 203; in
Utah, 207; Coolidge, Heywood,
Fullmer, and Babbitt appointed,
293; mentioned, 197
Turley, Theodore: builds first house
in Nauvoo, 44; Agricultural and
Manufacturing Association trustee, 149n; brewery of approved,
246; in Council of Fifty, 293
Tuttle, Smith, 132, 135
Twelve Apostles: Prophet instructs
on end of world, 9; gifts of land
to, 31; Prophet instructs on Zion,
49; enumerated, 58n; in British
Mission, 64, 71; recalled, 68; instructions to British emigrants,
90; settle British in Nauvoo, 90;
head land jobbing, 123; endorse
inheritances, 126; and Hotchkiss
Purchase, 134–136; urge gathering, 136–137; promote satellite
towns, 138; favor Prophet's emoluments, 160; institute debt forgiveness, 167–168; promote Nauvoo House, 189; on Temple rites,
192; promote Temple, 201; allay
anti-Mormon sentiment, 234; at
plural marriage, 247; purchase
Times and Seasons, 250–251;
charges of polygamy against,
262; propose mock congress,
289–290; in Council of Fifty,
293; and leadership succession,
311–320; opposition to, 316–319,
338; policies, 320–322; letter to
governors, 330; declaration on removal, 333; mentioned, 200

University (Nauvoo). *See* Nauvoo
University
Utah: economy, 178; tithe manage-
ment, 207; politics, 240–241;
Word of Wisdom in, 247; Coun-
cil of Fifty in government, 294;
Frémont's map of region, 298;

strategic concept of settlement, 304

Van Allen, Isaac, 32

Walker, Cyrus: visits Nauvoo, 224; counsel for Prophet, 233; on Mormon rights, 234; campaigns in Nauvoo, 235; mentioned, 106
Walker, G., 75
Ward, Thomas: action against, 85; death, 85; mentioned, 79
Warner, Charles, 169
Warren, Calvin, 168
Warren, Ill.: as satellite town, 138; Mormon troubles in, 141
Warren, W. B.: commissioner on Mormon problem, 329; disbands peace force, 339
Warsaw, Ill., 141, 221
Warsaw Signal: political view of Mormons, 221; call to arms against Mormons, 308
Wasson, Lorenzo D., 293
Weeks, William, 193
Weld, John F., 149n
Wells, Daniel H.: on city council, 101; land broker, 125; Agricultural and Manufacturing Association trustee, 149n
Wentworth, John, 297
Whig Party: in Illinois politics, 213, 231–232; in Hancock County elections, 220–221; on political views of Mormons, 226, 234; and election of 1842, 228; league with Bennett, 229; anti-Mormon feeling in, 239–240; influence of Mormon vote on, 239–240; and Mormons in Iowa, 240
White, Hugh, 35
Whitney, Newel K.: bishop at Commerce, 36; ward bishop, 44; in city council, 101; buys store goods, 161; instructed in secret rites, 271; receives endowment, 273; in Council of Fifty, 293

Wight, Lyman: solicits at conference, 44; in Nauvoo House revelation, 180; and Nauvoo House Association, 182, 322; heads "pinery," 185; political views, 217; accuses Babbitt, 252; Texas mission, 290, 293, 295; in Council of Fifty, 293; leaves Nauvoo, 295
Wightman, William, 138–139
Wisconsin "pineries": 158, 183–184; lumber from to Nauvoo, 156; proposed removal of colony to Texas, 290
Woodruff, Wilford: at Springfield conference, 27; missionary in Britain, 65–66; returns to America, 1846, 84; sells Nauvoo House stock, 189; baptizes for dead, 198; in Council of Fifty, 293
Woodworth, Lucian: Nauvoo House architect, 182, 189; promotes Nauvoo House, 186; in Council of Fifty, 293; embassy to Texas, 294
"Word of Wisdom": 244; economics, 247; mentioned, 243

Young, Brigham: settles at Nauvoo, 51; emoluments, 122n; land broker, 124; house, 156; fears arrest, 336; departs Nauvoo, 337; mentioned, 106, 197
— Economic leader: on British emigration business, 79–81; Trustee-in-Trust, 120n, 207; on Nauvoo poverty, 146; on water power development, 152; advocates cooperatives, 155; signs Kirtland note, 166n; sells Nauvoo House stock, 189; urges abandonment of Nauvoo House, 190; and Temple construction, 212; Temple fund raising, 203, 204; on tithe goods, 206; on Word of Wisdom, 247; plans for Nauvoo, 321–322

Young Brigham (*continued*)
— Political and governmental leader: theory of Kingdom, 280; in Council of Fifty, 293; on Texas colony, 295; on Prophet's candidacy, 302; opposes western colonies, 302–303, 320–321; expanded view of Kingdom, 303–304; concept of Utah settlement, 304; policies, 320–322; provides *ad hoc* government, 325; agrees to abandon Nauvoo, 330; plans for removal, 331–335
— Religious leader: senior Apostle, 11; in Missouri exodus, 12; urges regathering, 26; on obedience to counsel, 50, 277; missionary in Britain, 64; and priesthood, 108–109; endorses inheritances, 126; on Temple rites, 192; baptizes for dead, 198; dissent against, 243; admonishes forgiveness, 255; instructed in secret rites, 271; receives endowment, 273; and polygamy trial, 276; supported by Fifty, 293; succession to leadership, 313–320

Zarahemla, Iowa: decision to build, 38; stake appointed, 44; gathering to, 49; radicalism at, 55; as satellite town, 138; action against tipplers in, 245

Zion: in Jackson County, Missouri (Independence), 10, 23, 49; at Caldwell County, Missouri (Far West), 23; and Mormon communitarianism, 23, 280; in Great Basin, 24; related to New England towns, 24; inheritances in (Nauvoo), 45–46; in Missouri discontinued, 47; at Nauvoo, 47–49; in British Mission policy, 80; and Mutual Benefit Association, 81–83; Nauvoo House in stake of, 180; in Temple revelation, 191; expanded concept, 298. *See also* Kingdom of God